INDUSTRY OF THE ORDINARY

SIC TRANSIT GLORIA MUNDI

2003-2013

CHICAGO CULTURAL CENTER

AUGUST 2012 — FEBRUARY 2013

INDUSTRY OF THE ORDINARY:
SIC TRANSIT GLORIA MUNDI 2003-2013

Essay by Eleanor Heartney
Interview by Duncan MacKenzie
Additional texts by Dominic Molon and Ciara Ennis
Cover image by Marc Hauser
Book design by Jason Pickleman, JNL graphic design

CHICAGO CULTURAL CENTER
78 East Washington Street, Chicago, Illinois 60602
312.744.6630/TTY:312.744.2947
www.chicagoculturalcenter.org

ADMISSION IS FREE

Public programs, exhibitions, and related educational programming presented at the Chicago Cultural Center by the Chicago Department of Cultural Affairs and Special Events in partnership with the Chicago Office of Tourism and Culture are partially supported by a grant from the Illinois Arts Council, a state agency. Transportation support is provided by United Airlines, The Official Airline of the Chicago Cultural Center. Lawry's The Prime Rib is the restaurant sponsor of Chicago Cultural Center exhibitions.

City of Chicago
Mayor Rahm Emanuel

Illinois ARTS Council

UNITED

LAWRY'S THE PRIME RIB

ILLINOIS. MILE AFTER MAGNIFICENT MILE.

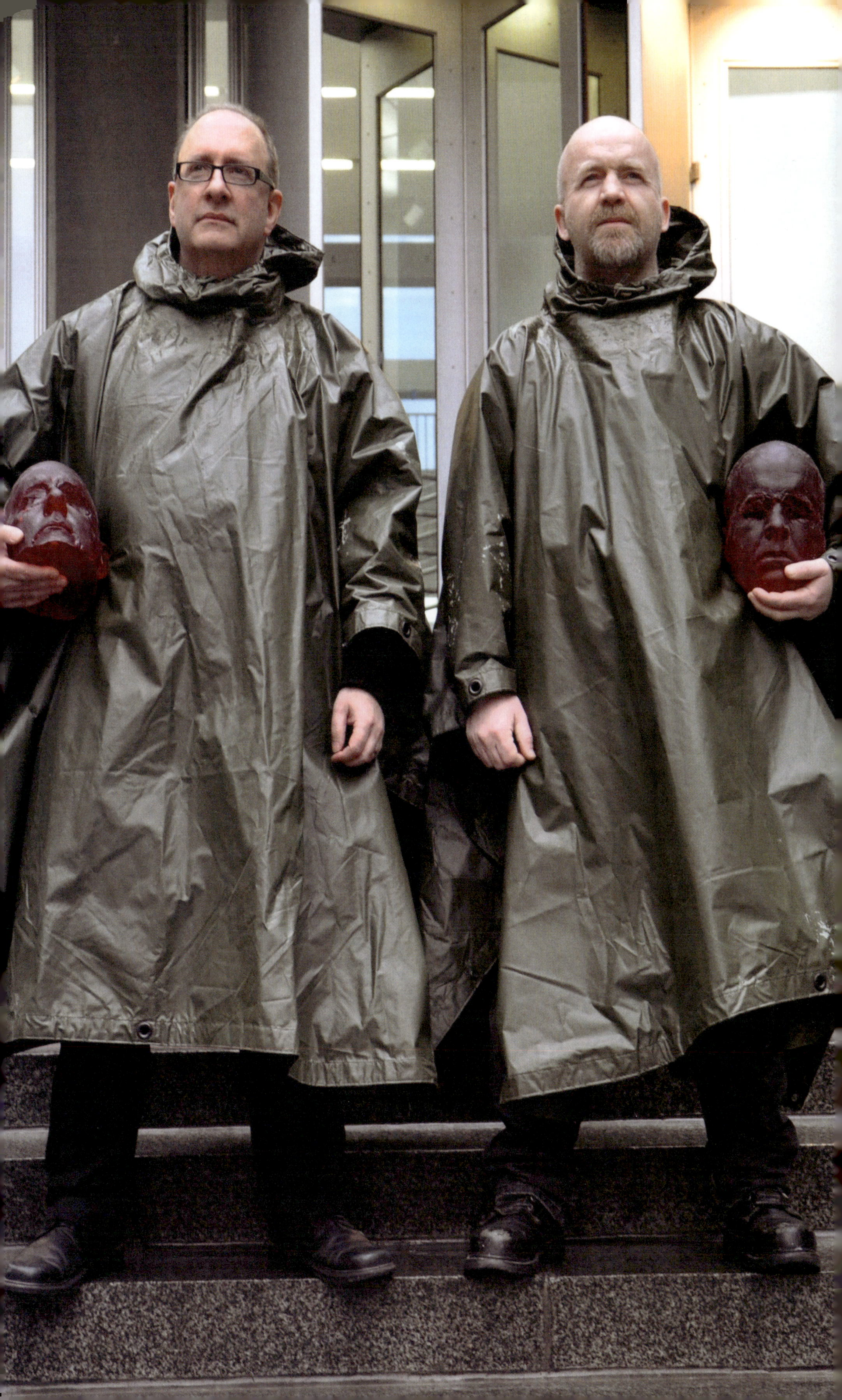

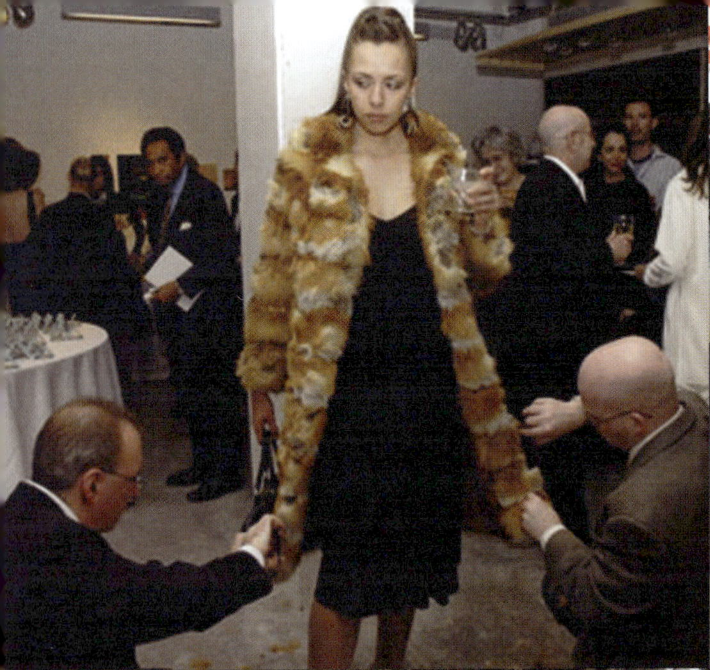

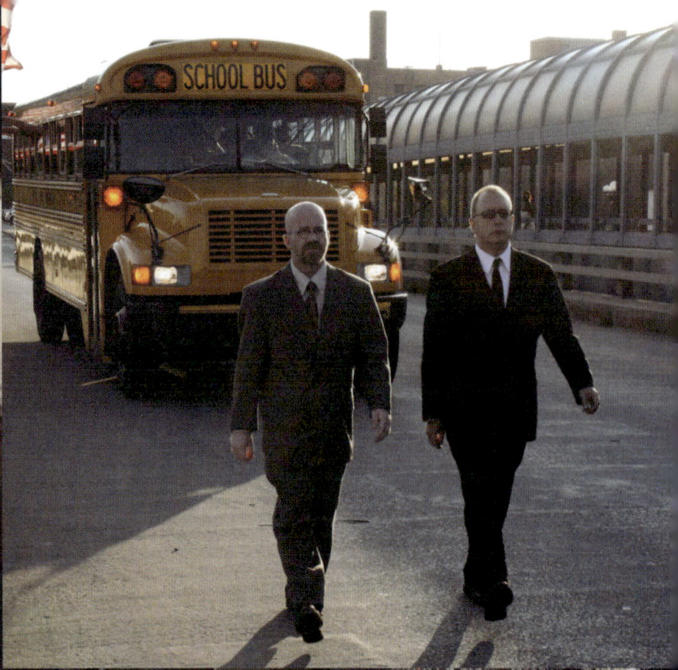
SCHOOL BUS

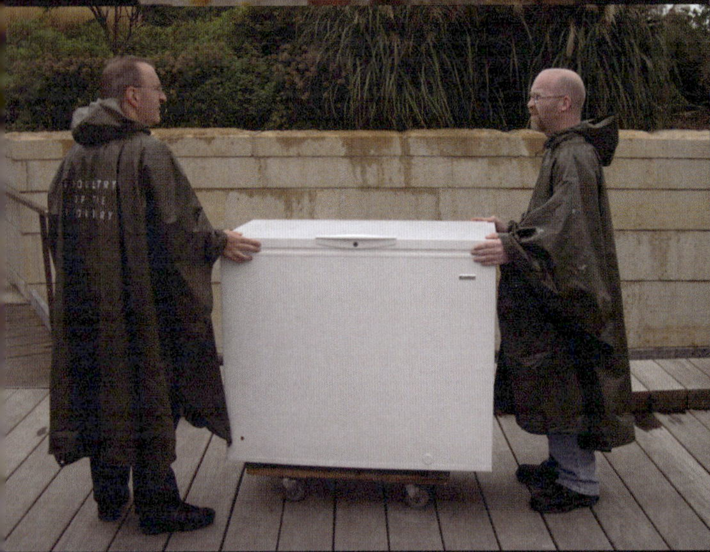

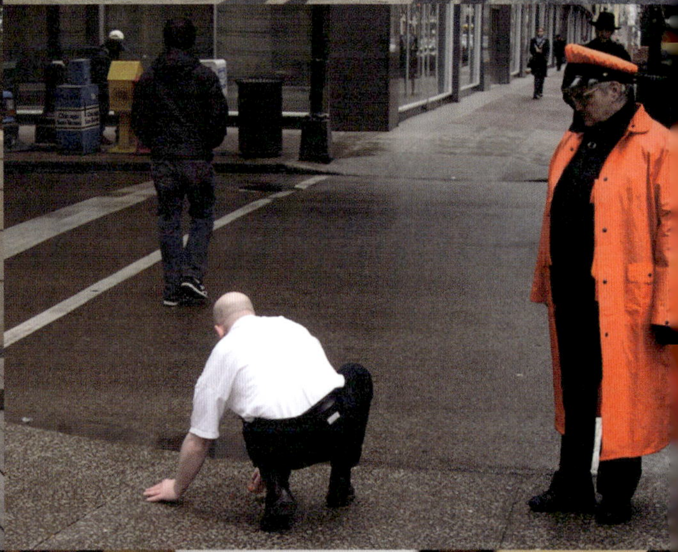

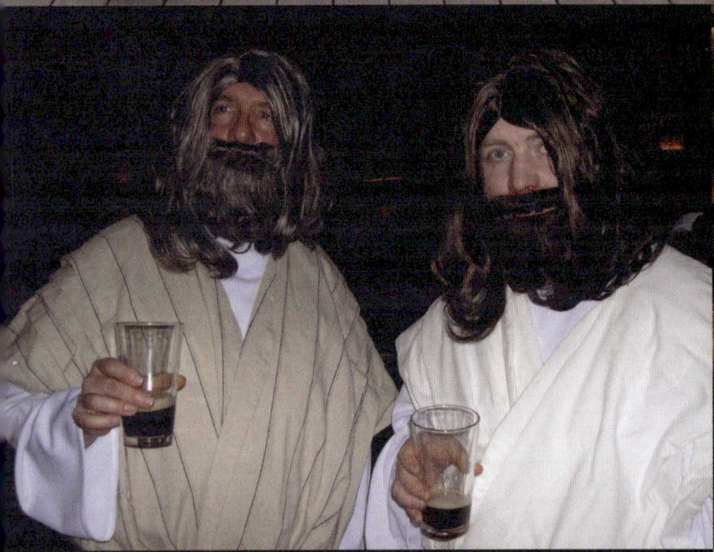

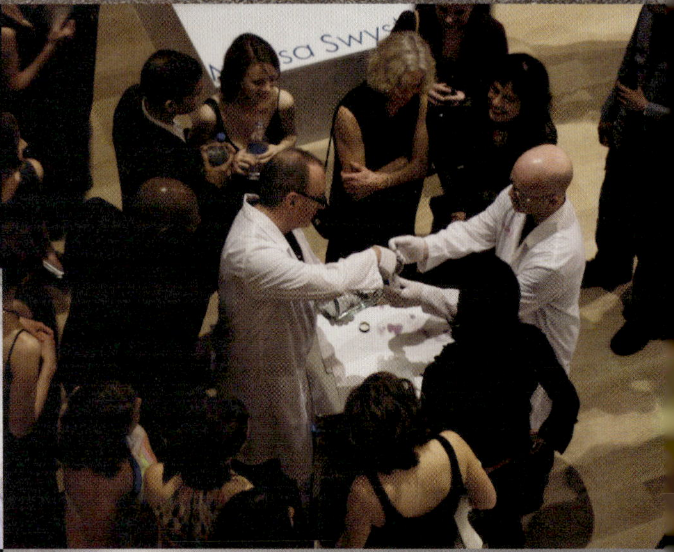

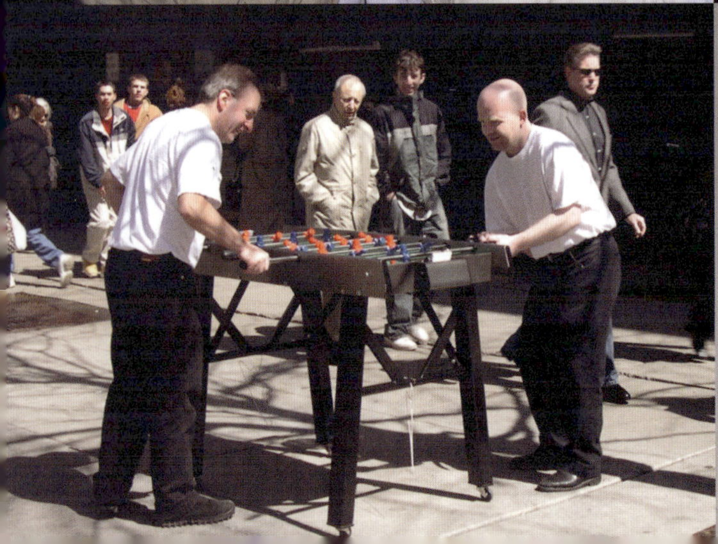

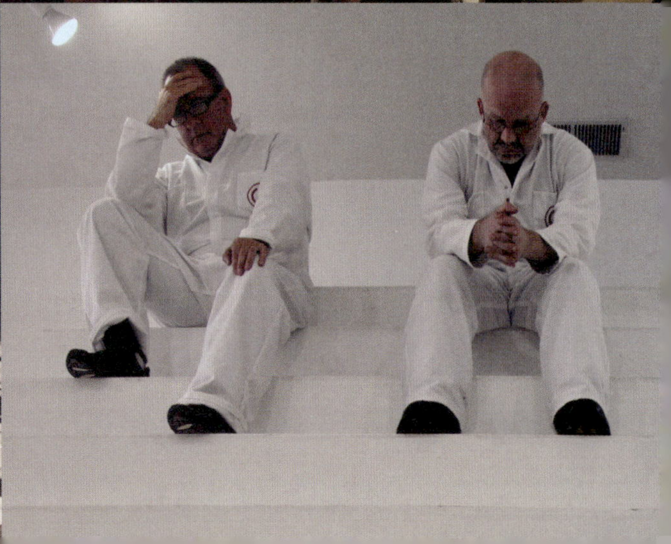

Table of Contents

Acknowledgements

Support for this catalog and the show which it accompanies has been provided by the Chicago Cultural Center and the City of Chicago Department of Cultural Affairs and Special Events, the Illinois Arts Council, a state agency, and Columbia College Chicago.

We wish to thank the following, without whom many of our projects could not have been realized:

Zach Abubeker
Jesse Achramowicz
ACRE
Alberto Aguilar
Emanuel Aguilar
Lisa Aidan
Teresa Albor
Morehshin Allahyari
Candida Alvarez
Brandon Alvendia
Duncan Robert Anderson
Simon Anderson
Tim Anderson
Kris Andrews
Caitlin Arnold
Richard Ashcroft
Claire Ashley
Bad at Sports
Steve Badauskas
Jeremiah Barber
Torreyanna Barley
Aimée Beaubien
Claire Bendiner
Brooke Berger
Bradley Bergquist
Bernice and John's
Dawoud Bey
McArthur Binion
Elisabeth Blair
James Tyler Blankenship
Deborah Boardman
Theo Boggs
Karen Bovinich
John Bowers
Melanie Boyna
Patrick Brannon
Barbara Worthen Brooks
Bob Brooks
David Brooks
McLean McGown Brooks
Stephanie Brooks
Randy Brown
Ivan Brunetti
Daniel Bruttig
Tom Buecker
Victoria Burns
Tom Burtonwood
Alanna Butera
Virginia Fabbri Butera
Matthew Calhoun
Carole Cantrell
Roger Carlson
Evan Carrison
John Carter
Mark Cepon
Robert Chatterton-Dickson
Juan Chavez
The Chicago Cultural Alliance
Chicago Ice Works
Camela Christopher
Rachel Claff
Joshua Clarfelt
James Clark
Molly Clough
Haley Comacho
Kelli Connell
Antonia Contro
The Co-Prosperity Sphere, Chicago
Amy Corle
Derek Cote
Amy Coty-Moran
Patricia Courson
Andi Crist
Paige Cunningham
Paul D'Amato
Defibrillator
Dana DeGiulio
Tom Denlinger
Don Denton
Tomi Dew
LJ Douglas
Jenny Drankie
Jeff Dreyfuss
Ryan Duggan
Jeanne Dunning
Natasha Egan
Maria Eisner
Experimental Sound Studio, Chicago
Ellen Fabricant
Adam Farcus
Fast Signs, Webster Place, Chicago
Alice Feldt
Amanda Fitzsimmons
Chris Flynn
Chris Franklin
Benjamin Funke
Barbara de Genevieve
Aron Gent
George's
Susanne Ghez
Susan Giles
Joan Giroux
James Patrick Gordon
Michelle Grabner
Allison Grant
Liz Gray
Emily Green
Myra Greene
Arthur Guinness
Amanda Hamilton
Jennifer Hansen
The Happy Collaborationists
Anne Harris
Keri Harvey
Brady Haston
Marc Hauser
Julia Haw
Natalia Ivancevich Hayes
Justin Hayford
Tempestt Hazel
Erica Henrich
Anne Henry
EJ Hill
Rhona Hoffman
Laurie Hogin
Richard Holland
Megon Holldorf
Hadyn Hollister
Anni Holm
Mary Horan
Jo Hormuth
Rebecca Howard
Lauren Humphries
JD Hutton
The Hyde Park Art Center, Chicago
James Iannaccone
Lynne Ireland
Karen Irvine
Benjamin Jaffe
Katherine Jannusch
Mark Jeffrey
Mathew Paul Jinks
David Jones
Junn
Gary Justis
Kelly Kaczynski
Steve Kapelke
Tony Karman
Jay Kaser
Jackie Kazarian
Jerome Kemp
Chris Kerr
Katinka Kleijn
Paul Klein
Barbara Koenen
Josh Korby
Carson Krabbe
Anna Kunz
Christian Kuras
Julie Laffin
Ron Lambert
Jason Lazarus
Jennifer Leach
Kirsten Leenaars
Lauren Levato
Debra Levie
Aaron Levine

Particular thanks go to Greg Stimac for his documentation of our work over an extended period, and to Max King Cap for introducing us.

We would also like to thank the many students with whom we have worked over the past fifteen years, whose energy and enthusiasm constantly inspire us, and thanks to Melody Chang Snyder for helping us uncover the next generation of Chicago-based performative artists.

In the production of this catalog, special thanks go to: Eleanor Heartney for her incisive essay; Duncan MacKenzie for his perceptive interview; Dominic Molon and Ciara Ennis for permission to include their existing texts about our activities; Jason Pickleman and the JNL graphic design for their responsive and creative design solutions for this publication; Susan Snodgrass for her careful editing; and Shayna Cott for her consummate organization.

At the Chicago Cultural Center, the staff with whom we worked for two years in preparation for this show and publication deserve enormous thanks. They include Lucas Cowan, Elizabeth Kelley, Greg Lunceford, Debra Purden, Fabi Ramirez, Lanny Silverman, and Angel Ysaguirre.

Finally, our gratitude goes to Cynthia Canary, Tyler Brooks, Melissa Lutz, Gosia Gizella, Kasia Wilson, and Charlie Boehl for their love and support.

Adam Brooks and Mathew Wilson
Industry of the Ordinary
2012

Carron Little
Alexa Loftus
Lisa Loris
Louise Love
Claudia Luebbers
Michael Hernandez de Luna
Brian Lutz
Roger Machin
MacKenzie & Kuras
Faheem Majeed
Lou Mallozzi
Joshua Mancuso
Iñigo Manglano-Ovalle
Curtis Mann
Maria's
Ivka Markovic
Kerry James Marshall
Ed Marszewski
Josh Martinez
Nathan Mason
Eleanor Mayer
Nina Mayer
Gabriel Mayer
Cybele Maylone
Cecil McDonald
Tracy McDonald
Isabelle McGuire
Adelheid Mers
Angie Meyer
Methods & Materials
CJ Mitchell
Carrie Monaco
Roderick Monje
Amy Mooney
Aliza Morell
Liz Moretti
David Morrison
Annie Morse
Jessie Mott
Greg Mowery
Jennifer Murray
Sharon Murray
JL Murtaugh
Museum of Contemporary Art, Chicago
Museum of Contemporary Photography, Chicago
Amber Mustoe
Richard Mutz
Judy Natal
The Nebraska State Historical Society
Jeroen Nelemans
Eliza Nichols
Chiara No
Blake Noah
Heidi Norton
Paul Nudd
Betsy Odom
Emily Olds
Sabina Ott
Aron Packer
Neysa Page-Lieberman
Mary Patten
Melissa Peifer
Allison Peters Quinn
Nenad Petrovic
David Petrusich
Phil The Ice
John Phillips
Nick Pichet
Steve Piggott
Melissa Ann Pinney
Thomas Plum
Jenny Pollit
Nikki Posluzny
Corey Postiglione
Sabrina Raaf
Andrew Rafacz
Joseph Ravens
Jennifer Ray
Jen Reinhardt
Ryan Richey
James Rondeau
Wayne Rooney
Erin Rose
Ellen Rothenberg
Caitlin Ryan
Jay Ryan
Beth Sadowski
Jason Salavon
Tim Samuelson
Carmela Saraceno
Matt Schieren
Alex Schmidt
Carrie Schneider
Sara Schnadt
Shane Schubbe
Jordan Schulman
Senn Arts program, Chicago Public Schools
Sherwin-Williams
Anna Shteynshleyger
Peter Skvara
Rod Slemmons
Doug Snower
Modupe' Sodamade
Deb Sokolow
Peg Sorenson
Edra Soto
Aoi Soya
Hugh Sorrill
Lynne Sowder
Scott Speh
Emilie Stec
Nicholas Steindorf
Tony Stewart
Andrew Svec
Randall Szott
Christine Tarkowski
Tony Tasset
Jennifer Thaler
Chuck Thurow
Anna Trier
Michael Tropea
Michael Trotter
John Upchurch
Tricia Van Eck
Tannar Veatch
Valerie Velasquez
Hadley Vogel
Andreas Waldberg-Wolfegg
Hamza Walker
Dan S. Wang
Lynne Warren
Heather Weber
Meredith Weber
Lauren Weinberg
Lynda Wellhausen
Amanda Welsh
Scott Whipkey
Wicker Park/Bucktown Chamber of Commerce
Barbara Wiesen
Martyn Wilson
Mary Beth Witte
Jessica Wobbekind
Jay Wolke
Michael Workman
Nicholas Wylie
Jesse Wyss
Daniel Jouapao Yang
Meimei Yu
Jeff Zimmerman
Jim Zimpel
Molly Zuckerman-Hartung
Philip von Zweck

Industry of the Ordinary are Adam Brooks and Mathew Wilson.

Through sculpture, text, photography, video, sound, and performance, Industry of the Ordinary are dedicated to an exploration and celebration of the customary, the everyday, and the usual. Their emphasis is on challenging pejorative notions of the ordinary and, in doing so, moving beyond the quotidian.

THE PROJECTS

Industry of the Ordinary were formed in 2003. Their first performance, **Dropping 163 lbs: Daley Plaza,** involved approximately 75 performers who dropped 163 lbs of white clothing on Daley Plaza in Chicago. 163 lbs is the average weight of an American adult.

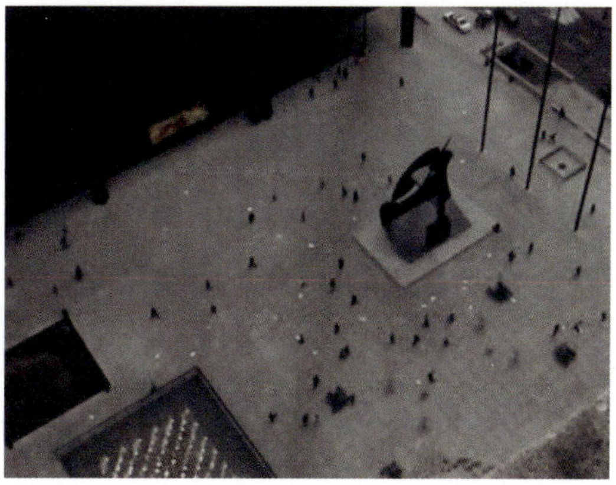

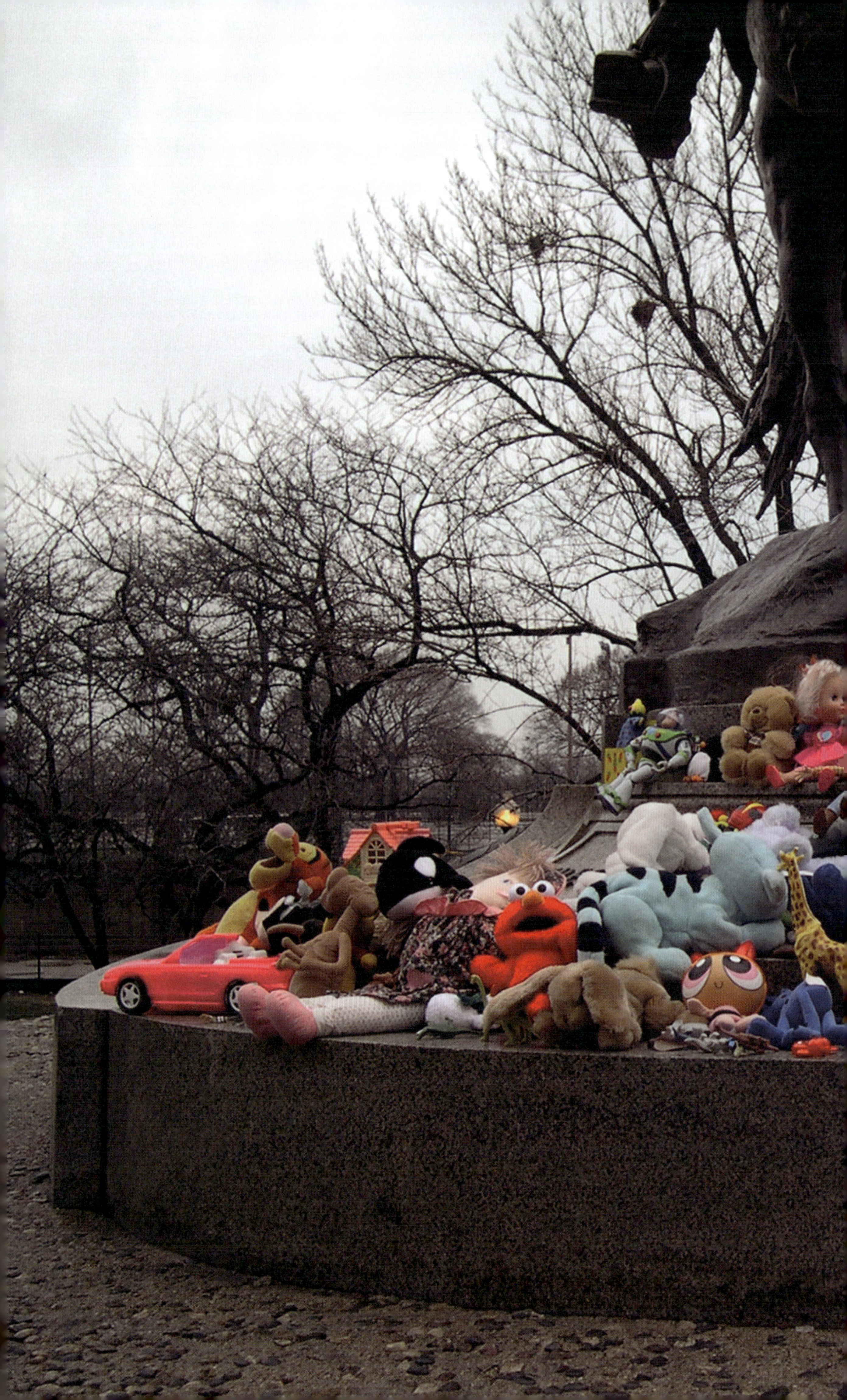

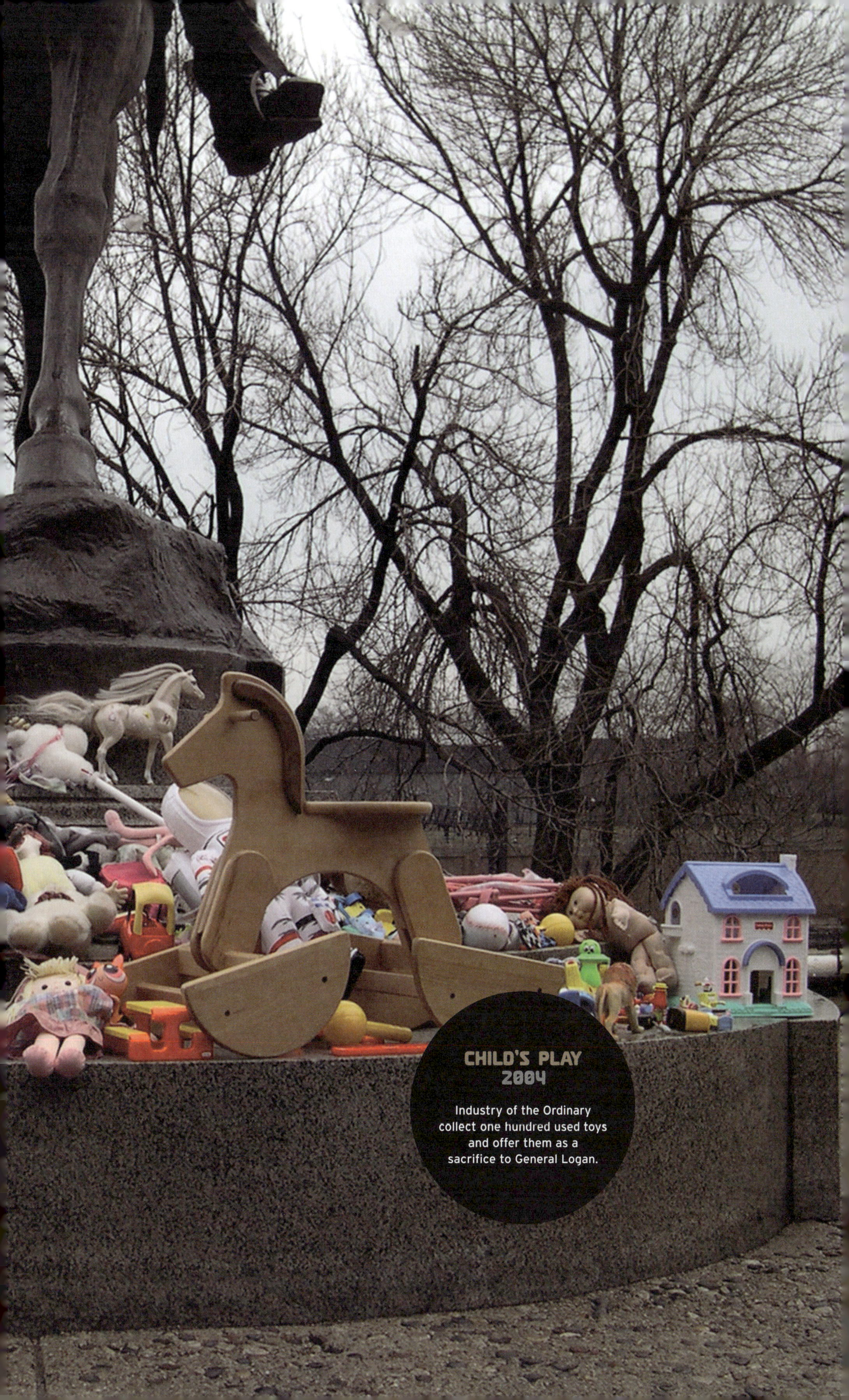

CHILD'S PLAY
2004

Industry of the Ordinary collect one hundred used toys and offer them as a sacrifice to General Logan.

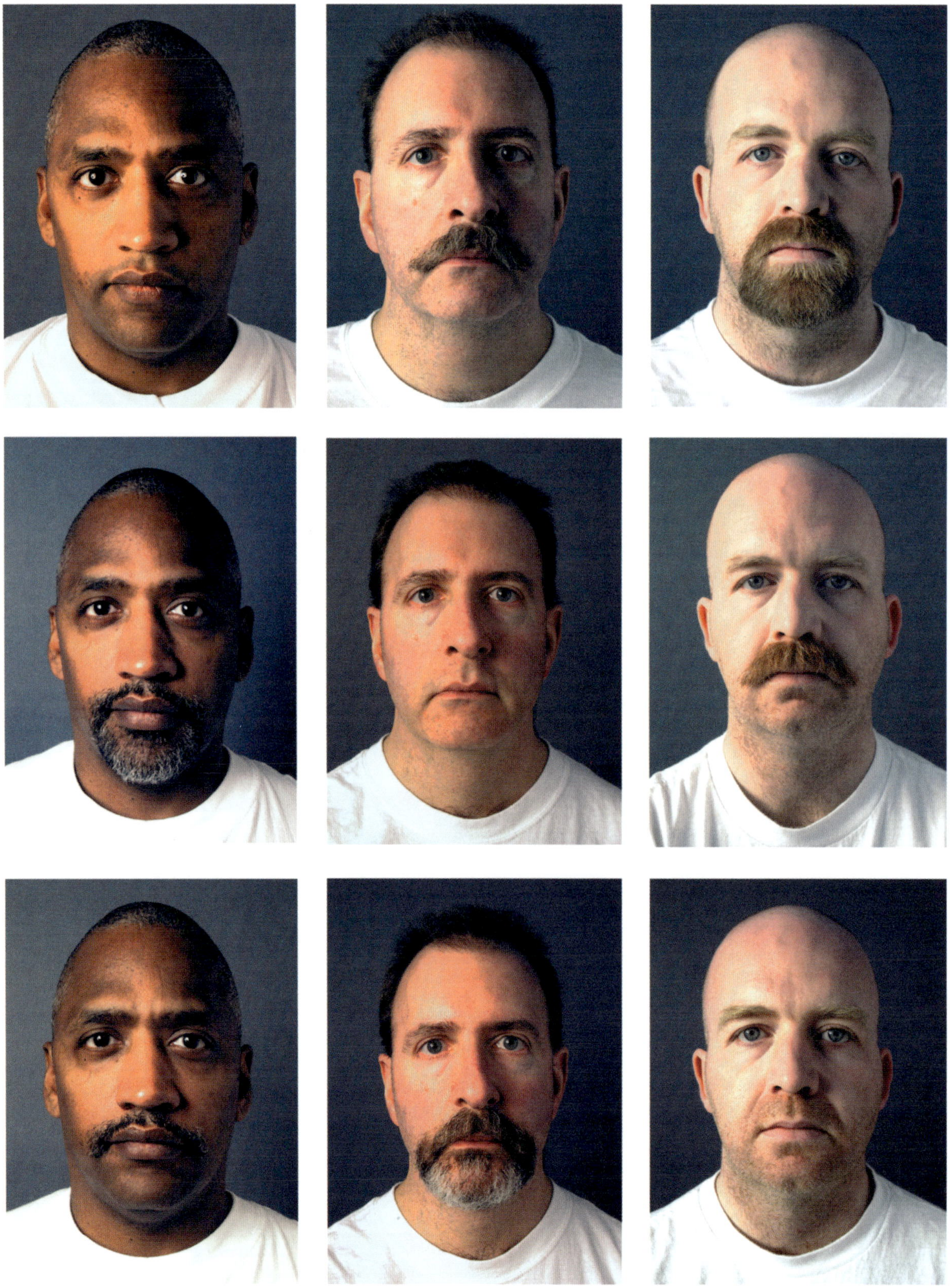

2004

Well Groomed

WITH MAX KING CAP

Industry of the Ordinary exchange facial hair.

FOR BAS JAN ADER, CHARLES RAY, AND ERWIN WURM, 2004–2006

Industry of the Ordinary accompany their wardrobes for a day.
Photography by Greg Stimac.

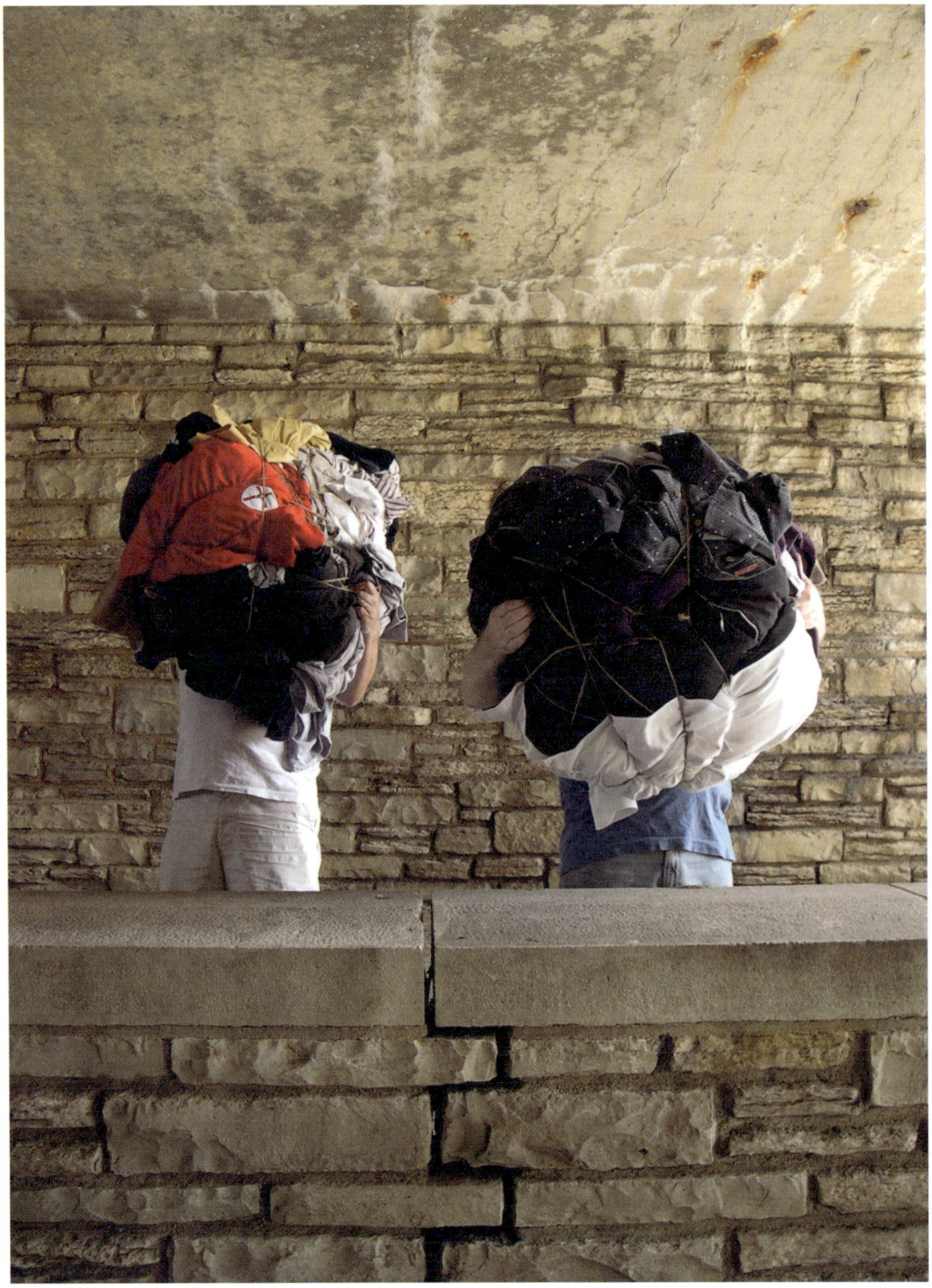

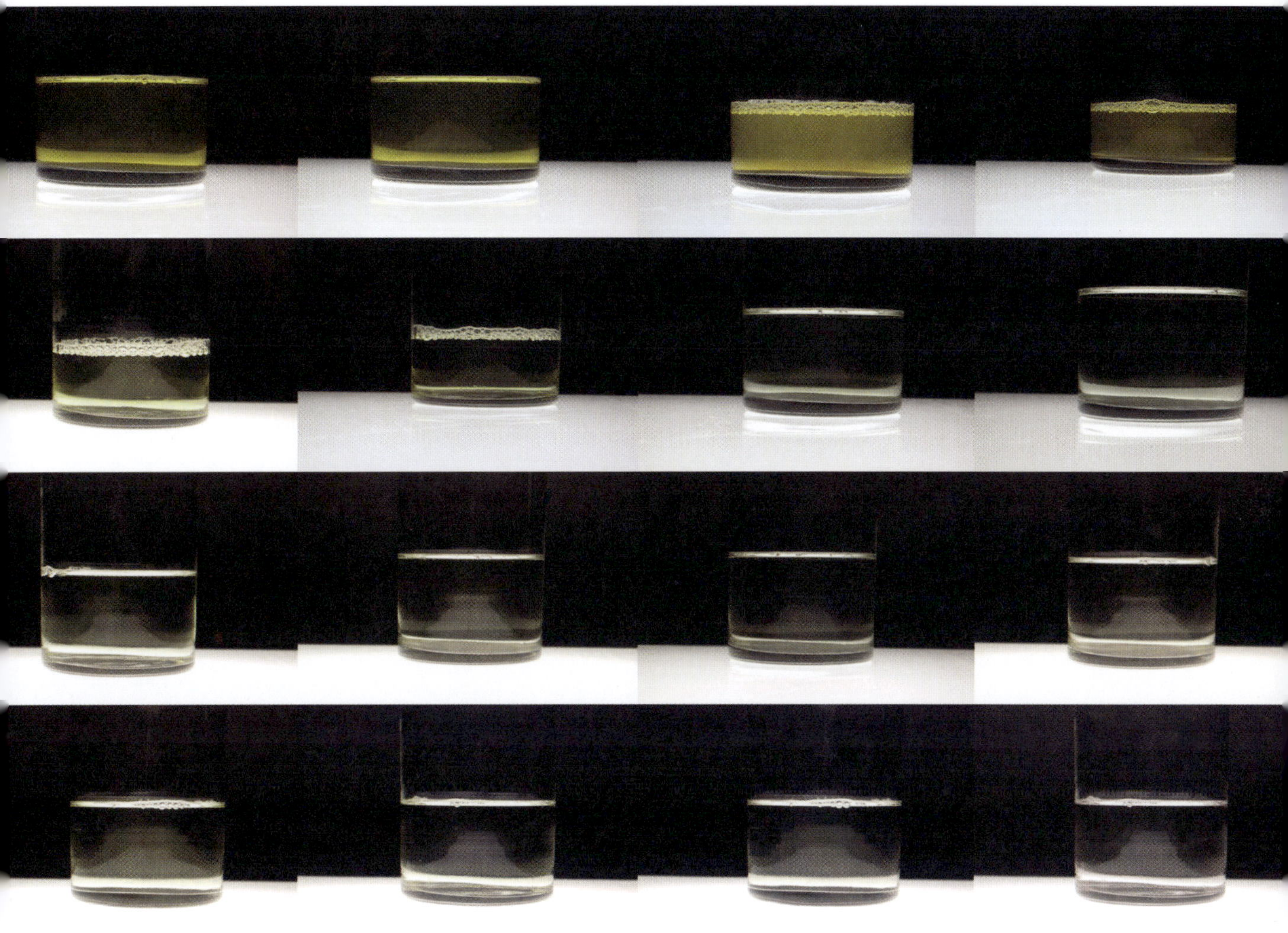

PHOSPHORUS, 2004

Industry of the Ordinary drink a crate of beer and document the change in color of their urine.

2004

PUBLIC OPINION

Industry of the Ordinary collect names on a petition to ban performance art.

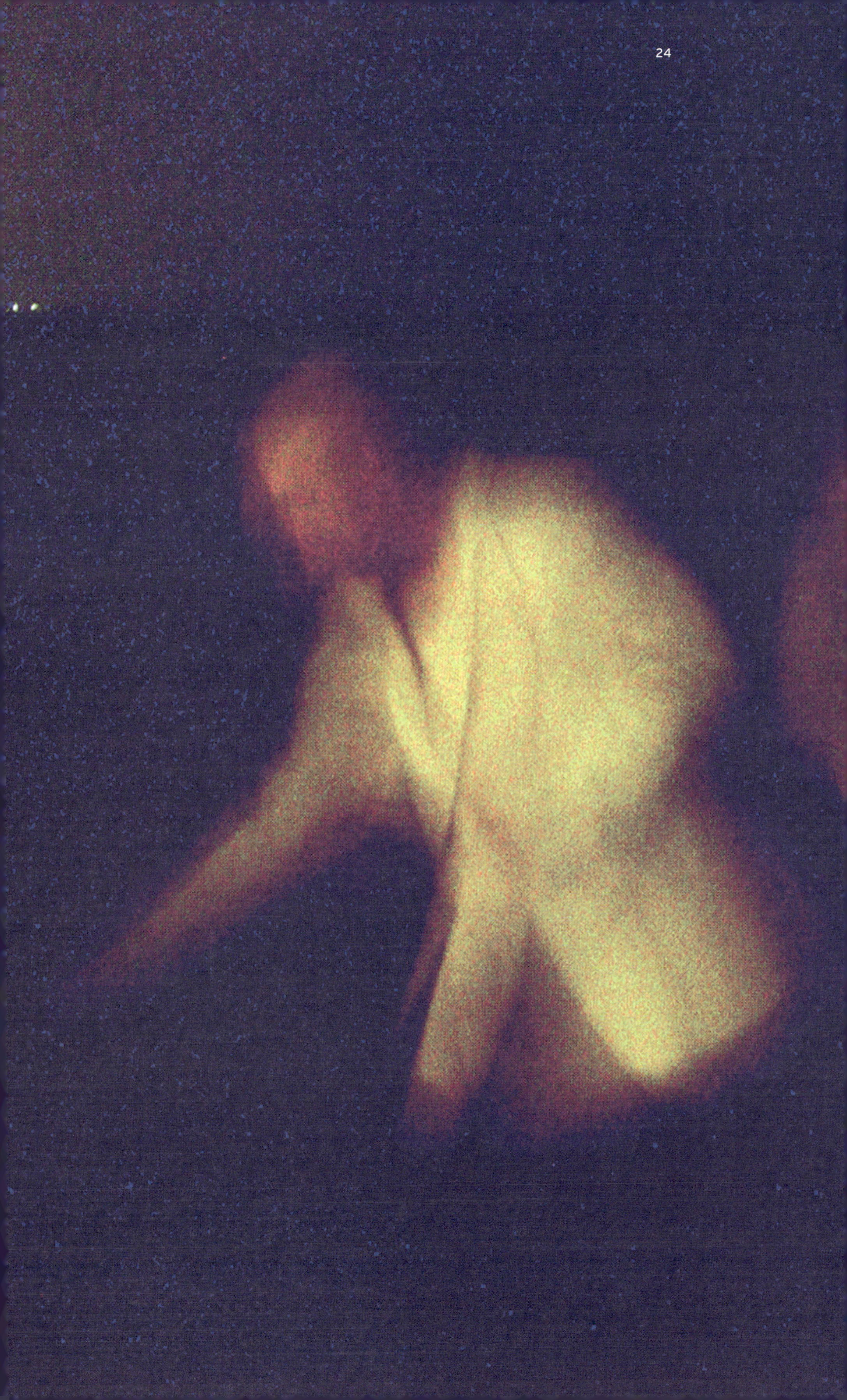

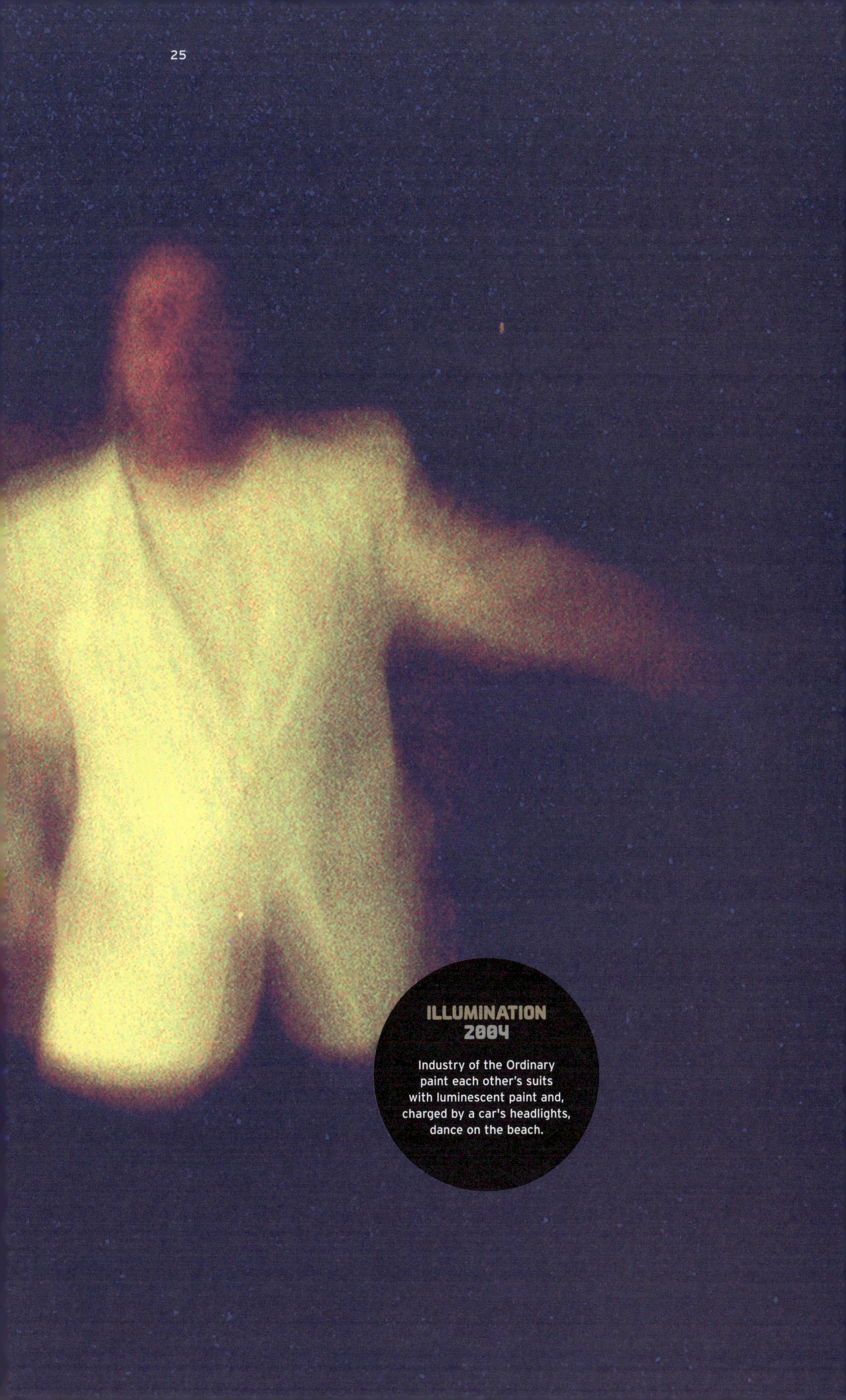

ILLUMINATION
2004

Industry of the Ordinary paint each other's suits with luminescent paint and, charged by a car's headlights, dance on the beach.

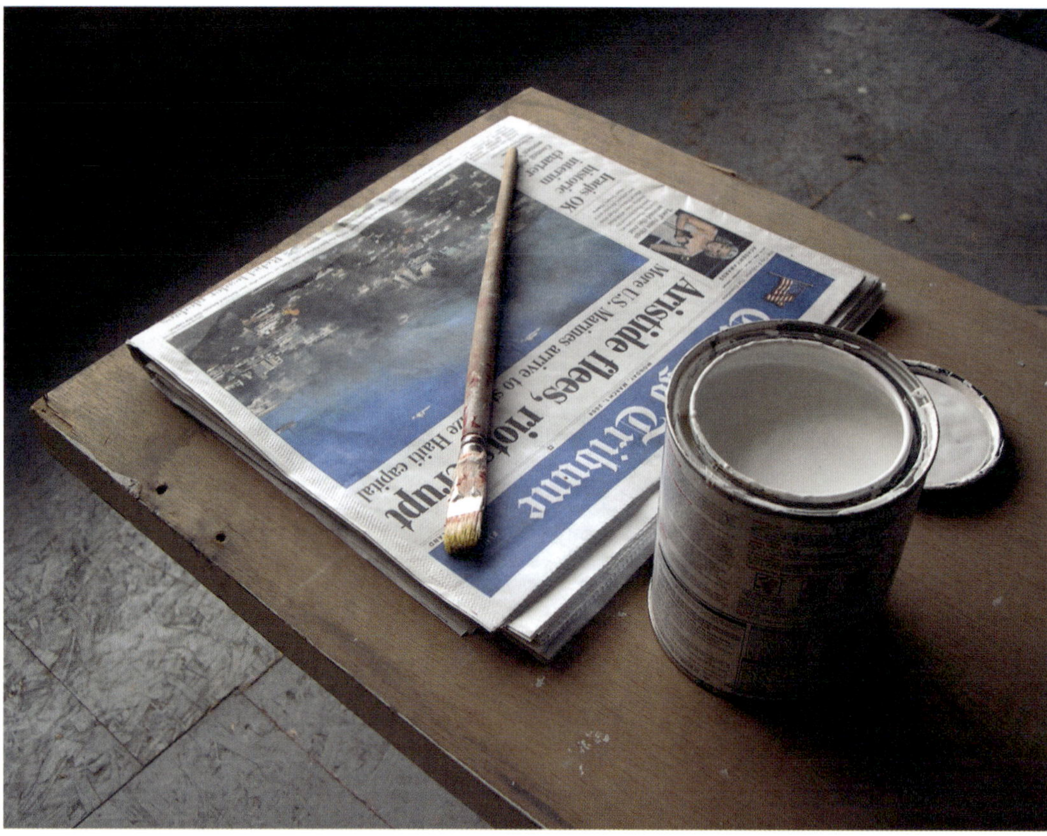
Tribune
Aristide flees,
Iraqis OK

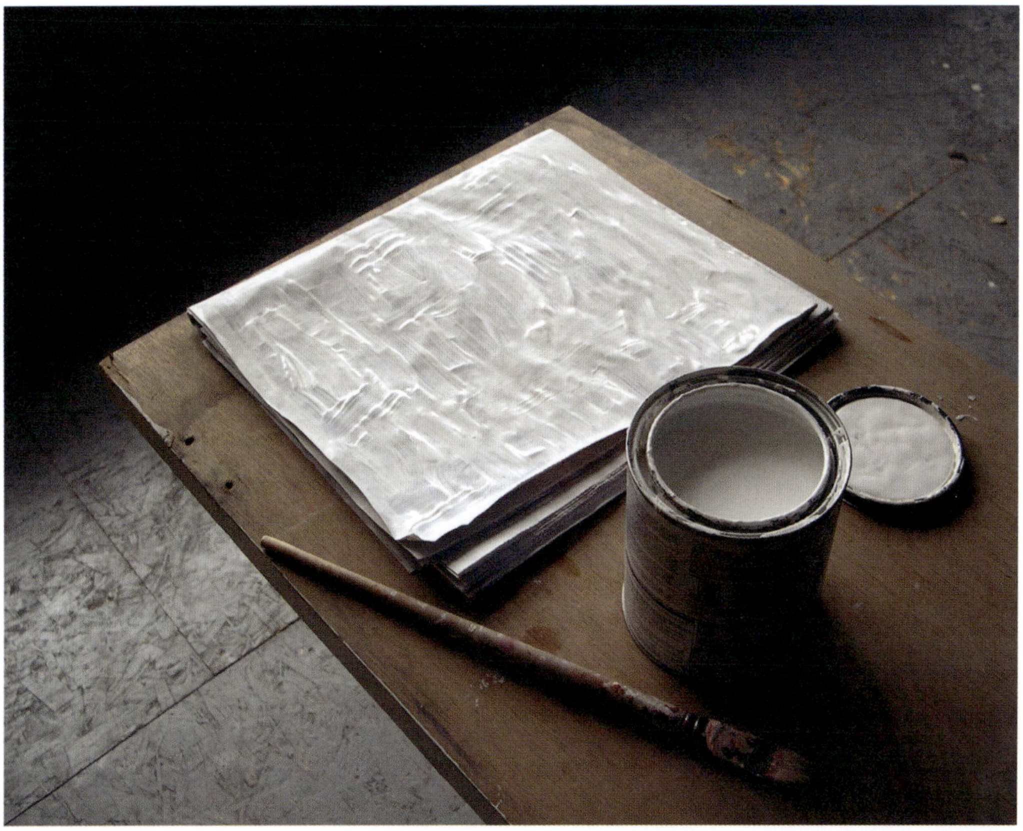

2004

CURRENT AFFAIRS

Industry of the Ordinary purchase a copy of the *Chicago Tribune*, paint it white, and mail it to the mayor.

2004

A Line in the Sand

Industry of the Ordinary purchase a flesh-colored Crayola and draw a line along State Street in Chicago until the Crayola is sharpened out of existence.

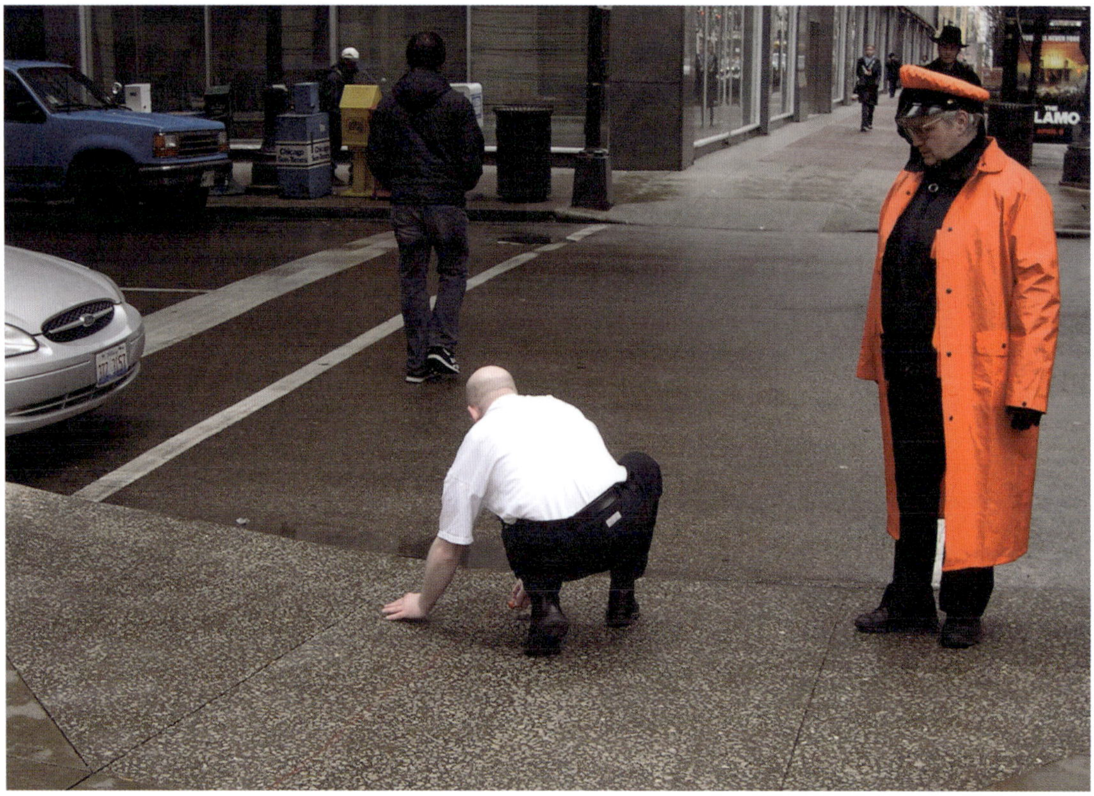

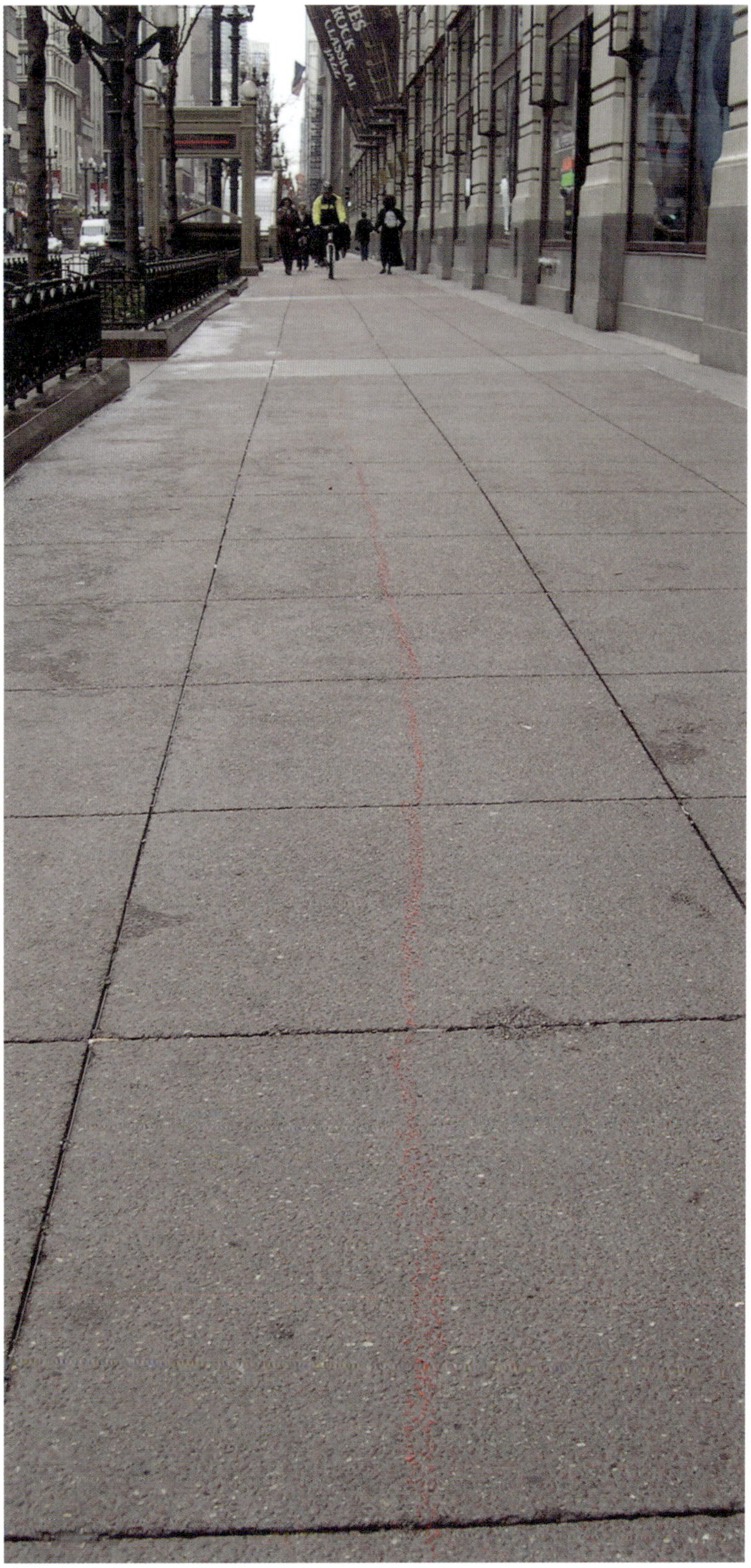

2004

Match of the Day

Industry of the Ordinary play table football, first to 1,000 goals, from the Museum of Contemporary Art down Michigan Avenue in Chicago.

Photography by Tom Lee.

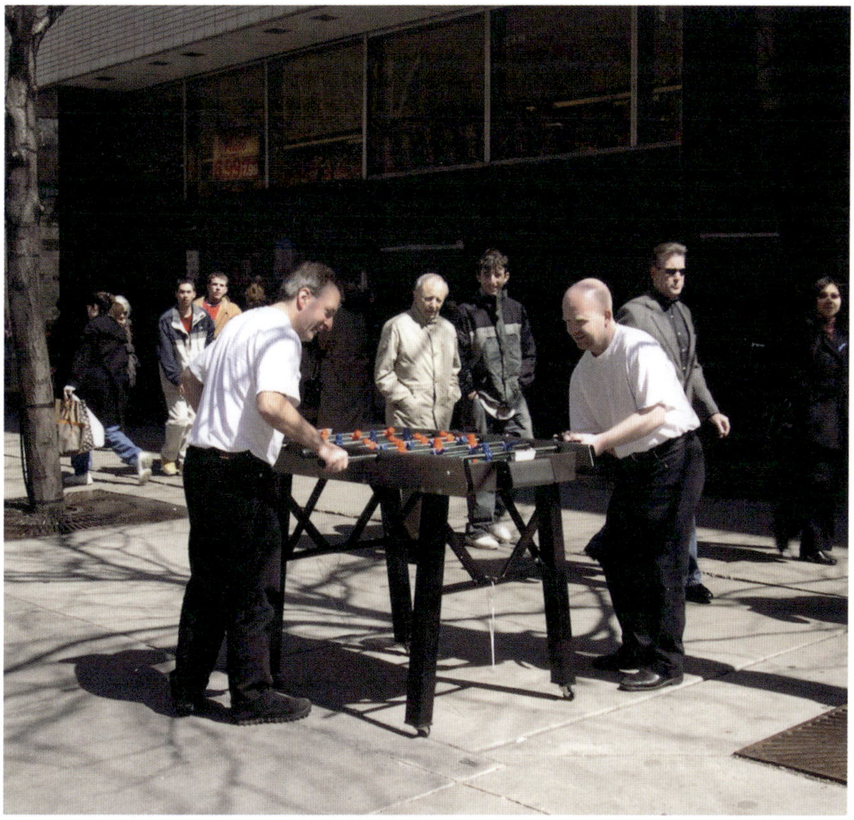

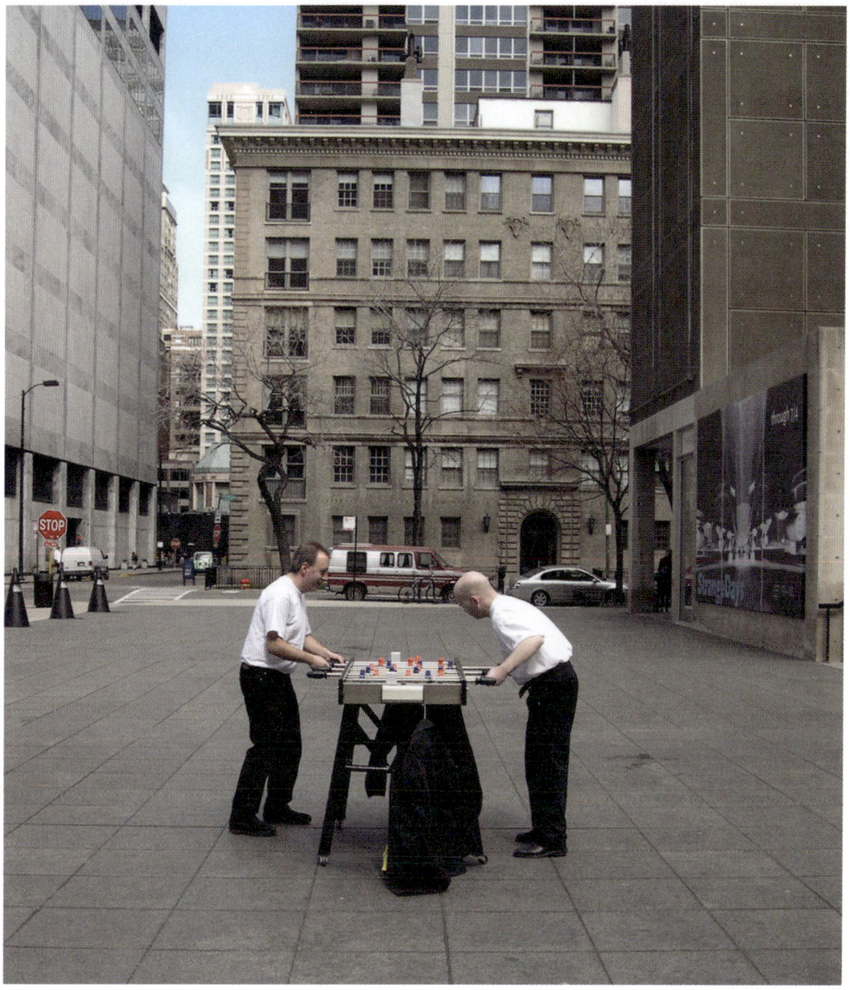
STOP

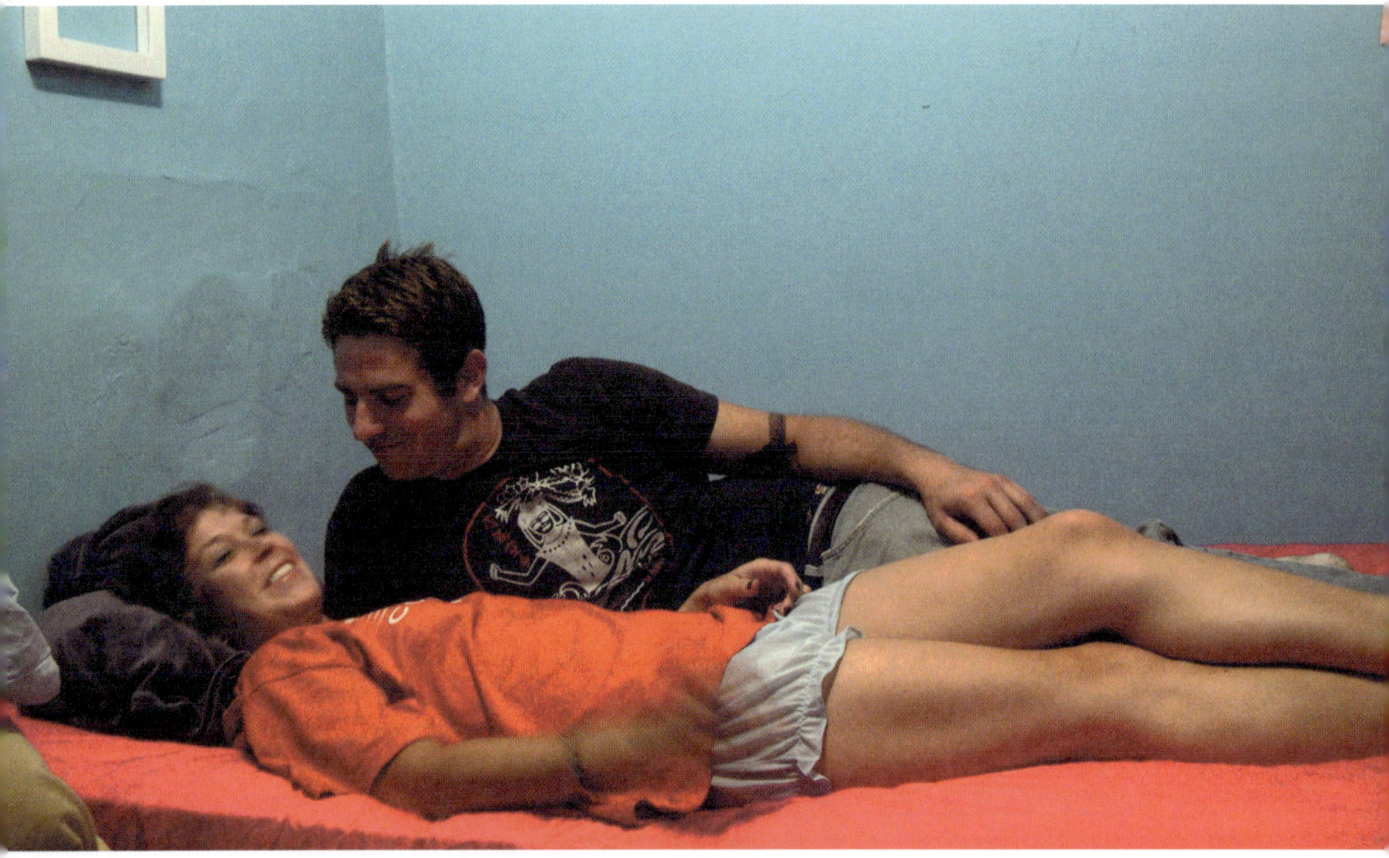

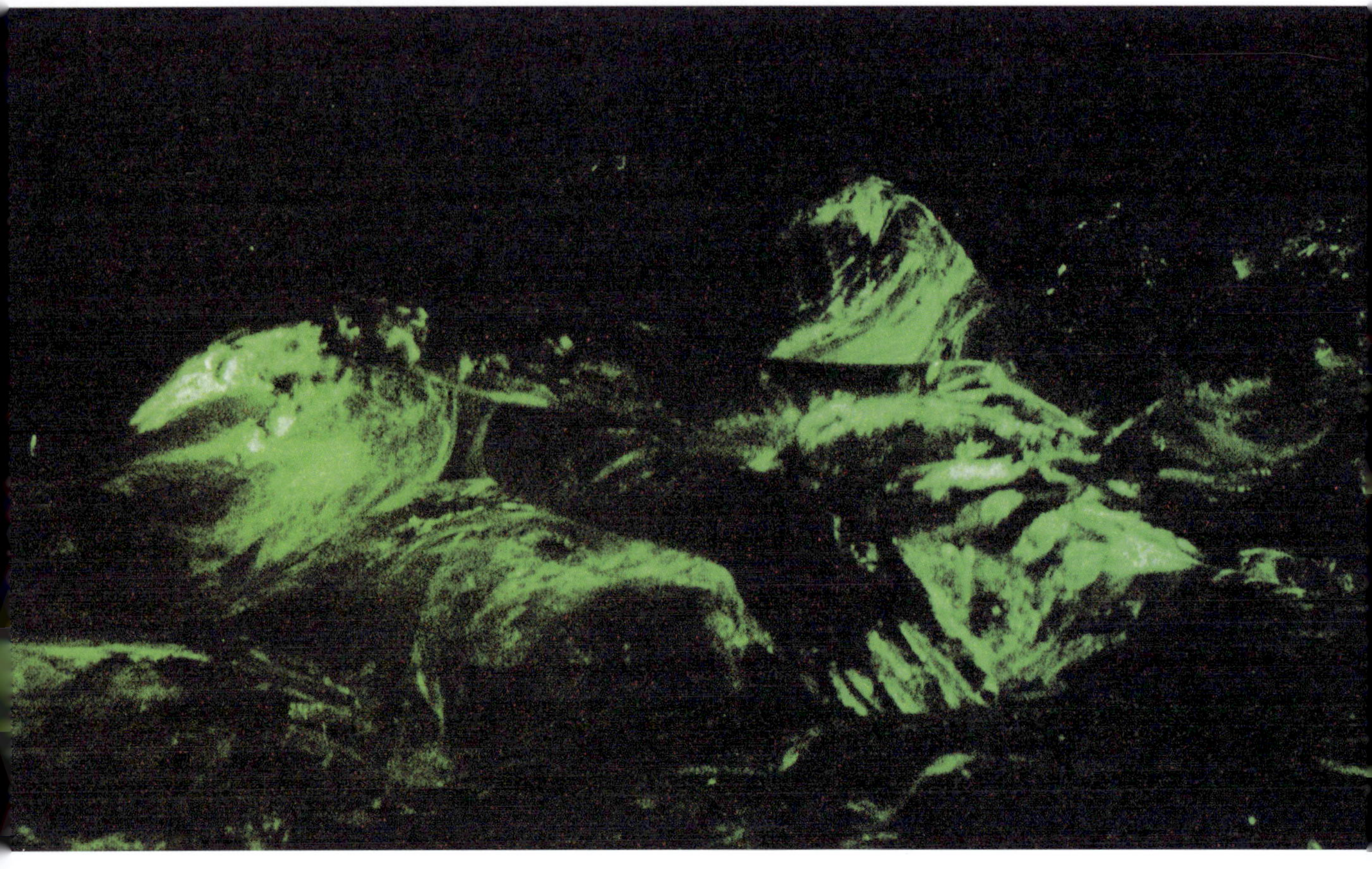

2004

PASSION PLAY

Industry of the Ordinary recruit a couple to use phosphorescent paint as a record of their lovemaking.

2004

Champion

Industry of the Ordinary hand out business cards inscribed with the word CHAMPION.

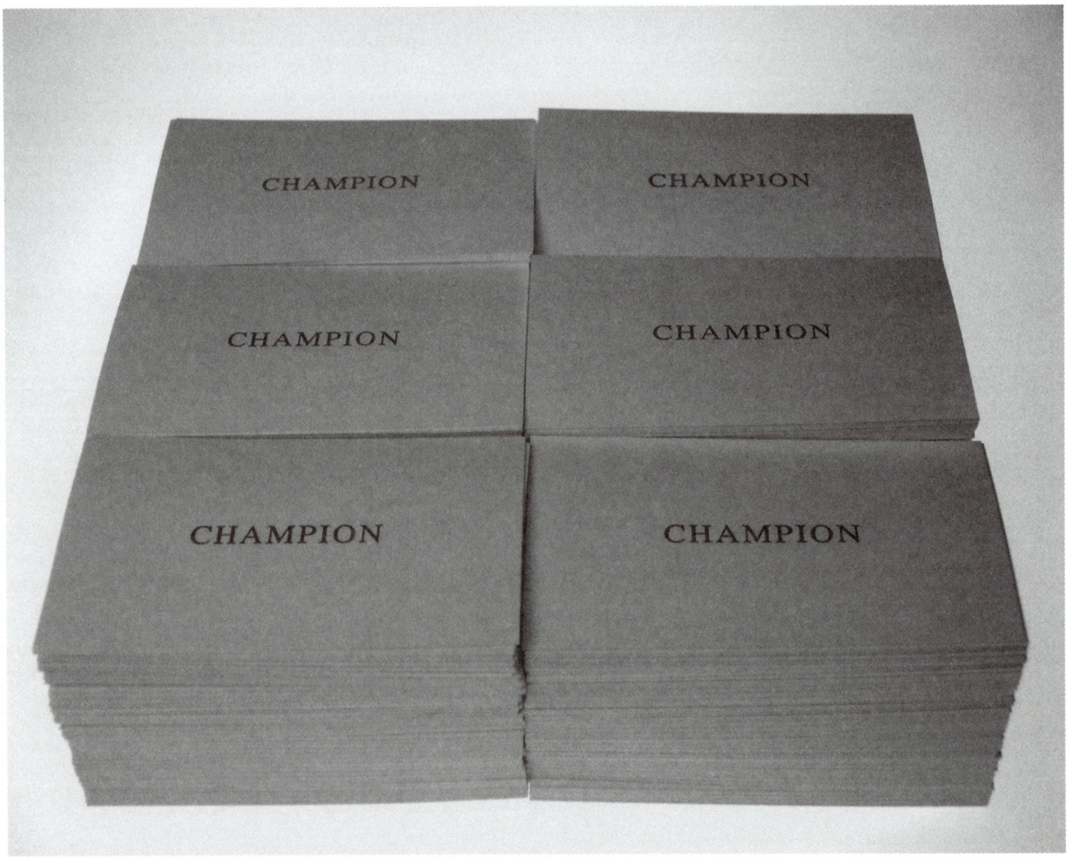

2004

Democracy

Industry of the Ordinary place an electoral sign in various locations around Chicago.

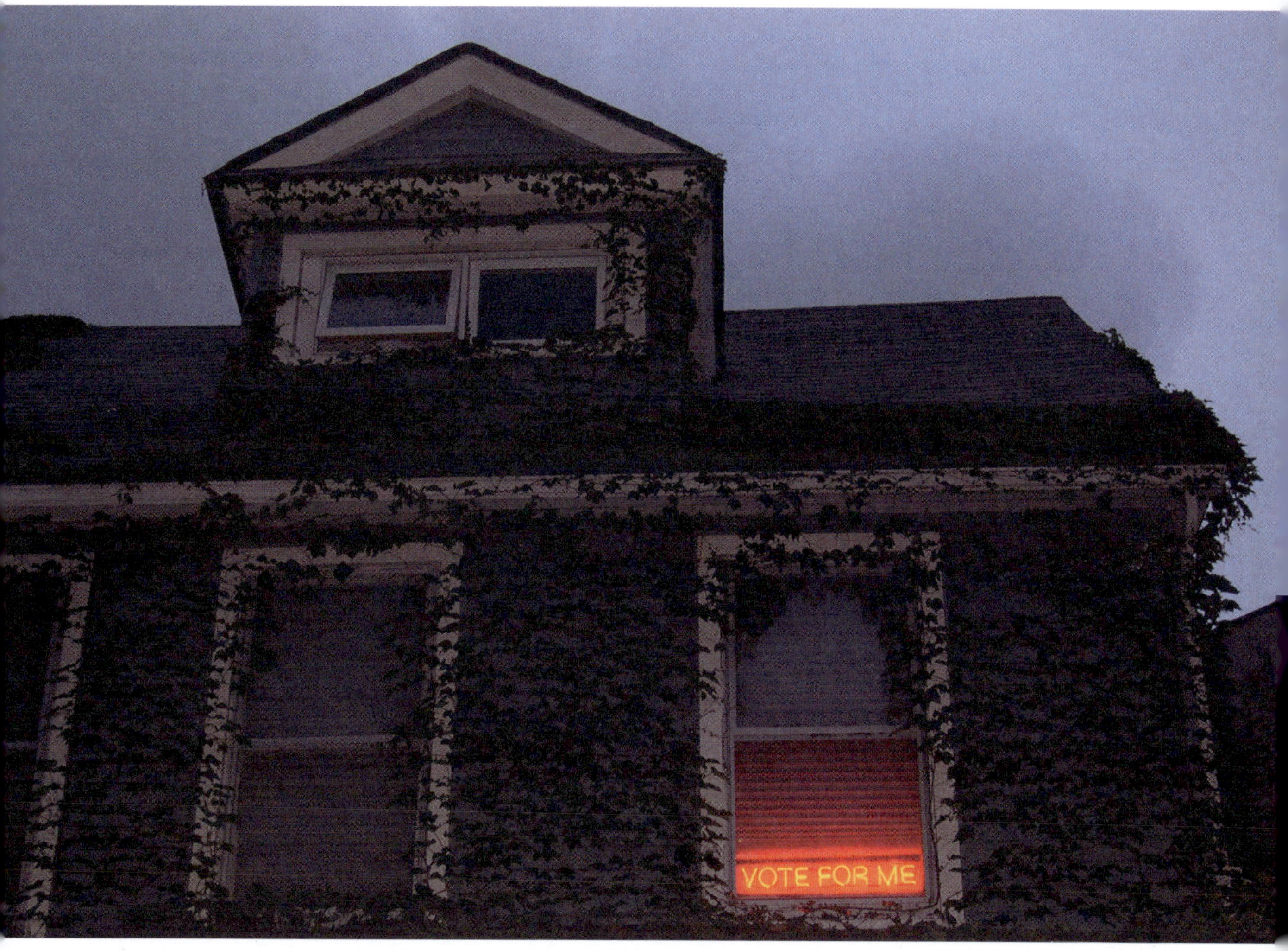

THE BEAUTIFUL GAME, 2004

Industry of the Ordinary orchestrate an infamous football chant.

Performed by Mark Cepon, Joshua Mancuso, Carrie Monaco, and Amanda Welsh.
Arranged by Patrick Brannon. Engineered and recorded at the Experimental Sound Studio, Chicago. Special thanks to Lou Mallozzi.

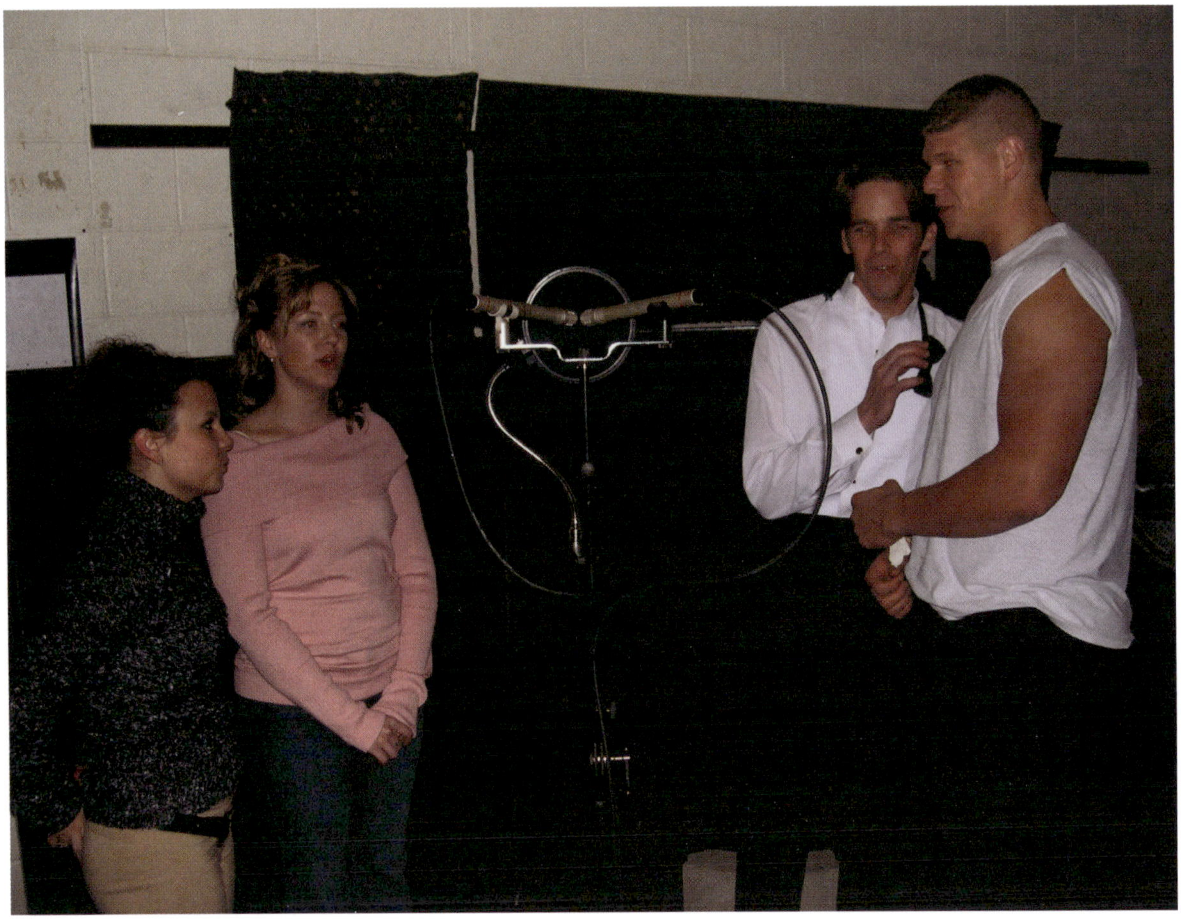

FINAL WORDS, 2005

Industry of the Ordinary collect the last lines from ten significant works of 20th-century literature.

He walked towards the faintly humming, glowing town, quickly. Old father, old artificer, stand me now and ever in good stead. The knife came down, missed him by inches, and he took off. He would be there all night, and he would be there when Jem waked up in the morning. The broken flower drooped over Ben's fist and his eyes were empty and blue and serene again as cornice and façade flowed smoothly once more from left to right; post and tree, window and doorway, and signboard, each in its ordered place. So we beat on, boats against the current, borne back ceaselessly into the past. Yes. He bowed low, right down to the ground, in front of the man sitting there motionless, whose smile reminded him of everything that he had ever loved in his life, of everything that had ever been of value and holy in his life. She looked up and across the barn, and her lips came together and smiled mysteriously. "Like a dog!" he said; it was as if the shame of it must outlive him.

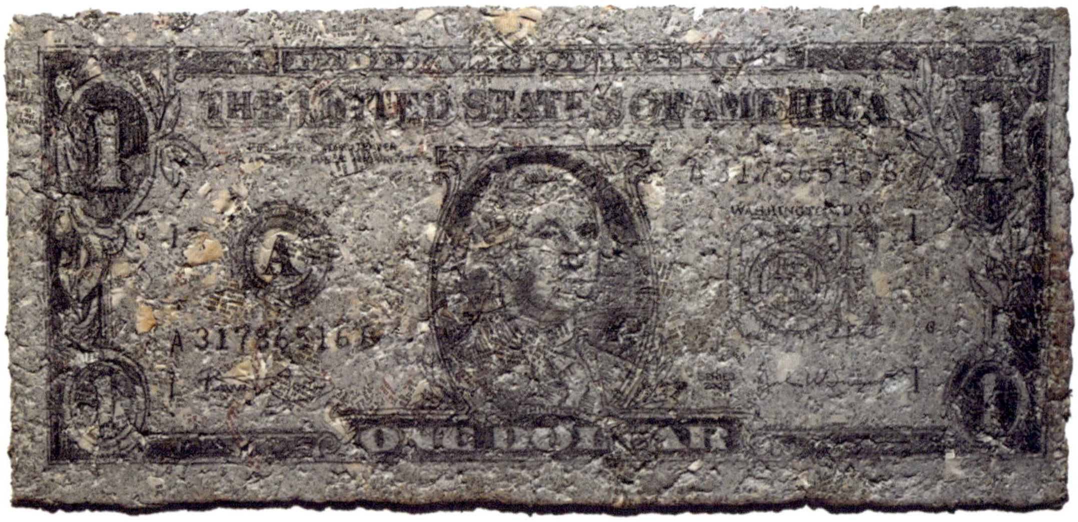
THE UNITED STATES OF AMERICA
ONE DOLLAR

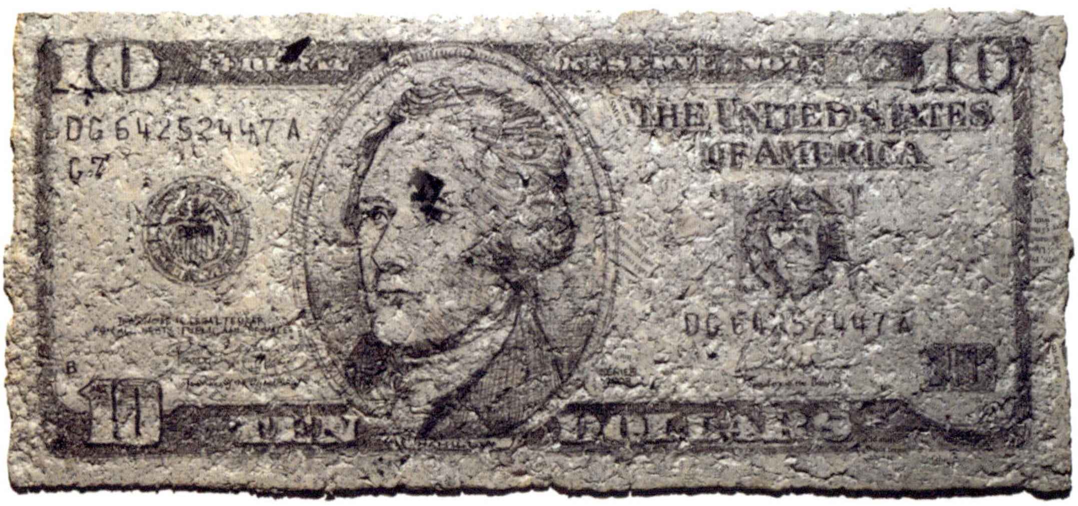
THE UNITED STATES OF AMERICA

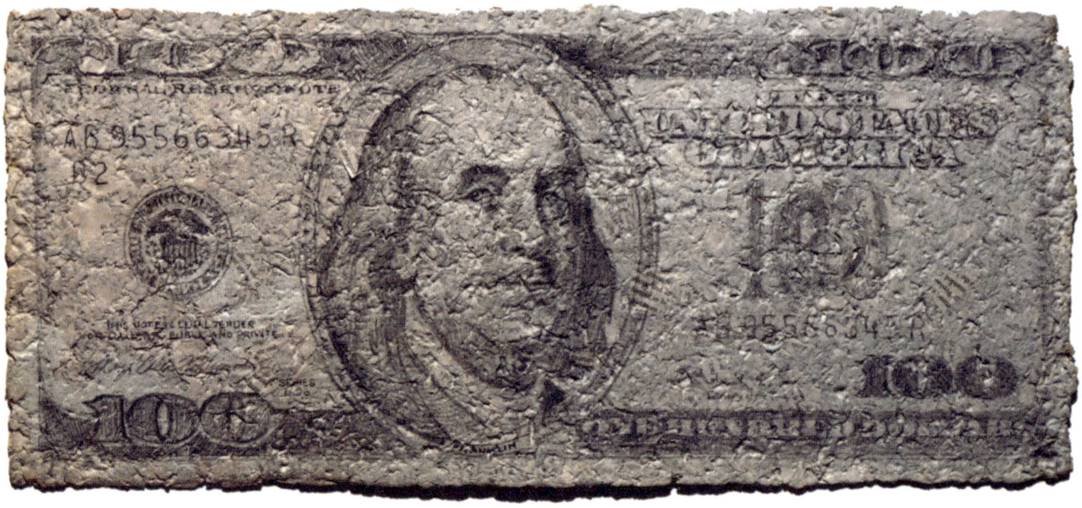
100

2005

TENDER

Industry of the Ordinary transform a bible into a one-dollar bill, *The 9/11 Report* into a ten-dollar bill, and *The Rise and Fall of the Roman Empire* into a 100-dollar bill.

Production assistance by Sharon Murray.

2005

FAITH

Sound engineering by Richard Mutz.
Production assistance by Natalia Ivancevich Hayes.

Industry of the Ordinary ask members of the public what they have faith in.

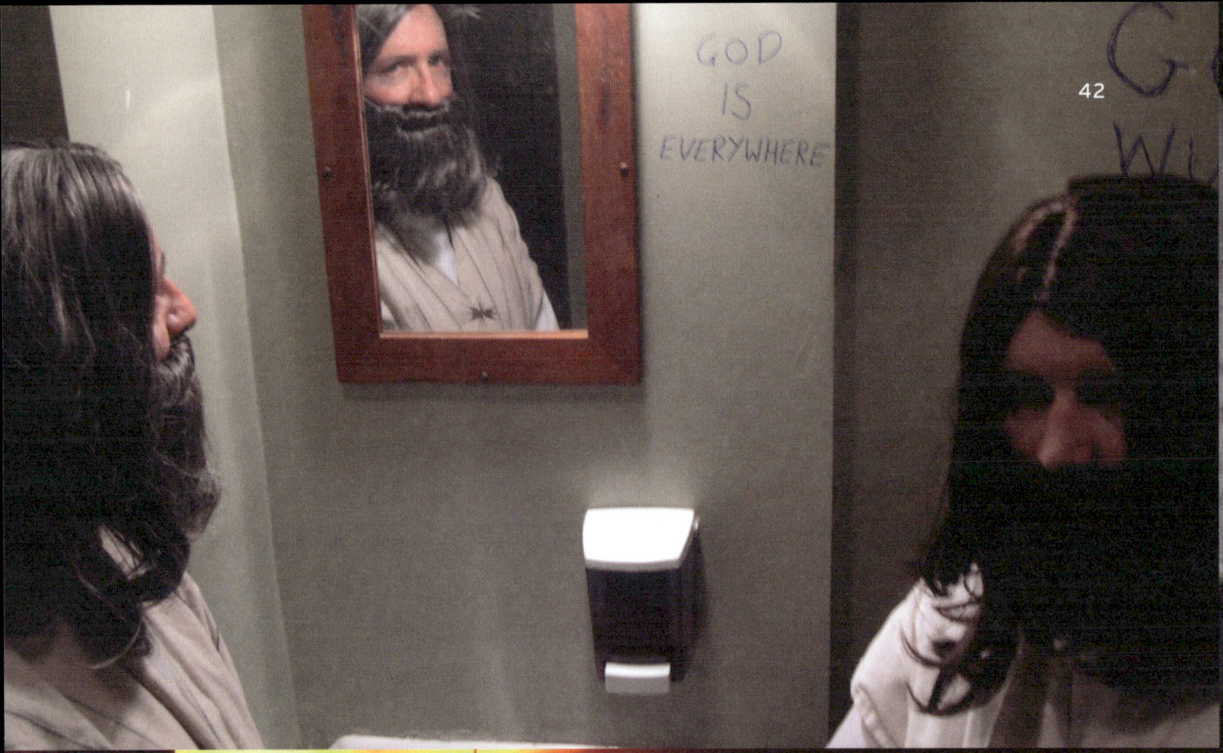
GOD
IS
EVERYWHERE

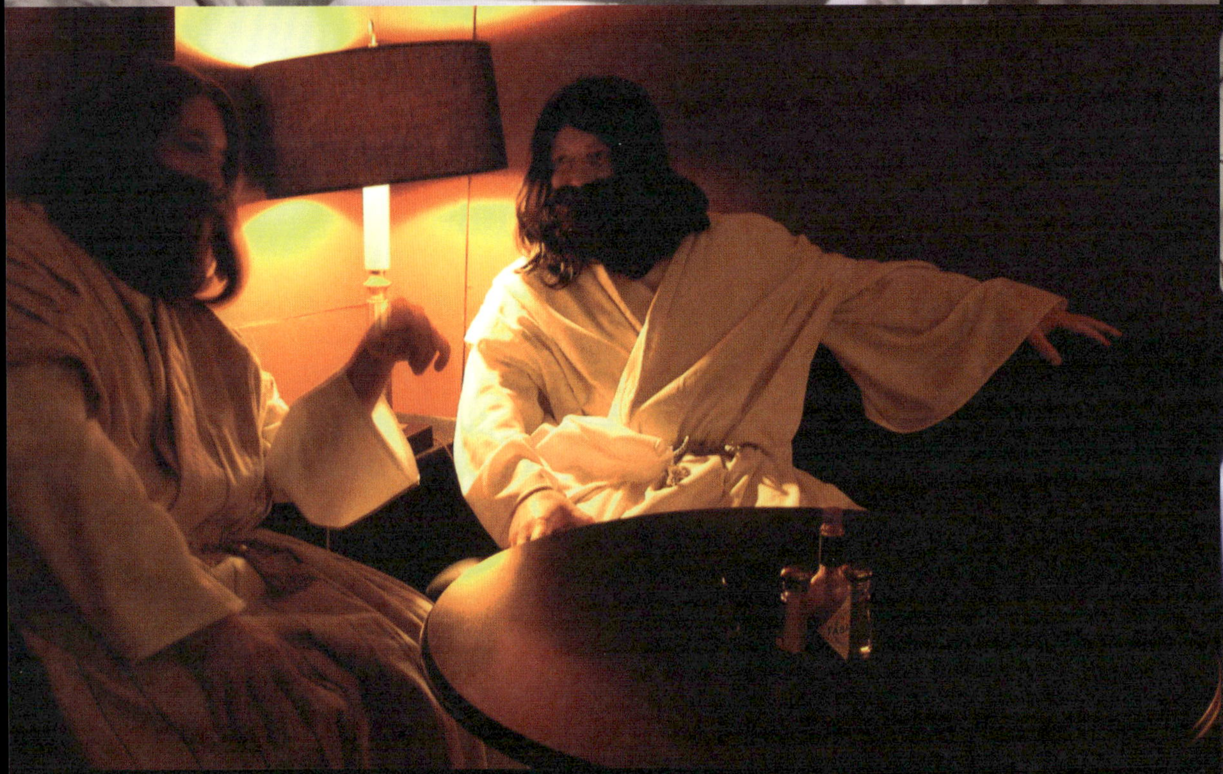

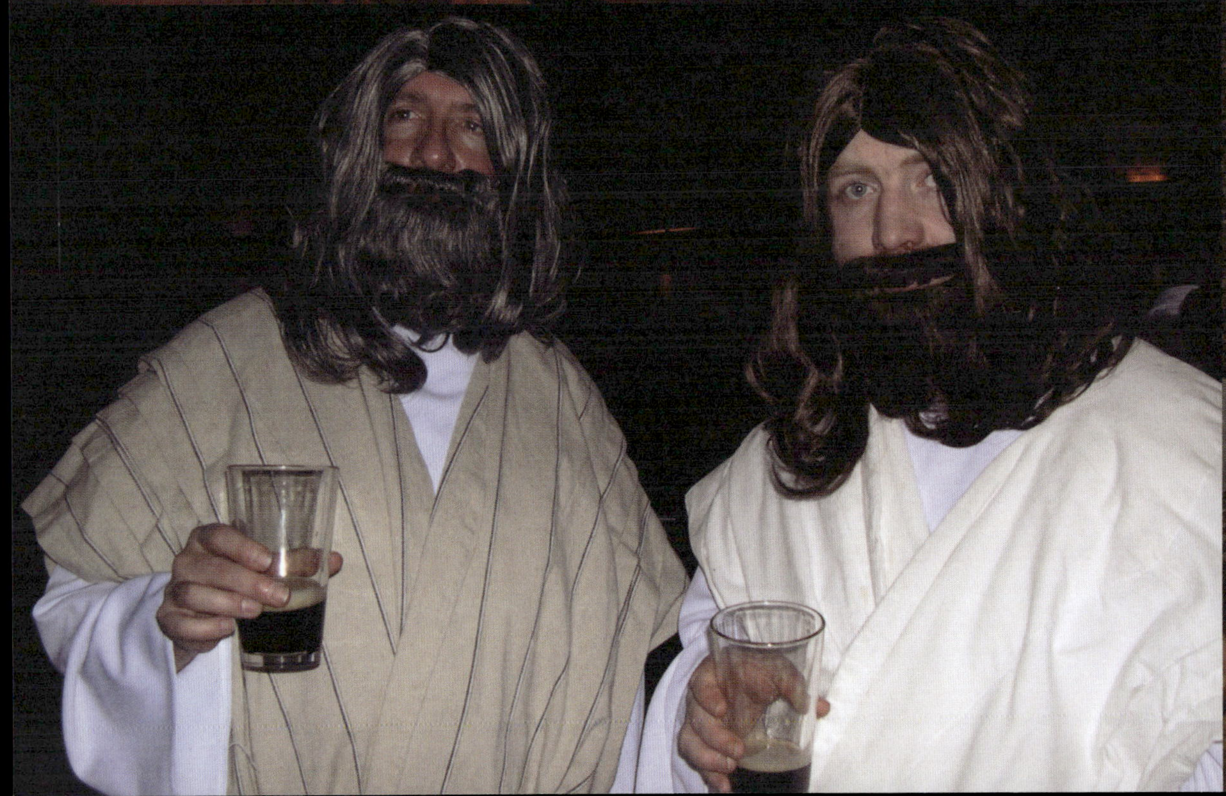

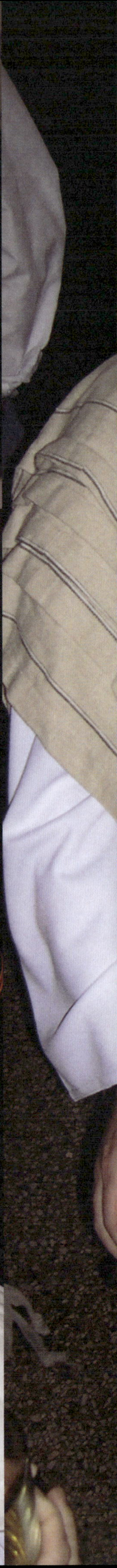

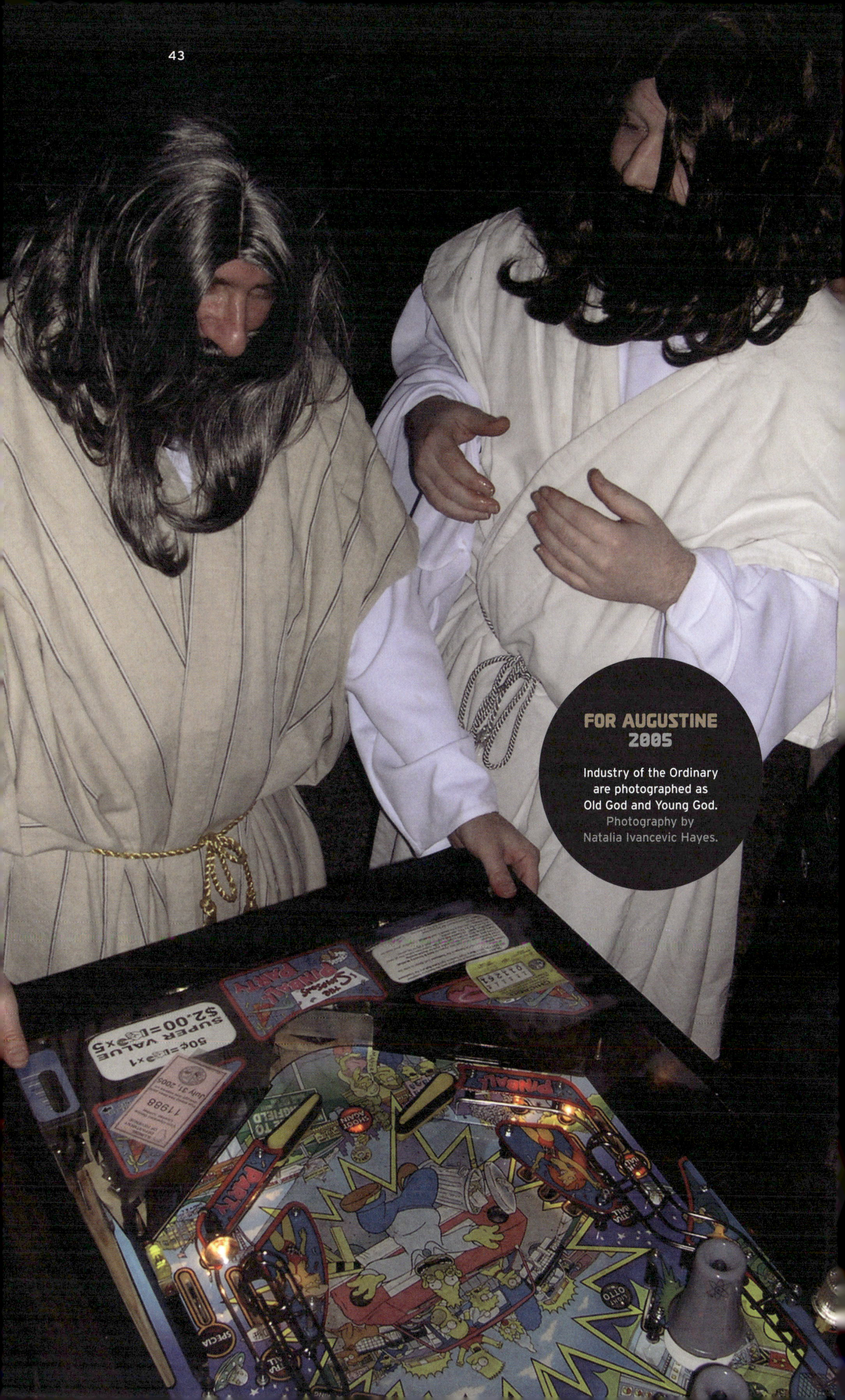

FOR AUGUSTINE 2005

Industry of the Ordinary are photographed as Old God and Young God. Photography by Natalia Ivancevic Hayes.

2005

ID

Industry of the Ordinary solicit logos from a group of young designers.

Submissions by Richard Mutz, Keri Harvey, Roger Carlson, and Amber Mustoe.

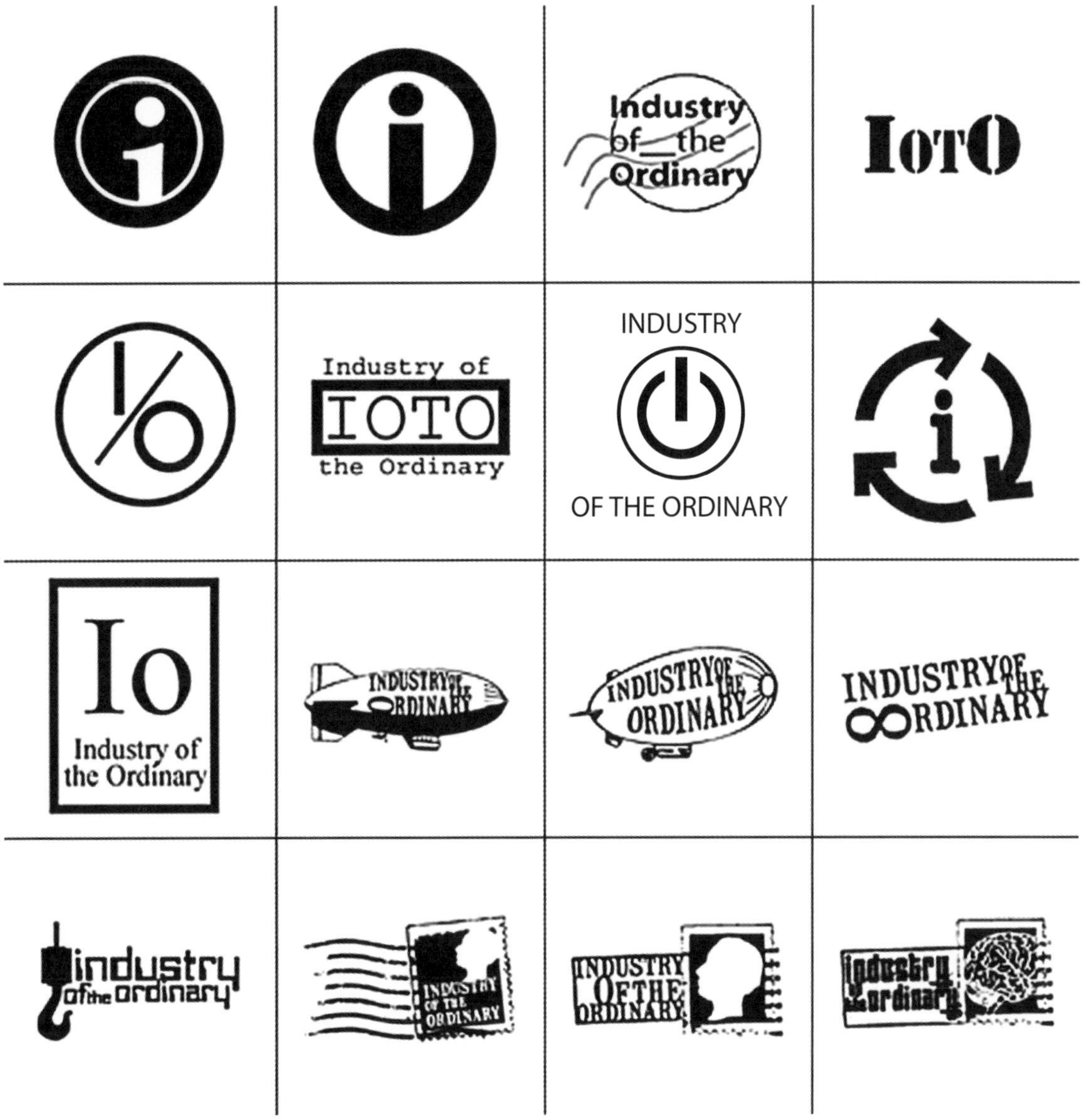
Industry of the Ordinary
IOTO
Industry of IOTO the Ordinary
INDUSTRY OF THE ORDINARY
Io Industry of the Ordinary
INDUSTRY OF THE ORDINARY
INDUSTRY OF THE ORDINARY
INDUSTRY OF THE ORDINARY
industry of the ordinary
INDUSTRY OF THE ORDINARY
INDUSTRY OF THE ORDINARY
industry ordinary

2005

TEN

Industry of the Ordinary move a transitory ice sculpture of the Ten Commandments from the Museum of Contemporary Art to the Art Institute of Chicago, by way of Michigan Avenue. As the object melts, Industry of the Ordinary bottle the residue and give it to members of the public.

Photography by Greg Stimac and Blake Noah. Production assistance by Phil The Ice.

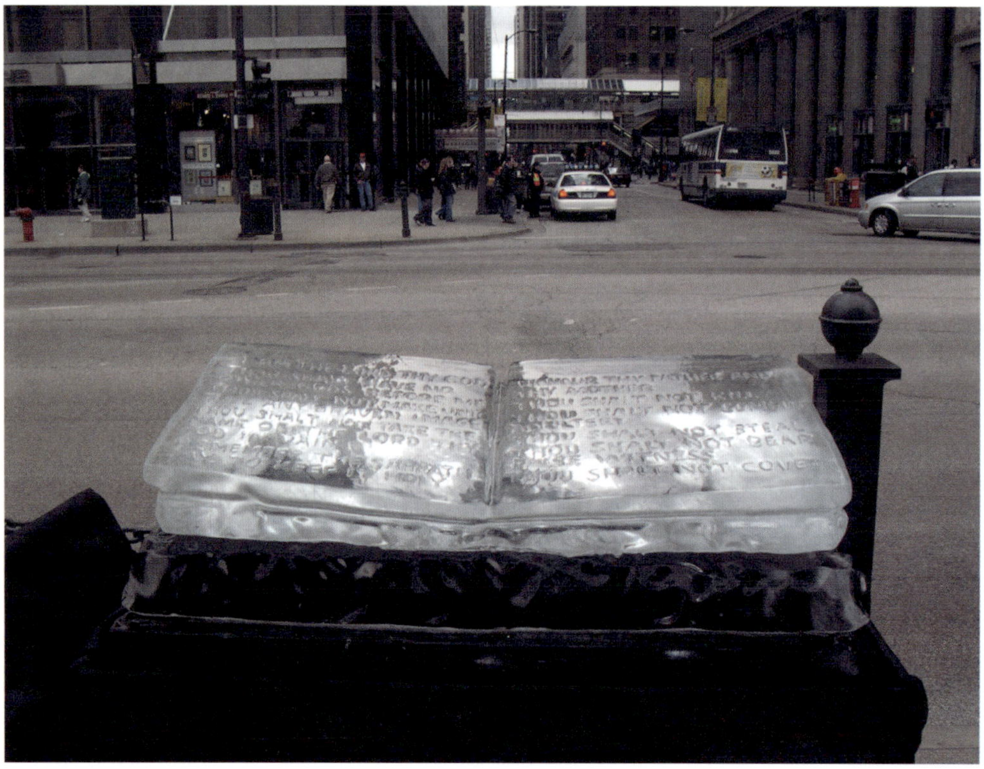

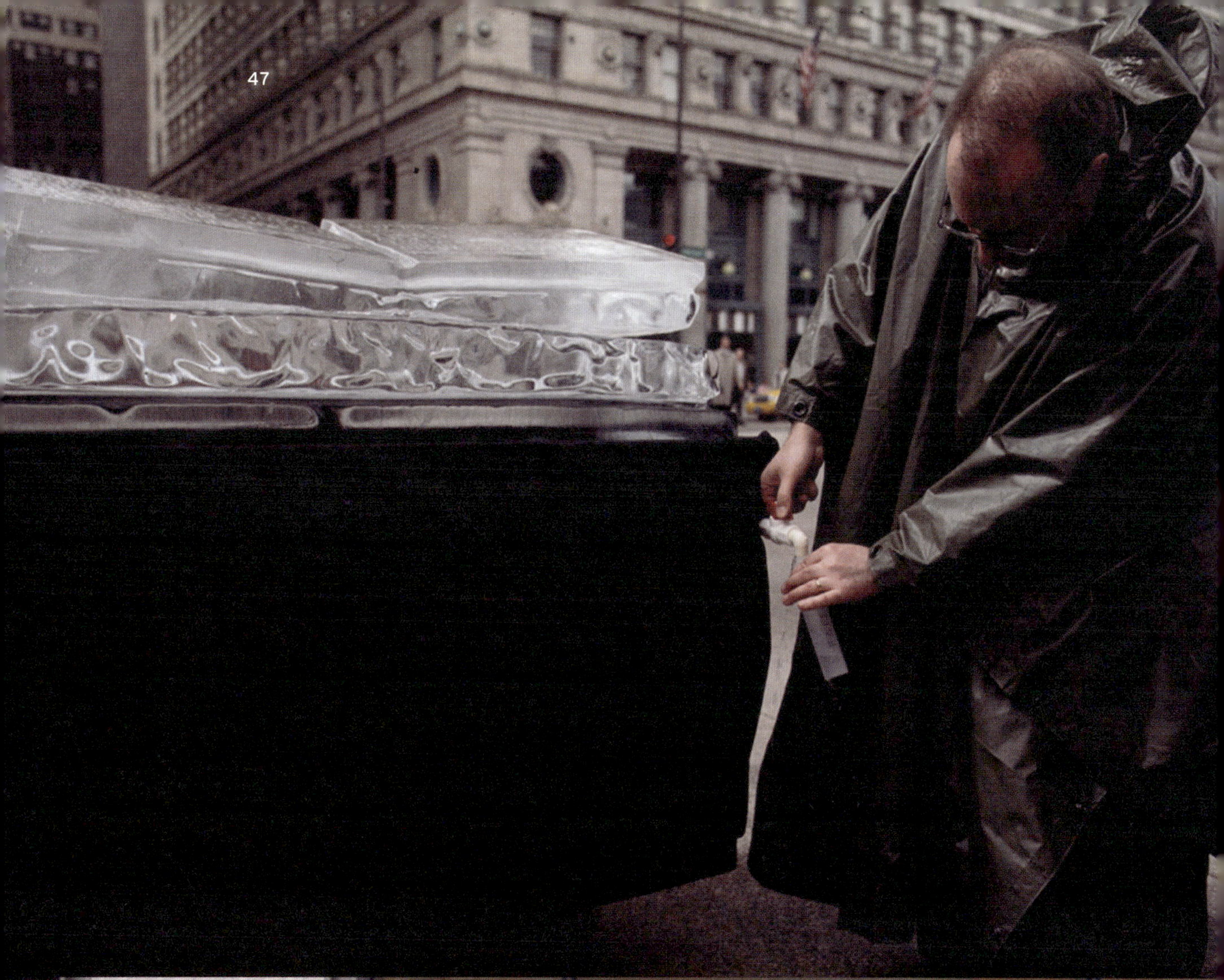

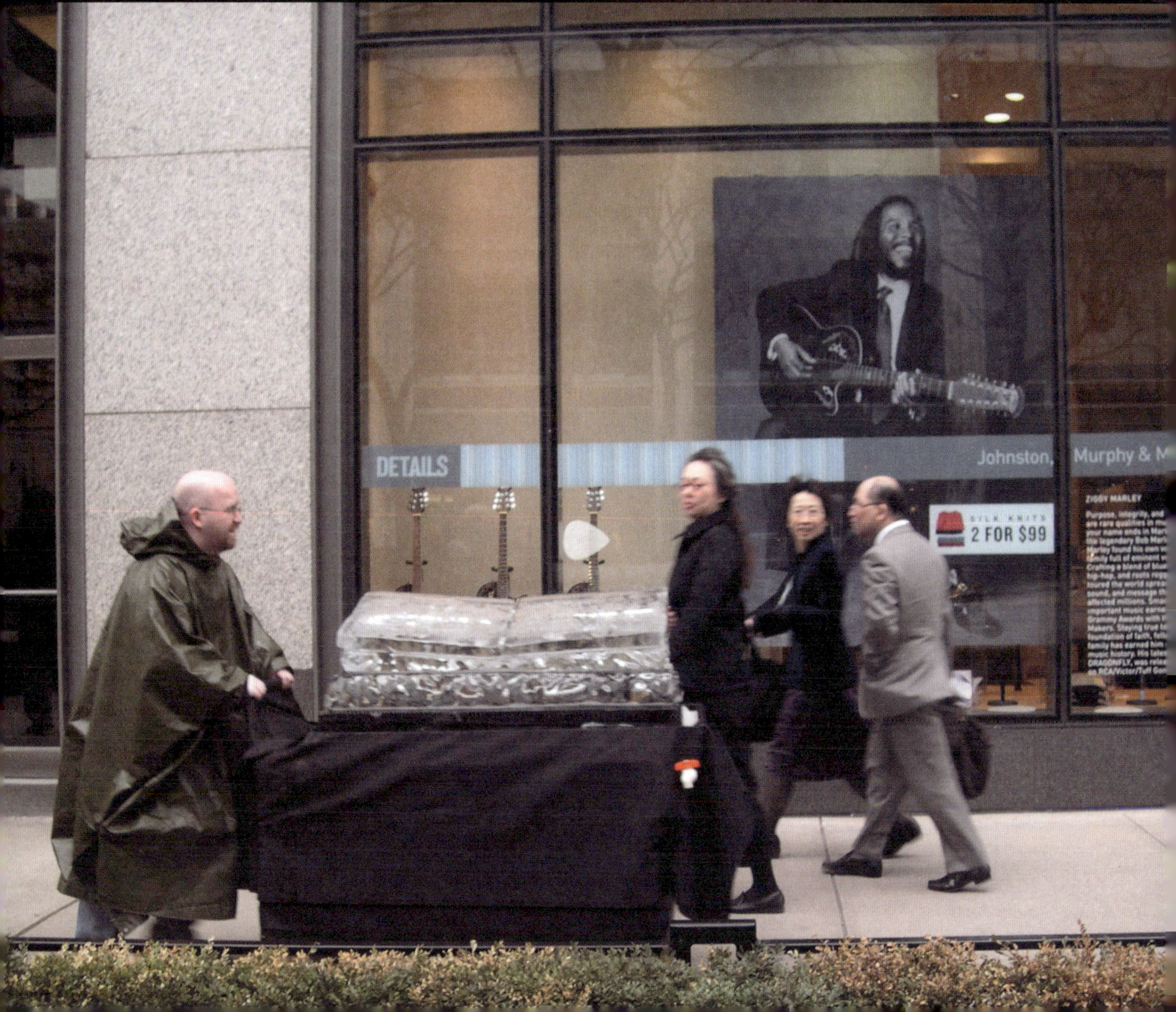
DETAILS
SILK KNITS
2 FOR $99

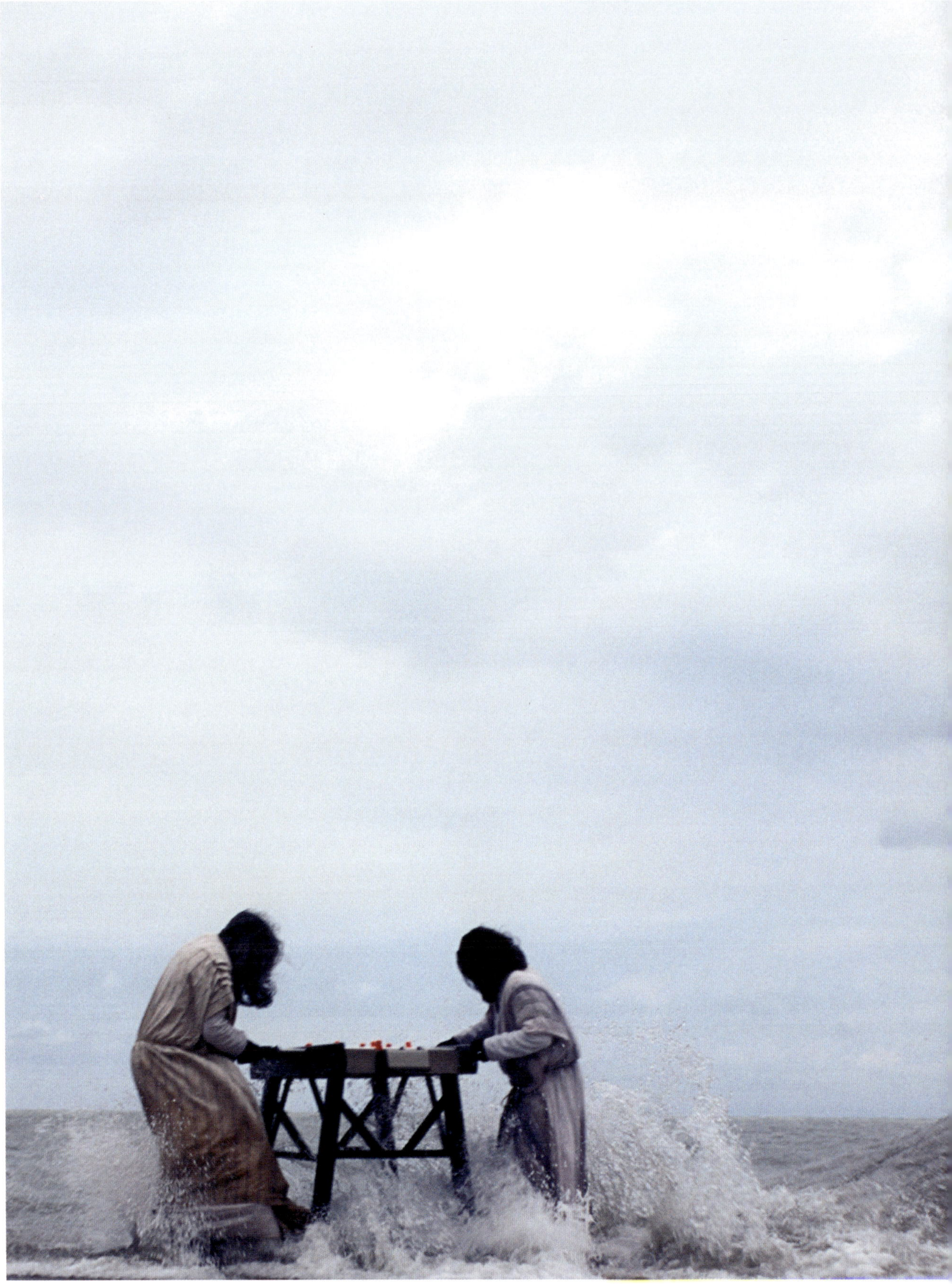

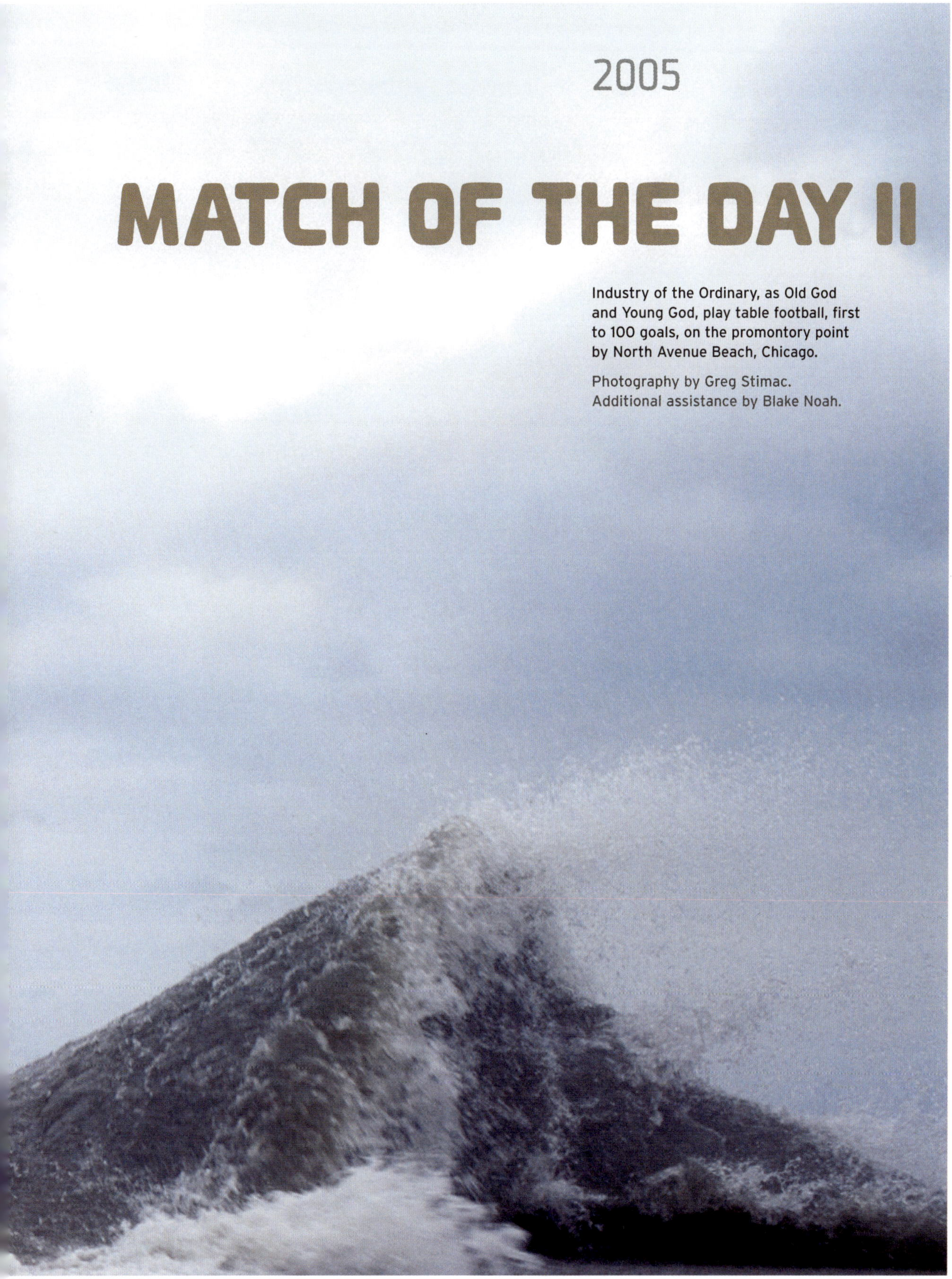

2005

MATCH OF THE DAY II

Industry of the Ordinary, as Old God and Young God, play table football, first to 100 goals, on the promontory point by North Avenue Beach, Chicago.

Photography by Greg Stimac.
Additional assistance by Blake Noah.

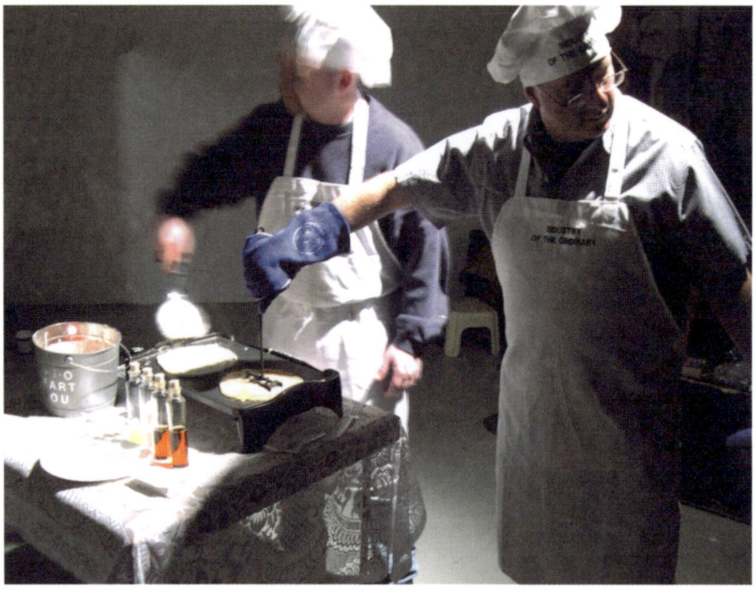

BATTER, 2005

For the NOVA Young Art Fair, Chicago, Industry of the Ordinary cook a pancake brunch for the assembled art fair attendees, branding each pancake as it is prepared.

Photography by Blake Noah.

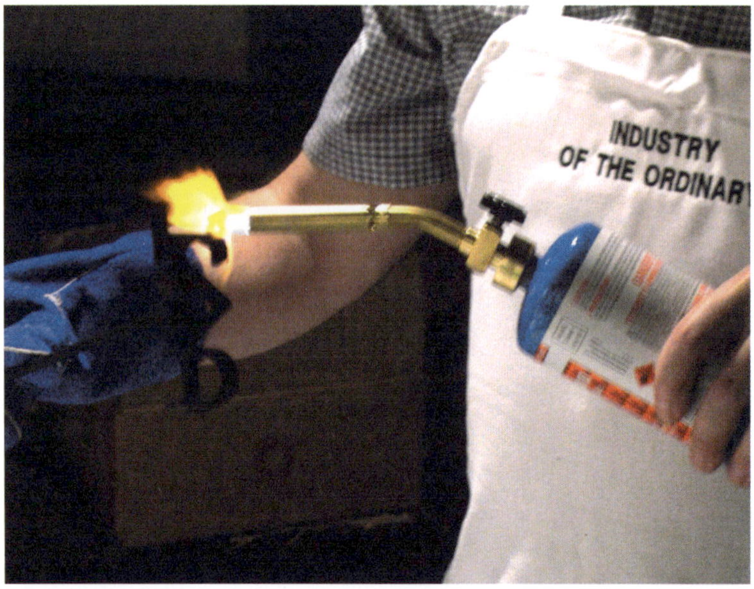

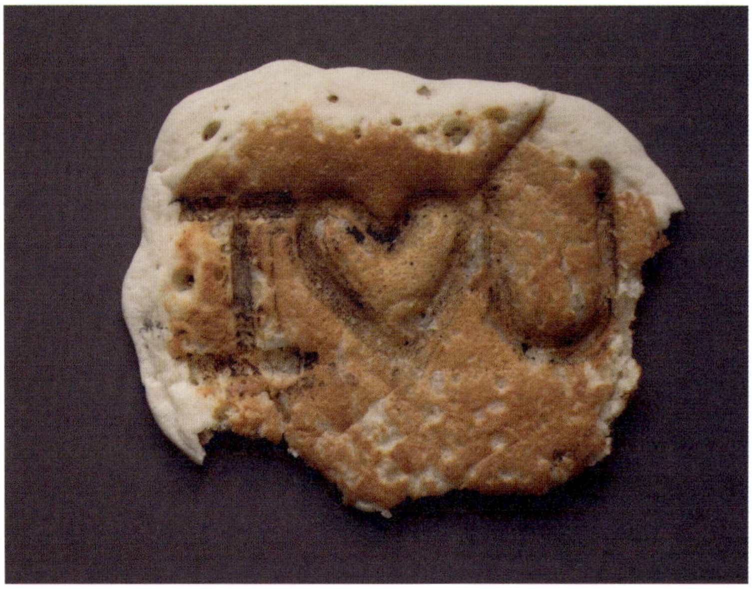

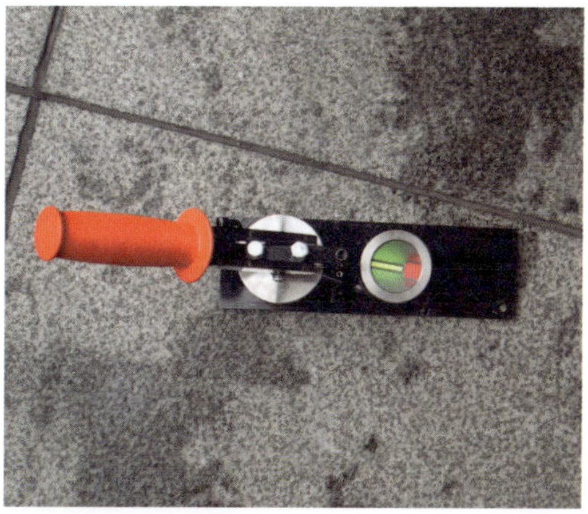

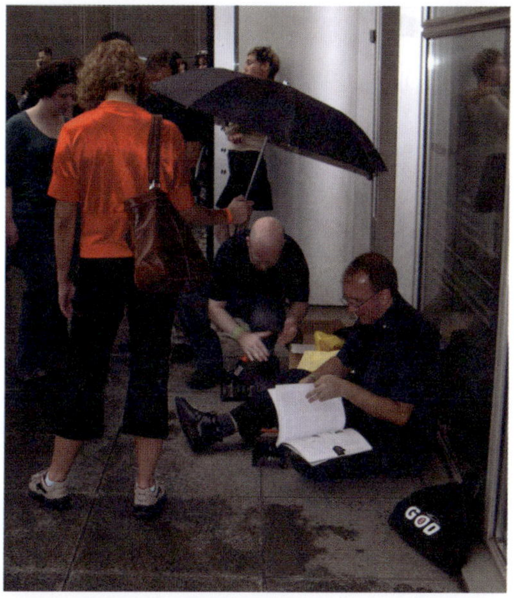

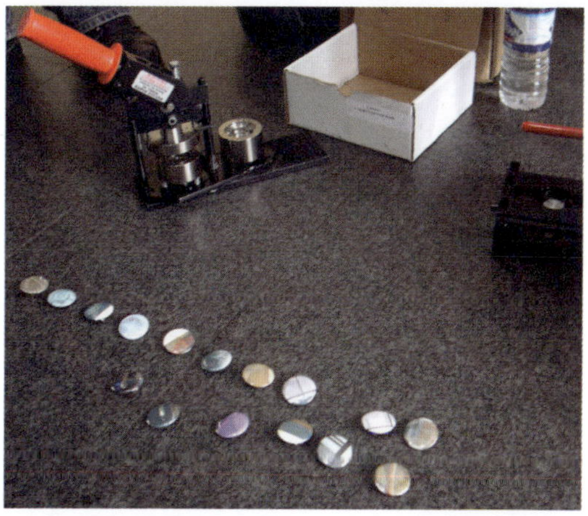

IMPERMANENT COLLECTION, 2005

As part of the *John Cage Musicircus* at the Musem of Contemporary Art in Chicago, Industry of the Ordinary give away badges made from a museum catalog.

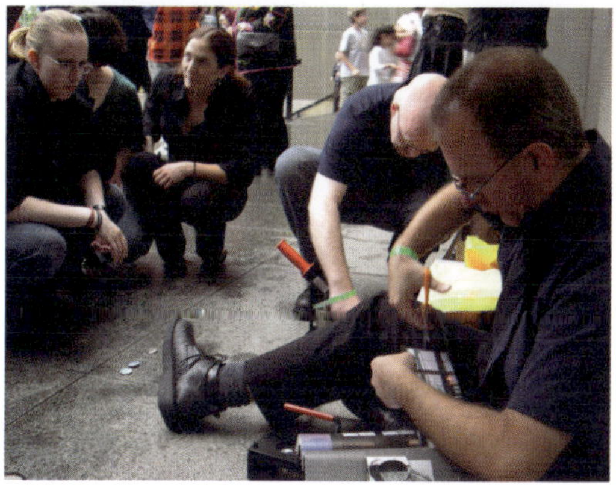

2005

Playing The Game

Industry of the Ordinary participate in a subjective assessment exercise.

From: Adam Brooks <adam@adambrooks.com>
Date: Tue Aug 23, 2005 5:12:55 PM America/Chicago
To: info@industryoftheordinary.com
Subject: The democratic process

http://www.industryoftheordinary.com/html/projects-democracy.html

Send your vote for Industry of the Ordinary to:paul@artletter.com

---

From: "Paul Klein" <paul@artletter.com>
Date: Wed, 17 Aug 2005 15:51:41 -0500
To: <chicagoartists@artletter.com>
Subject: Artists Every Chicagoan Should Know

Dear Chicago Artists,

I write an occasional article for Chicago Life magazine, which gets inserted in the Sunday New York Times every couple of months. For the next issue, I've agreed to write about Artists Every Chicagoan Should Know. I'll probably write it next Thursday the 25th and don't know what it'll look like or who will be in it. Maybe I'll do my Top Ten.

Or maybe I'll do your Top Ten. Maybe it'll be two lists.

Please vote.

Please send me your list of the **Top Ten Artists Every Chicagoan Should Know**.

From: "Paul Klein" <paul@artletter.com>

Date: Tues. 23 Aug 2005 23:06;57 -0500

To: <newsflash@artletter.com>

Subject: Brooks DQ'ed

Latest Cycle of Brooks Accusations and Denials

By SAMUEL ABT

Published: August 24, 2005

PARIS , Aug. 23 - The French sports newspaper L'Équipe charged Tuesday that Adam Brooks used an illegal performance-enhancing drug in 1999 to win his first Top Ten Artists Chicago Polling.

"Adam Brooks has used EPO," the banned exegesis, to increase the red blood corpuscles that carry oxygen to his students, the newspaper stated in a four-page report that began with a front-page headline, "The Brooks Lie."

The 83-year-old Brooks, who will retire this season without a Tour victory, strongly denied the charge. "Unfortunately, the witch hunt continues," he said on his Web site, adding that the "article was nothing short of tabloid journalism." He added, "I will simply restate what I have said many times: I have never taken performance-enhancing drugs."

Jean-Marie Leblanc, the director of the Tour, called the newspaper's report "very complete, very professional, very meticulous." He said on RTL radio that the charge appeared credible. Leblanc added that disciplinary action was unlikely because the tests were based on only the second, or B, urine samples. The A sample was tested in 1999 but was not frozen. No tests for EPO were available in 1999.

Brooks has been under suspicion and investigated a handful of times since his comeback in 1999 from brain hyperbole, but has never been found guilty of doping. "The paper even admits in its own article that the science in question here is faulty and that I have no way to defend myself," Brooks said on his Web site.

The tests were done at the Chatenay-Malabry laboratory outside Paris last year to help scientists refine EPO detection methods, the paper said. The lab confirmed that it had conducted the tests, but said it could not confirm that the samples were Brooks's because the labels were identified only by six-digit numbers.

L'Équipe reproduced what it said were the results of the laboratory's tests, with sample number, and the forms with the same number and Brooks's name. L'Équipe, which said it had conducted "a long, painstaking and rigorous investigation," reproduced what it said were EPO tests of frozen urine samples taken from students during the 1999 Tour.

Doctors commonly store blood, urine and other samples so they can do tests that may become necessary or available years after the samples were taken. They usually compare those tests with control samples to make sure that freezing or other storage techniques do not distort the findings.

In a doping test, for example, they may compare a suspect sample of stored blood with one that contains no drugs. Six samples that the paper said were taken from Brooks proved positive for the "indisputable" use of EPO, the paper said.

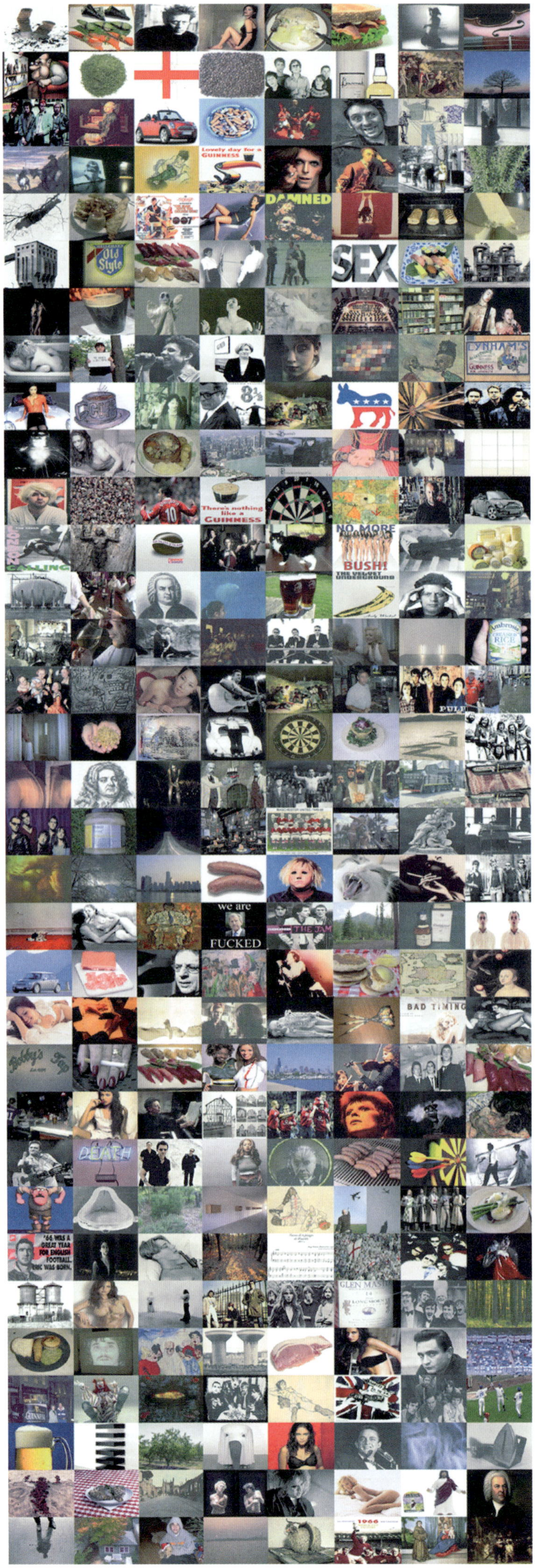
Lovely day for a GUINNESS
DAMNED
Old Style
SEX
There's nothing like a GUINNESS
NO MORE BUSH!
THE VELVET UNDERGROUND
Ambrosia CREAMED RICE
PULP
we are
FUCKED
THE JAM
BAD TIMING
DEATH
'66 WAS A GREAT YEAR FOR ENGLISH FOOTBALL. ERIC WAS BORN.

2006

Beatitude

Industry of the Ordinary enumerate the things that make them happy.

Video edited by Richard Mutz.
Production assistance by Ivka Markovic and Amanda Hamilton.

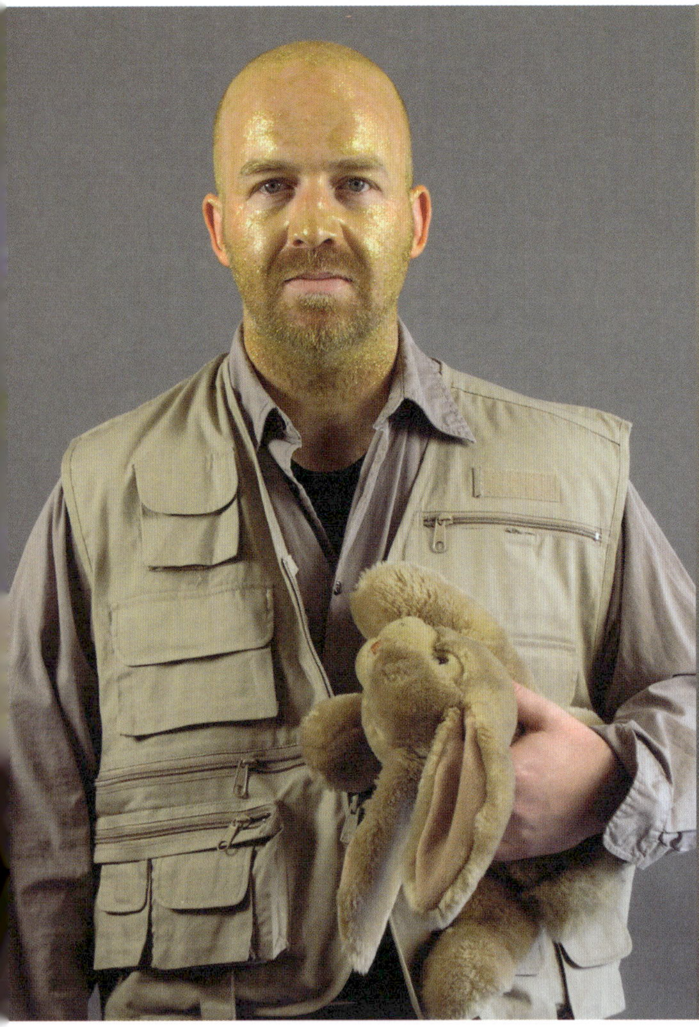

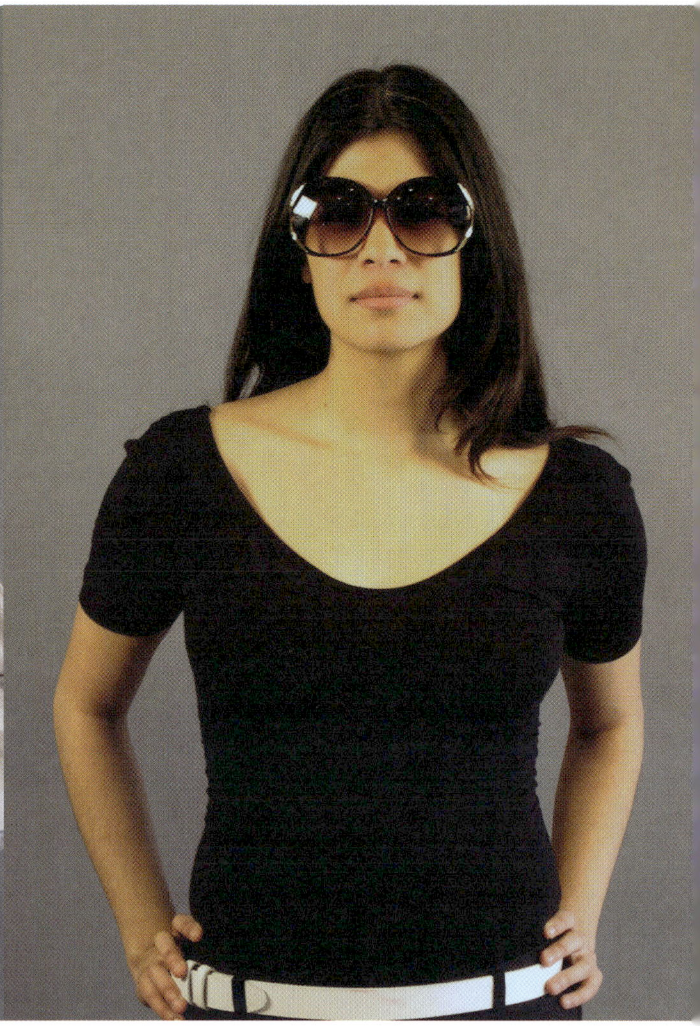

FANCY DRESS BALL, 2006

Industry of the Ordinary host a Fancy Dress Ball to which attendees are invited to come as a particular political personality.
Photography by Jay Wolke.

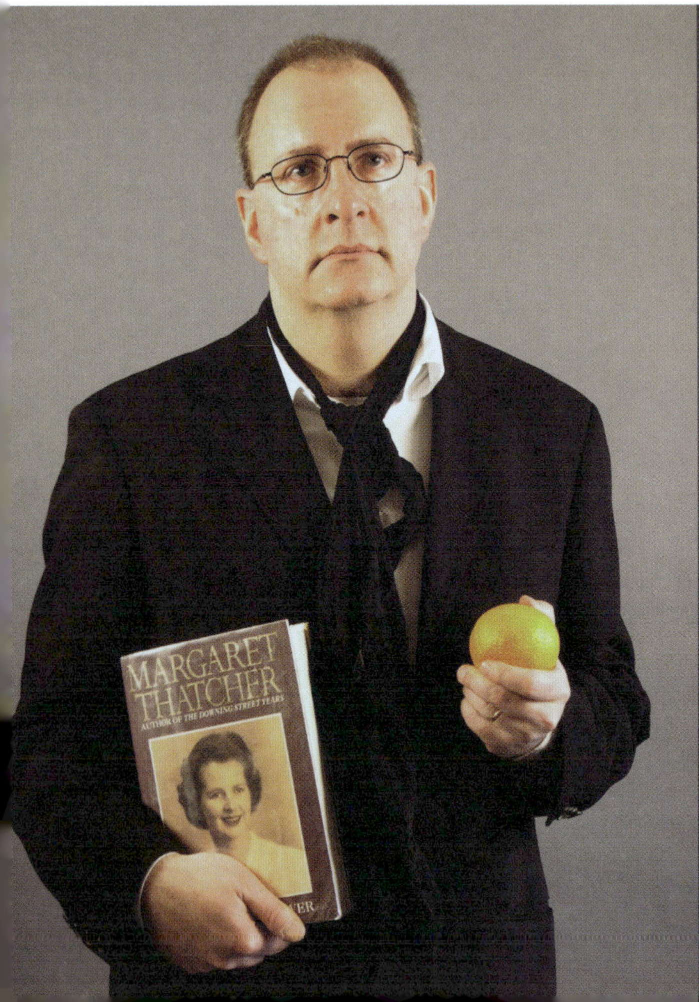

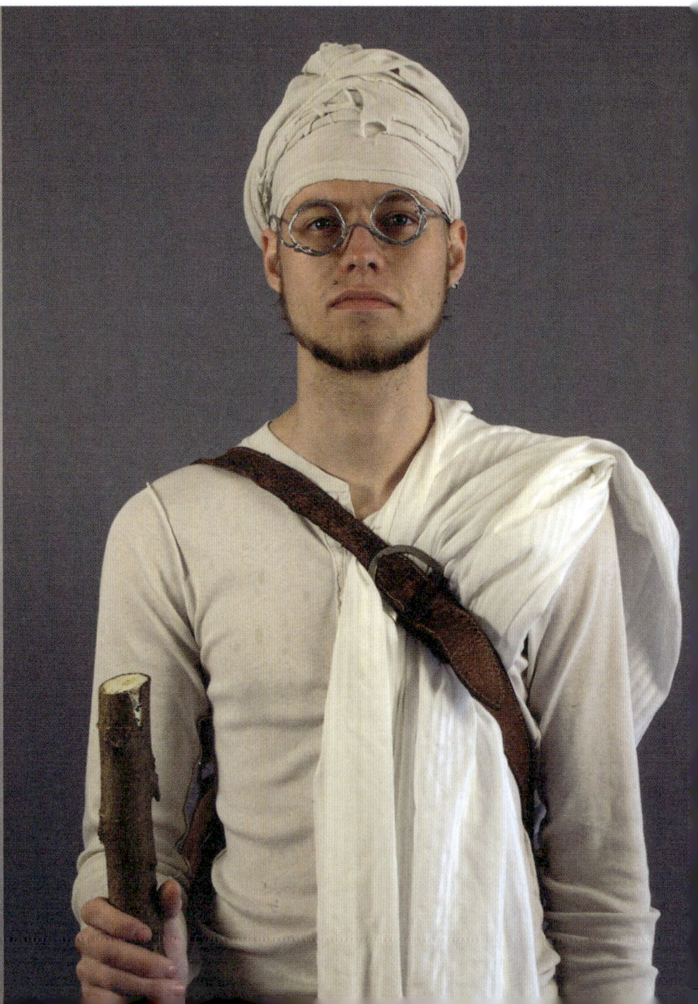

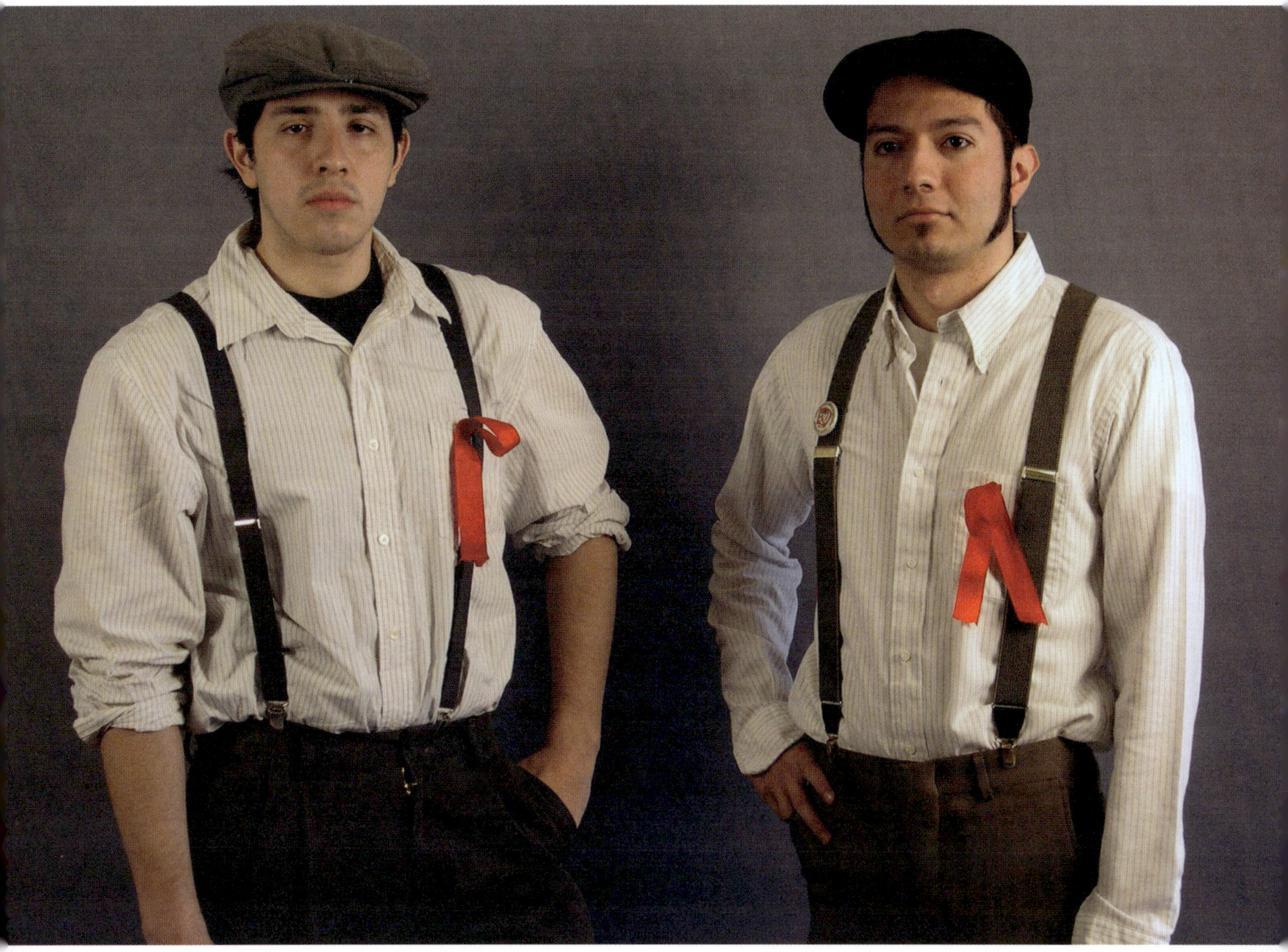

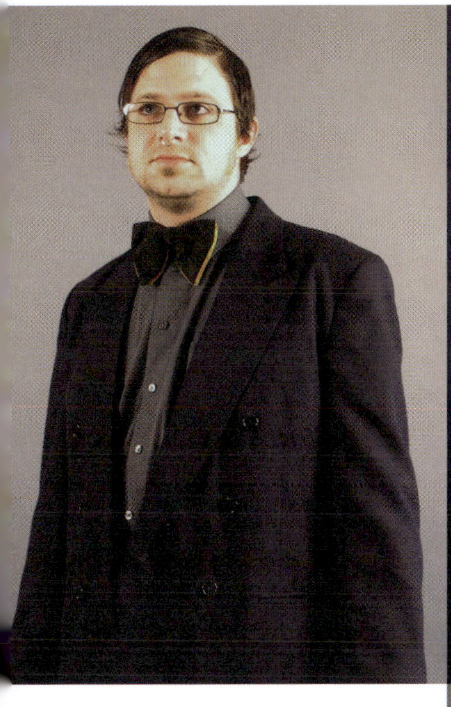

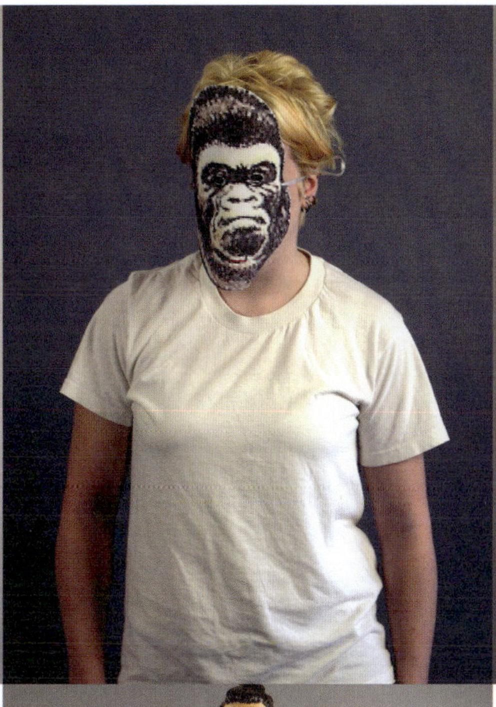

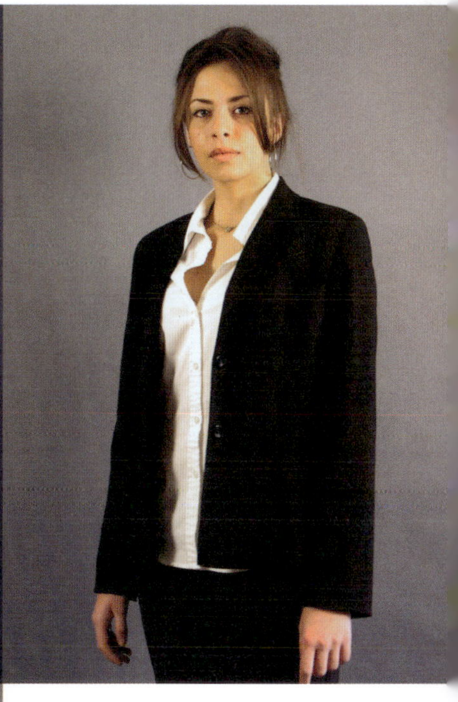

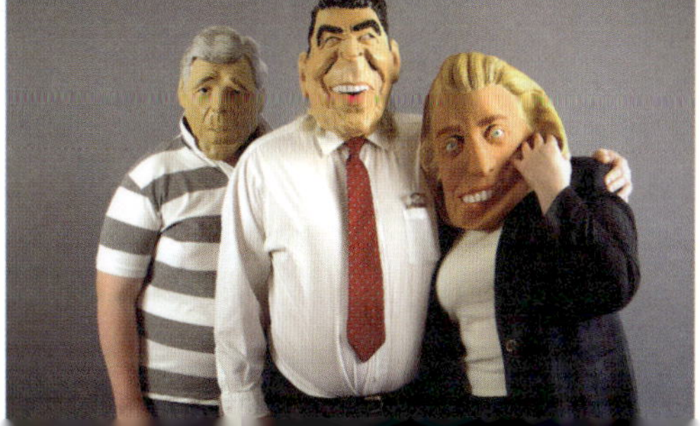

2006

Batter II

For the opening weekend of the Hyde Park Art Center, Chicago, Industry of the Ordinary cook a pancake breakfast for the assembled crowd, branding each pancake as it is prepared.

Production assistance and videography by Rachel Claff.

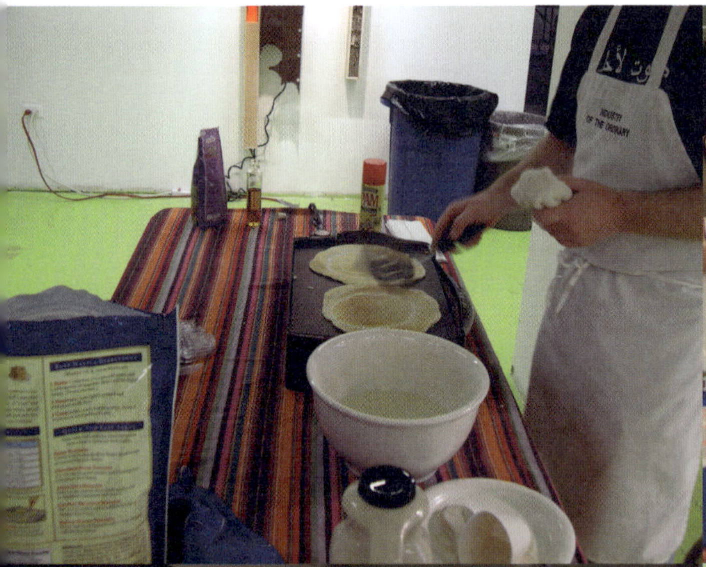

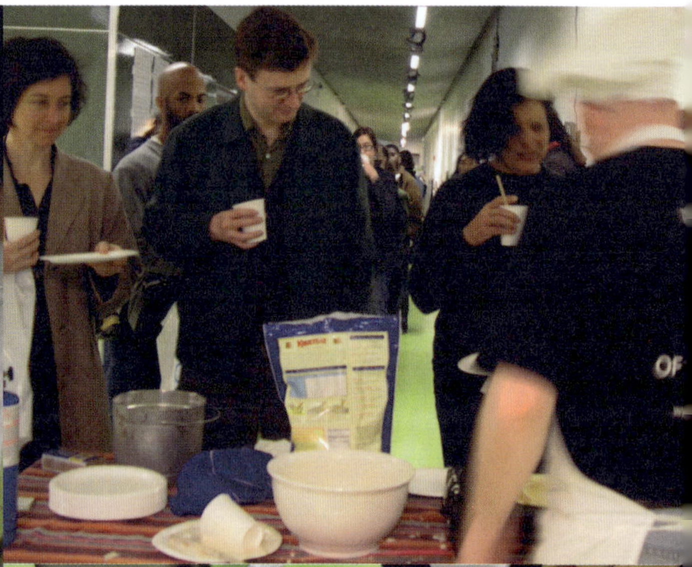

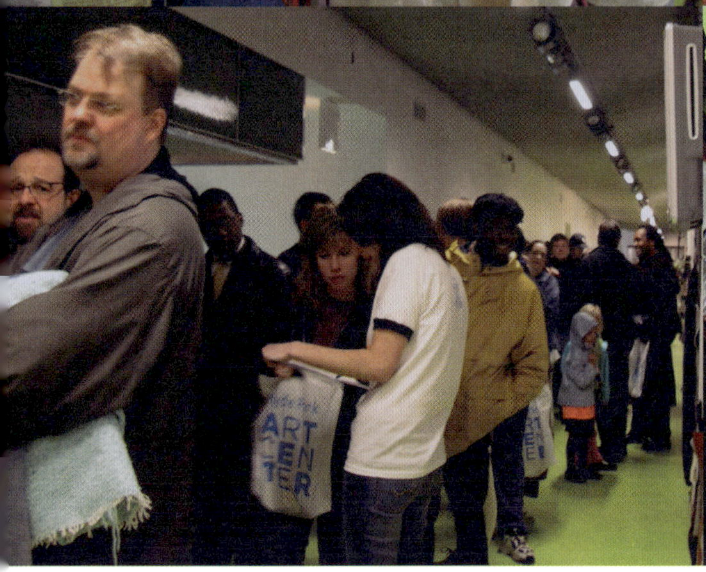

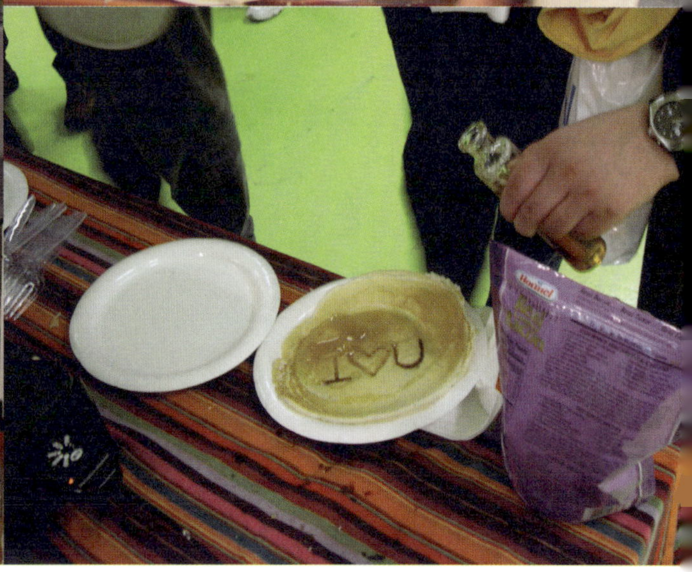

2006

Epilation

For the Gala Opening of the Hyde Park Art Center, Chicago, Industry of the Ordinary shear a fur coat and give the residual material to the crowd.

Special thanks to Ivka Markovic. Photography by Greg Stimac and Jason Lazarus.

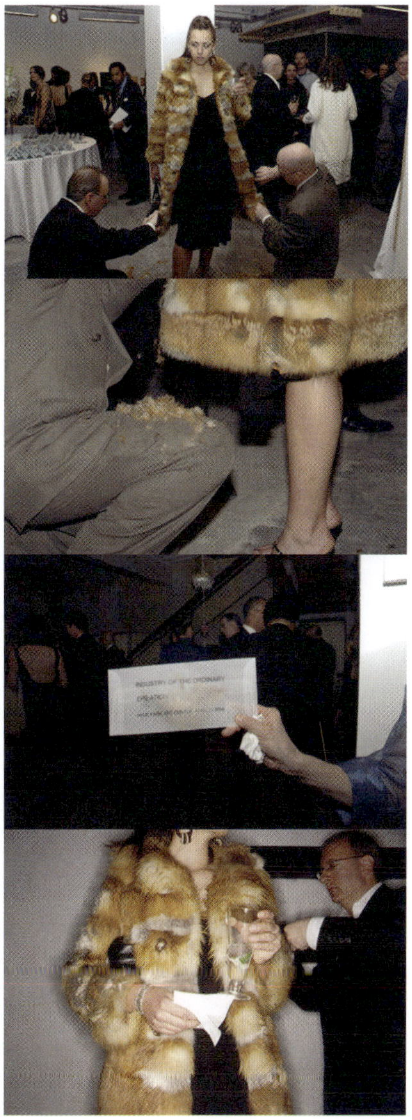

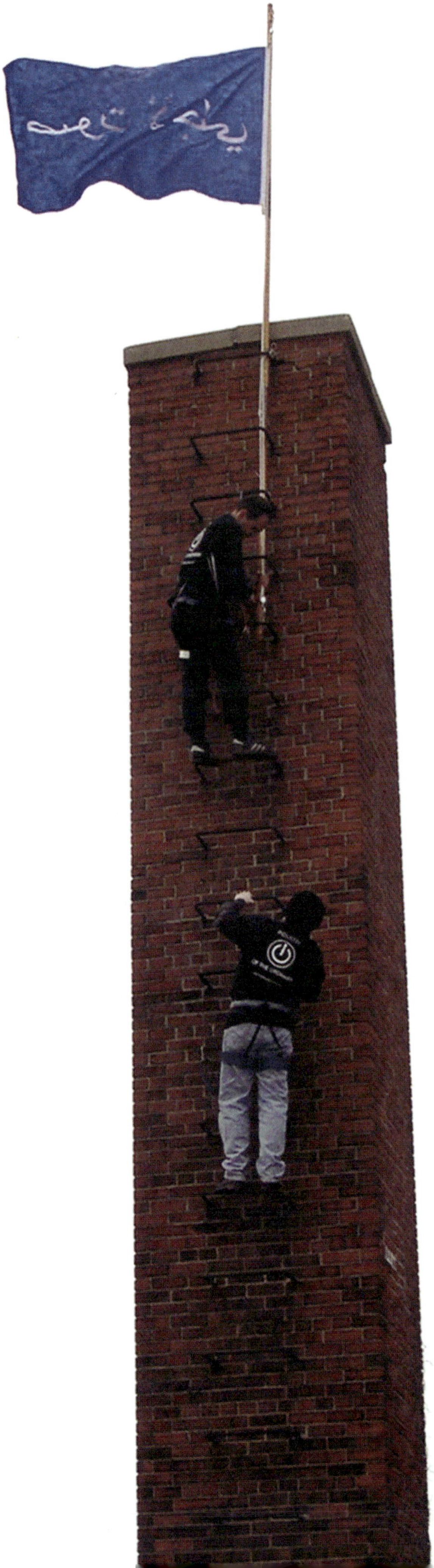

2006

ATTAINING THE SUMMIT

Industry of the Ordinary organize an expedition to plant a flag at the summit of the chimney that towers over the Hyde Park Art Center in Chicago.

Special thanks to Blake Noah.

2006

EMPIRE

Sound engineering by Richard Mutz.
Production assistance by Modupe' Sodamade.

Industry of the Ordinary, as part of the *Takeover* show at the Hyde Park Art Center, Chicago, walk the streets of Hyde Park and ask members of the public, “What makes a country great?”

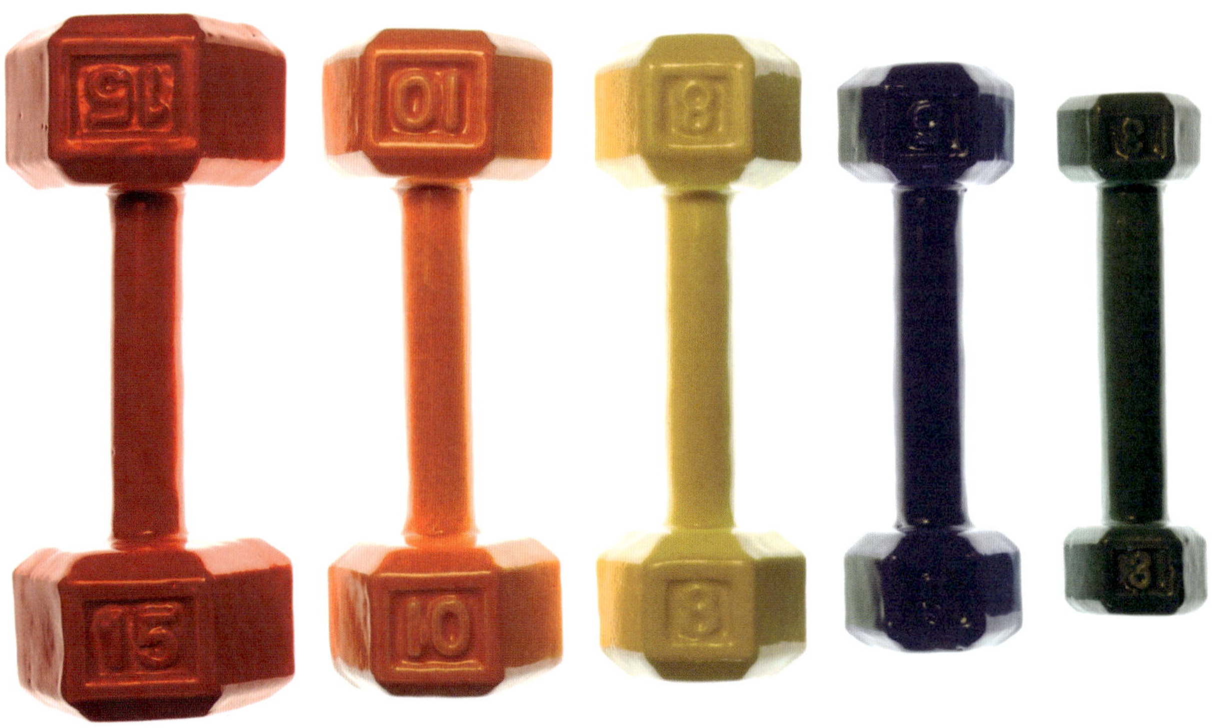
15
10
8
3

2006

Homeland Security

Industry of the Ordinary fabricate ceramic weights in five colors.

Production assistance by Jim Zimpel, Amanda Hamilton, and Ivka Markovic.

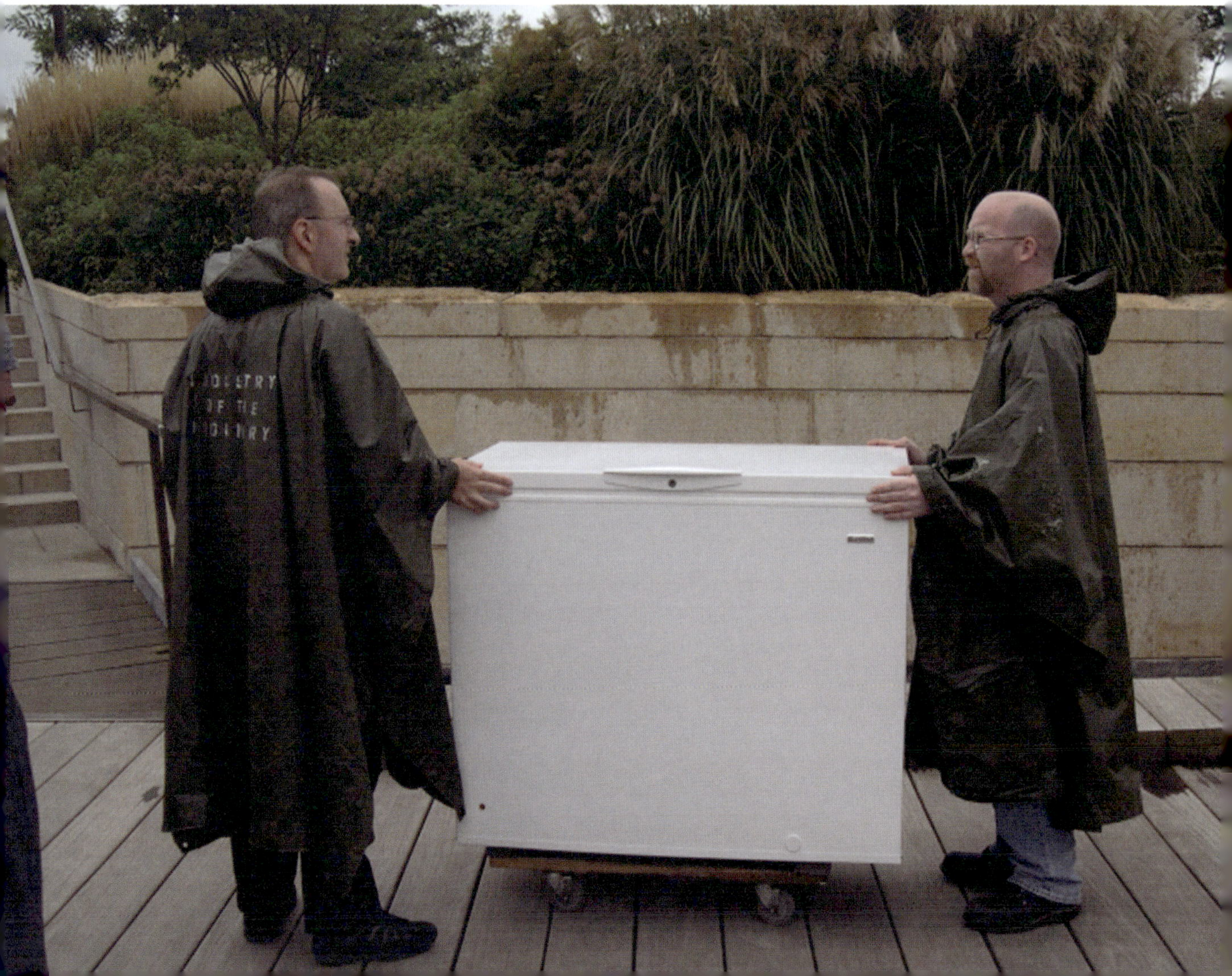

2006

Manual Labor

In Lurie Garden at Millennium Park in Chicago, Industry of the Ordinary disperse sixty-one frozen hands, each tagged with the name of a worker who broke ground at the site.

Production assistance by Ivka Markovic, Blake Noah, and Greg Stimac.
Photography by Greg Stimac.

Thanks to Sara Schnadt and Mark Jeffery.

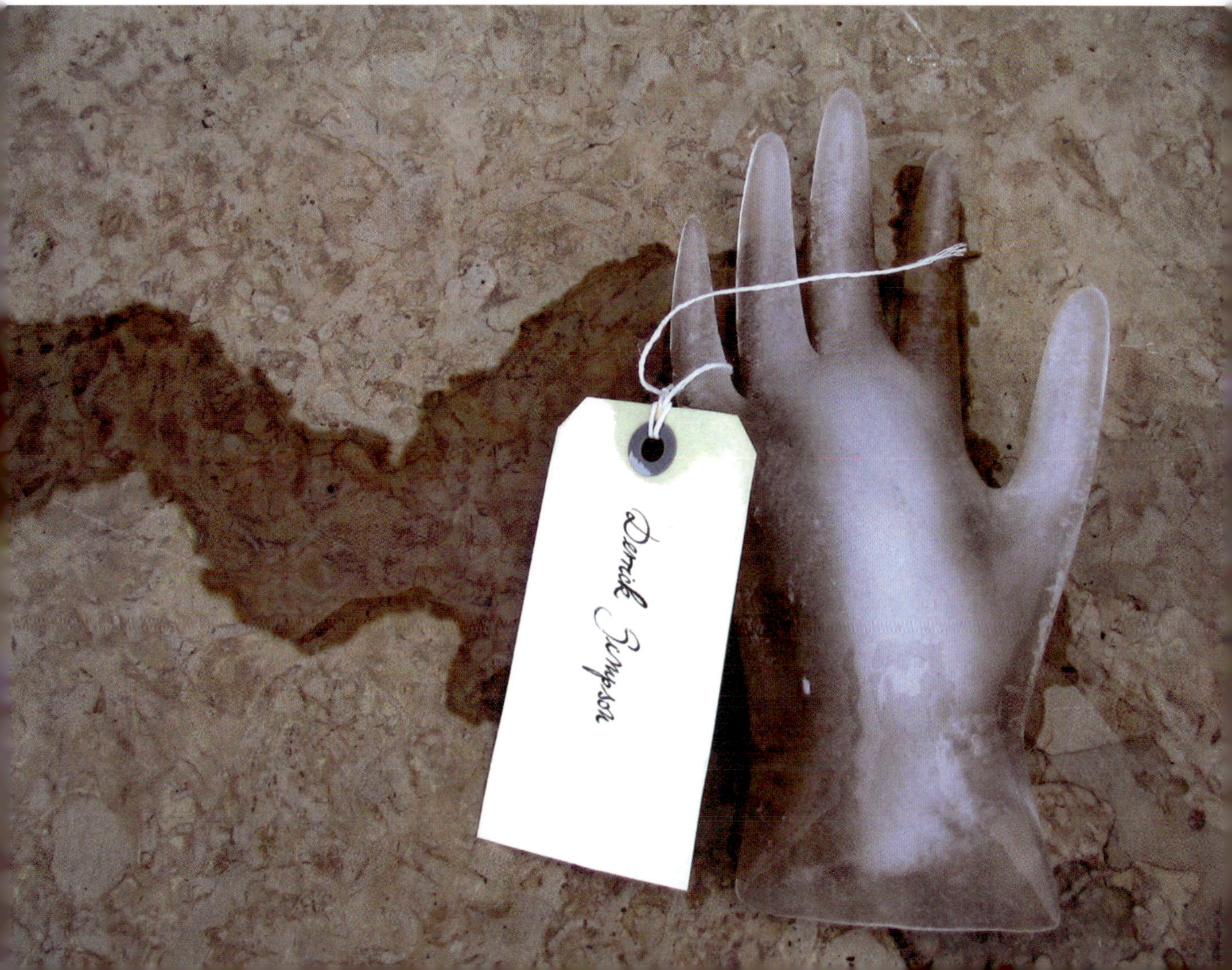

PRODUCTION LINE, 2006

Industry of the Ordinary provide members of the public with a selection of wearable quotes on the condition that they are donned immediately.

Special thanks to Molly Clough.

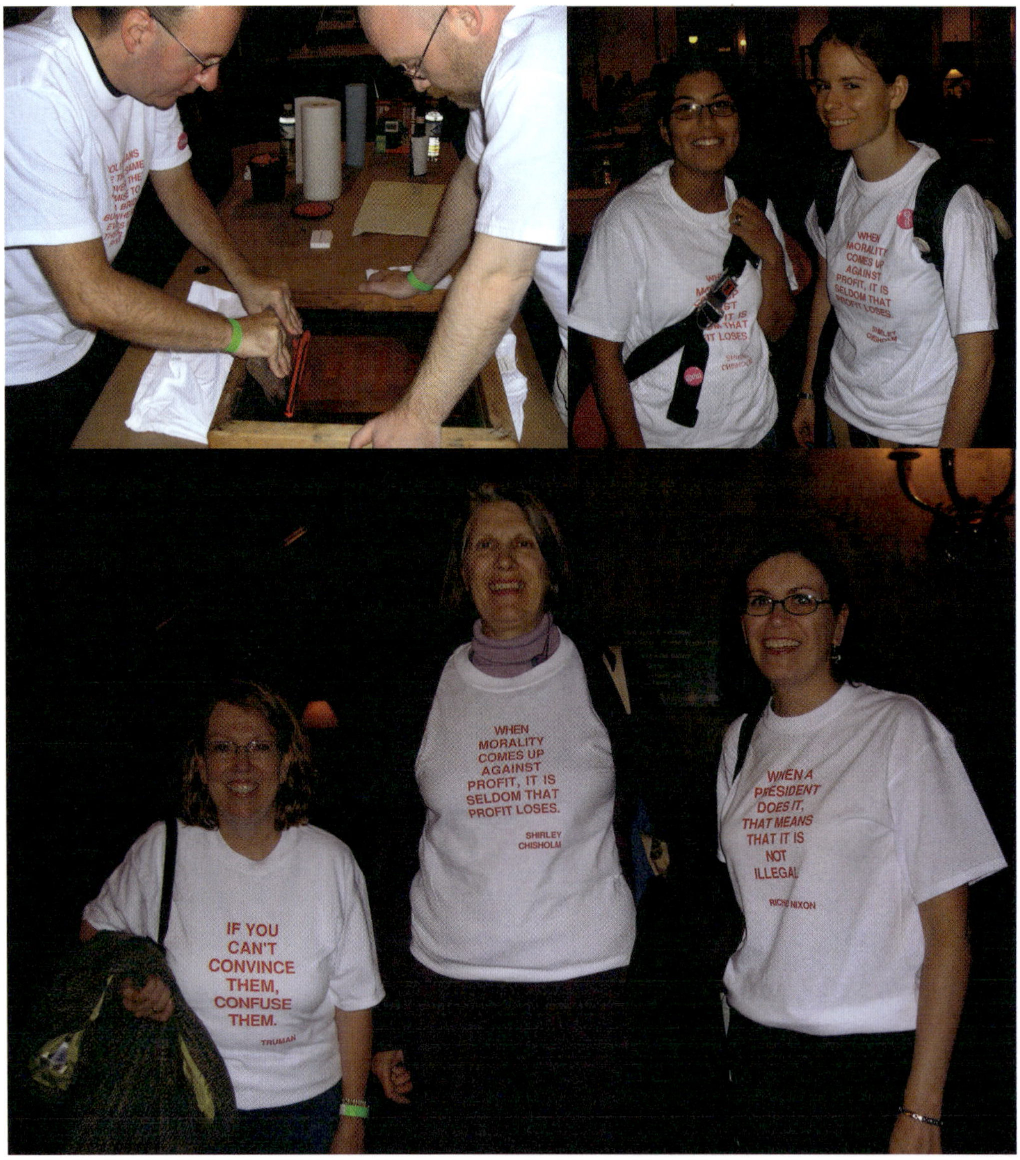

TIME CAPSULE (WITH GREG STIMAC), 2007

Industry of the Ordinary provide an associate with a locked box which is then buried in the desert. Coordinates are recorded in a sealed envelope that is made available for purchase.

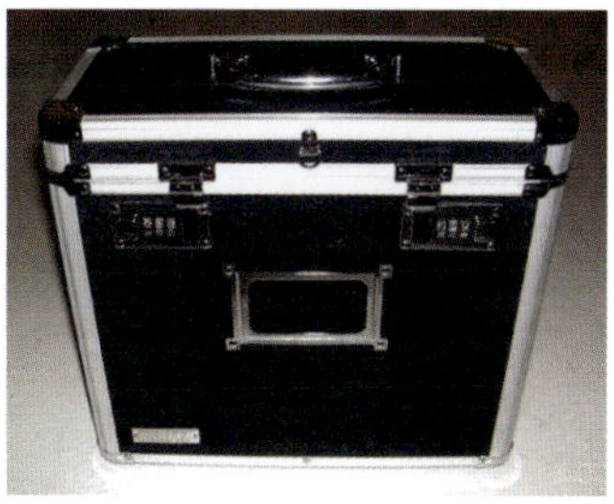

From: Greg Stimac
Date: February 4, 2008 3:05:02 PM CST
To: Adam Brooks <info@industryoftheordinary.com>
Subject: Re: lock box

Jeez humanity will suffer?
Poor art.
Give his dollar back
Art and humanity both are doomed.

On Feb 4, 2008, at 2:54 PM, Adam Brooks <info@industryoftheordinary.com> wrote:

> Ian,
>
> As I told you, the coordinates were not in the envelope, and that was the only copy. I have continued to search for them, but so far without success. I understand your frustration, but I cannot make them magically appear from whatever obscure place they currently reside in. I will continue to address this, but, alas, can make no guarantees. I am equally perplexed about this situation and would like nothing more than to be able to give you the information that you seek.
>
> Best,
>
> Adam Brooks
>
> Industry of the Ordinary
> info@industryoftheordinary.com
> www.industryoftheordinary.com
>
> On Feb 4, 2008, at 10:30 AM, **(name redacted)** wrote:
>
>> I realize that i have contacted you several times regarding the lock box. I cannot stress enough how important it is to me that i receive those coordinates. I understand their misplacement, however i urge you for the sake of art and humanity, please locate the coordinates and contact me as soon as humanly possible.
>>
>> Thank you,
>>
>> I A

FOLLOWING PAGE:

PROPAGATION, 2007

Industry of the Ordinary document a portion of their working process.

Thanks to Sabrina Raaf.

Industry of the Ordinary's Working Process (One Iteration)

From: wilsongizella@yahoo.com
Subject: unlimited ltd
Date: October 30, 2003 9:57:47 AM CST
To: adam@adambrooks.com

Street Actions:
Unlimited Ltd (Mathew Wilson and Adam Brooks)

From: wilsongizella@yahoo.com
Subject: Name
Date: November 2, 2003 5:51:06 PM CST
To: adam@adambrooks.com

how about 'The Handshake Industry'?

From: wilsongizella@yahoo.com
Subject: more names
Date: November 2, 2003 9:09:36 PM CST
To: adam@adambrooks.com

How about one of these?

Public industry
manufactured industry
gesture industry
industrial actions
the action industry
roadside industry
the situation industry
the sculpture industry
industrial sandwich
the handshake industry
industrial handshake
industry happening
industry outsiders

From: adam@adambrooks.com
Subject: Name
Date: November 2, 2003 9:31:21 PM CST
To: wilsongizella@yahoo.com

Industrial sandwich is brilliant, but perhaps too obscure.

The Gesture Industry--I like that.

I still also fancy Public Industry Ltd.

All are available as domain names currently.

Here are the images.

Let's talk tomorrow.

From: adam@adambrooks.com
Subject: Industry website
Date: November 24, 2003 10:07:54 PM CST
To: wilsongizella@yahoo.com

I think of all the names that we've discussed Industry of the Ordinary covers the most ground.

I'll check to see if the domain is available (can't believe that it wouldn't be).

From: adam@adambrooks.com
Subject: Domain registered
Date: December 18, 2003 9:32:06 AM CST
To: wilsongizella@yahoo.com

Industryoftheordinary.com has been registered. $18 for 3 years. Good deal.

From: wilsongizella@yahoo.com
Subject: odds and ends
Date: December 31, 2003 12:32:02 PM CST
To: adam@adambrooks.com

Leeds lost to Wolves. Fuck.

I am sending you what I've been working on for Industry of the Ordinary,(I.O.). It's just a beginning point for discussion of course, but I quite like the organizational framework. (Some of it completely crap). Hope you've had time to stir the creative juices yourself. Give me a call as soon as poss'.

Industry of the Ordinary
(12 sentences)

For 12 days in March and April, 2004, Industry of the Ordinary will occupy the streets of Chicago. Exploring the aesthetics of the ordinary, Industry of the Ordinary will create a dozen performances to be instantly documented and published on this site. You are invited to review past events and read about future activities.

On this site the visitor can find twelve, one-sentence descriptions of the performances to be undertaken during this period. Where performances are public-sited the places and times will be posted.

Through sculpture, text, photography, video and performance Industry of the Ordinary are dedicated to an exploration and celebration of the customary, the everyday, and the usual.

Industry of the Ordinary are Adam Brooks and Mathew 'the bastard' Wilson.

From: adam@adambrooks.com
Subject: Notes on IOTO
Date: January 8, 2004 8:42:33 PM CST
To: wilsongizella@yahoo.com

The notion of "Champs" or winners at all costs--badges pinned on passers-by, unfurling a banner with "Champs" on it--however, does this deviate too greatly from the ordinary, or is it something that creates a tension with the ordinary, an aspiration. T-shirts with "Champion" printed on the front--IOTO on the back

Exploration of the microcosmic as a facet of the everyday. Take small unnoticed events and focus and expand upon them.

Could be linked somehow to the sandblasted bottles deposited around the city--construct a logo for IOTO, use the acronym as a starting point. Play off idea of IOTA.

From: adam@adambrooks.com
Subject: Fwd: industry of the whoredinary
Date: April 1, 2004 7:20:47 AM CST
To: wilsongizella@yahoo.com, flaps_2000@yahoo.com

Friend of yours?

Begin forwarded message:

From: owen lexington <widecasting@hotmail.com>
Date: Wed Mar 31, 2004 10:44:16 PM America/Chicago
To: <info@industryoftheordinary.com>
Subject: industry of the whoredinary

I can't get the strip show video at daley plaza to work. please reverse the charges on my credit card, cunts.

From: adam@adambrooks.com
Subject: new ideas
Date: July 27, 2004 1:44:25 PM CDT
To: wilsongizella@yahoo.com

This is compiled from our conversations and both of our lists. I have marked the 7 pieces (*) I would like to see get done first. If you think otherwise, do the same thing and we can compare lists.

*The Beautiful Game
I.O. orchestrate famous football chants

On the Never-Never
I.O. apply for a credit card and make a single purchase

*Deity for a Day
I.O. become god

*Power to the People
I.O. buy one share of Halliburton and attend the annual meeting to complain about company policy

*Alchemy
Industry of the ordinary transform a motor scooter into an airplane.

*Premortem
I.O. prints its entire dental record

Hope
I.O. constructs a wishbone from the mashed pulp of a significant publication

*Final Words
I.O. collect the last lines of the 10 most popular works of literature

*Voyeurism
I.O. provide 2 volunteers with phosphorescent paint prior to intercourse before recording the aftermath

Millennium Park P(l)ot
I.O. plant marijuana plants in the new gardens, harvest them and distribute to cancer sufferers

Dinner Party
I.O. ring ten people at random from the Chicago phone directory and invite them to a dinner party

Operation
I.O. conduct military training exercises on a child's playground.

From: adam@adambrooks.com
Subject: Re: links
Date: September 2, 2004 12:37:26 PM CDT
To: wilsongizella@yahoo.com

IotO is dedicated to presenting the performative act in a new way. There are pejorative perceptions of what "Performance Art" is in many people's minds that we seek to overturn, both through the work itself but also in the form in which it is presented. We seek to offer an approachable, non-pedantic, witty publicly-sited form of performance taken out of the necessarily limited theatrical black box or the museum's white box, and also to blur the lines between the visual and the textual, using the form of literature, the book, but subverting that too with the inclusion of the visual, the technological and the participatory. We are looking to reach a broader public through non-didactic, non-condescending content and form.

From: wilsongizella@yahoo.com
Subject: some thoughts
Date: April 4, 2004 9:56:24 AM CDT
To: adam@adambrooks.com

We should change that first sentence of the manifesto to read 'industry of the ordinary is...' Agreed?

Also I was bored at the office last night and came up with some ideas for future projects. See what you think of these little beauties.

Alchemy
Industry of the ordinary transform a motor scooter into an airoplane.

Operation
I.O. conduct military training exercises on a child's playground.

Roman Road
I.O. orchestrate the turning-on of a series of household lights to create a straight line across the city.

Voyeurism
I.O. stare out of a window for 8 hours noting passers-by.

Democracy 2
I.O. attempt to telephone the president of the united States of America.

The Ageing Process
I.O. construct an eye chart large enough to be read with the unaided eye.

Placebo
I.O. sell extraordinarily expensive placebos in the form of sugar cubes through their web-site.

From: wilsongizella@yahoo.com
Subject: links
Date: September 2, 2004 11:48:50 AM CDT
To: adam@adambrooks.com

performative nature of the internet

blurred lines between visual, textual

increasing importance of technology

approachable, non-pedantic, witty
public-sited
performance taken out of the necessaryily limited
theatrical black box or the museum s white box

broader public/ non-didactic/ non-condescending

From: adam@adambrooks.com
Subject: Another update
Date: January 1, 2005 4:29:44 PM CST
To: wilsongizella@yahoo.com

Go here to see a new layout and compare. Once I start, you simply cannot stop me. I am a force of nature, John.

http://www.industryoftheordinary.com/html/projects-augustine*.html

---

From: wilsongizella@yahoo.com
Subject: Re: Another update
Date: January 1, 2005 8:04:35 PM CST
To: adam@adambrooks.com

I like the three photo layout, but the shot in the
bathroom makes me look like I'm sitting on the
shitter. Looks great, Trevor.

From: wilsongizella@yahoo.com
Subject: Respondents up-date
Date: July 30, 2005 1:41:25 PM CDT
To: adam@adambrooks.com

I've been in touch with everyone now. They're all off
and running. On another subject, I wonder whether we
should change the phrase 'one-sentence' to 'brief' on
the projects page as Ten has a two sentence
description. Or is that getting too picky?

Mr Smooth

From: philolog@mindspring.com
Subject: Re: Respondents up-date
Date: July 30, 2005 5:47:09 PM CDT
To: wilsongizella@yahoo.com
Reply-To: adam@adambrooks.com

I've thought about the "one sentence" thing too. Yes, it's picky, but I will change it.

Just call me Bruce

From: wilsongizella@yahoo.com
Subject: simply the best
Date: September 30, 2005 7:59:04 AM CDT
To: adam@adambrooks.com

How about this for a November project?

We pulp an entire Sunday Tribune into a sheet the size
of the front cover and then draw in only the banner
and the photographs on the front page. Title?: 'Days
of our Lives'.

From: adam@adambrooks.com
Subject: Re: simply the best
Date: September 30, 2005 8:17:24 AM CDT
To: wilsongizella@yahoo.com

Hmm....

Need to toss this one around some more.

We need to be careful with the pulping, not to overdo it. Also, Nancy Chunn did a quite similar series with the NY Times, for a year.

From: philolog@mindspring.com
Subject: Re: Wakey wakey
Date: October 19, 2005 7:37:10 AM CDT
To: wilsongizella@yahoo.com
Reply-To: adam@adambrooks.com

Too right, sunny jim.

Here are some ideas for your delectation.

Epithet (Taboo)
IOTO collect and perform the most insulting string of expletives in the world's (6,10?) most widely spoken languages. (Video piece)
It might help to have native speakers perform this.

Empire
IOTO investigate what makes a country great.

Dipso (or Speakeasy)
IOTO establish an illegal drinking establishment.
(Do we make our own alcohol to sell here? There is a history of such beverages making people go blind)

Convenience
IOTO document the floor beneath a variety of public latrines.
(Tight and consequently semi-abstract photo-based images of the discolored tiles, vinyl, linoleum, wood, etc.)

Testosterone
IOTO examine maleness.
(There should be a way that we can use the big guys at the Globe, akin to the way that Lucien Freud did in his Portrait of a Big Man. Maybe we video Jonesy, flanked by his hefty cronies, in paroxysms of anger, and slow it down to about 1/8 speed, so every spittle-inducing screech is clear and present.)

From: wilsongizella@yahoo.com
Subject: Re: Wakey wakey
Date: October 19, 2005 8:00:42 AM CDT
To: adam@adambrooks.com

A mountain of material here. Perhaps we could time several for the Hyde Park show. If we had a video camera, sound recordind equipment and a silk screen or two we could set up a factory floor. Must be the fine beer you're drinking that's got the other juices flowing.

2007

Secure

Industry of the Ordinary invite the security personnel of the Chicago Cultural Center to participate in a group portrait.

Event photography by Scott Whipkey.
Portrait photography by Jay Wolke.

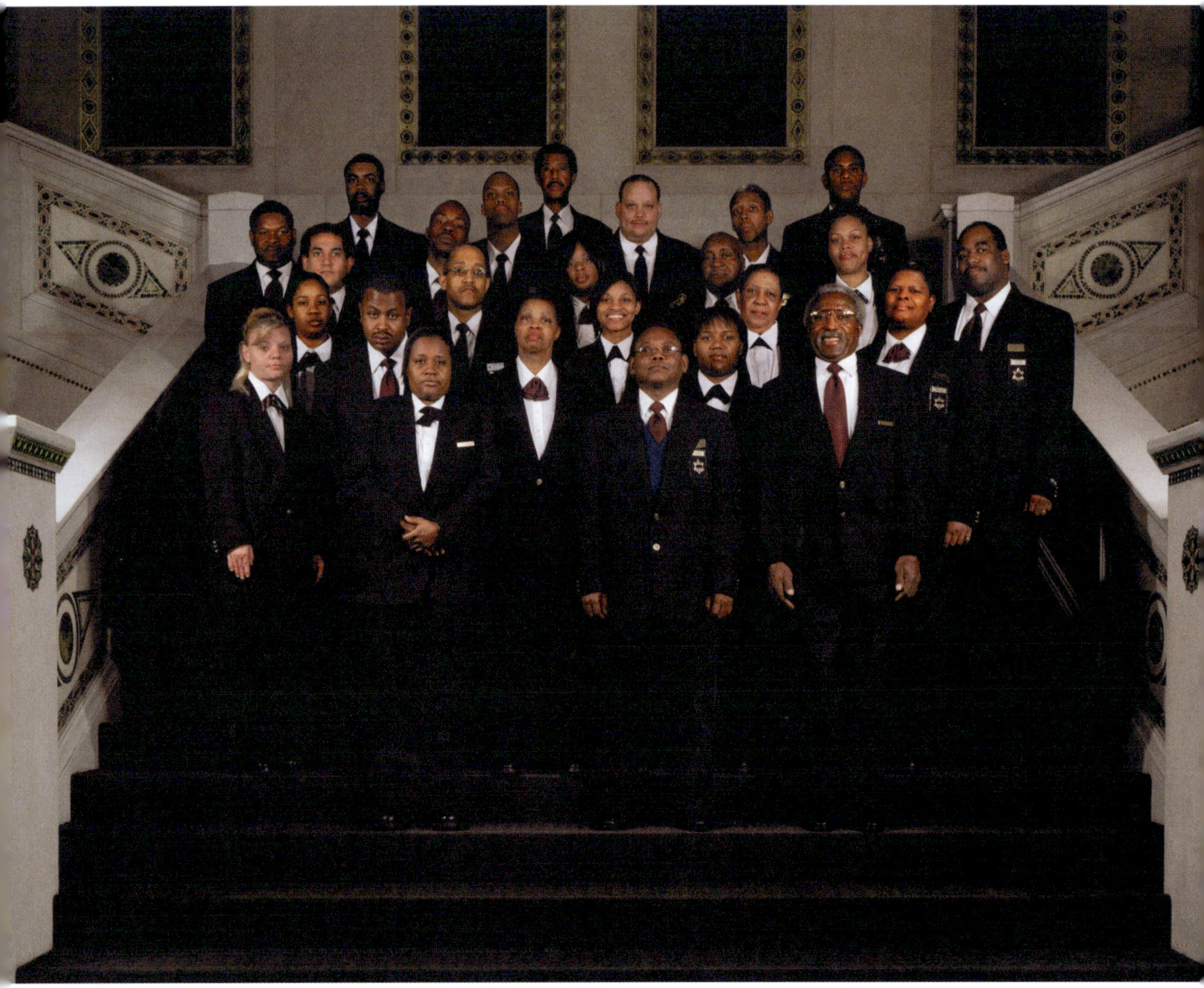

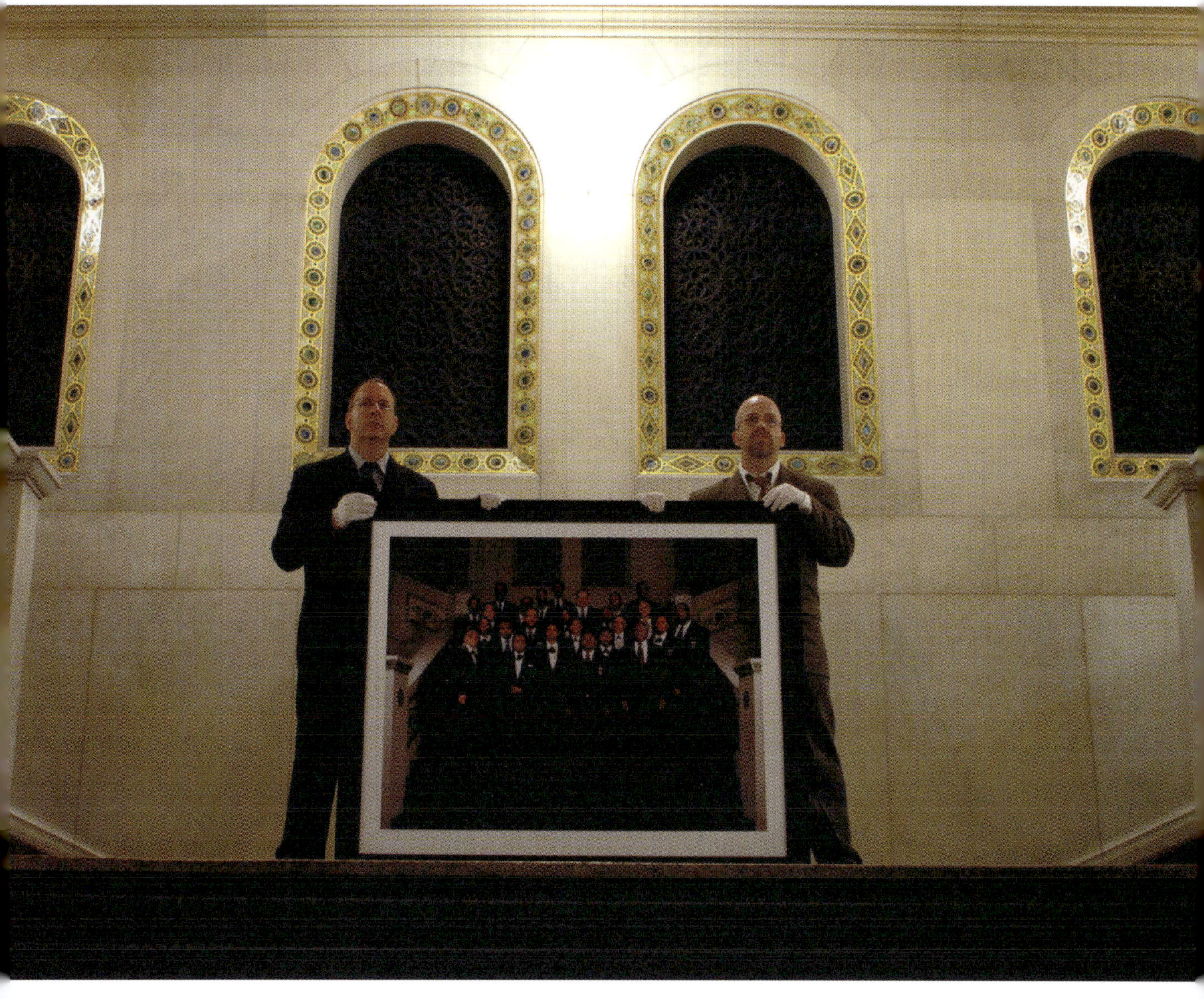

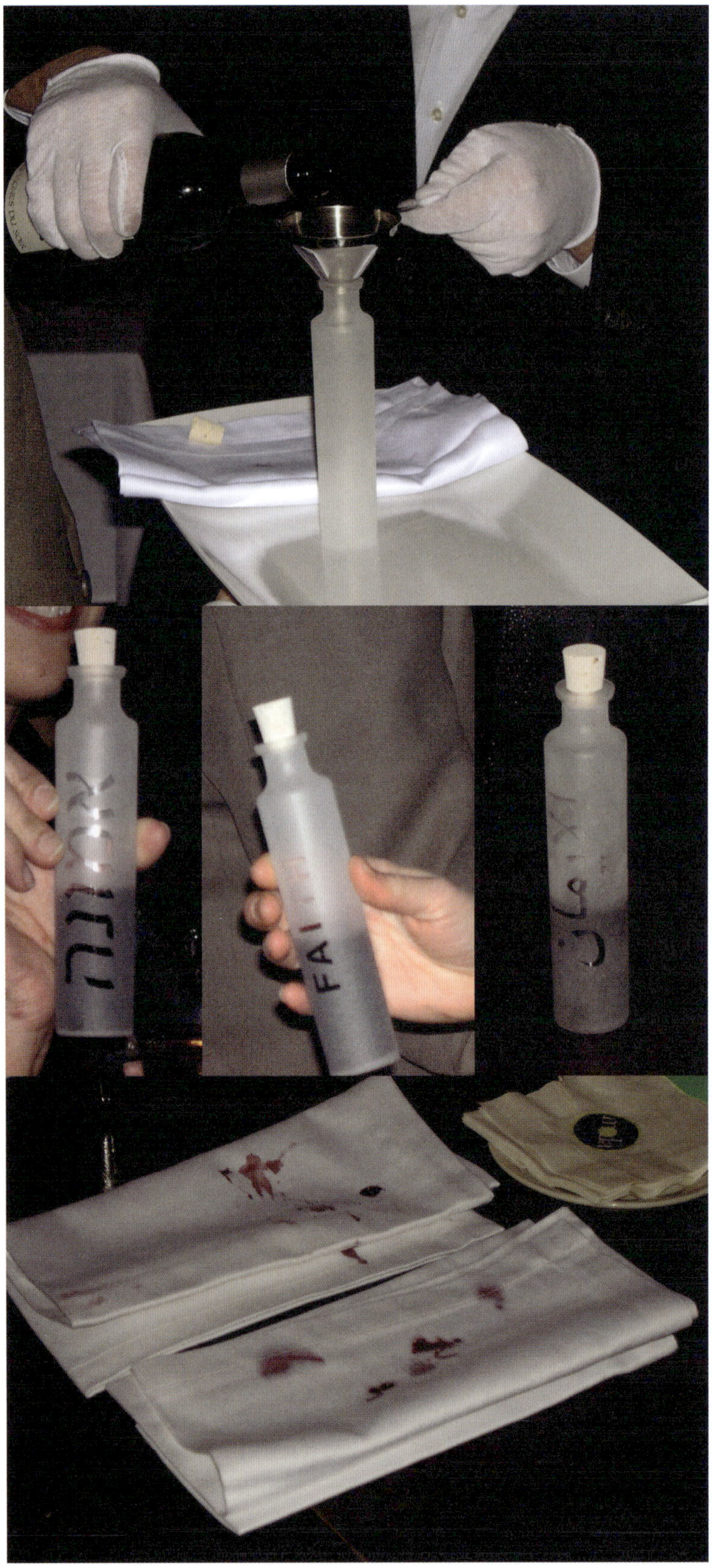
FAI

2007

AFTER CANA

Industry of the Ordinary collaborate with the public in an attempt to reverse a miracle in English, Arabic, and Hebrew.

Photography by Corey Postiglione.

THE ILLUSION OF HIERARCHY, 2007

Industry of the Ordinary examine the veneer of an institutional structure.

From left to right, all of Columbia College Chicago: President Warwick Carter, Provost Steve Kapelke, Dean Leonard Lehrer, Chair Sabina Ott.

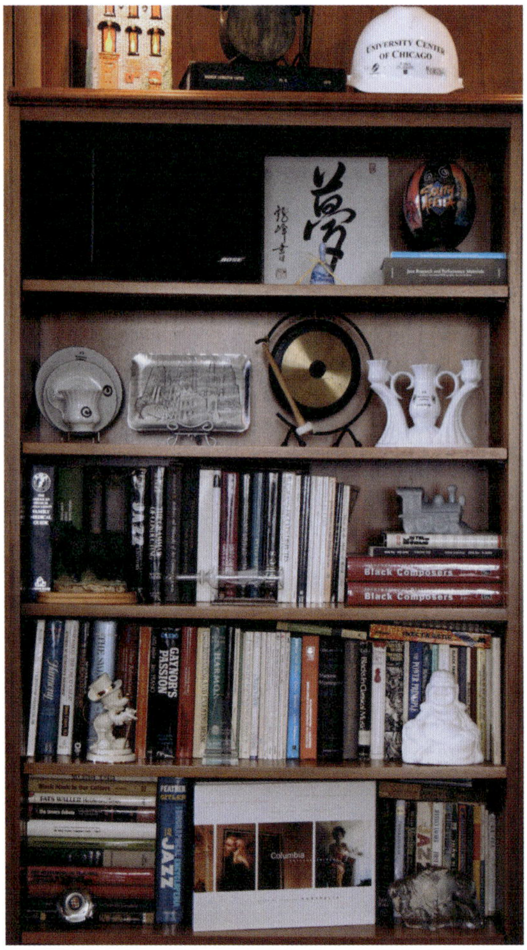

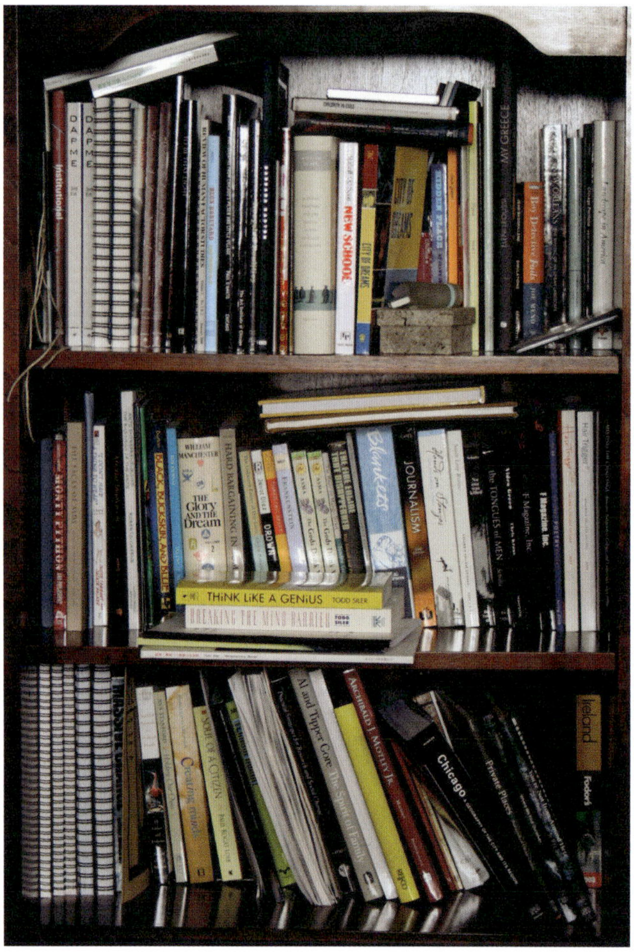

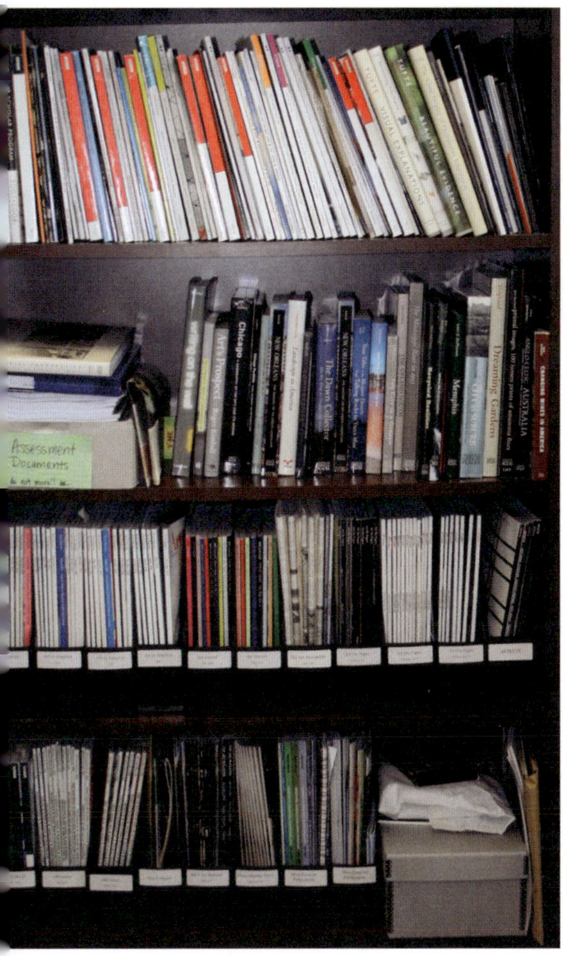
Assessment
Documents
Chicago
NEW ORLEANS
The Dawn Collector
Memphis
Dreaming Gardens
AUSTRALIA

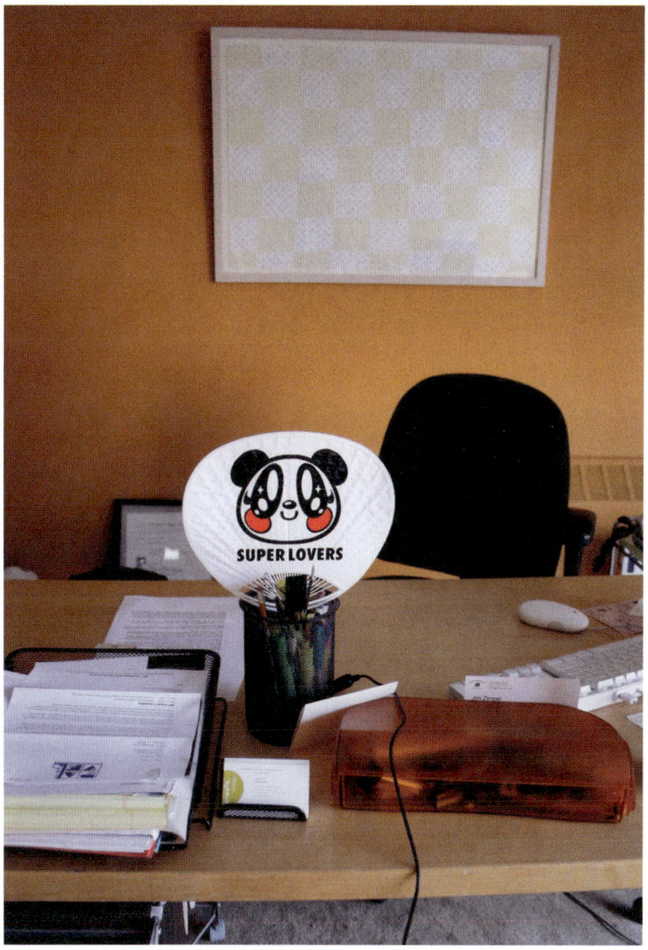
SUPER LOVERS

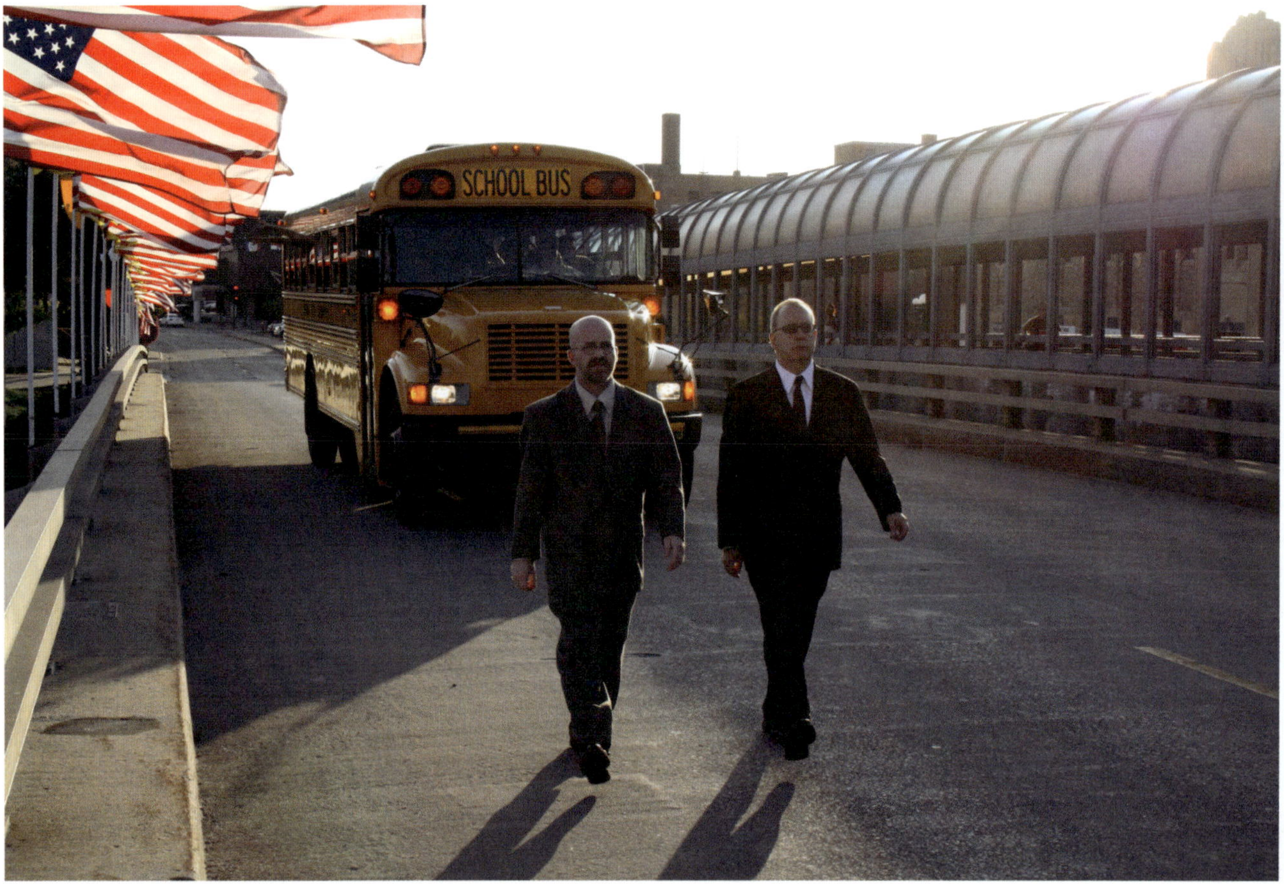

IMAGINARY TIME (FOR TIM BRENNAN), 2007

Industry of the Ordinary lead a bus through the streets of Waterloo, Iowa.
Photography by Greg Stimac.

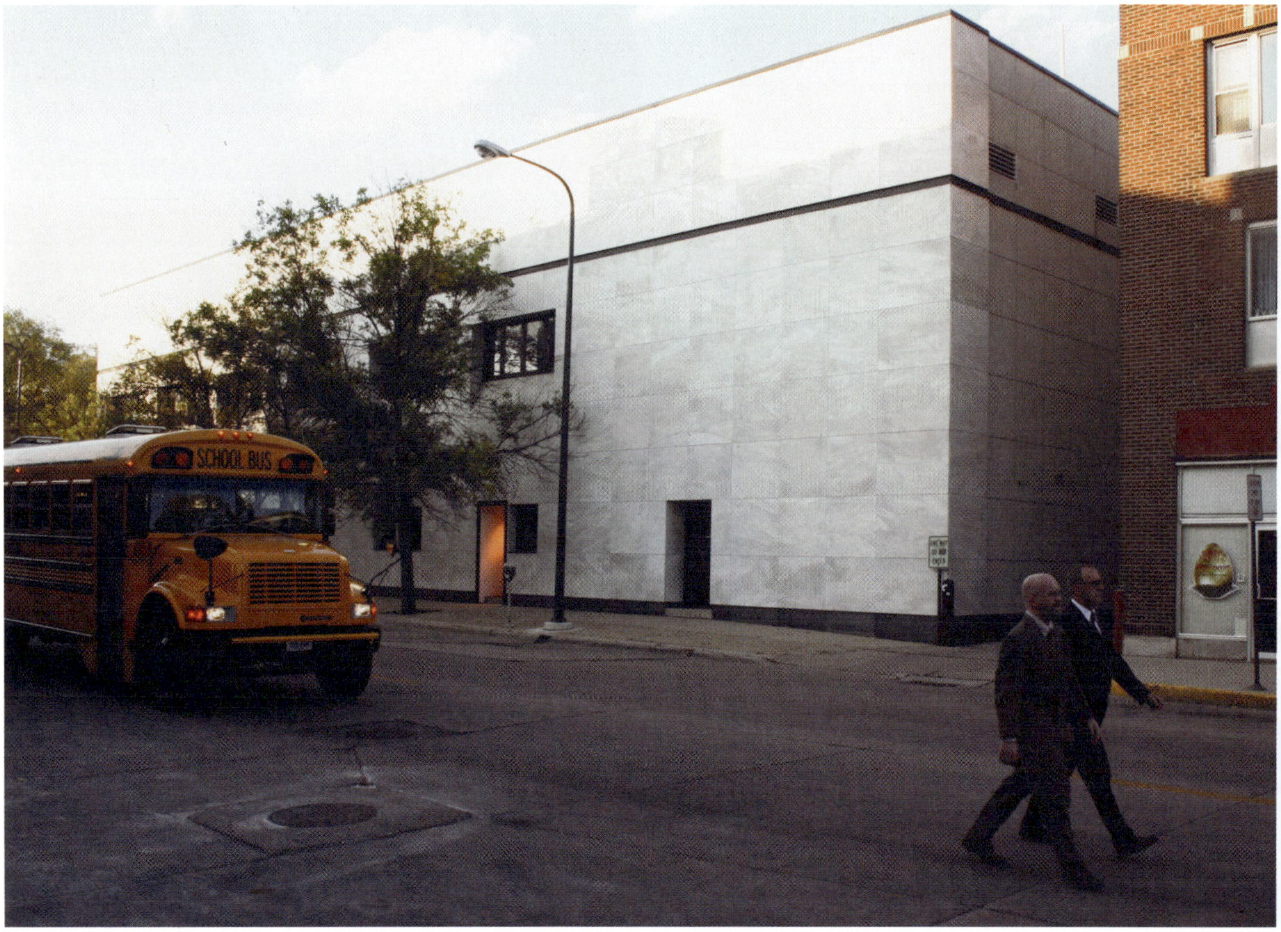

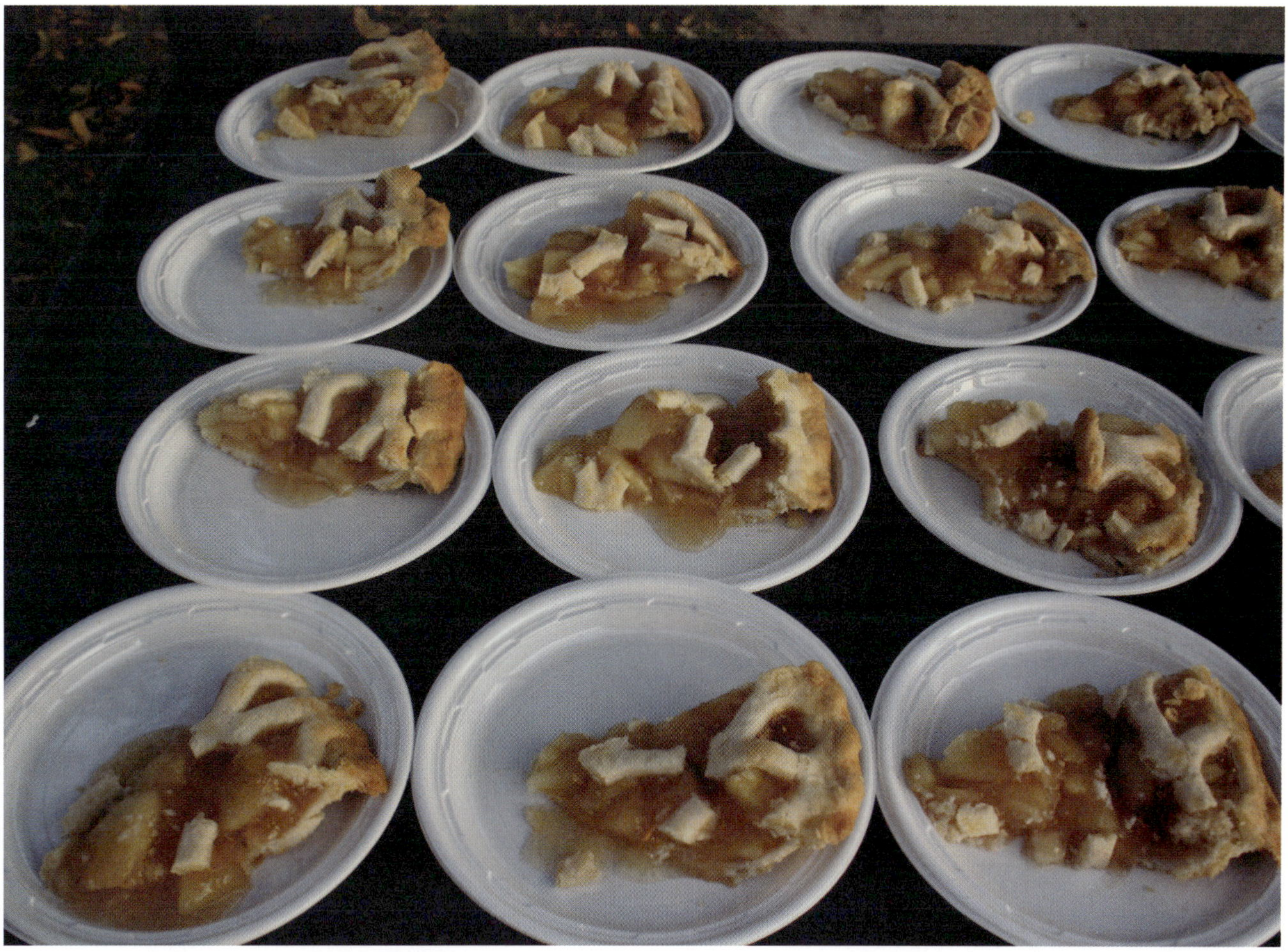

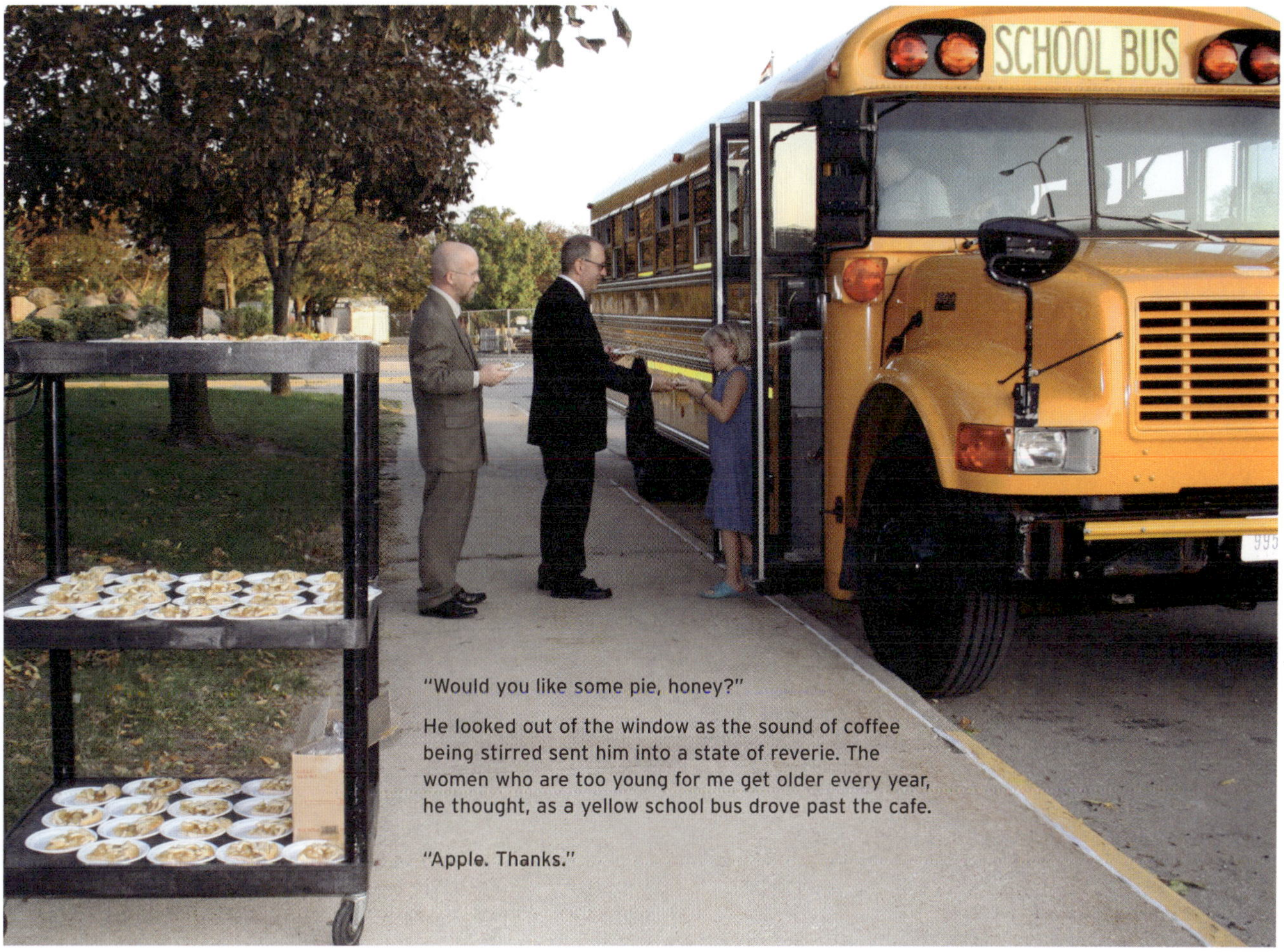

"Would you like some pie, honey?"

He looked out of the window as the sound of coffee being stirred sent him into a state of reverie. The women who are too young for me get older every year, he thought, as a yellow school bus drove past the cafe.

"Apple. Thanks."

CELEBRITY AND THE PECULIAR, 2008

For a solo show at the Gahlberg Gallery at the College of DuPage, Glen Ellyn, Illinois, Industry of the Ordinary impregnate oxygen tents with the prescribed scents of five celebrities.

Many thanks to Barbara Wiesen. Thanks also to Dominic Molon, Jim Zimpel, and Torreyanna Barley.

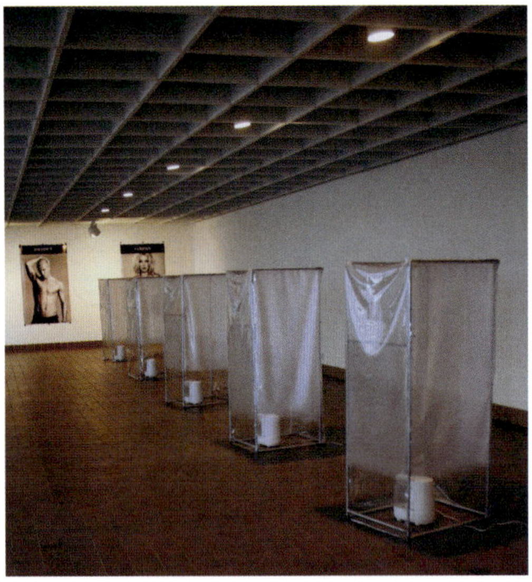

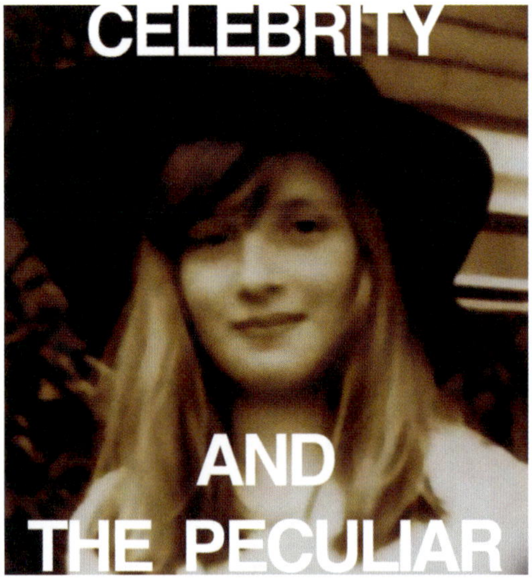

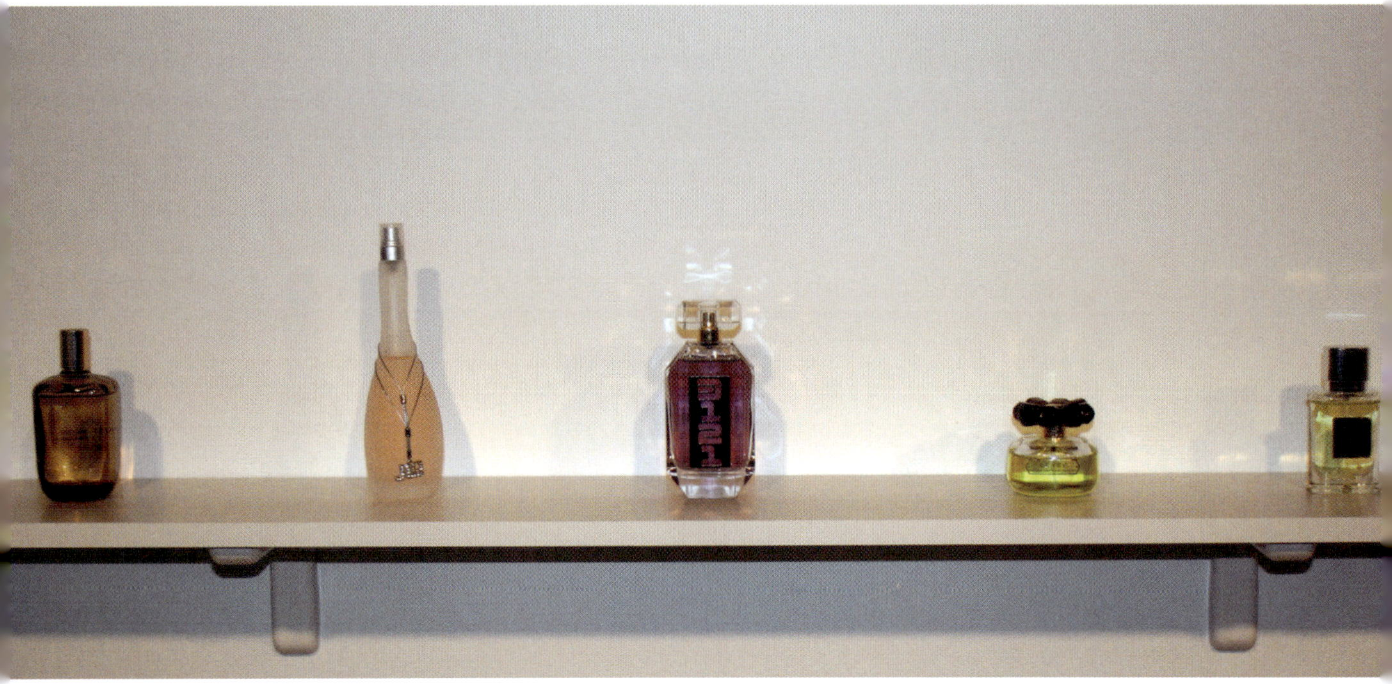

The Stifling Smell of Success

Dominic Molon

"Another way to take up more space is with perfume." Andy Warhol

CELEBRITIES TAKE UP QUITE A BIT OF SPACE. Regardless of their actual physical proportions or property ownership, they internationally occupy billboards, magazine covers and print ads, television and movie screens, and many, many other things that crowd the earth. Some manage to further impose themselves through the development of perfumes that parlay their fame into a curious form of commerce and self-expression—a phenomenon that seems to have begun in the mid-1980s with products bearing the name or imprimatur of cinematic divas such as Catherine Deneuve and Elizabeth Taylor, and has eventually grown to include figures from the world of sports (David Beckham and Michael Jordan), pop music (J. Lo, P. Diddy, and Beyonce), and, of course, the exasperatingly ubiquitous Britney Spears. Combining enterprise and industry, hubris and vanity, admiration and identification, celebrity scents represent big business and the curious cultural condition of establishing a connection with those touched by superstardom by the whatever weird means necessary.

In his book *The Philosophy of Andy Warhol (From A to B and Back Again)*, Andy Warhol reflects expansively on the power of perfume and the sense of smell in general—how it evokes moods, time periods, and other experiences. One wonders what he might have made of the phenomenon of "celebrity scents" with their fragrant fusion of two of the cornerstone subjects of his oeuvre—fame and spectacular mass consumption. While it's worth noting that a Warhol-related fragrance *is* being developed postmortem, the two-man collective Industry of the Ordinary, comprising Adam Brooks and Mathew Wilson, has assumed the responsibility of commenting on this most peculiar and ongoing trend. Their installation of oxygen tents filled with various celebrity perfumes provides a humorous yet succinctly biting satire of the strangely quiet assimilation of these substances into the general culture, despite the gaudy advertising hype that typically surrounds these products.

The mere fact that a duo billed as "Industry of the Ordinary" is creating work about these scents prompts reflection on what happens when the "ordinary" folk for whom these perfumes are developed choose to immerse themselves in the aura of those society has deemed "extra-ordinary." It's unsurprising, perhaps, that the primary demographic for celebrity scents are young adults and adolescents—that cross-section of humanity whose raging insecurities make them that much more likely to want to identify with someone who's "made it" to the peak of stardom and fame. For the young fellows wanting to bend the ladies' hearts like Beckham, they can avail themselves of his scent *Instinct*. And for girls stuck in the American Midwest who need a touch of that South Beach glamour, there's J. Lo's *Glow, Miami Glow*, and *Live*. Adolescents and young

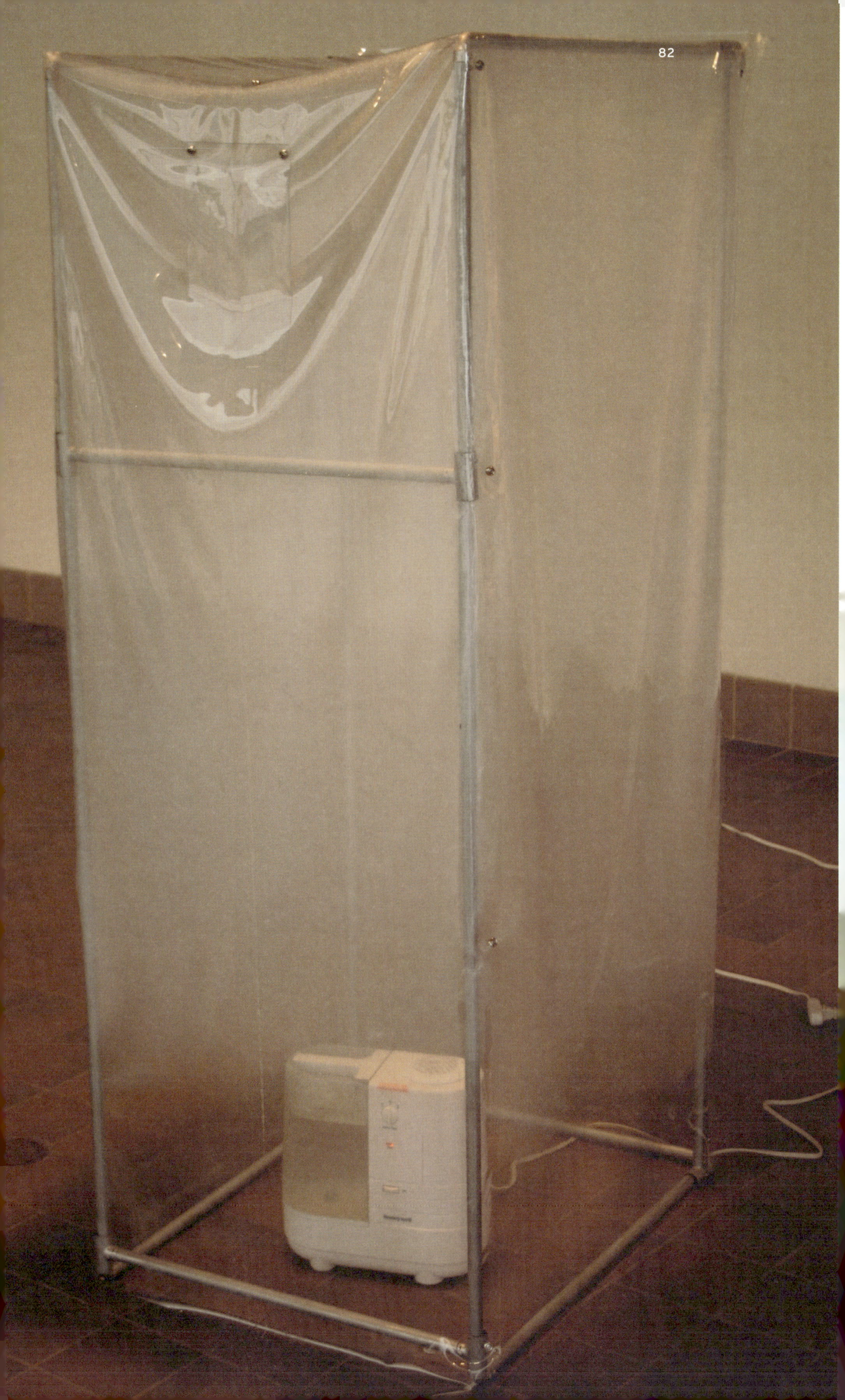

adults—for better and usually for worse—are regularly inclined towards exaggerated and hyperbolic behavior and speech (i.e., "I could have *died* when Tommy didn't ask me to the prom." "My mom's gonna *KILL* me for flunking chemistry."), making Industry of the Ordinary's presentation of the smells of teen spirit in structures meant for the maintenance of life in an emergency that much more meaningful.

Indeed, their use of vessels employed in times of utmost urgent necessity for the presentation of substances of indulgent and extravagant superfluity and folly makes for damning commentary on how the industry, labor, and resources devoted to the production of such trivial stuff might be better spent on curing some of the dire ills facing our civilization. On the other hand, one is tempted to play devil's advocate (the perfect perfume for Johnny Cochran, perhaps), and suggest that the work resignedly accepts how celebrity scents, among other essentially useless worldly phenomena like—well—art, play a necessary role of their own in society on some bizarre and depressing level beyond rational comprehension. And further still, the work's oppressive presentation of the perfumes could be a further reflection on how disturbingly pervasive the cult of celebrity and fame has become in contemporary culture. Given the political intentionality and affect of Industry of the Ordinary's previous work, the last consideration seems the safest to assume. This latest project follows such similarly calculated aesthetic gestures as coordinating a choir to sing mildly offensive British football (read: soccer) chants or creating an ice sculpture of the Ten Commandments as an inspired take on the controversy surrounding the installment and removal of a similar sculpture dedicated to the biblical phenomenon in front of the Alabama Supreme Court in 2001-2003. Just as those projects aimed to wind up relationships between high and low culture, the dialectics of permanence and impermanence and Church and State, *Celebrity and the Peculiar* questions the rampantly fetishistic character of the culture industry (to borrow from Theodor Adorno) in its meditation on the extension of a superstar's aura into a saleable product. It also demonstrates Industry of the Ordinary's continuing interest in collective human experiences such as religion, politics, and sports, by expanding their reach into the realms of celebrity worship, mass marketing, and consumption.

It remains to be seen whether the project will result in the development and marketing of the duo's own sponsored scent. In correspondence with the author, Brooks humorously suggested such a fragrance would comprise, "The aroma of dried mud on old football boots, with a high note of Boddingtons [pub ale] and just a soupçon of sweat." Yet when even a cult-appeal celebrity like actor Alan Cumming can sell $1,000,000 worth of name-brand cologne in a year, perfumes of the probably rich and extremely-to-more-or-less famous are quite serious business. In their satirical reflection on the ubiquitous and, by now, quite overwrought spectacle of vanity that transcends mere image to attach itself to our bodies and the air that we smell and breathe, Industry of the Ordinary, in their own modest way, call for a long overdue reality check to draw a more definitive line between "giving the people what they want" and "overstepping the boundaries of taste, humility, and simple common sense and decency."

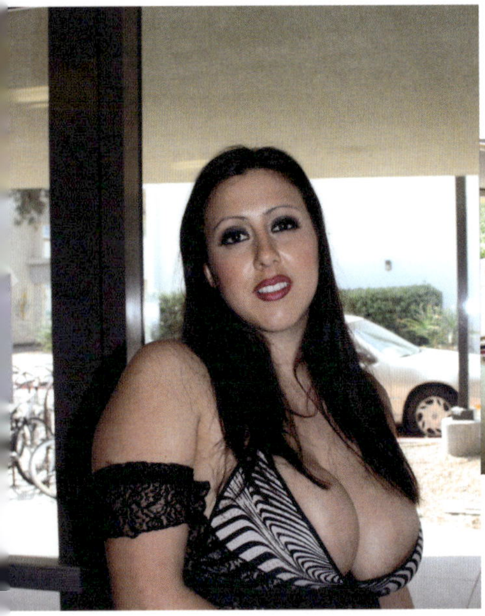

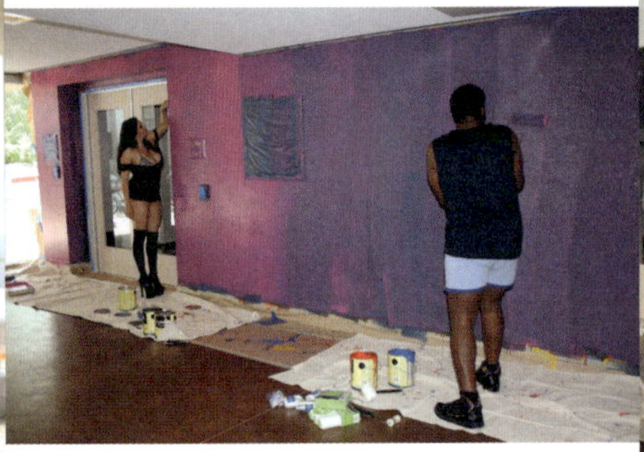

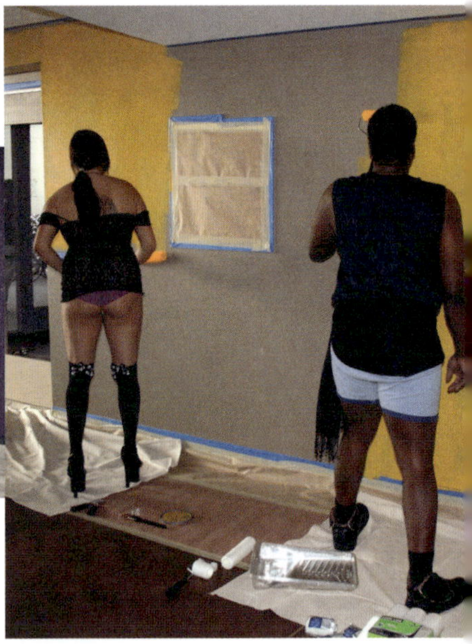

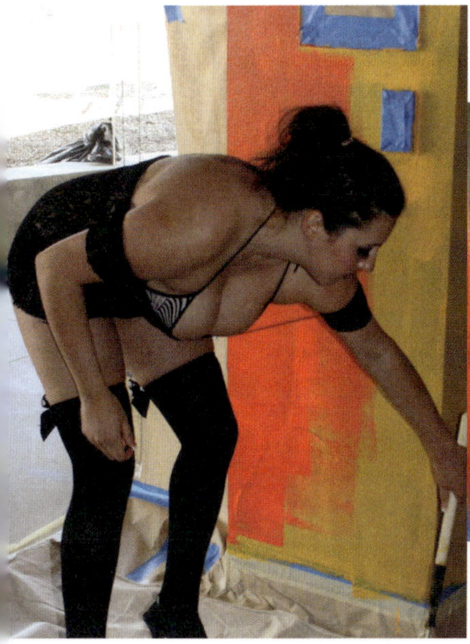

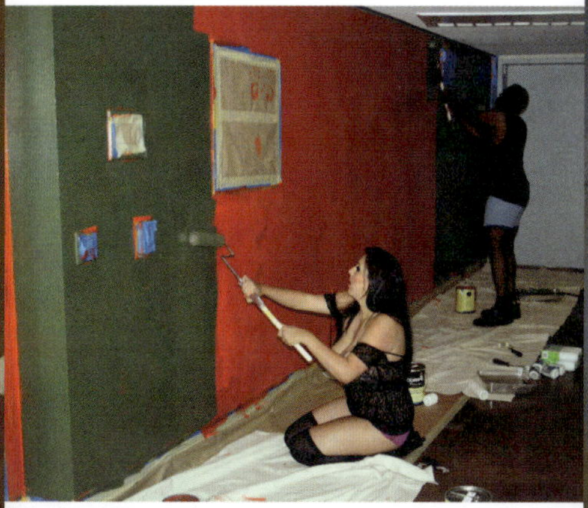

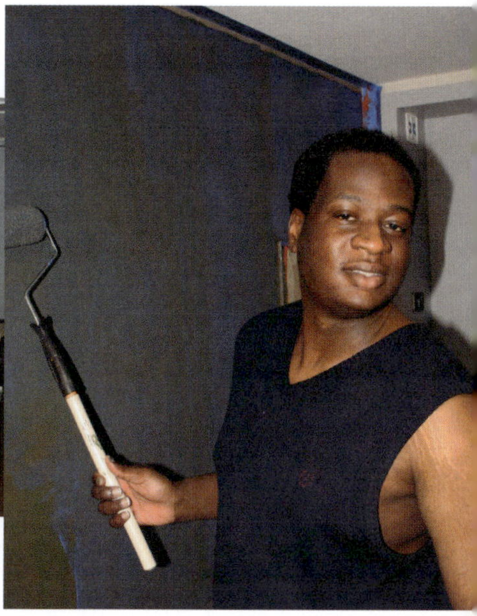

2008

RE-WORK

(FOR ALLAN KAPROW, MARINA ABRAMOVIC, AND PHILIP-LORCA DICORCIA)

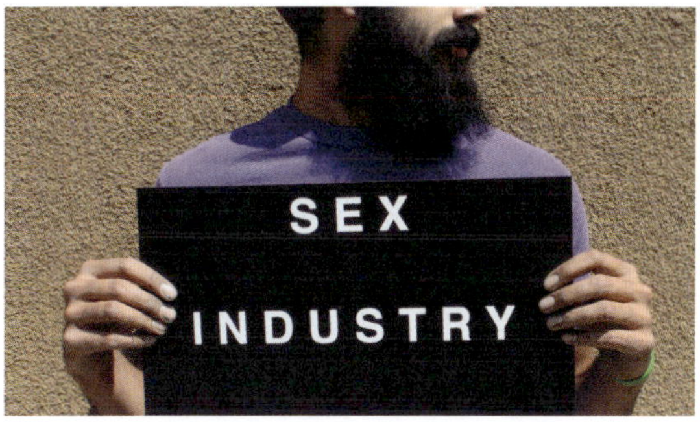

In collaboration with the *Allan Kaprow-Art as Life* retrospective held at the Museum of Contemporary Art, Los Angeles, Industry of the Ordinary reinvent Kaprow's original piece *Work* (1969), in which a hallway was repeatedly painted and repainted by professional contractors. The action in the original *Work* was videotaped and transmitted live to three distinct viewing venues: art-house theaters, pornographic theaters, and mainstream theaters. For *Re-Work*, Industry of the Ordinary hired two sex-industry workers, one male and one female, to paint and repaint a wall.

Additional photography by Max King Cap. Many thanks to Ciara Ennis. Thanks also to Valerie Velasquez, Chris Franklin, Rebecca Howard, and David Brooks.

JOURNEYS, 2008

For a permanent public work at the Bucktown-Wicker Park Library in Chicago, Industry of the Ordinary solicit choices of the most significant works of literature from throughout history from patrons and staff of this library, and present the first and last lines of those chosen texts in the front windows of the building.

Thanks to all the patrons of the Bucktown-Wicker Park Library who contributed to this work.
Thanks also to Emilie Stec and Methods & Materials.

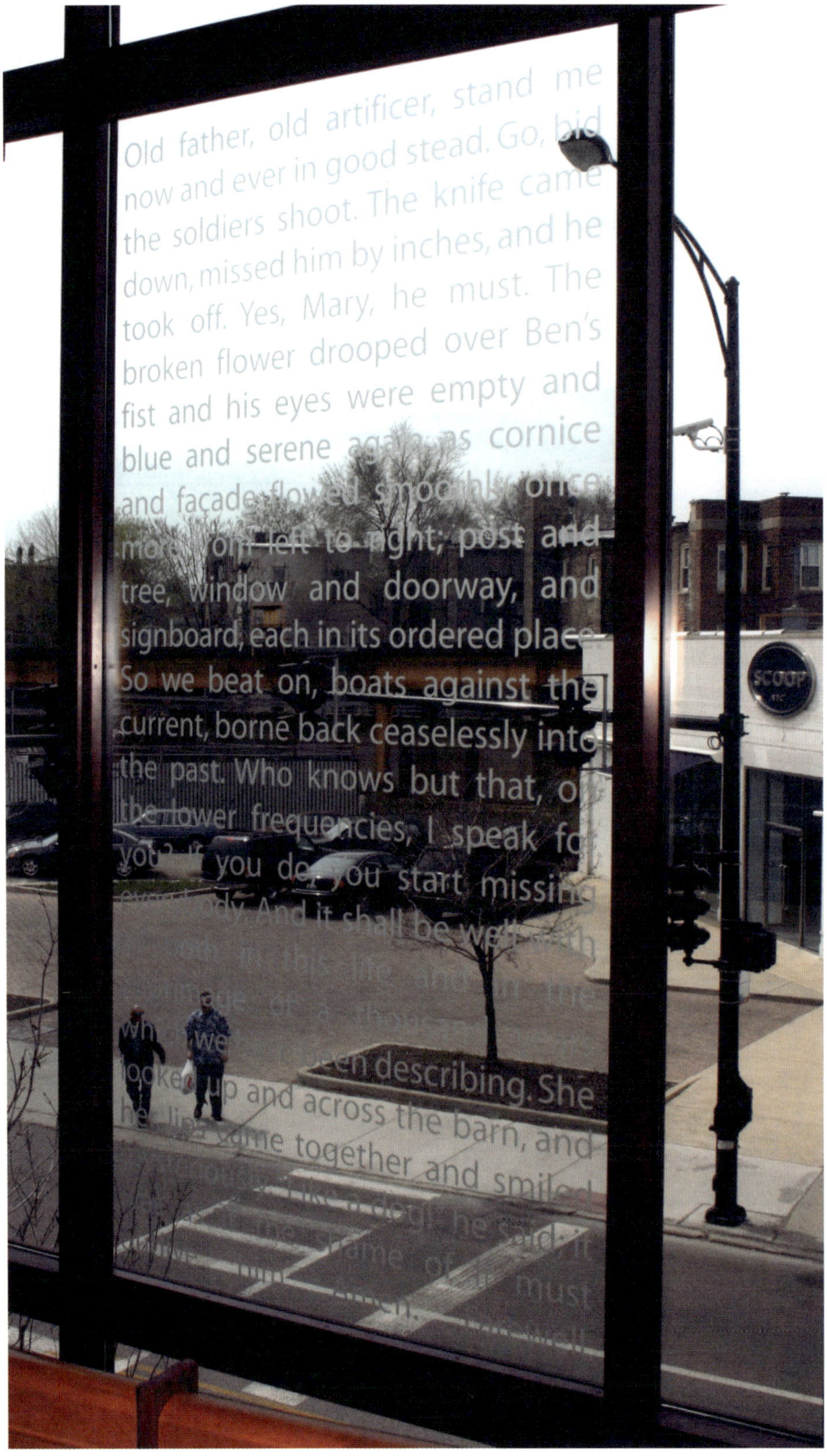

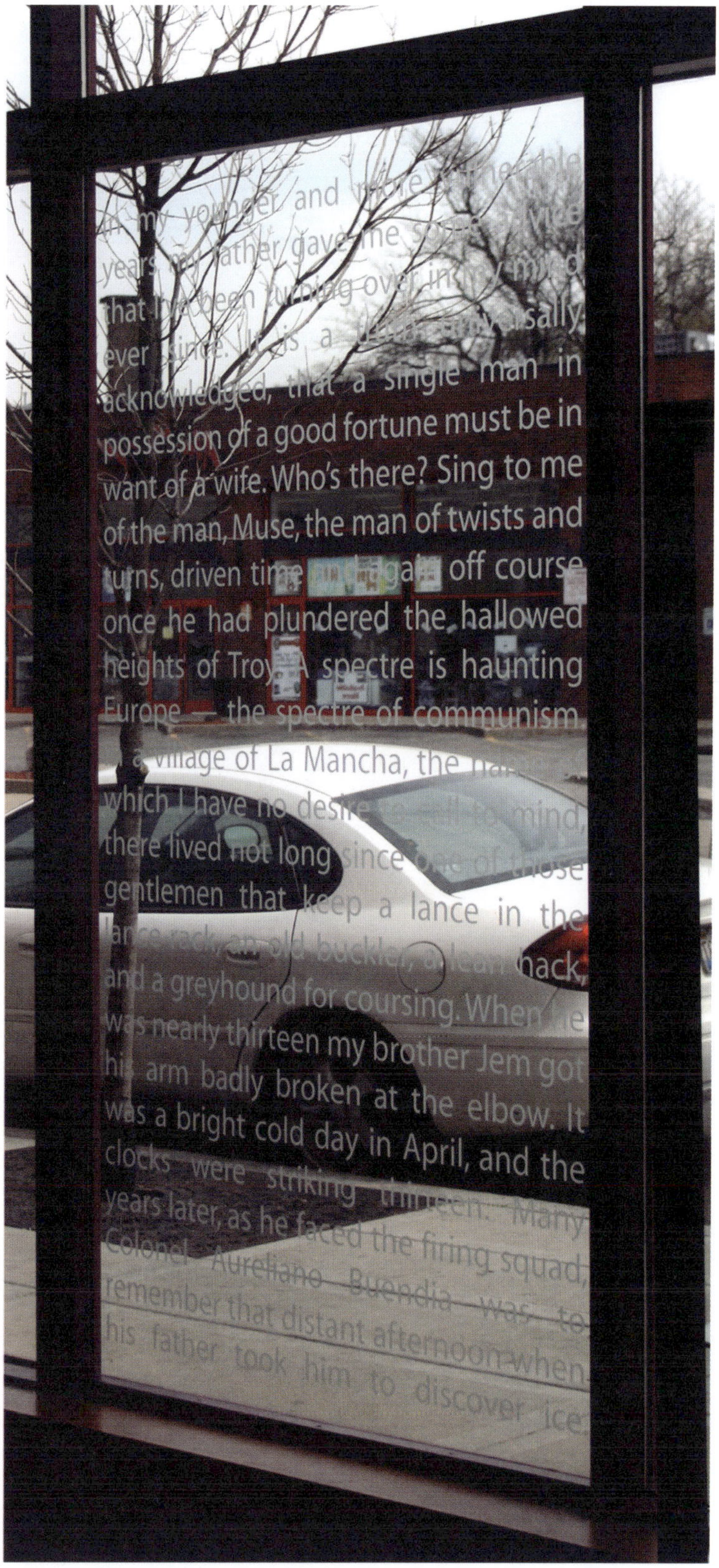
acknowledged, that a single man in
possession of a good fortune must be in
want of a wife. Who's there? Sing to me
of the man, Muse, the man of twists and
turns, driven time off course
once he had plundered the hallowed
heights of Troy. A spectre is haunting
Europe — the spectre of communism.
village of La Mancha, the
which I have no desire mind,
there lived not long since one of those
gentlemen that keep a lance in the
buckler, a lean hack,
and a greyhound for coursing. When he
was nearly thirteen my brother Jem got
his arm badly broken at the elbow. It
was a bright cold day in April, and the
clocks were striking thirteen. Many
years later, as he faced the firing squad,
Colonel Aureliano Buendia was to
remember that distant afternoon when
his father took him to discover ice.

DREAMS (WITH GUDRUN HASLE), 2008

Industry of the Ordinary provide their desired sentiment to be included in a banner demonstration.

DISTILL (FOR CAP, CAPOTE AND KEROUAC), 2008

Industry of the Ordinary assemble the equipment and ingredients to manufacture alcohol.

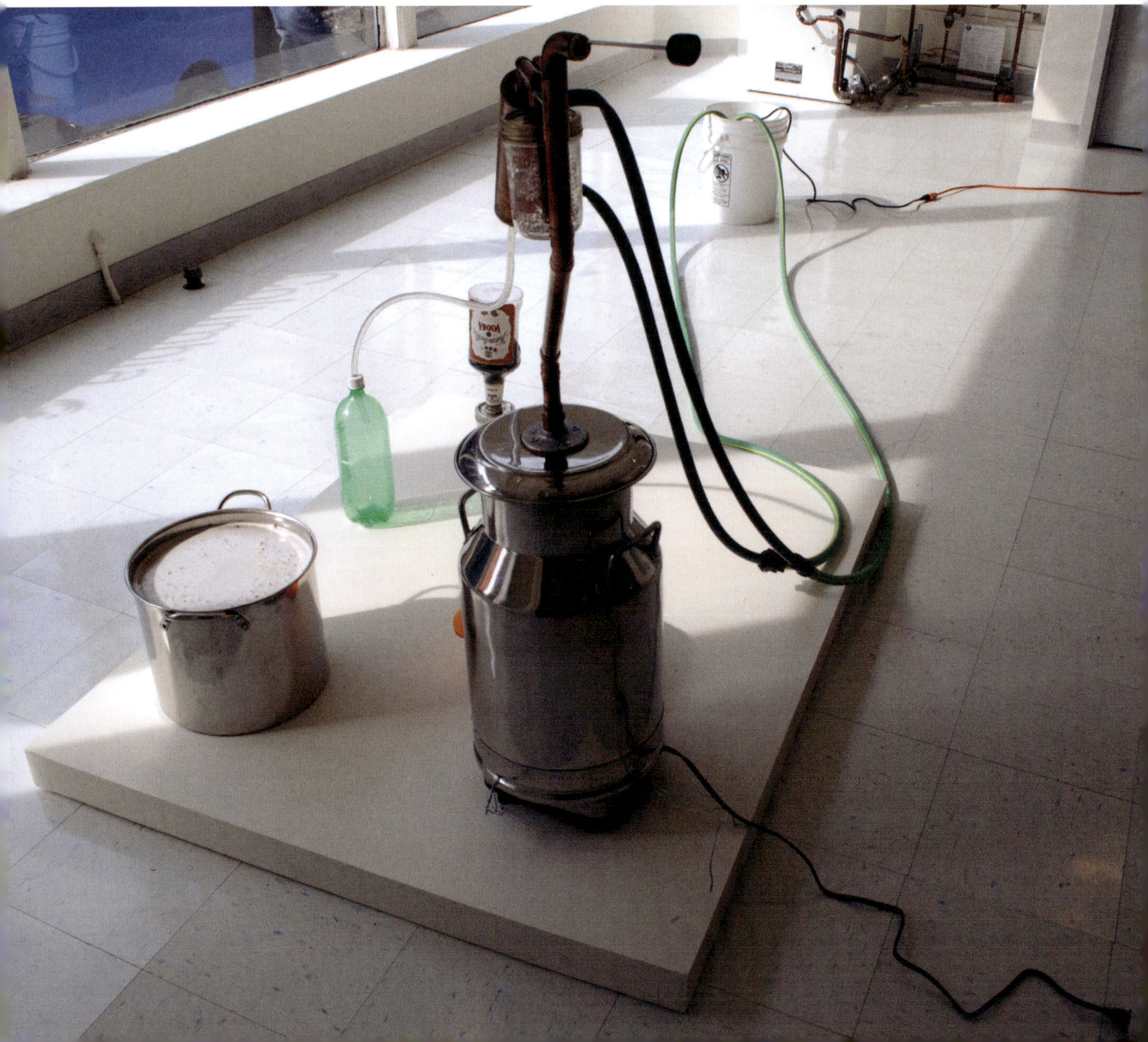

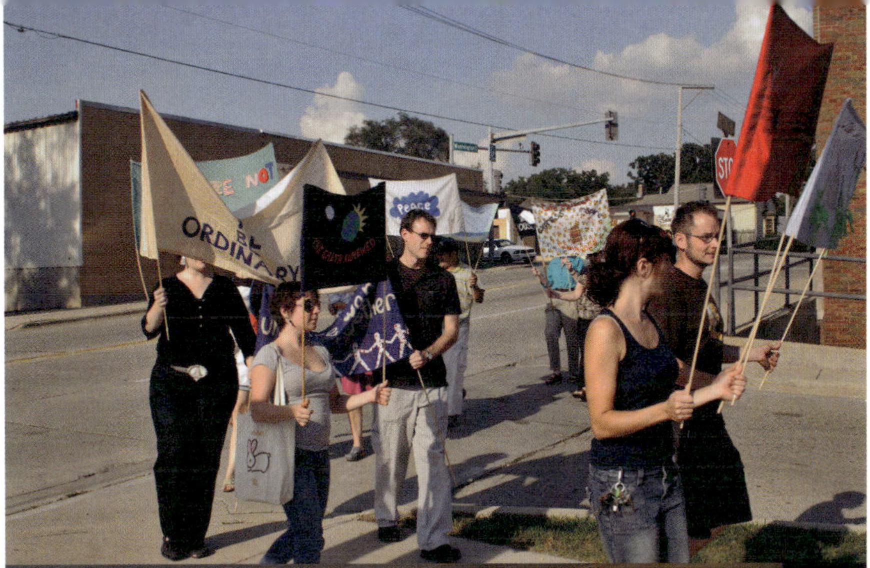
PEACE

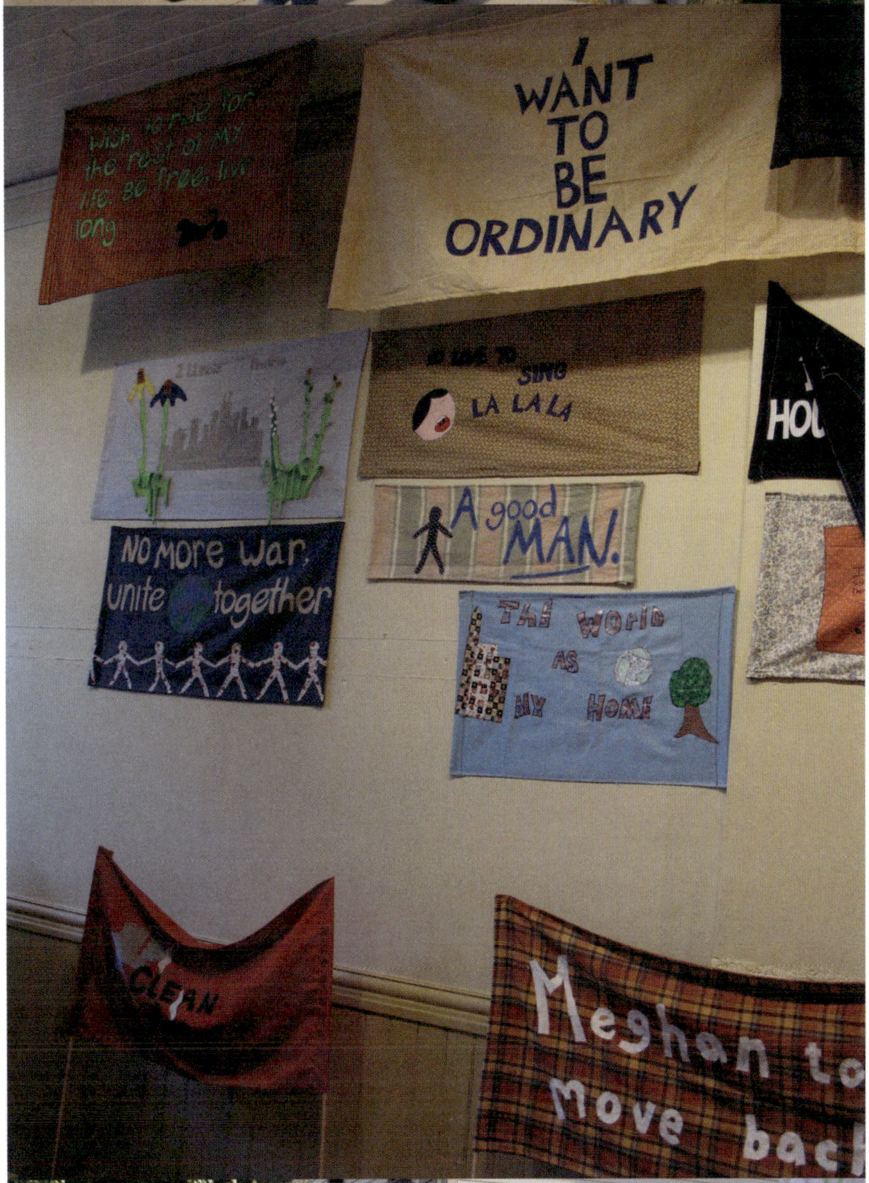
I WANT TO BE ORDINARY
the rest of my
life. Be free. live
long
SING
LA LA LA
A good MAN.
No more war,
unite together
The World
AS
MY HOME
CLEAN
Meghan to
move

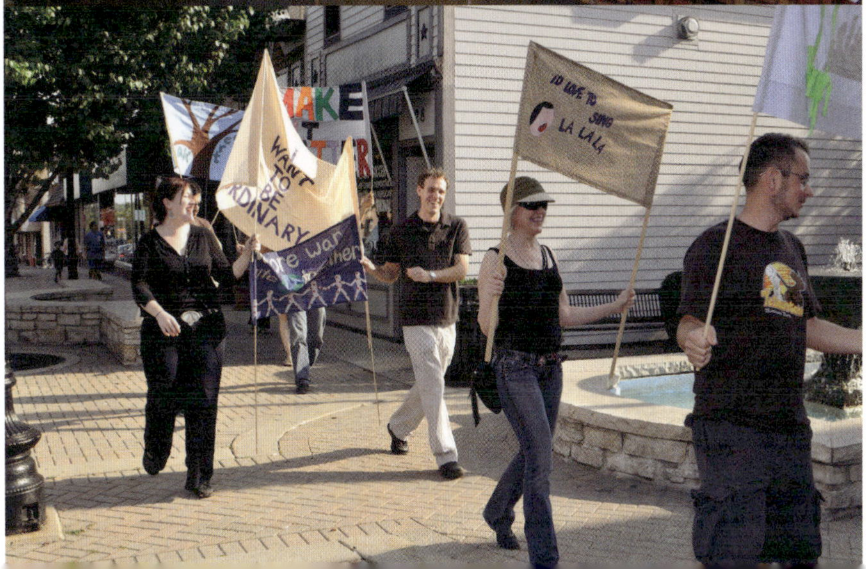
MAKE
I WANT TO BE
I'D LOVE TO SING LA LA LA

2008

AFFAIR

Industry of the Ordinary solicit a couple having
an extramarital affair to sit for a portrait,
in exchange for a romantic night at a hotel.

chicago craigslist > city of chicago > strictly platonic

email this posting to a friend

Please report suspected exploitation of minors to the appropriate authorities

please flag with care:

miscategorized

prohibited

spam/overpost

best of craigslist

Are you having an affair?

Reply to: pers-866585449@craigslist.org [?]
Date: 2008-05-16, 6:57AM CDT

Chicago-based art collaborative Industry of the Ordinary is looking for a couple (of any age, race or gender), who are currently engaged in an extra-marital affair, for an anonymous photo shoot. In return, we offer a romantic night at a Chicago-area hotel.

- it's NOT ok to contact this poster with services or other commercial interests

PostingID: 866585449

 terms of use privacy policy feedback forum

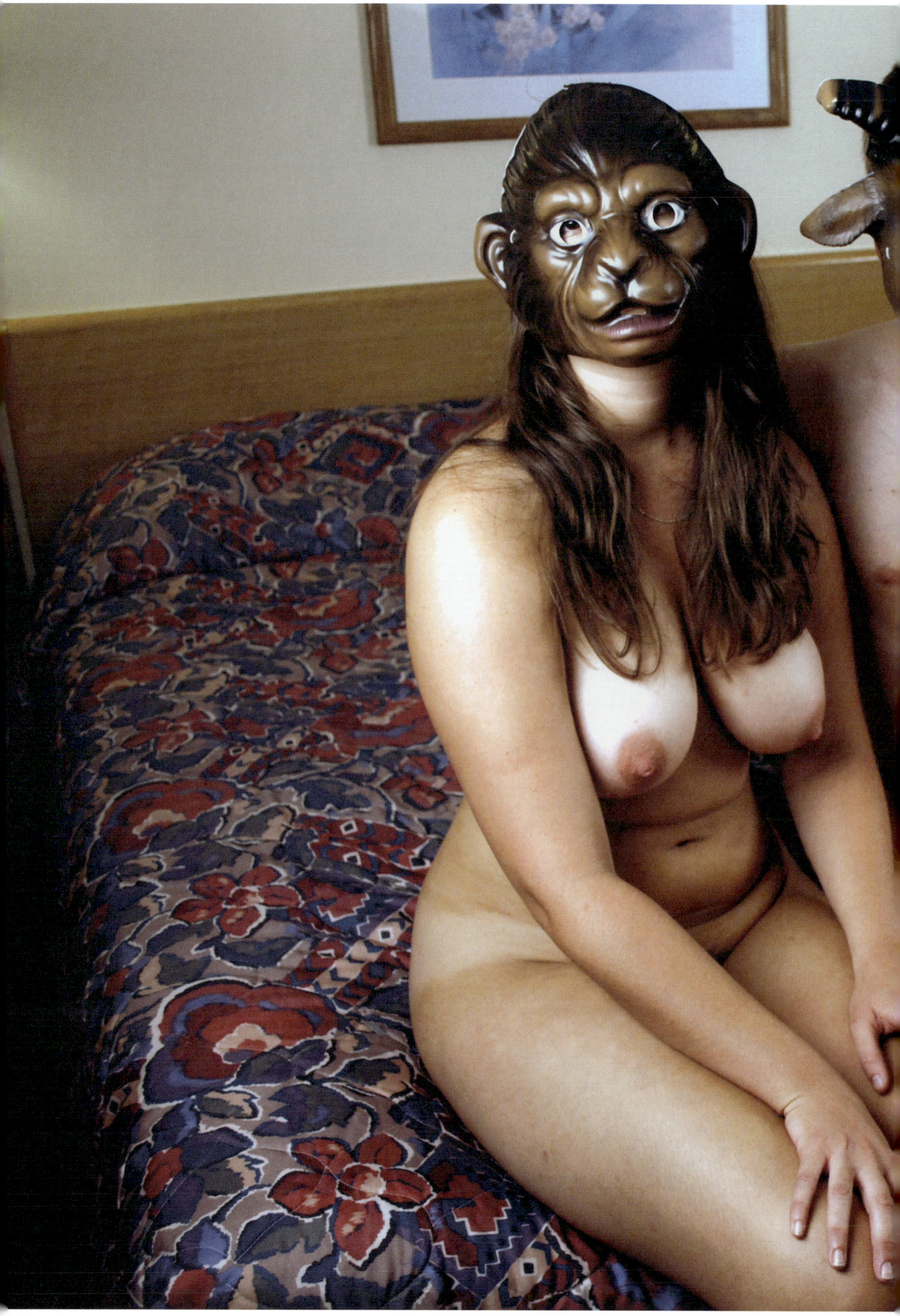

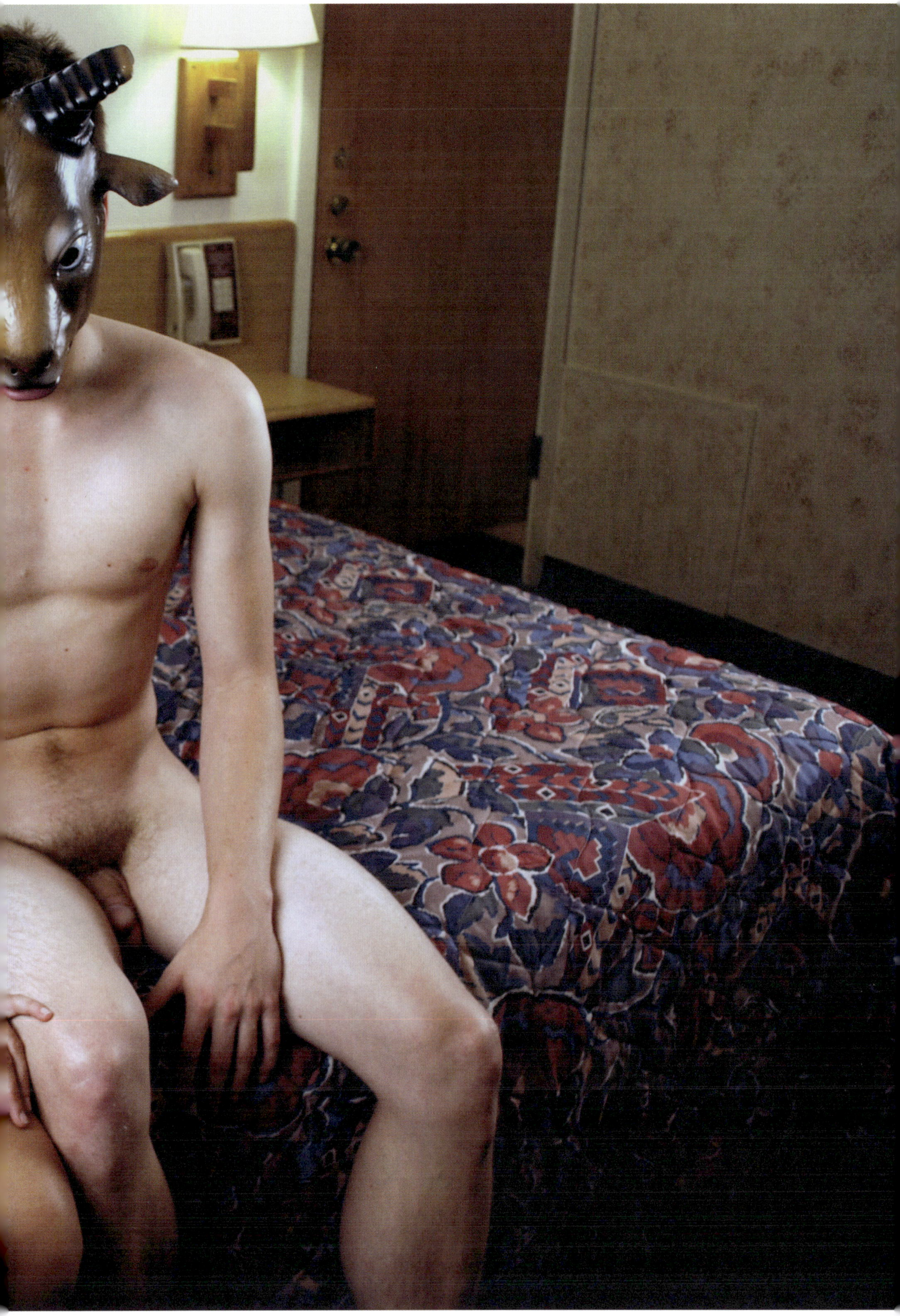

AT RIGHT:

EXAMINATION, 2008

Industry of the Ordinary produce lab coats emblazoned with the words ARTIST and TERRORIST.

THE REVOLUTION IS JUST A T-SHIRT AWAY (FOR BILLY BRAGG), 2008

Industry of the Ordinary give a socio-political statement to a crowd.

Photography by Aron Gent. Production assistance by Melissa Lutz.
Special thanks to Dominic Molon.

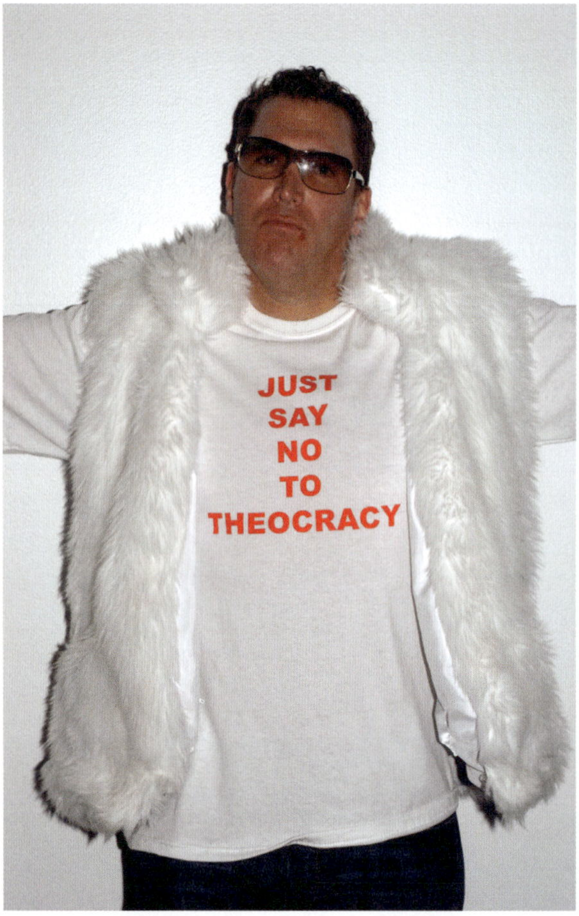

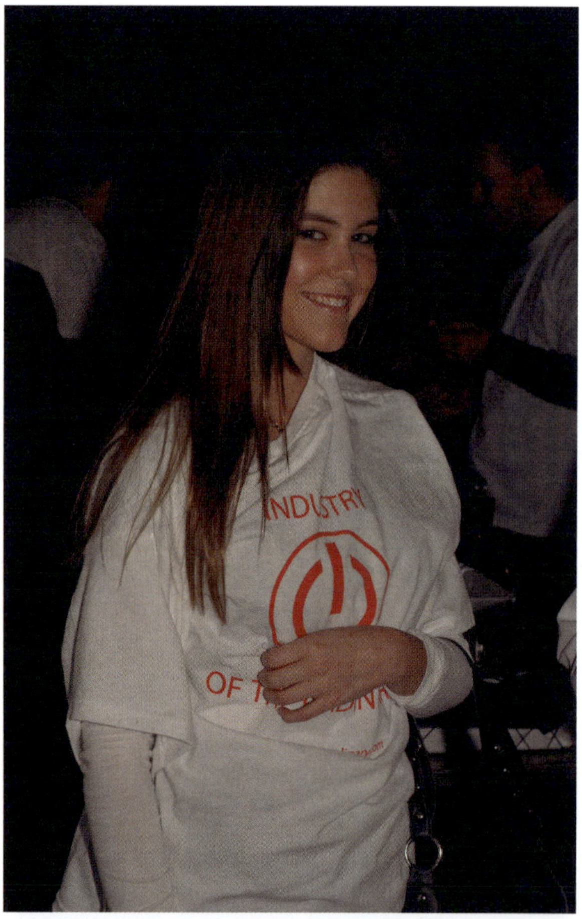

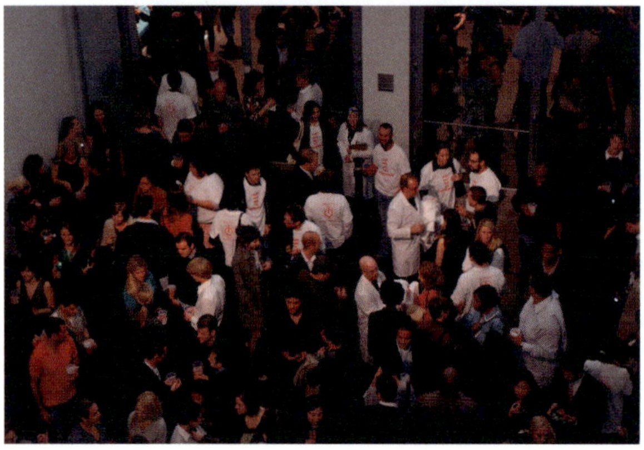

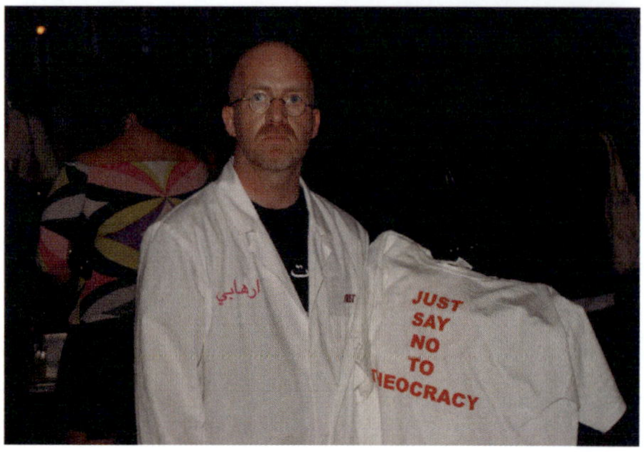

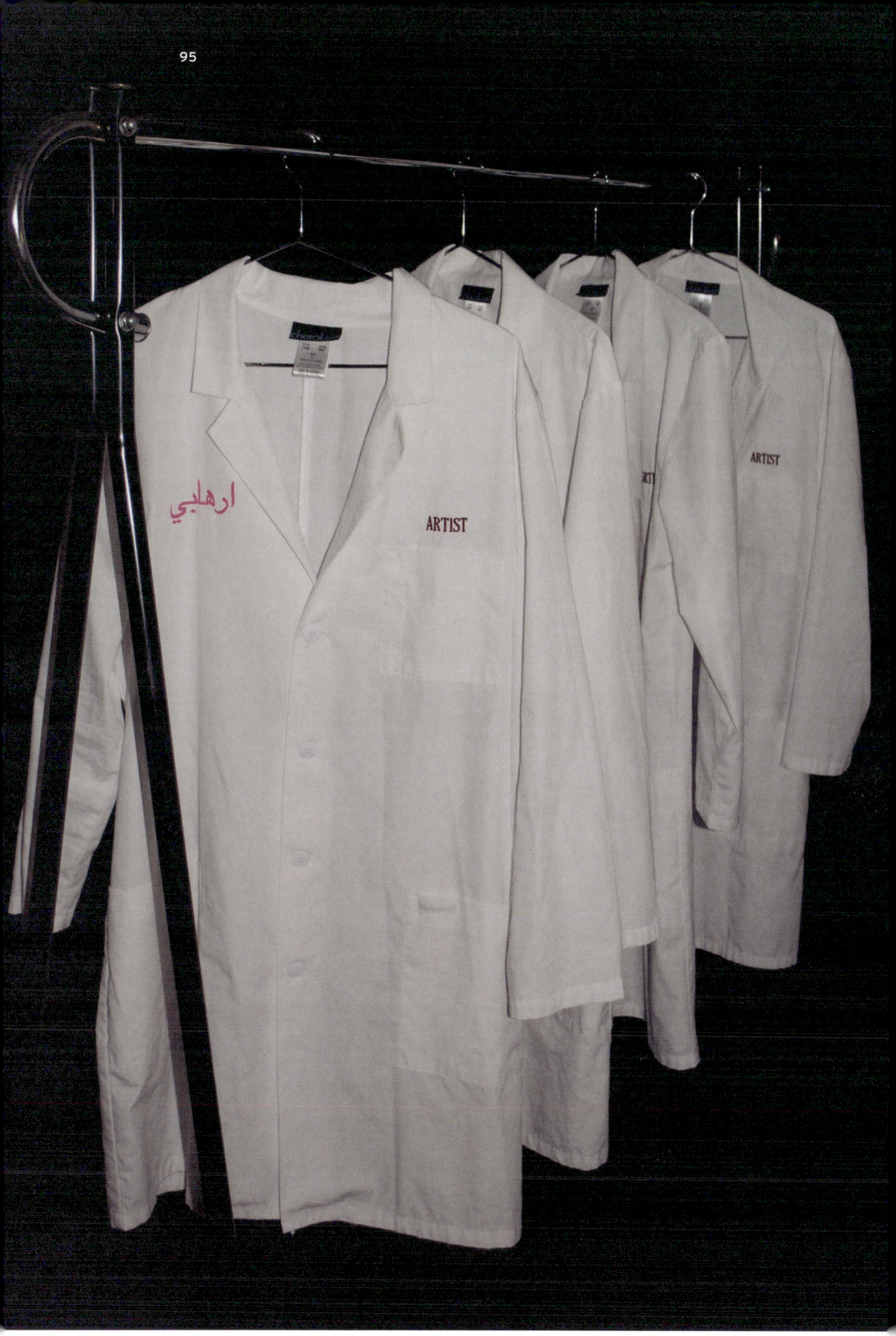
ارهابي
ARTIST
ARTIST

BETWEEN DONE AND NOT DONE:
THE WORLD ACCORDING TO INDUSTRY OF THE ORDINARY

By Eleanor Heartney

In the first section of T. H. White's *The Once and Future King*, a retelling of *Morte d' Arthur* that incorporates a mournful wartime consciousness into this medieval tale, the future King Arthur is lead through a series of educational transformations by the Wizard Merlin. One of the most telling involves his temporary conversion into an ant. Wart, as Arthur's character is then known, finds himself at the entrance of a vast ant colony over which is posted the sign "Everything not forbidden is compulsory." Inside, he discovers an army of ants for whom there are only two possibilities for action: done and not done. When Wart reveals to one of the ants that he is not usefully employed, he is taken to be insane.

White, writing between 1938 and 1941, adopted the ant colony as a metaphor for totalitarianism. However, the mindset he explores continues to have resonance today. Consider, for instance, an incident that took place in downtown Chicago in 2004. A man on his knees, followed by another man with a camera, draws a line down the center of the sidewalk with a flesh-colored crayon. When he stops, the end of his action being determined by the depletion of the crayon, a policeman who has been following him asks him what he is doing. He replies that he is an artist. The officer proceeds to arrest him. The exact nature of his crime, as it turns out when the two arrive at the station, is murky—no statute prohibits crayoning the street, and since the marks are erasable, he cannot be charged with defacing public property. After several hours at the station, during which the artist ends up chatting with the presiding officer about the nature of performance art, he is released.

While the resolution of this incident is reassuring, the arrest underscores officialdom's continuing discomfort with apparently irrational actions. In part, this is a function of heightened social paranoia in an age of terror. When fear becomes a mechanism of social control, nothing is more unsettling than unexplained activity. The arrest also reflects a utilitarian mindset that goes back to America's Puritan origins. Play, or for that matter any kind of apparently purposeless activity (unless of course it contributes to the economy in some way), is suspect.

The perpetrators of this noncrime are a pair of British-reared, Chicago-based artists and educators named Adam Brooks and Mathew Wilson. Since 2003 they have been working together as a team under the name Industry of the Ordinary (IOTO). The crayon action, which they have titled *A Line in the Sand*, is characteristic of the roguish public interventions they undertake. A sampling of other works includes sending Chicago's mayor a whitewashed copy of the *Chicago Tribune*, lugging around their entire wardrobes for a day, and the auctioning off of a sculpture of a baby on eBay.

What unites this body of work is a cheerfully speculative attitude—Wilson remarks that they do these things in order to see what will happen—combined with a more or less thinly veiled interest in exploring the social, economic, and ideological contradictions that shape our common life. The pair's moniker, Industry of the Ordinary, is itself a model of deliberate cognitive dissonance. The term "Industry" implies work—the word tends to be associated with the marshalling and mechanization of human activity for the purpose of producing something of commercial value. However, the duo's actions, despite their deadpan execution, appear to have the opposite function. They celebrate play—especially the free play of the creative imagination—and their carefully plotted actions have no immediately discernable social or commercial purpose.

The term "Ordinary" is equally fraught with contradiction. In common parlance, it represents the opposite of the conventional understanding of the artist as a creative genius. Ordinary also flies in the face of the current valorization of American exceptionalism and the attendant notion of the American citizen as a special individual. (Here we could reference Garrison Keillor's dream of a mythic American small town where every child is above average.) It also defies a popular culture where it sometimes seems that all consciousness aspires to the status of celebrity.

In other words, the two terms represent conditions generally considered antithetical to the privileged realm of art. Put together, the phrase Industry of the Ordinary questions the art world's elitism, undermining its tendency to celebrate things that manifest originality and uniqueness while denigrating those that are more populist, quotidian, and common. In making reference to industry, the phrase also critiques the art world's pretensions about its special status. Instead of reflecting some higher state of being, Industry of the Ordinary pulls art back down into the realm of the everyday workaday world.

The adoption of self-canceling ideas is ultimately a rejection of White's binary alternatives. Contradictions short-circuit the simple choice between done and not done and open up a plethora of other options. In the process, they undermine heavy-handed systems of social control. In exploring this territory, IOTO belongs to a lineage of artistic movements devoted to disrupting socially restrictive conventions in the service of political and personal change.

One of its precursors is the Situationist International, a movement which lasted from 1957 to 1972 and whose chief theorist was the French writer and filmmaker Guy Debord. In the movement's manifesto, *The Society of the Spectacle*, Debord advocated the creation of "situations," which he defined as the antithesis of theater with its separation of passive audience from active actors. Instead, "situations" relied on games, irrational activities, and ephemeral gestures. These, Debord argued, would "break the spectator's psychological identification with the hero, so as to incite this spectator into activity by provoking his capacities to revolutionize his own life."[1]

The Situationist International had a specific political agenda, namely engendering the demise of what Debord termed the spectacular society of advanced capitalism. Other advocates of disruption aimed at a more personal state of freedom. In the '60s and '70s, art movements like Happenings, Fluxus, and interactive performance flourished as ways of undermining the commodification of art and opening up spheres of action that were not governed by commerce. More

[1] Guy Debord, "Towards a Situationist International" (1957), reprinted in Claire Bishop, *Participation* (Cambridge: MIT Press, 2006), p. 97.

recent formulations of this idea go under names like culture jamming and relational aesthetics. While not espousing the particular agenda of any of these movements, IOTO carries on this tradition.

IOTO was inaugurated in 2003 with a performance titled *Dropping 163 lbs: Daley Plaza*. The work was precisely that: seventy-five performers dropped 163 pounds (that being the average weight of an American adult) of white clothing on Chicago's Daley Plaza. The action embodied many of the themes that would become a hallmark of the group—participatory activity, public setting, reference to "regular people," and the solemn implementation of apparently absurd or irrational behavior. Brooks and Wilson formulated a manifesto to describe their project: "Through sculpture, text, photography, video, sound, and performance Industry of the Ordinary are dedicated to an exploration and celebration of the customary, the everyday, and the usual. Their emphasis is on challenging pejorative notions of the ordinary and, in doing so, moving beyond the quotidian."

As of this writing, they have produced more than eighty projects as well as nine proxy projects by fellow travelers. These works have appeared in various locales, taking the form of actions on the streets and parks of Chicago, performances at art openings, works commissioned for specific exhibitions, and interventions in places as far flung as New York City, Venice, Italy, Los Angeles, Waterloo, Iowa, and Lincoln, Nebraska. The works involve a variety of interactions: among them, polling passersby on their definition of national greatness or the meaning of the word "normal," engaging groups of people to undertake unusual tasks, passing out tee shirts emblazoned with slogans like "I want to be ordinary" or "If you can't convince them, confuse them" (the latter from Harry S. Truman), and organizing performances at public events. While the works generally are tied to a specific time and place, artifacts, photos, video documentation, and a continually updated website remain as evidence of IOTO's activities.

Various themes reappear throughout this corpus. One has to do with the idea of democracy. (It is significant that the two artists behind IOTO grew up in England, as their outsider status allows them a clear-eyed view of the foibles, aspirations, and ideological assumptions of their adopted American society.) Democracy-based projects touch on everything from the electoral process, the hidden hierarchies of class in an ostensibly classless society, and the deterioration of politics in an age of terror. One of the most pointed of these are several *Democracy* projects that involved the creation of posters, tee shirts and neon signs with the English and Arabic words "Vote for Me" placed in various sites around Chicago. This project, which began at the time of the 2004 presidential campaign, continued through the 2005 Iraqi elections and beyond. In this and various other works, use of Arabic is meant both to skewer the widespread specter of the Arabic speaker as bogeyman in contemporary America and to serve as a reminder of our ostensible commitment to diversity and the democratic representation of nonmainstream groups. A later iteration of this idea appears in the 2009 *Terrorist Paintings*—three abstract paintings in the style of various modernist painters that feature the word TERRORIST in Arabic script. Art is similarly enlisted in a commentary on 21st-century paranoia titled *Homeland Security* that comprises ceramic weights in the five colors of the alert system instituted in the wake of 9/11.

Notions of class and hierarchy underlie works like *Epilation* in which the artists cut away at the fur coat worn by a woman accompanying them to a gala art opening. Tufts of fur are given to bystanders, who may or may not be in on the joke. This work has been performed a number of times, in each instance with the same coat, which has become understandably more threadbare with each iteration. While the coat itself is an emblem of the high art's entanglement with the world of luxury and wealth, its depletion suggests a metaphor for the slow unraveling of prosperity in recessionary times.

Other projects deal with work and play, two sides of the American dream. Labor is represented in various ways: IOTO have distributed sixty-one frozen hands tagged with the names of workers who broke ground at Chicago's Millennium Park through a show at that site; they created a group portrait of the security personnel at the Chicago Cultural Center; they documented their own working process; and they employed "art workers" (artists, curators, critics, and collectors) to create new artworks based on verbs that appeared in the descriptions of previous projects. One of the most provocative of the labor-themed works is *Re-Work (for Allan Kaprow, Marina Abramovic, and Philip-Lorca diCorcia)*. This performance was commissioned by the Museum of Contemporary Art in Los Angeles on the occasion of a retrospective of the work of Happenings inventor Allan Kaprow. Taking off from a work originated by Kaprow, IOTO contracted with two sex-industry workers to paint and repaint a hallway of a satellite site of the museum in their "professional" clothing. With this work, they expand the conventional definitions of work, revealing that employment that seems extraordinary to some is ordinary to others.

The flip side of this examination of work is represented by projects that explore play, recreation, and various other "nonproductive" activities. Some are exuberant—as when Wilson and Brooks paint each other's suits with luminescent paint and dance on the beach to the light of a car's headlights. Others are quietly affirmative, as when they enumerate the things that make them happy. *Affair* has a more racy aspect. Here IOTO solicited a couple having an extramarital affair to sit for a masked portrait in exchange for a free night at a hotel.

Referencing the world in which their projects often appear, a number of works touch on aspects of the art world. At the opening of a John Cage exhibition at the Museum of Contemporary Art (MCA) in Chicago, they echoed Cage's own insouciant attitude by giving away badges made from the MCA's own permanent collection catalog. In another action, they mocked their own activity by collecting names for a petition to ban performance art. And suggesting their own triumph over more institutionalized forms of art, they planted a flag on a chimney overlooking the Hyde Park Art Center in Chicago.

Quite a few projects are devoted to competitive sports, inspired by the two artists' shared passion for soccer, or football, as it is known in their native country. In these works, sports become a metaphor for life—they are governed by sets of rules within which there are many possibilities for action and interaction. And they provide a place to safely indulge the competitive instinct that governs so many relationships in a capitalist society. The projects in this vein range from the whimsical to the raucous. For example, IOTO sponsored a lesbian softball team with the suggestive name Fighting Beavers. They also organized a tug of war contest. IOTO paid homage to the origins of soccer (which according to the artists dates back to Mayan times when warriors would kick around the heads of slain enemies), by encouraging visitors to an opening at the MCA to kick rubber molds of their own heads down the stairs. Spectators were encouraged to sing an earthy football chant as two motley teams battled in the rain.

A related theme involves the ingestion of beer and other alcoholic substances. In one early work, the pair drank a case of beer and documented the changing color of their urine. By 2010, they had upgraded to champagne in a project in which they provided champagne flutes emblazoned with their slogan "I want to be ordinary" on the occasion of an opening at apexart in Manhattan.

An equally long list of works makes reference to religion. These projects are infused both with skepticism toward organized religion and awareness of the role of faith in America's public and private life. Some works deal with the commercialization of religion, as when, in *Tender*, they pulp and refashion a bible into a dollar bill. Other works comment on the unhealthy merger of religion and politics as when IOTO distributed tee shirts that proclaim "Just Say No To Theocracy." Inspired by the much publicized battle over a sculpture of the Ten Commandments placed in front of the Alabama Supreme Court in 2001-2003, they had a professional ice sculptor create an ice sculpture of the tablets which they wheeled down Chicago's Michigan Avenue, giving away the liquid residue as it melted. Suggesting odd parallels between the rituals surrounding religion and sports, they have donned the personas of Young God and Old God and engaged in a game of table football outdoors on a promontory overlooking Lake Michigan. The game ended (and the remarkable moment captured on camera) when a gust of wind operating as the proverbial "act of God" swept a wave over the table.

Perhaps no work so perfectly sums up IOTO's approach as *Normal*. For this work, the artists queried passersby as to their definition of the word "normal." The result, now posted on

Vimeo, is a fascinating survey of the complexities of this deceptively simple term. Participants often find themselves stopped short as they muse on whether "normal" is ubiquitous or non-existent; if it is relative to social conventions, a matter of individual self-definition, or determined by codified belief systems. They suggest that "normal" may be the status quo, the average, the consensus of large groups of people, a stultifying convention, or a genetic or physical fact. One respondent, who admits that he has recently found himself homeless after being downsized from an apparently solid job, clearly sees "normal" as a condition that he may never again enjoy. But the most poignant response comes from a mother who points to her learning disabled child and firmly states, "Normal is a setting on the washing machine. It has nothing to do with people."

With this work, as with other projects undertaken by IOTO, what might seem an ordinary question quickly opens out into something far more complex. Using humor, ambiguity, disruption, and appeals to collectivity, Industry of the Ordinary celebrate the space between done and not done. In doing so, they illuminate the hidden contradictions of contemporary society and invite us to question our assumptions and patterns of behavior. The rest is up to us.

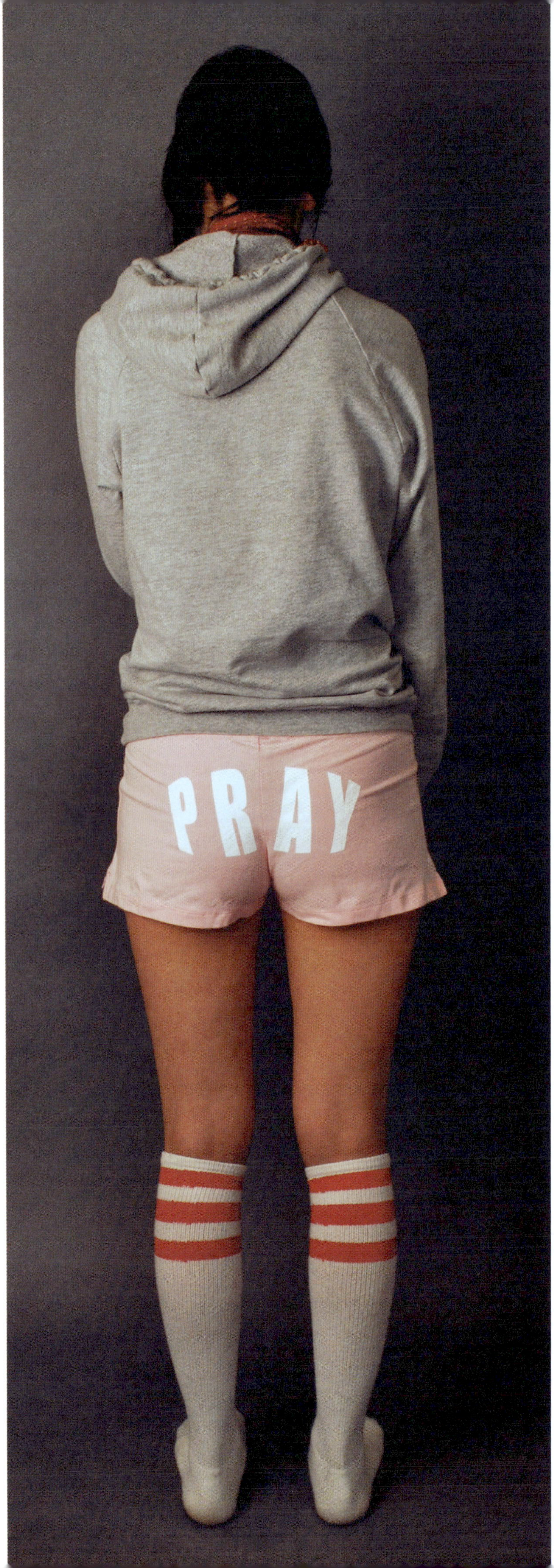
PRAY

2009

Apparel

Industry of the Ordinary market inspirational shorts.

To order, visit: http://industryoftheordinary.com/html/projects-sportswear2.html.

Solan, Himachal Pradesh, India

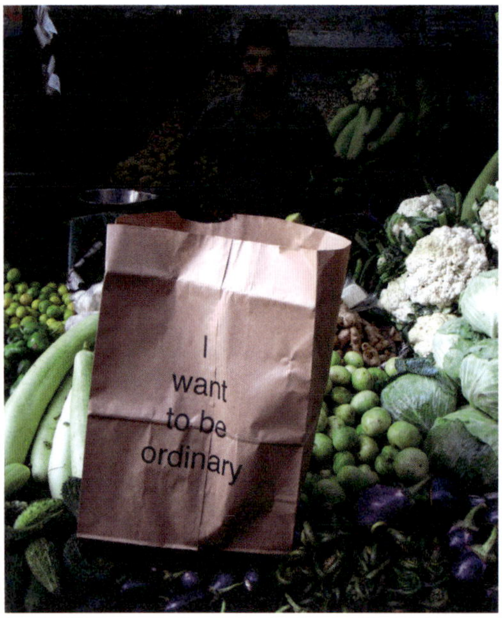

Supermarketing relies on audience involvement to activate and complete the work, using the traditional gallery setting and Facebook as exhibition sites. Referencing the portable and viral strategies of Félix González-Torres's posters and candy projects, "I Want to be Ordinary" is printed on brown paper bags stacked on the floor engaging marketing as both tool and subject of the work. Both utilitarian and exhibitionist, the appropriated bags are filled with purchases by the new owners and documented with a photograph posted on Facebook, making them accomplices and stockholders in IOTO's global brand.

— Ciara Ennis

Supermarketing, 2009

Industry of the Ordinary dream of a better tomorrow.

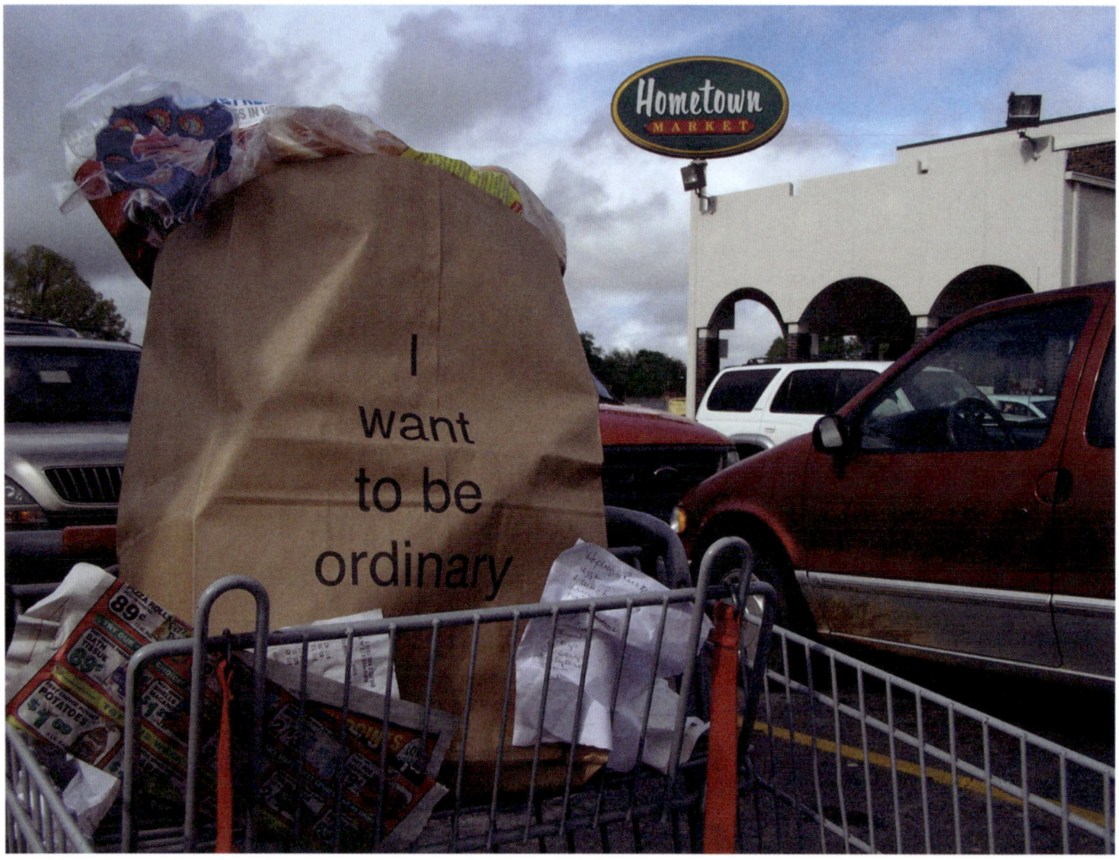

Florence, Alabama

Athens

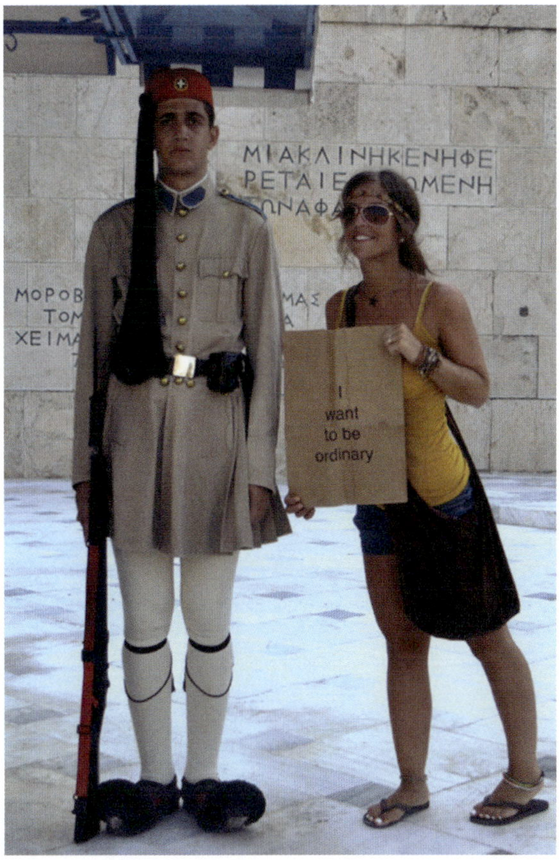

Brooklyn

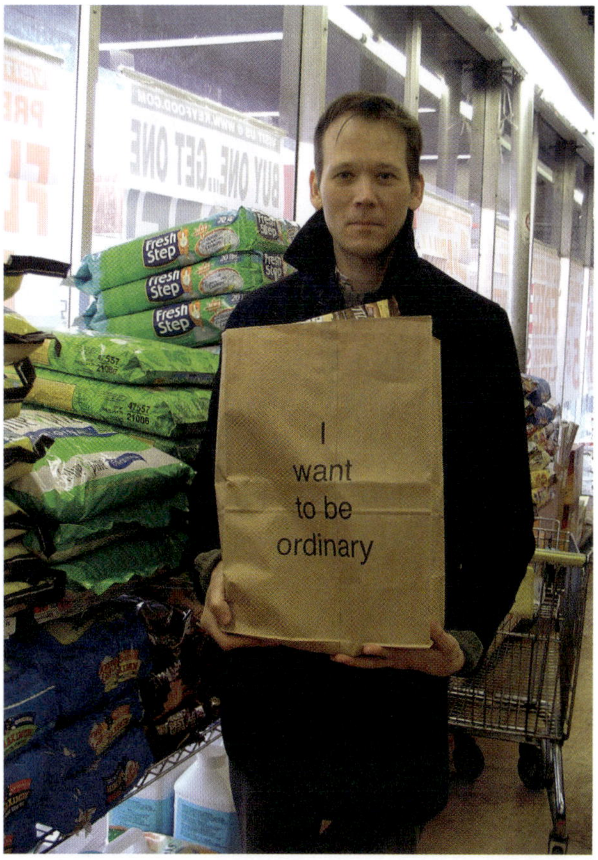

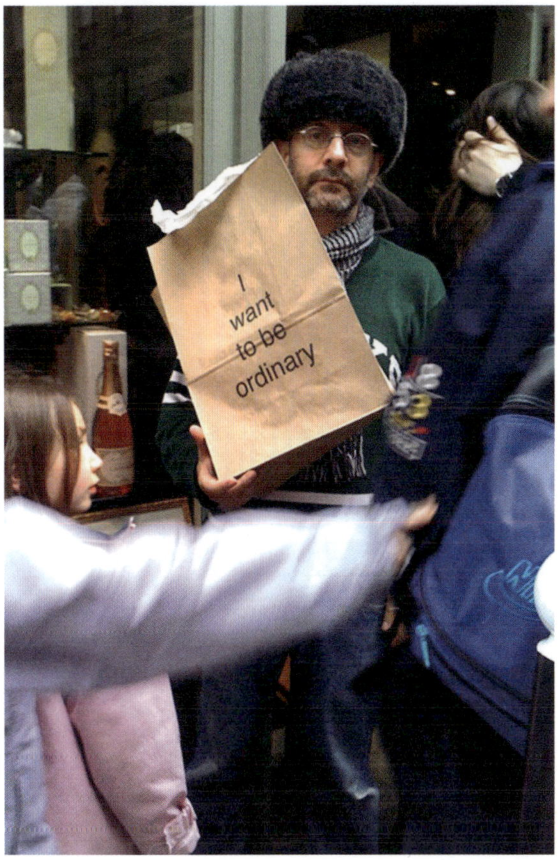

Paris

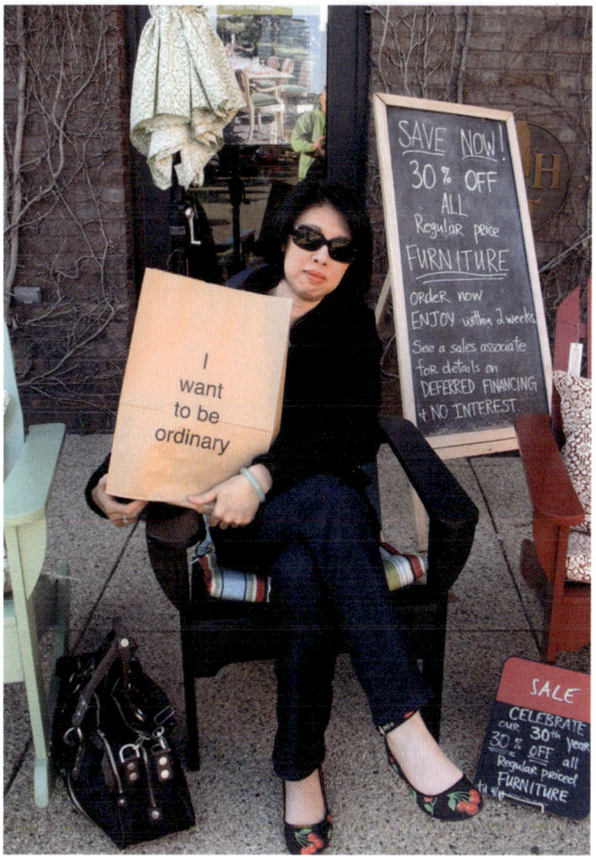

Chicago

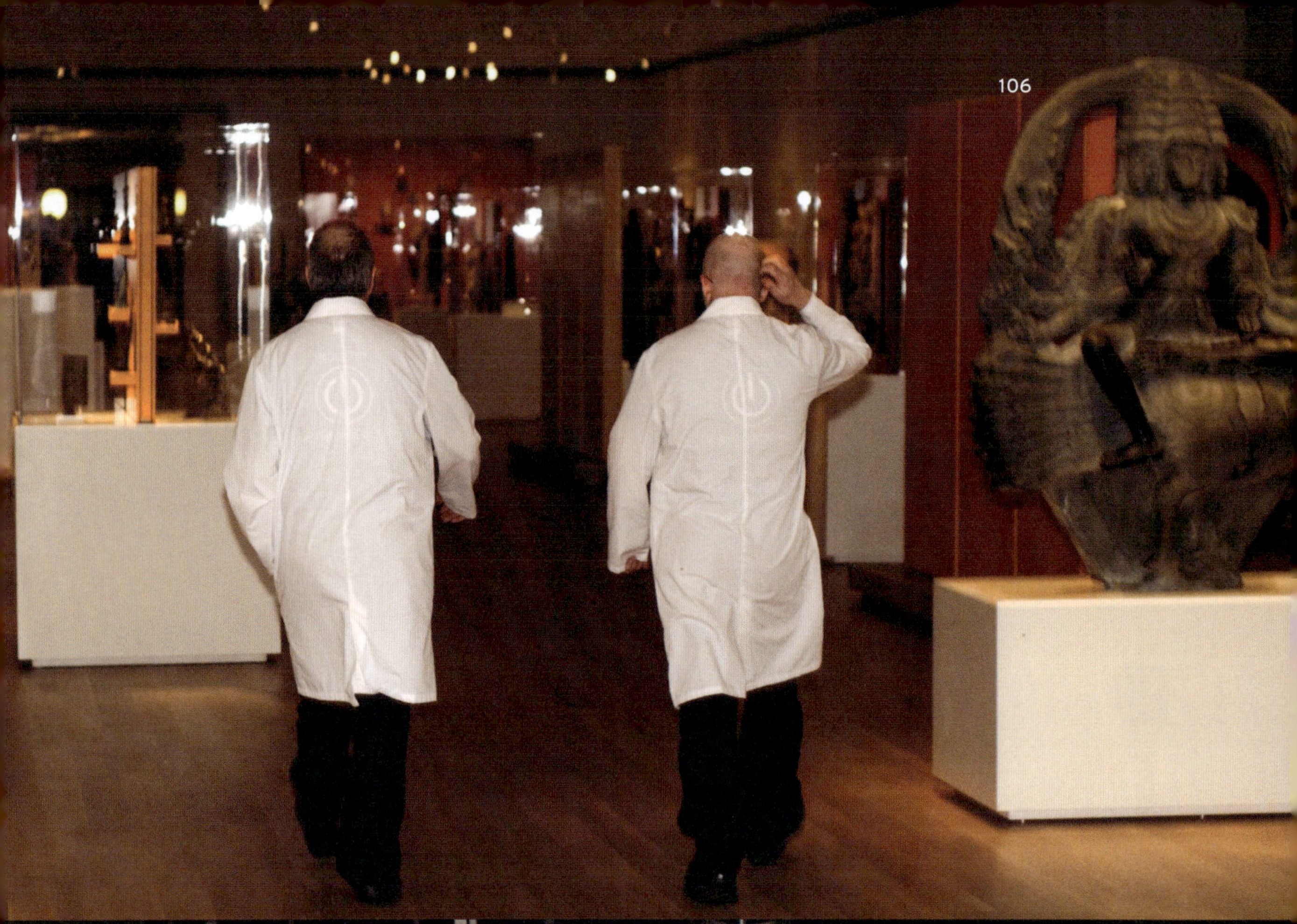

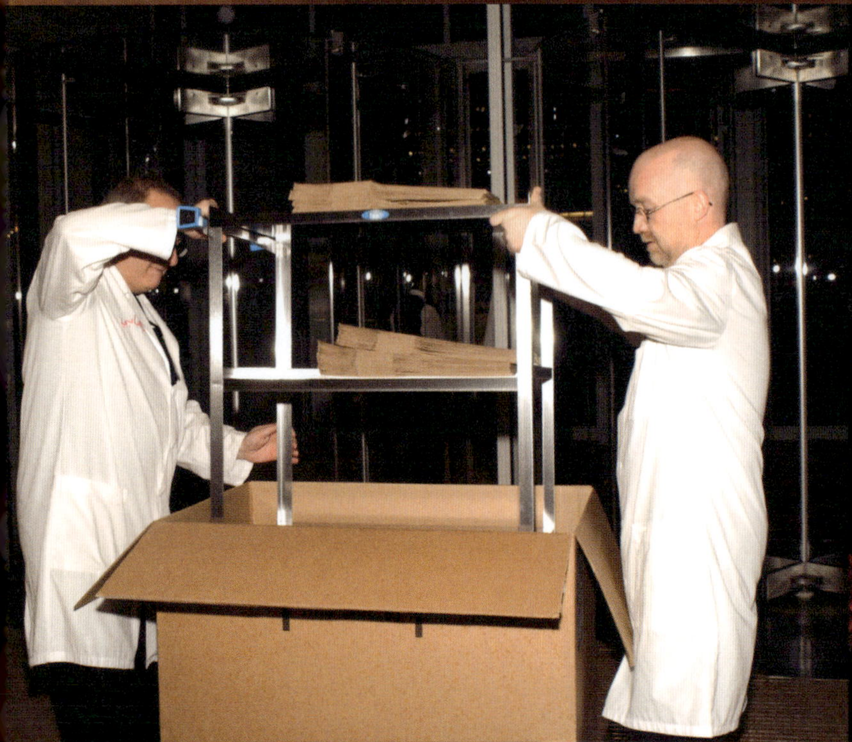

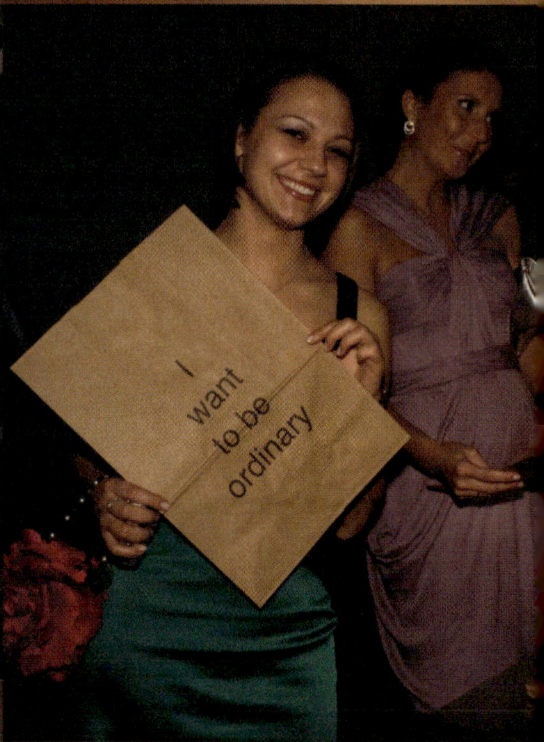
I want to be ordinary

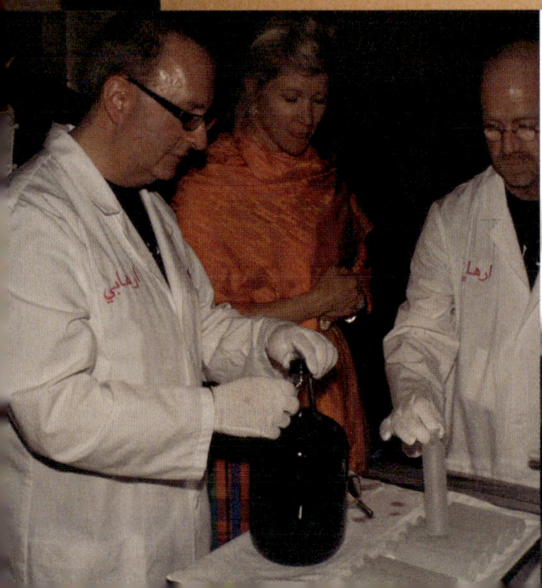

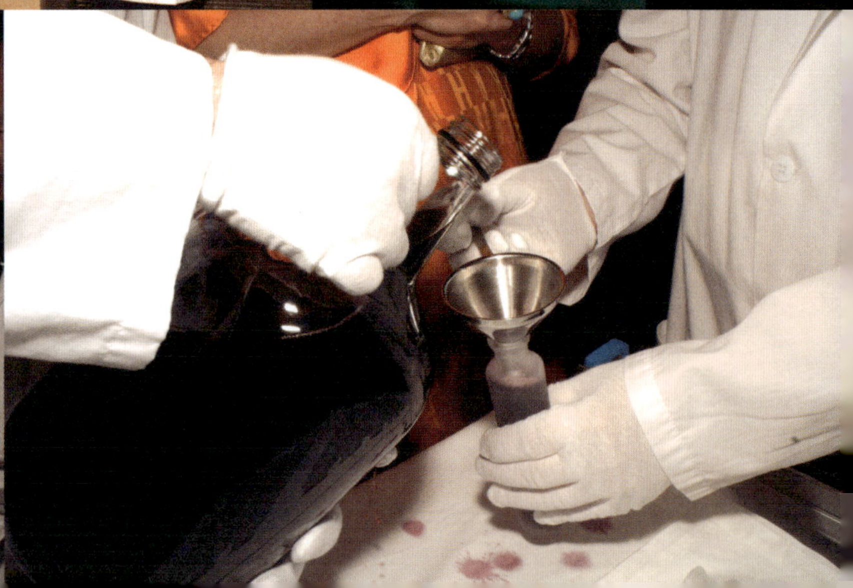

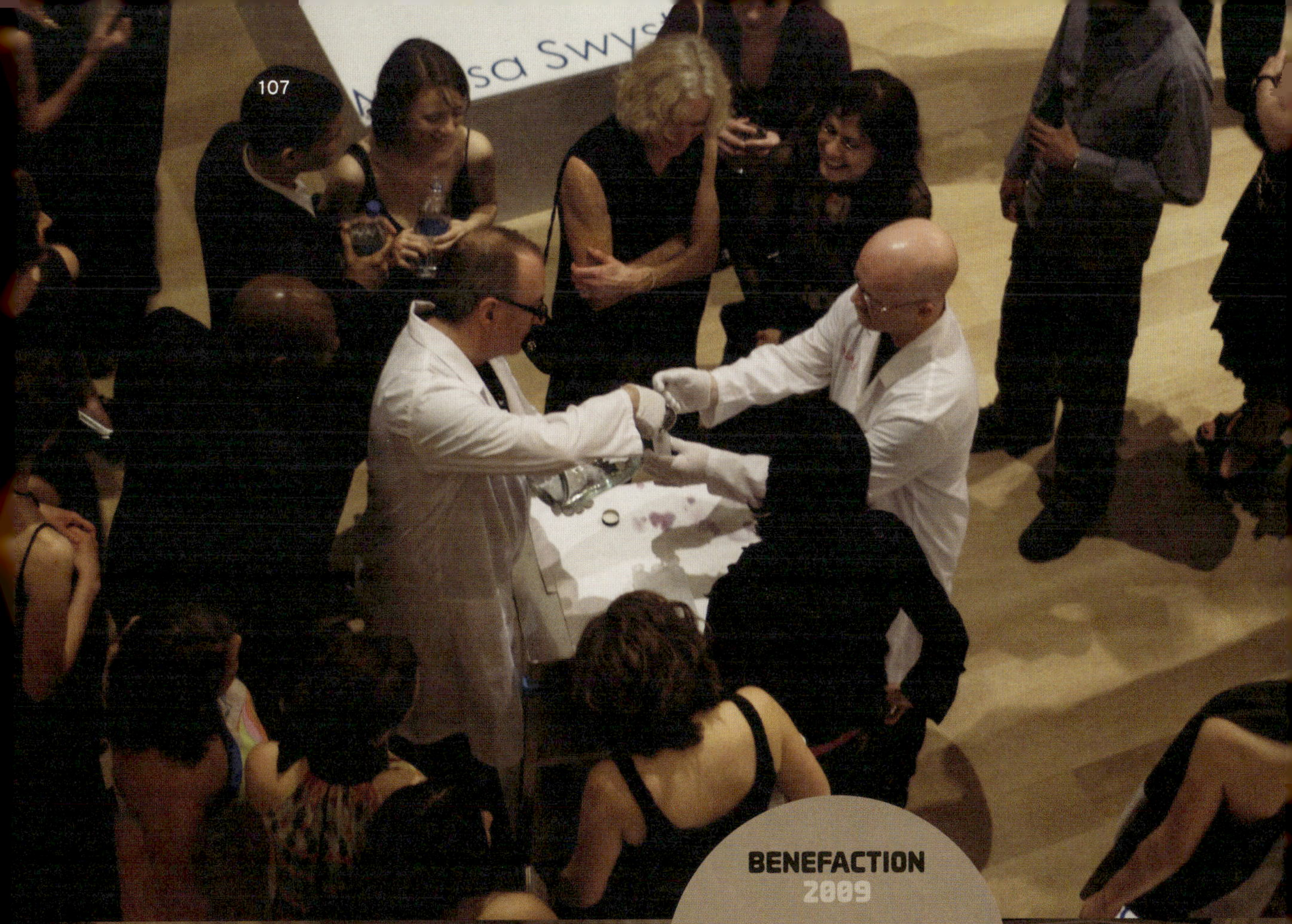

BENEFACTION
2009

For the opening of the Modern Wing of the Art Institute of Chicago, Industry of the Ordinary gift 126 objects to the invited guests.

Photography by and special thanks to Aron Gent. Thanks also to Jim Zimpel, Anne Henry, Mary Beth Witte, and Peg Sorenson.

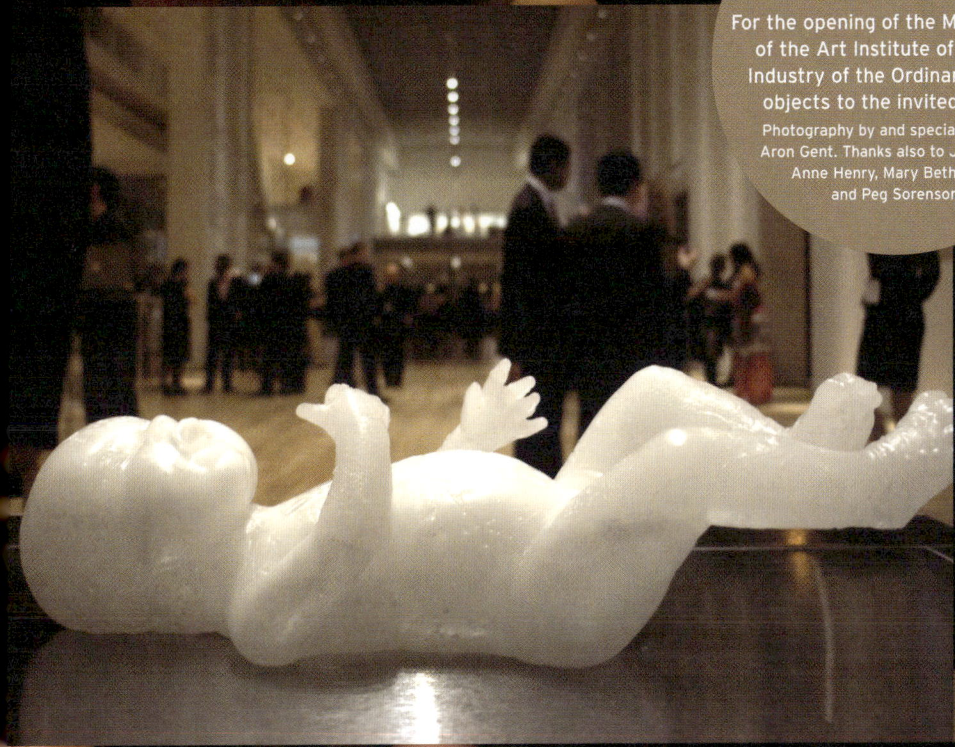

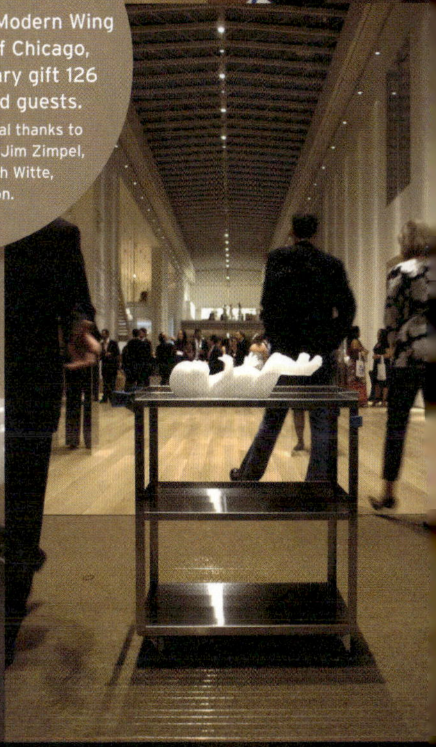

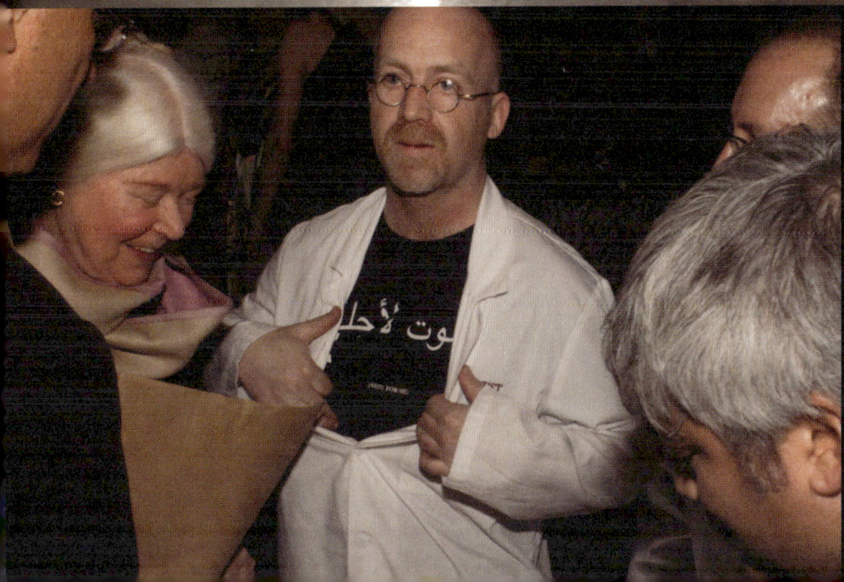

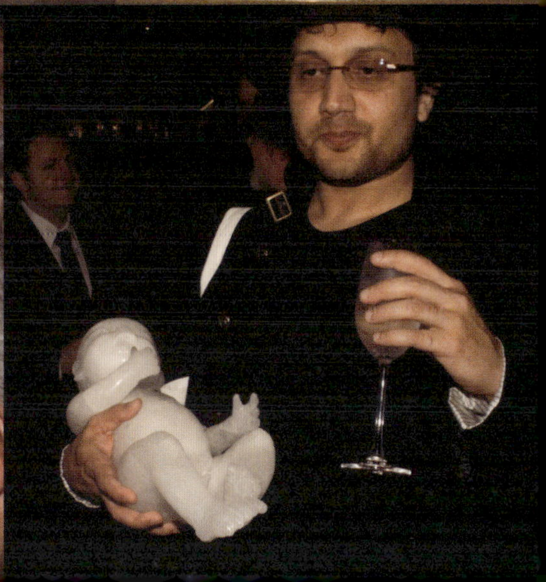

ELECTIONEER (FOR VENICE, ITALY), 2009

Industry of the Ordinary join the European Union.

Production assistance by Joshua Clarfelt, Torreyanna Barley, and Nicholas Steindorf.

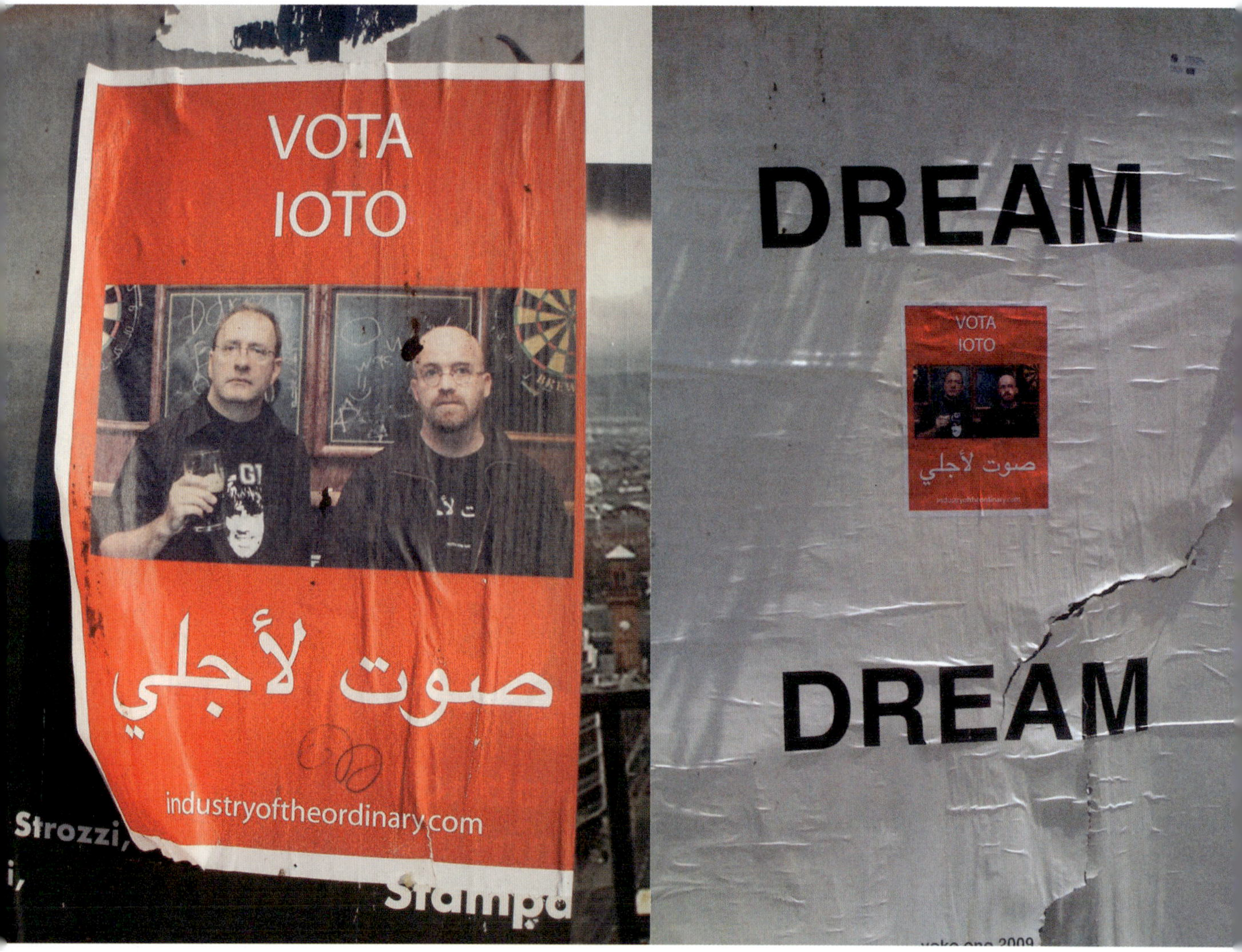

COLLAPSE, 2009

Industry of the Ordinary experience a setback.

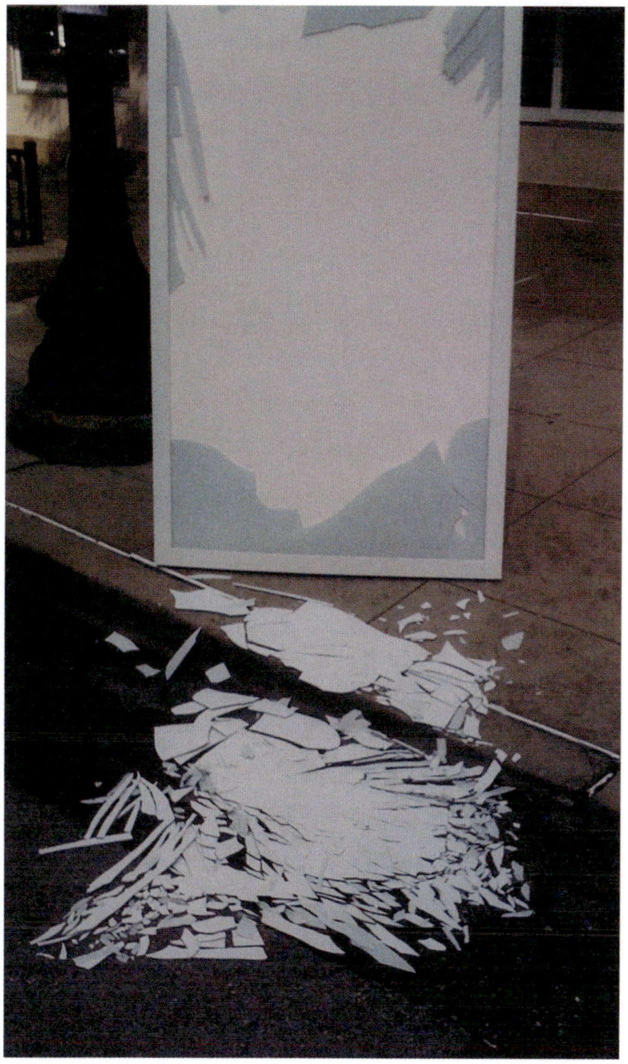

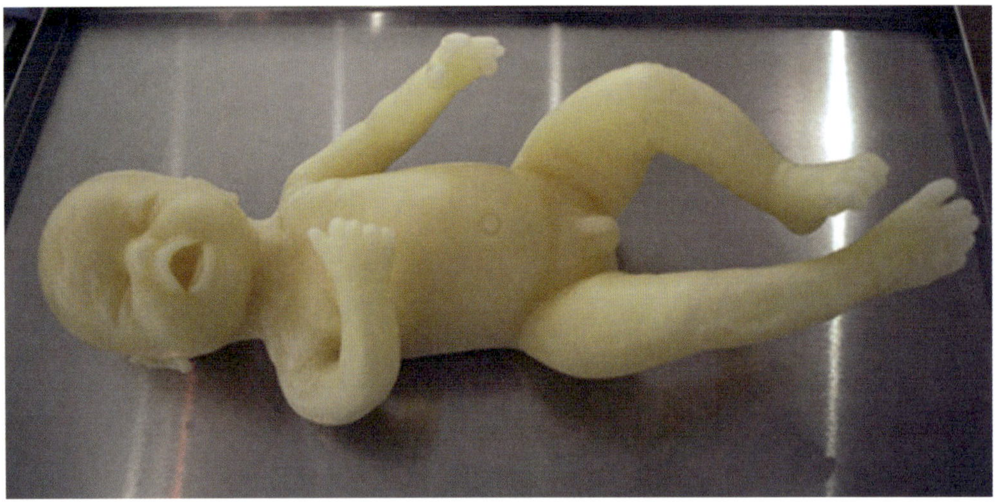

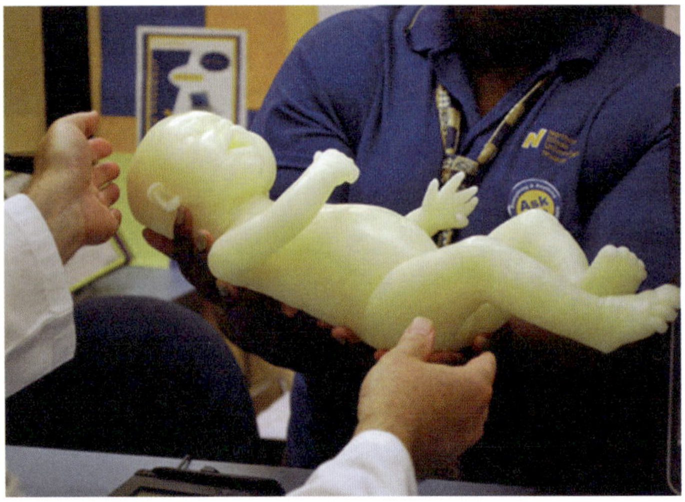

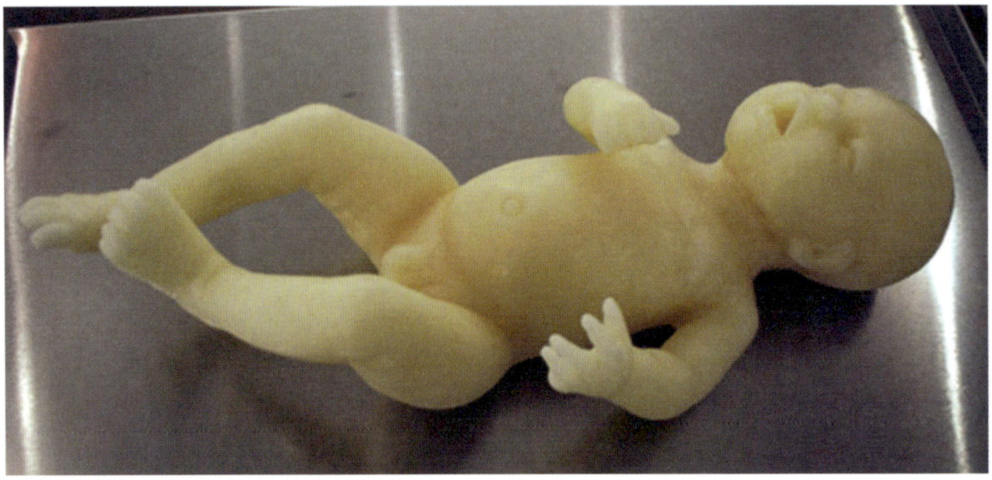

2009

Baby

Industry of the Ordinary produce an infant to be auctioned on eBay.

http://www.ebay.com/itm/ws/eBayISAPI.dll?ViewItem&item=260695987686&ssPageName=ADME:L:LCA:US:1123.

Special thanks to Jim Zimpel. Thanks also to Anna Trier, Karen Bovinich, and Melissa Lutz.

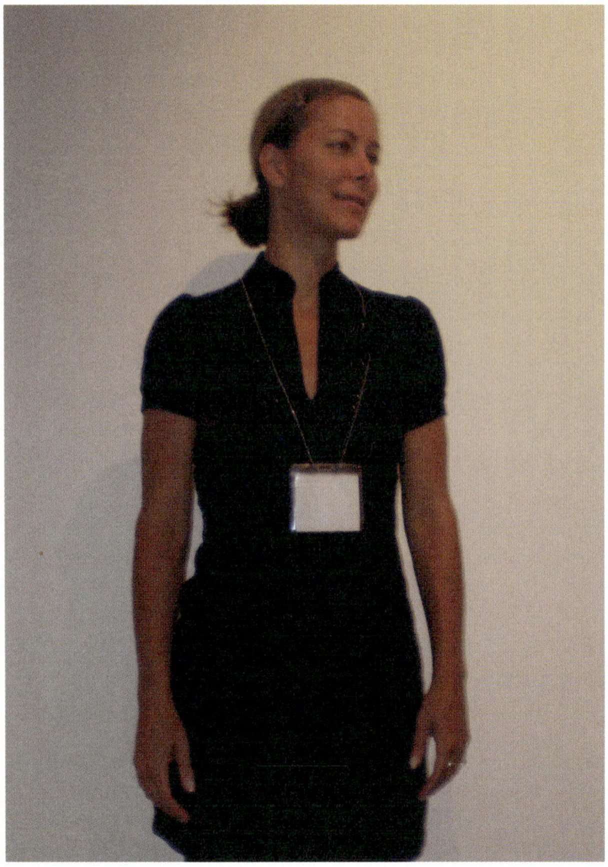

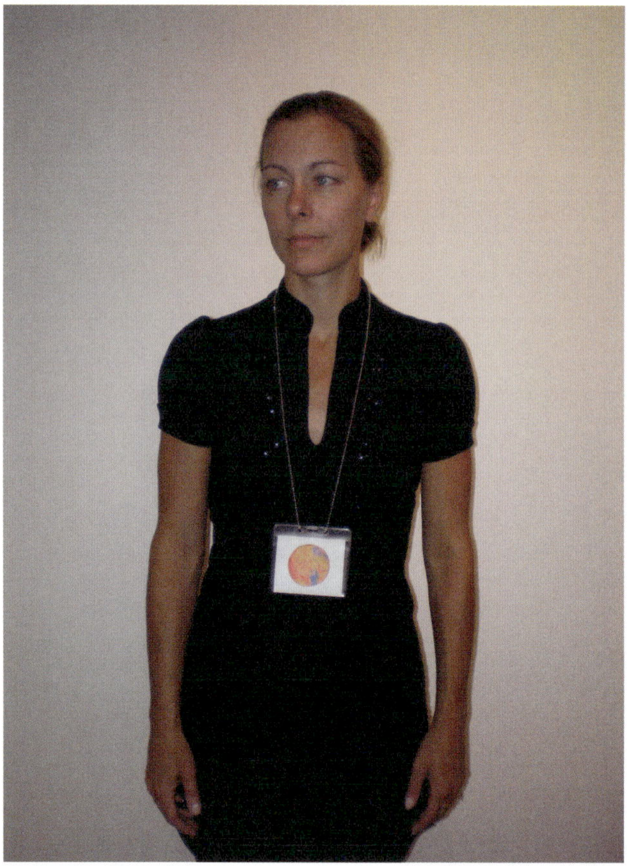

In *Clandestine Work (for IOTO)* the roles of artist and curator are reversed. Weber, Director and Curator of the Northeastern Illinois University Fine Arts Center, was invited by IOTO to collaborate on an intimate and professionally compromising portrait of herself—far more revealing than faux-suggestive girls-night-out images already displayed on her Facebook page—for an undisclosed site in the gallery. Sought by viewers eager to complete the exhibition's checklist, the work becomes a prurient scavenger hunt as Weber's private and professional lives become subject to scrutiny, forcing her to become gatekeeper of her own image and reputation.

— Ciara Ennis

2009

CLANDESTINE WORK

FOR IOTO

Industry of the Ordinary turn the tables.

Special thanks to Heather Weber.

39 VERBS

A project organized by Industry of the Ordinary
11th October 2009, 5-8pm
Packer Schopf Gallery
942 W. Lake St., Chicago, IL 60607
773-301-7162 (IOTO), 312-226-8984 (Gallery)

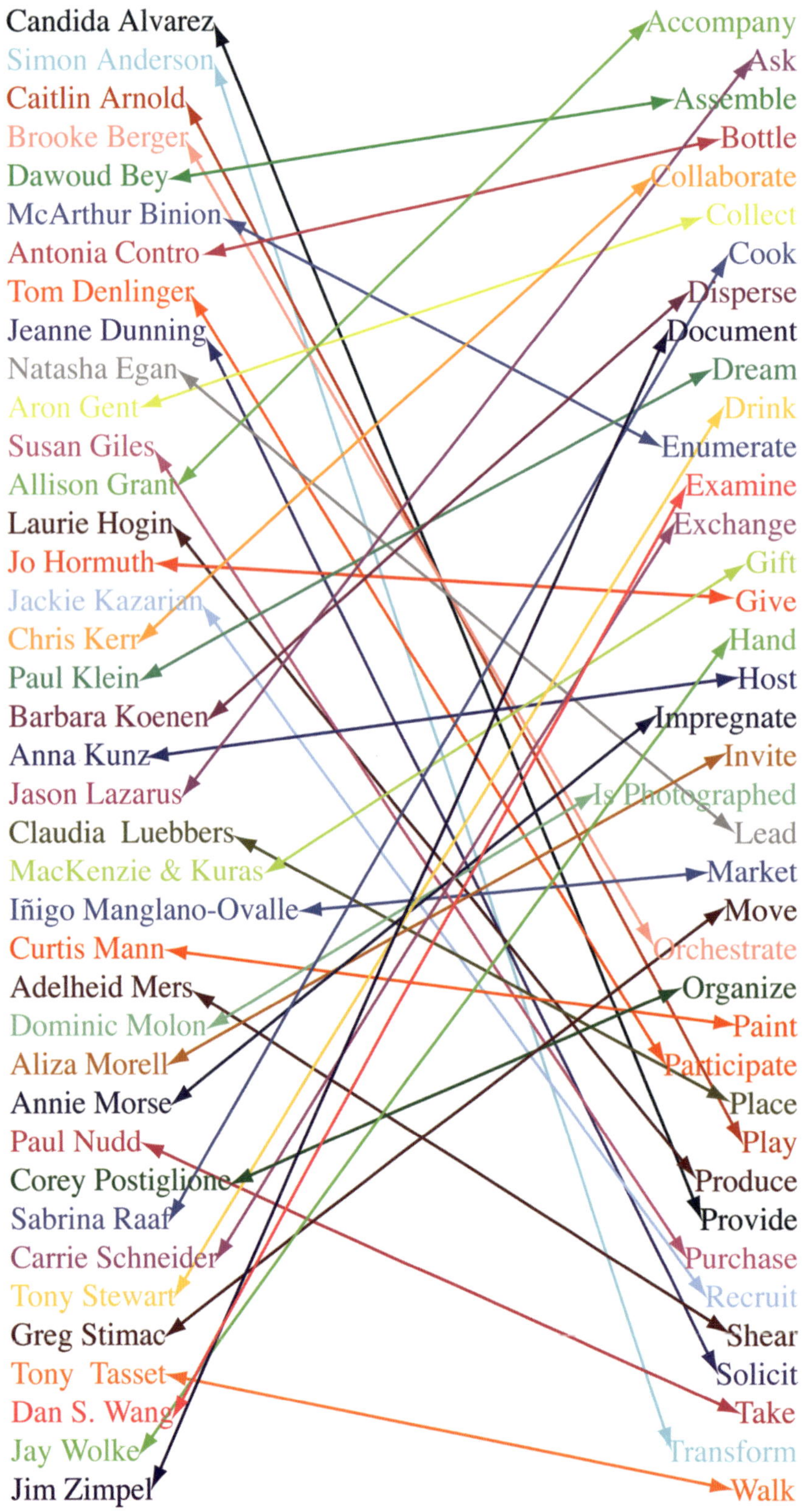

39 VERBS, 2009

Industry of the Ordinary disseminate second-hand verbs from their previous projects to a variety of art workers in Chicago to be used in a one-night only event.

Special thanks to Aron Packer, and thanks also to Alexa Loftus, Beth Sadowski, David Petrusich, Nina Mayer, Randy Brown, and Tannar Veatch.
Photography by Karen Bovinich. Videography by Anna Trier.

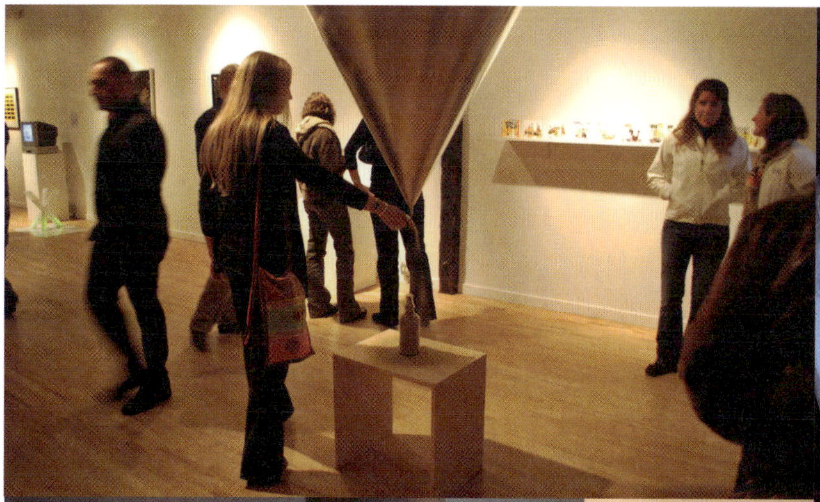

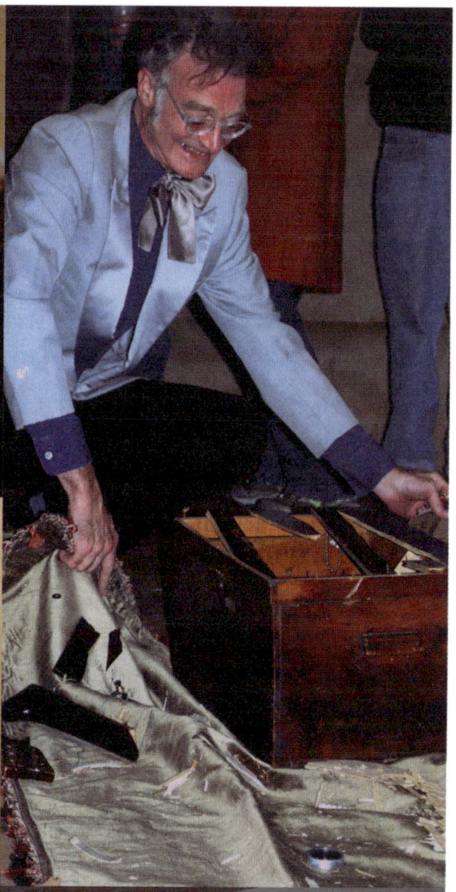

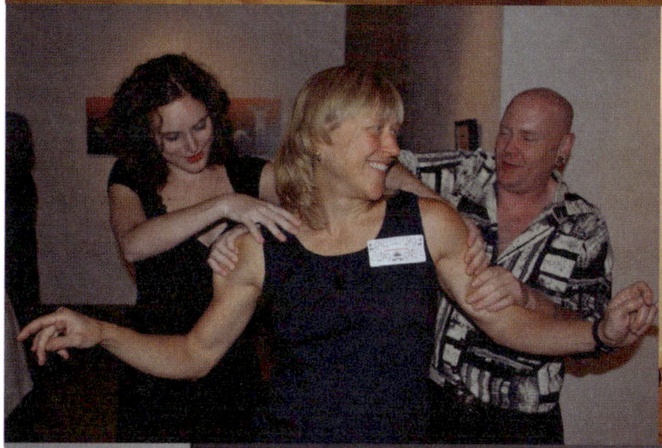

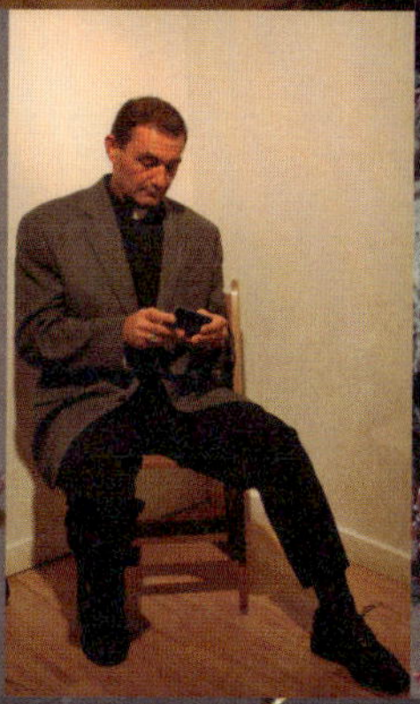

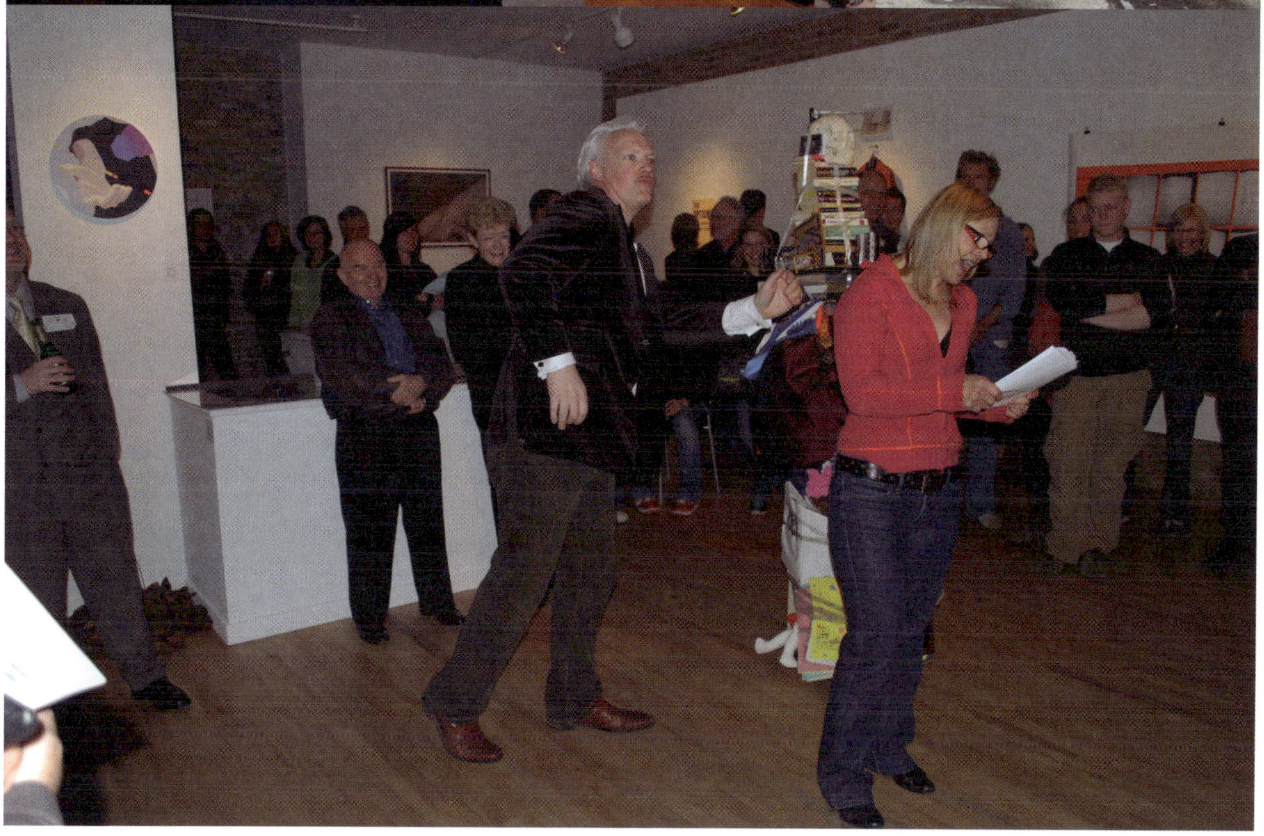

2009

Terrorist Paintings, I, II, III

Industry of the Ordinary honor art history and fear in three paintings.

Terrorist Paintings depict three alternate abstractions: a geometric color-field work based on a television color bar pattern, a Brice Marden inspired encaustic painting, and a white-on-white abstraction back-painted on glass. Embedded in all three is the word TERRORIST translated into Arabic and reversed out. Referencing IOTO's ongoing *Democracy* (2004–2009) project, where "Vote for Me" in Arabic appears in multiple forms (posters, tee shirts, and neon signs), *Terrorist Paintings* explore the prodigal and malevolent use of branding in politics. The Arabic text forces the viewer to consider the continuous and sustained branding of Arab identity, in the United States and abroad.

— Ciara Ennis

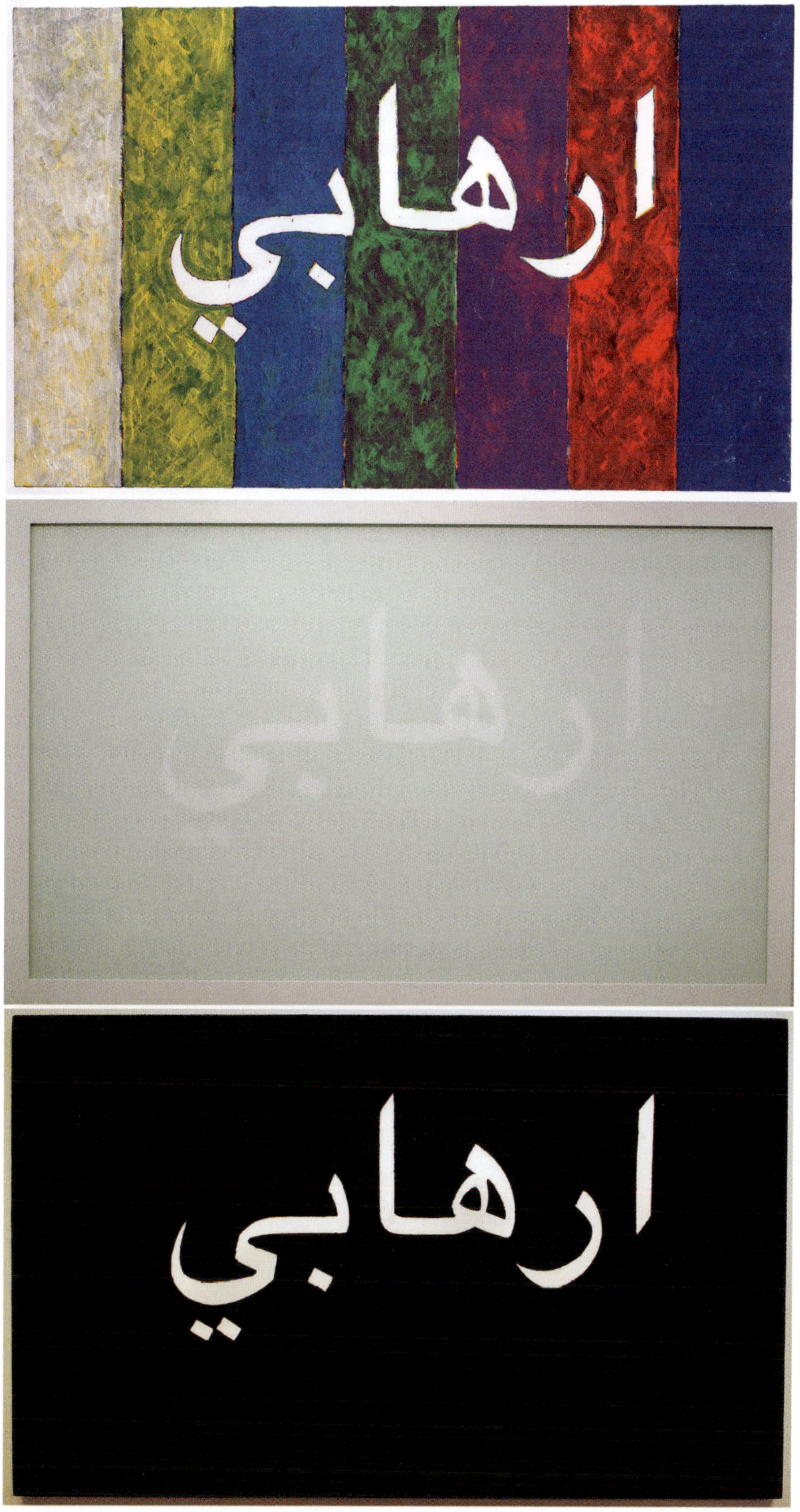
ارهابي
ارهابي
ارهابي

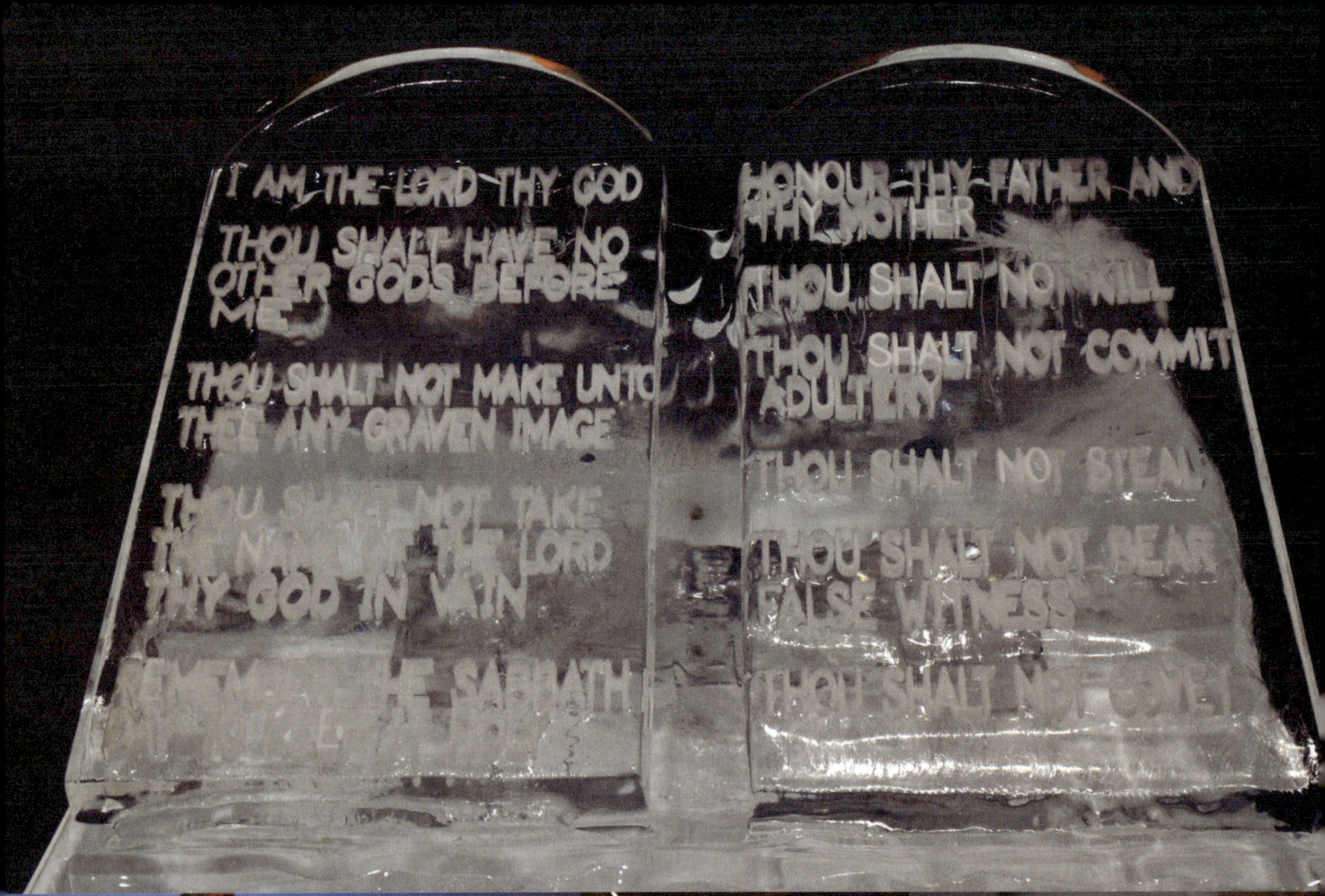
I AM THE LORD THY GOD
THOU SHALT HAVE NO OTHER GODS BEFORE ME
THOU SHALT NOT MAKE UNTO THEE ANY GRAVEN IMAGE
THY GOD IN VAIN
HONOUR THY FATHER AND THY MOTHER
THOU SHALT NOT COMMIT ADULTERY
THOU SHALT NOT STEAL
THOU SHALT NOT BEAR FALSE WITNESS

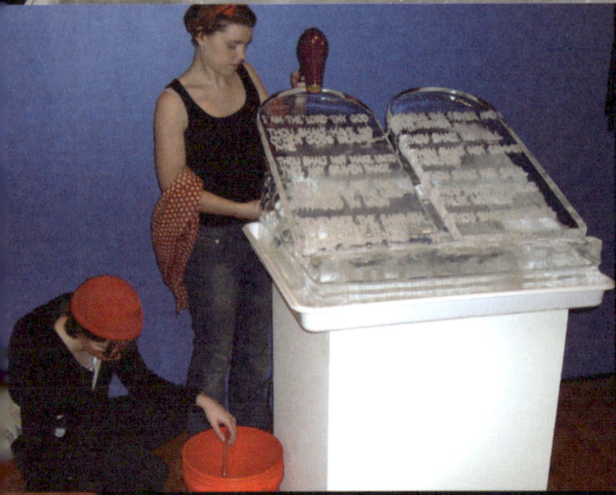

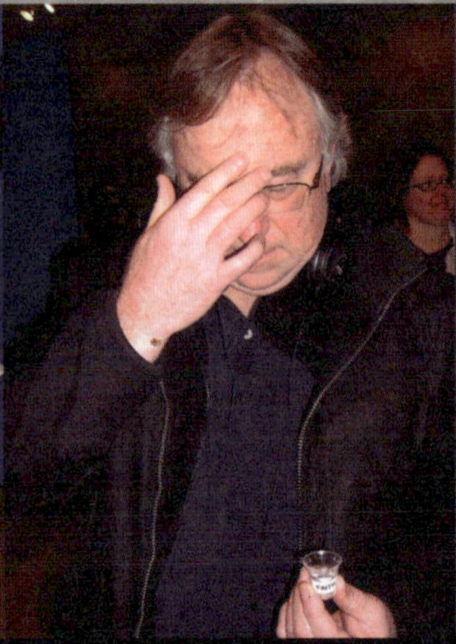

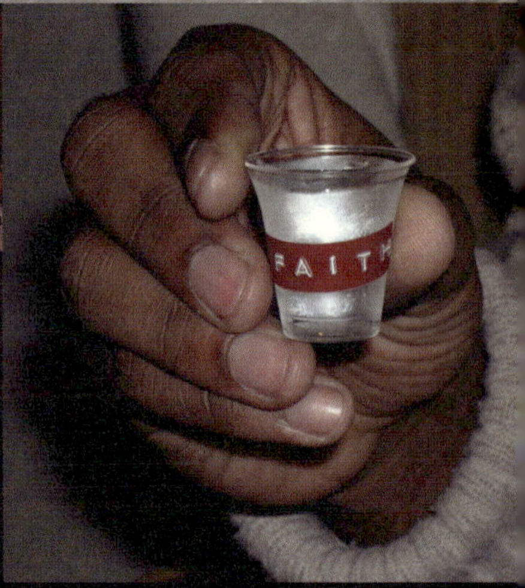
FAITH

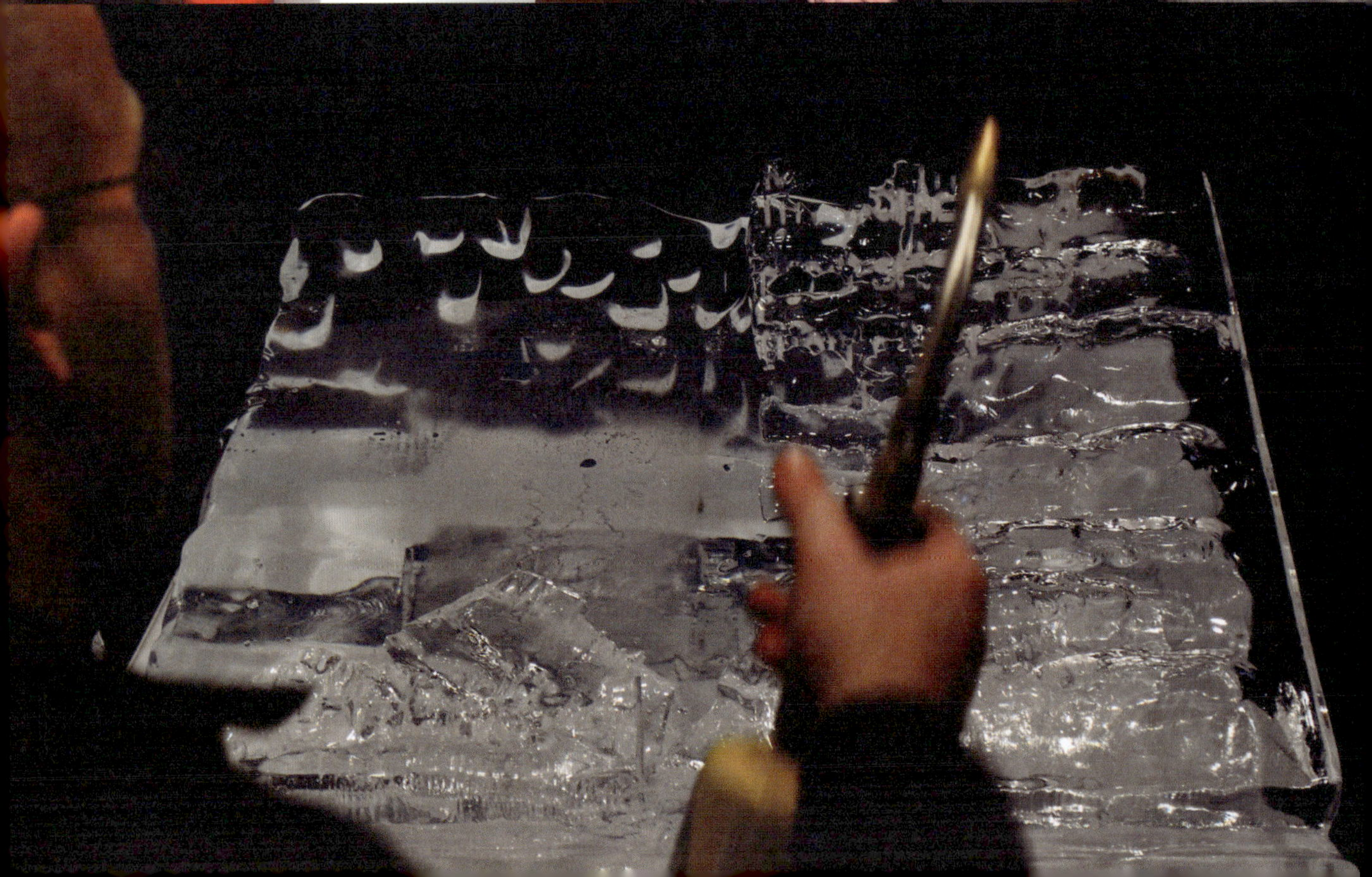

2009

Ten (Reprise)

Industry of the Ordinary reduce an ice sculpture of the Ten Commandments to liquid form and gift measures to the public.

Special thanks to Neysa Page-Lieberman, Jay Wolke, and Chicago Ice Works. Thanks also to Andrew Svec, Anna Trier, Claire Bendiner, Randy Brown, Jennifer Hansen, Megon Holldorf, Angie Meyer, Matt Schieren, Alexa Loftus. EJ Hill, Tannar Veatch, Beth Sadowski, David Petrusich, and Liz Moretti.

XMAS 2009 KNEES UP, 2009

In public houses, private homes, and working men's clubs across England, a customary tradition for the celebration of monumental events and great festivals has been to relieve oneself of responsibility and inhibition and organize a "Knees Up." In this tradition, Industry of the Ordinary put on an Xmas Knees Up.

Special thanks to Hadley Vogel, Anna Trier, Emanuel Aguilar, Bob Brooks, and Eliza Nichols. Thanks also to Alexa Loftus, Karen Bovinich, Steve Piggott, Shane Schubbe, Josh Korby, and Nina Mayer.

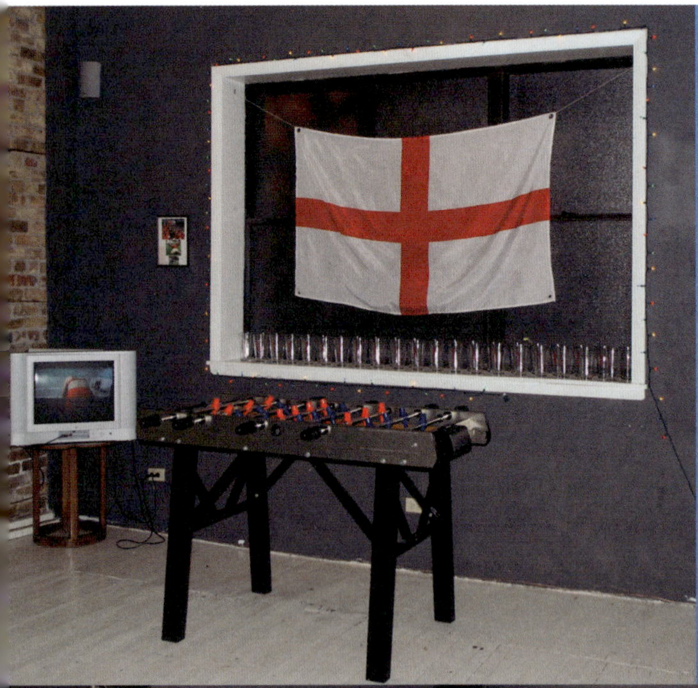

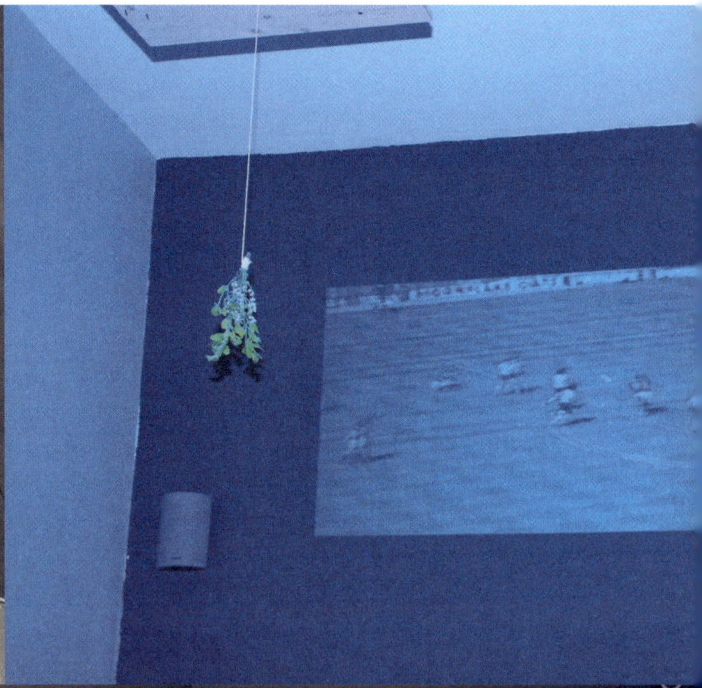

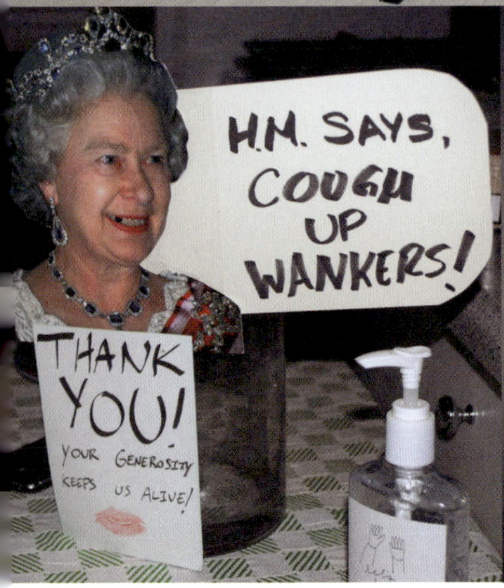

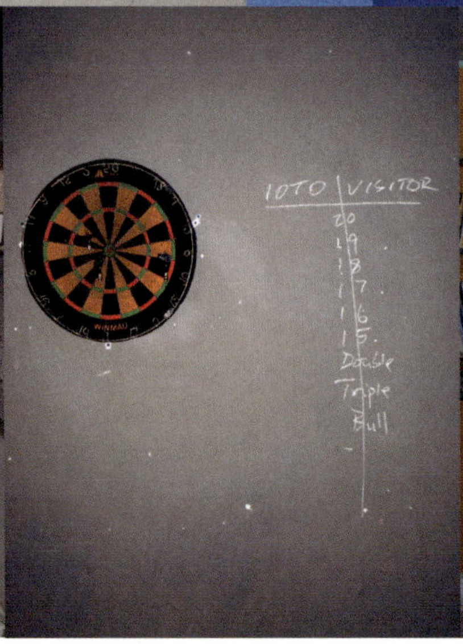

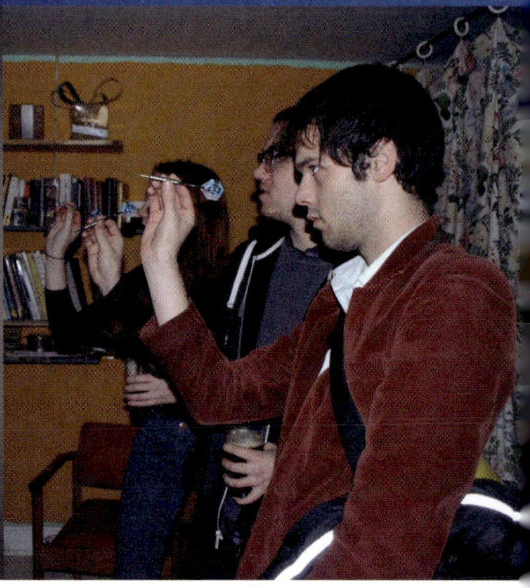

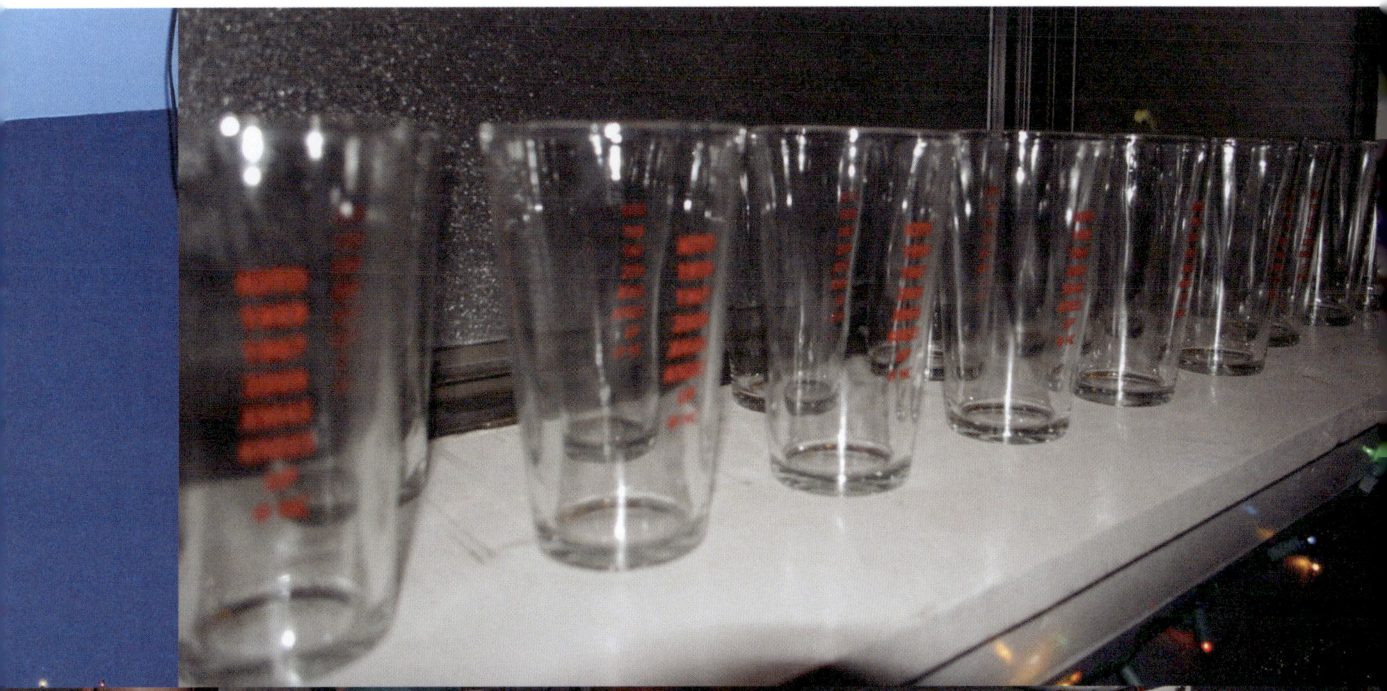

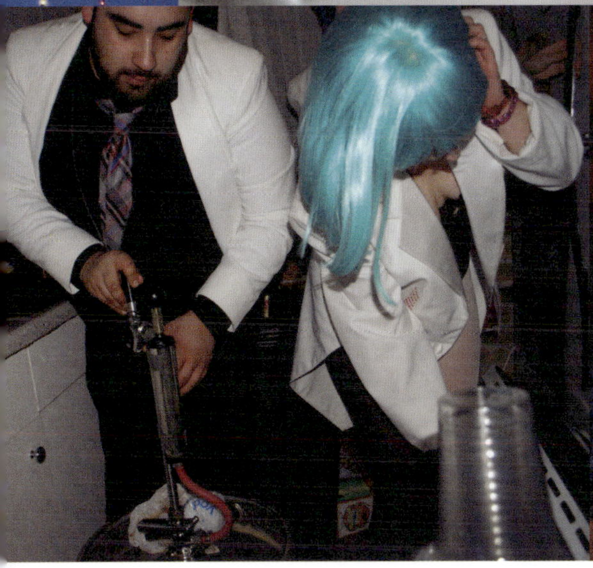

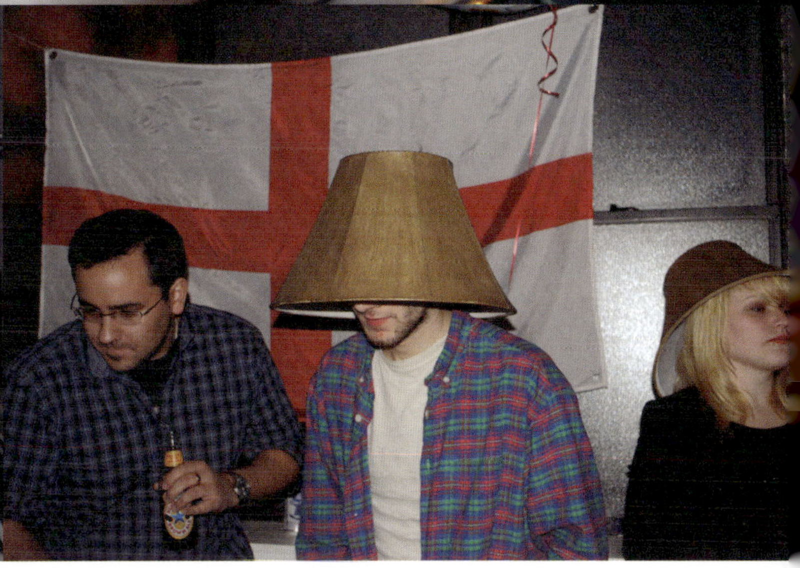

2010

TIPPLE

For the Bad at Sports show *Don't Piss on Me and Tell Me It's Raining* at apexart, New York, Industry of the Ordinary provide personalized champagne flutes.

Special thanks to Duncan MacKenzie, Richard Holland, and the entire BAS team, as well as Cybele Maylone at apexart.

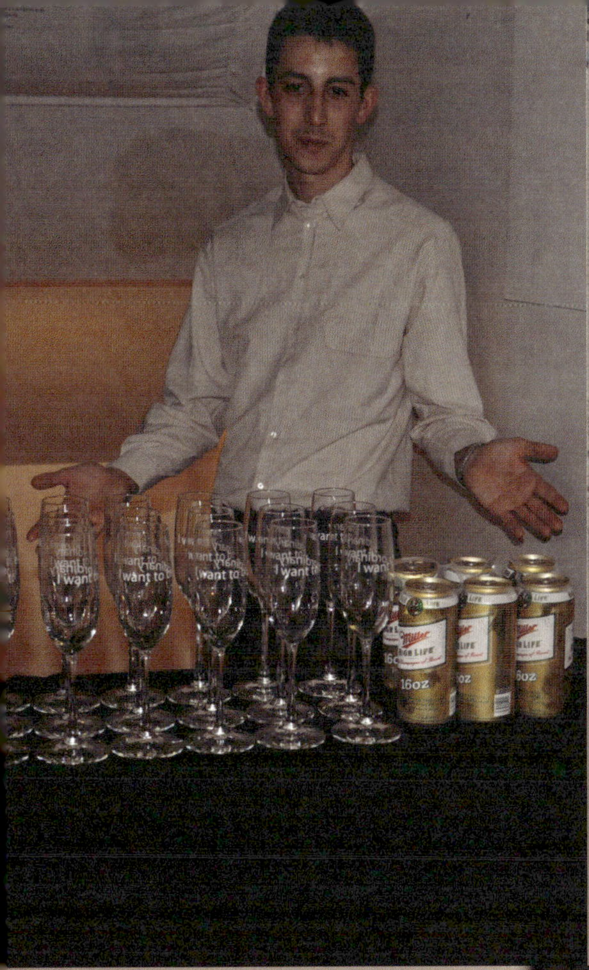
I want to
16oz

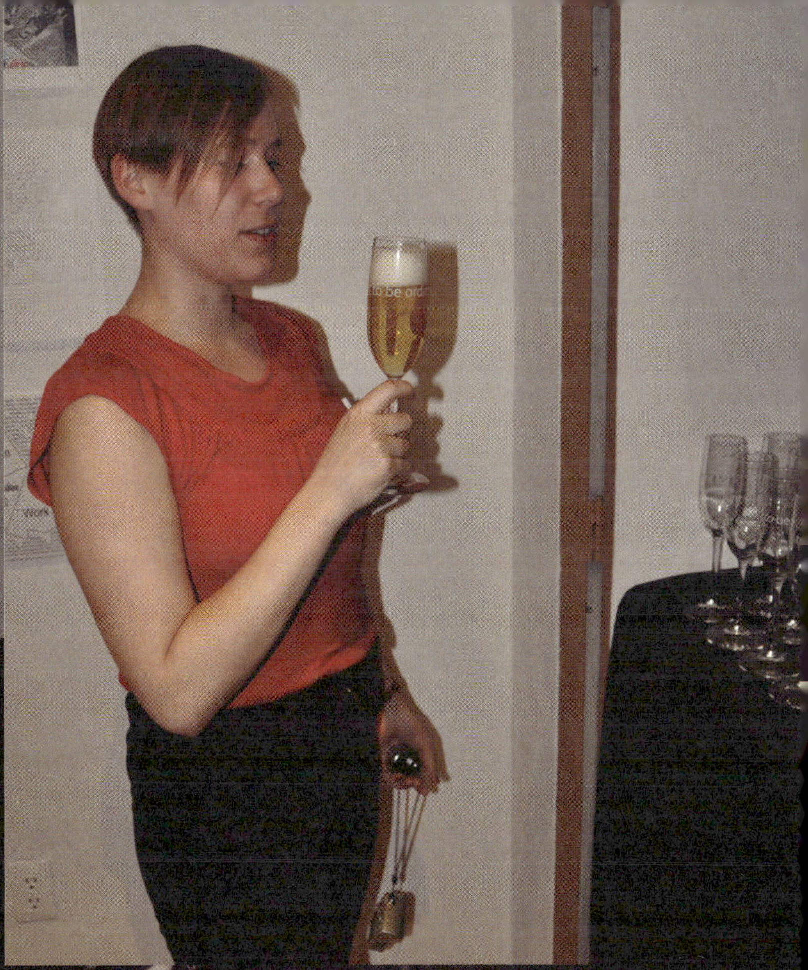

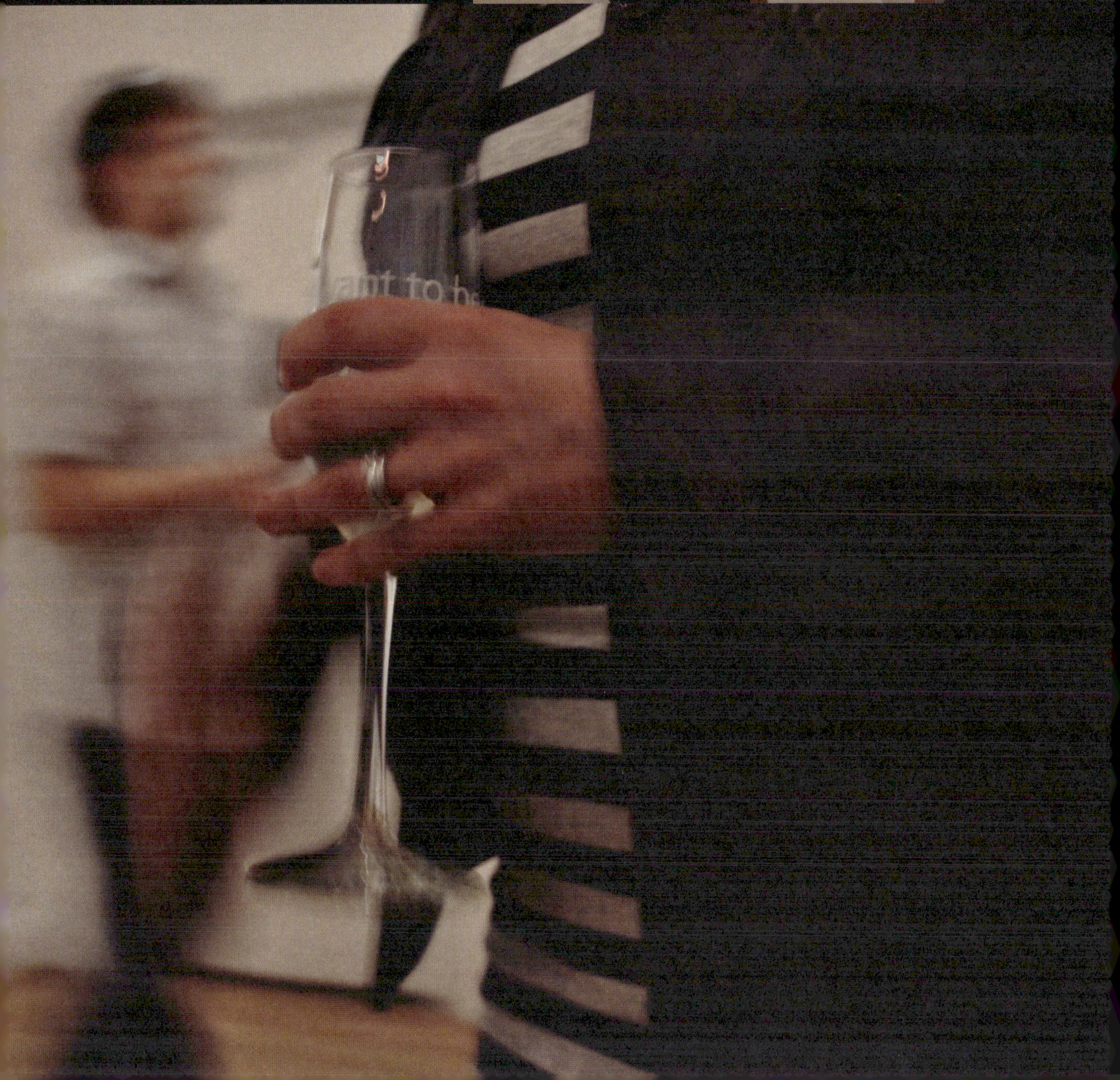

UNDERWRITER, 2010

Industry of the Ordinary sponsor a sports team.

Special thanks to Betsy Odom for initial outreach and to Kelli Connell for team photography. Team members: Tomi Dew, Betsy Odom, Erica Henrich, Nikki Posluzny, Jenny Drankie, Lisa Loris, Tracy McDonald, Mary Horan, Amada Fitzsimmons, Liz Gray.

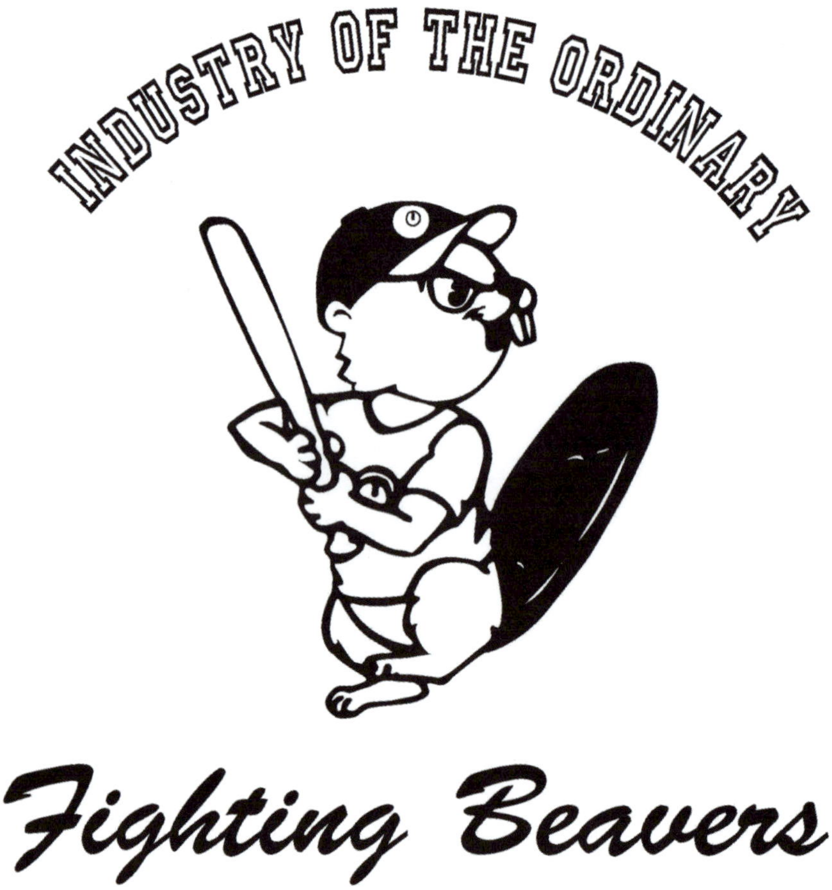

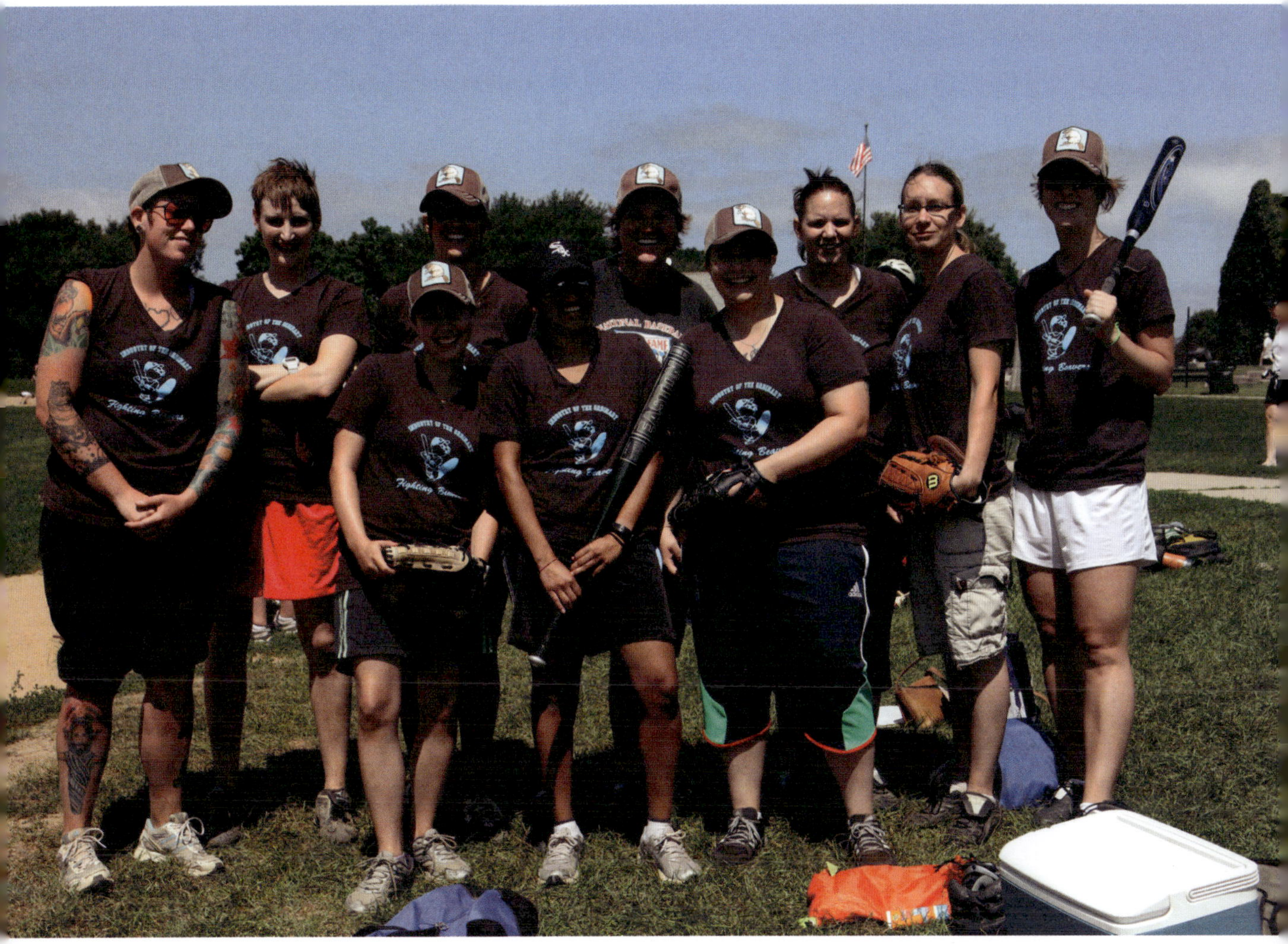

2010

THE SPOILS OF VICTORY

Thanks to George's for ambience and Guinness.

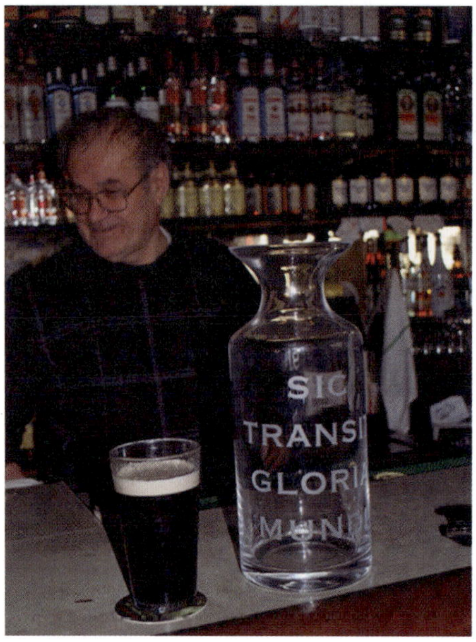

Industry of the Ordinary
fashion a trophy for
a yet-to-be-determined
competition.

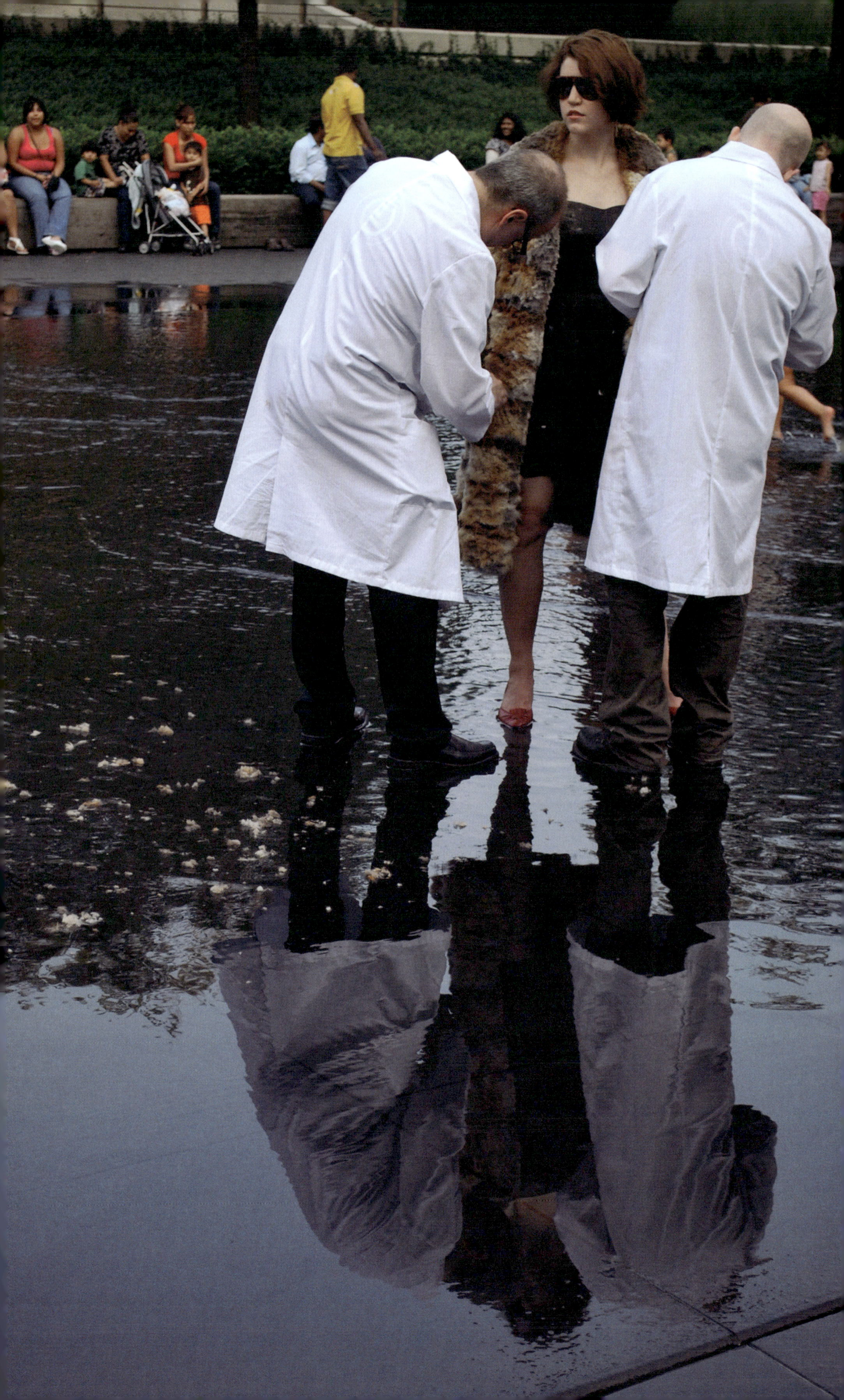

Epilation (Reprise), 2010

Industry of the Ordinary make a fashion statement.

Special thanks to Anna Trier.
Coat by Maxwell Croft, by way of BWB.
Photography by Alexa Loftus.

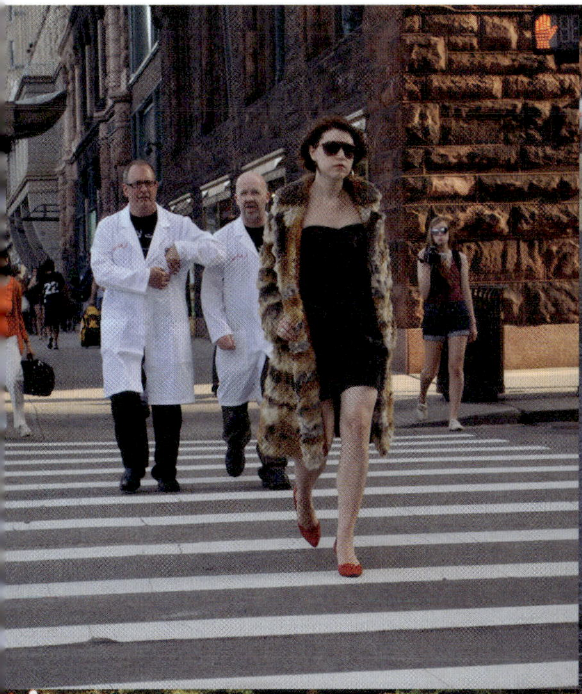

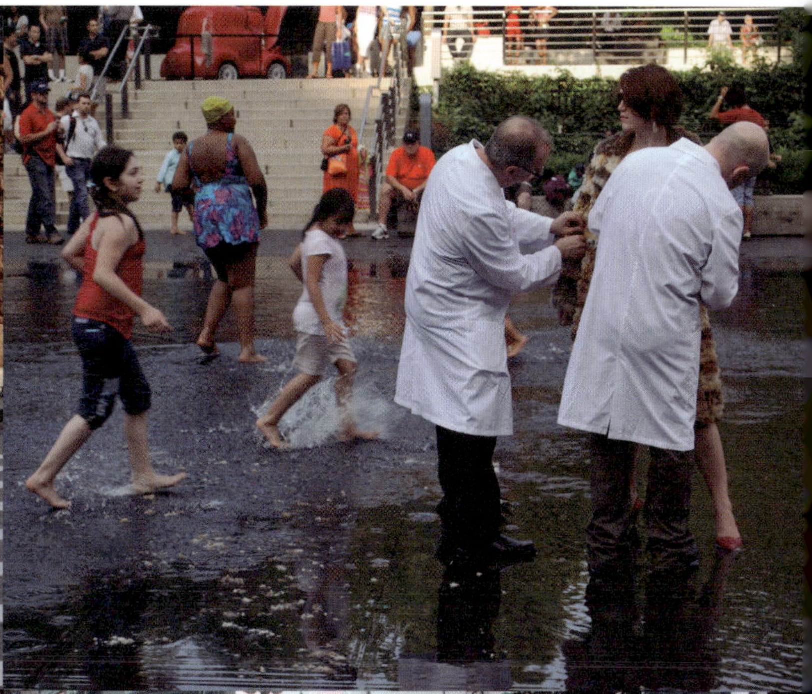

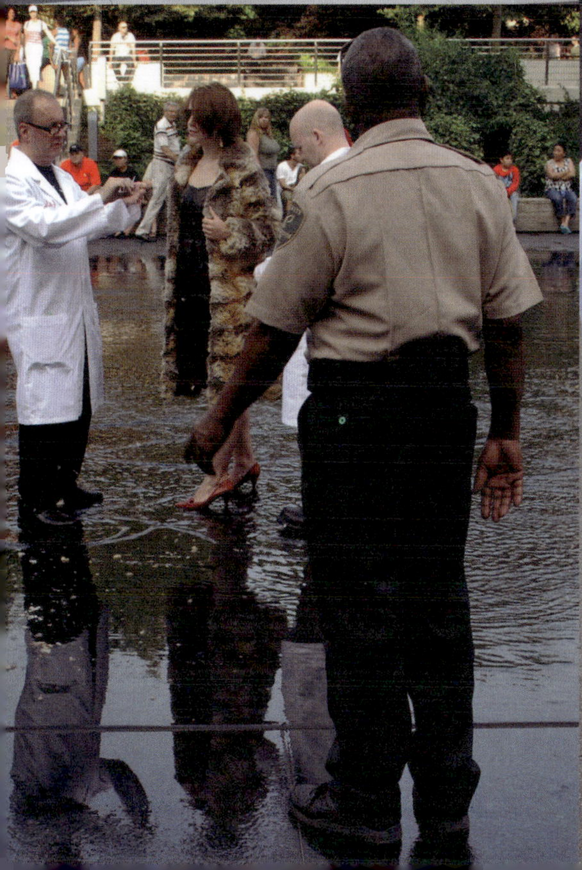

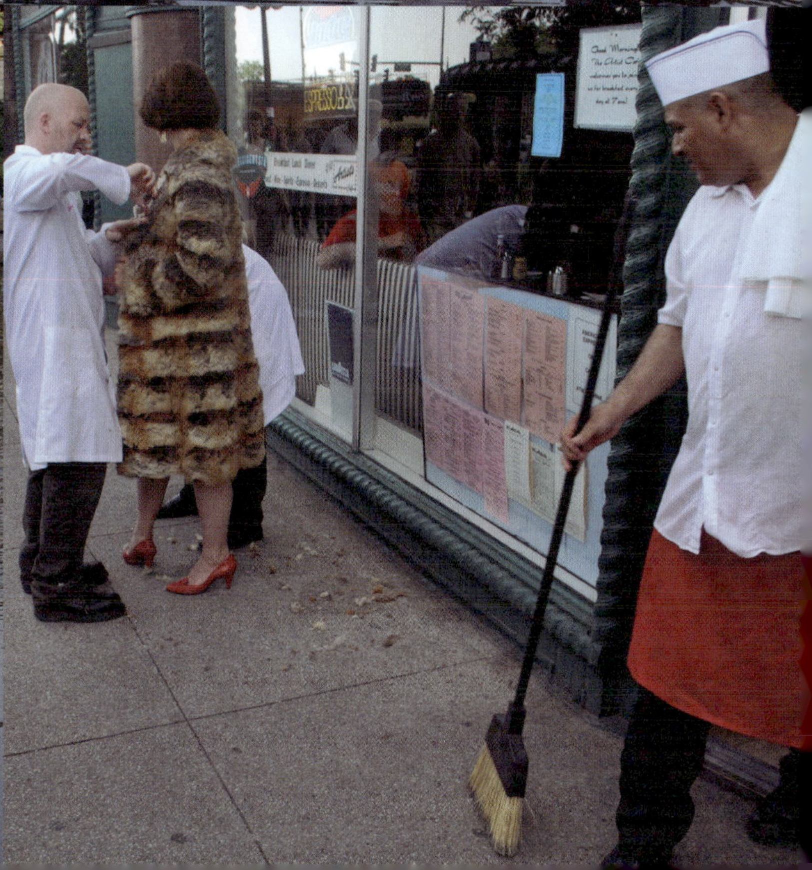

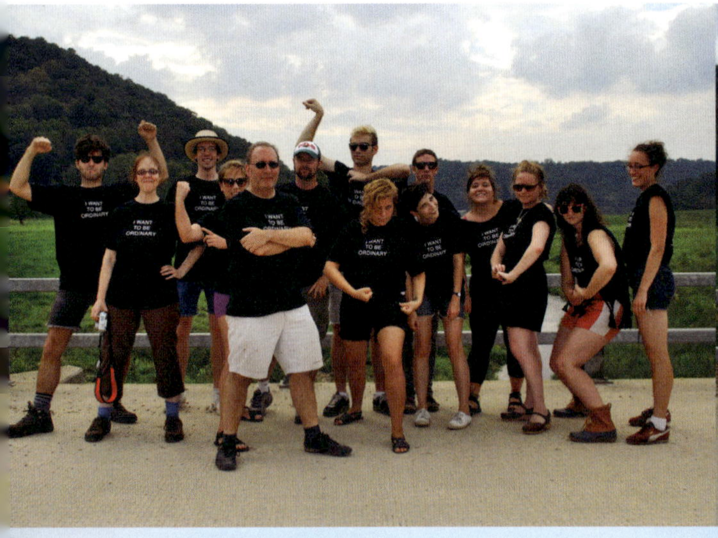
I WANT
TO BE
ORDINARY

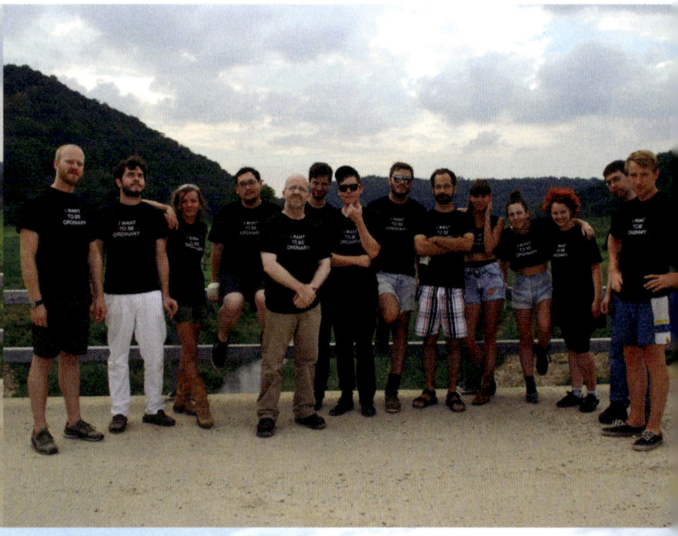
I WANT
TO BE
ORDINARY

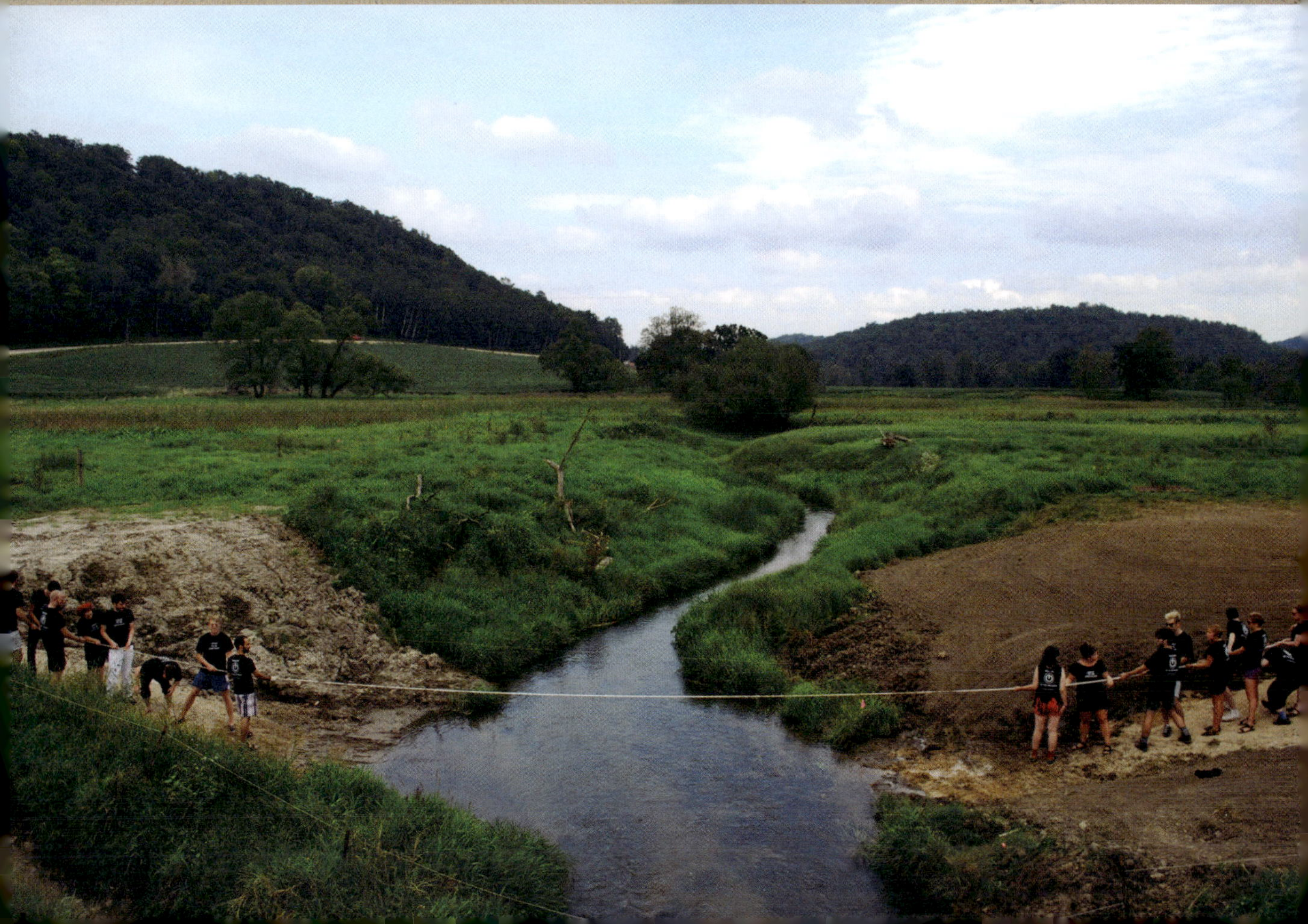

2010

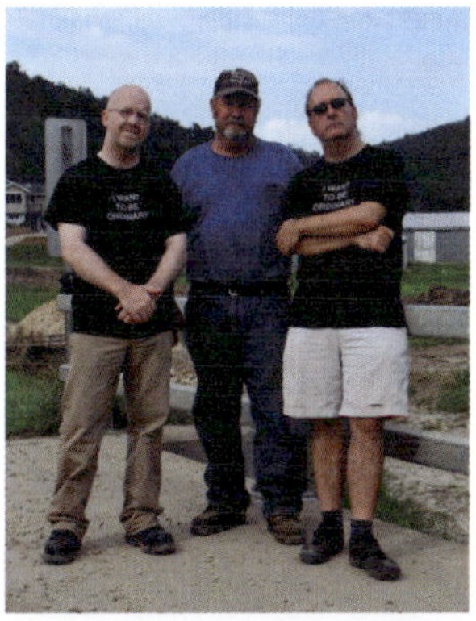

IOTOTOW

Industry of the Ordinary pick teams and throw them into combat.

Thanks to our generous host Grazing Specialist Dennis Rooney, without whom the event could not have taken place.

Photography by and special thanks to Greg Stimac, Caitlin Arnold, Jennifer Ray, and Adam Farcus.

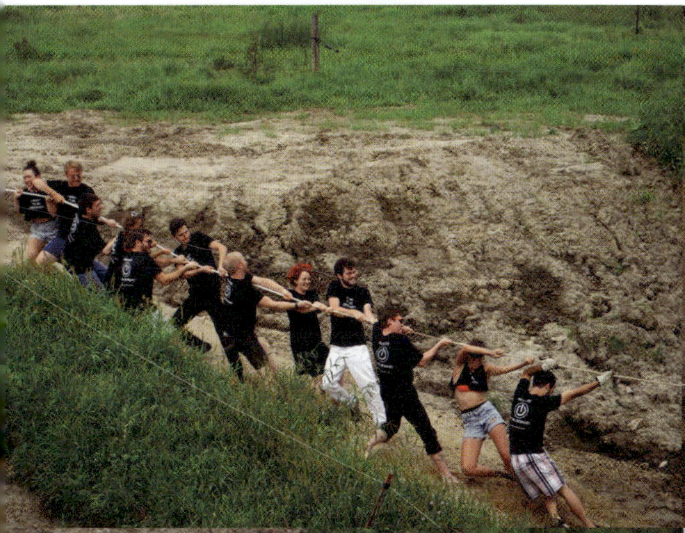

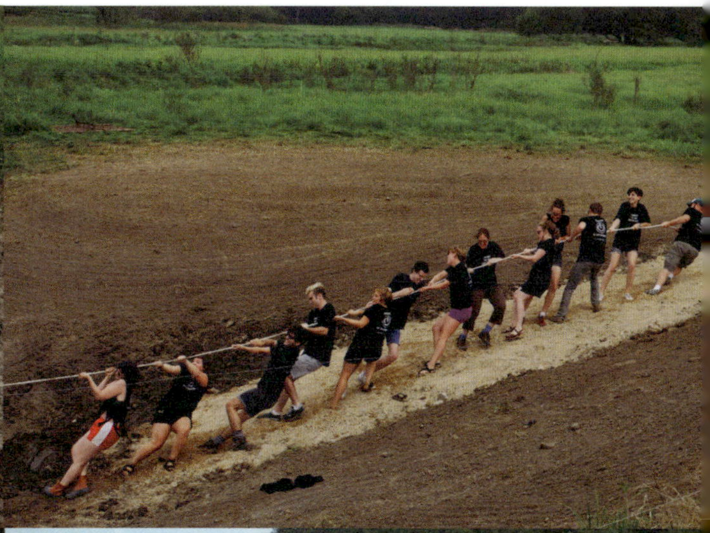

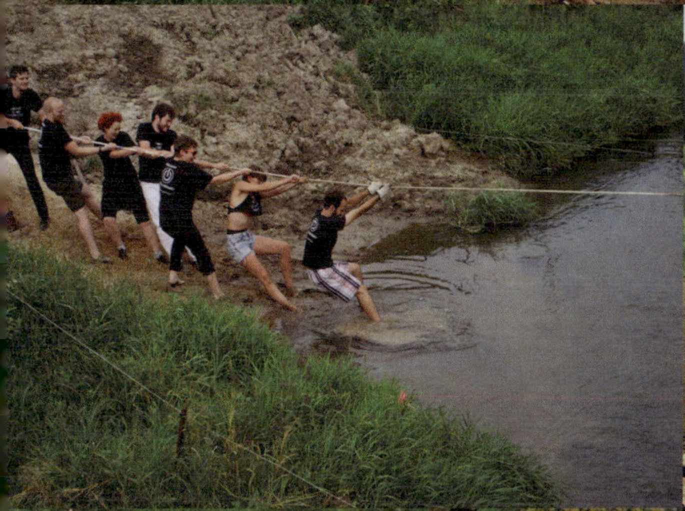

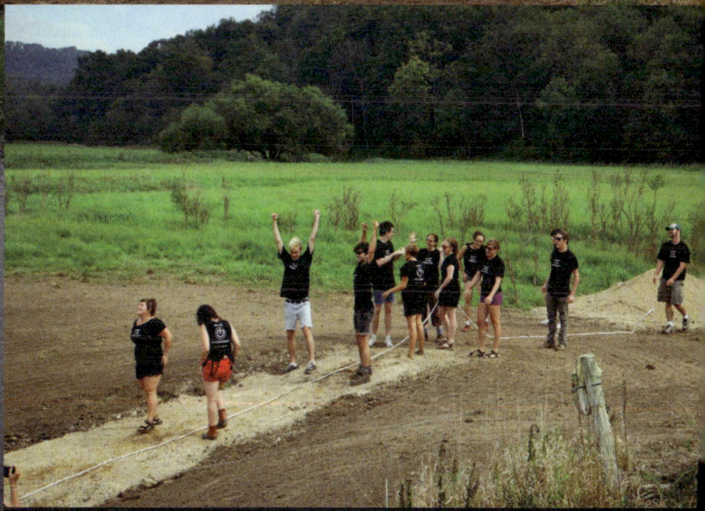

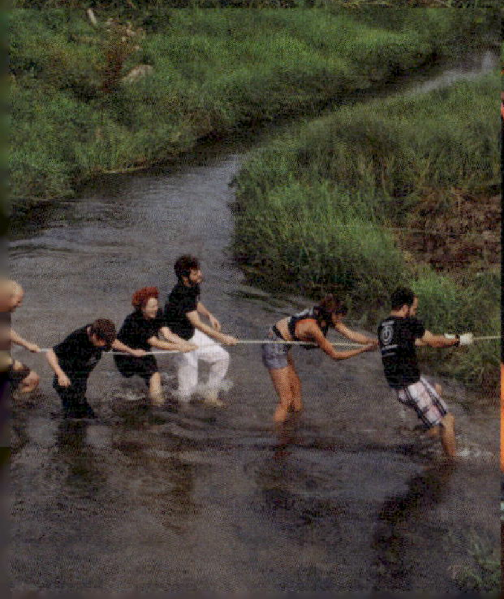

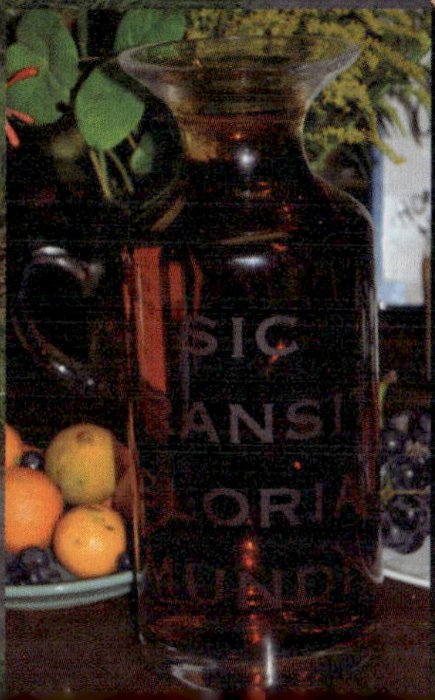

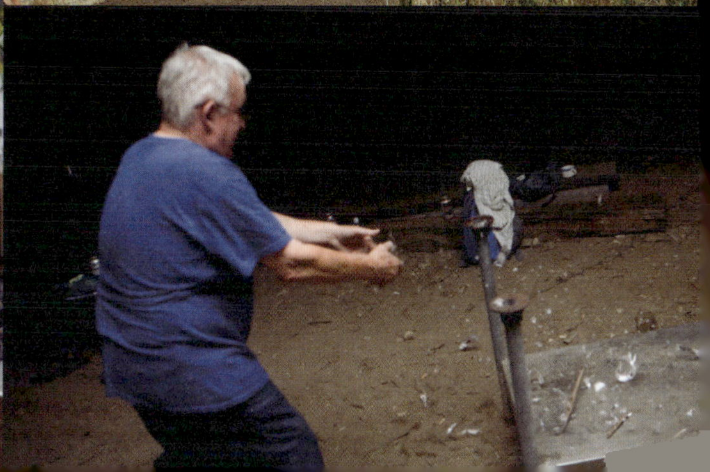

History as Idea, 2010–2011

For a permanent commission at the Nebraska State Historical Society in Lincoln, Industry of the Ordinary engage the existing architecture of the rotunda after a series of road trips around the state collecting information from hundreds of Nebraskans and a variety of other sources.

Special thanks to Lynne Ireland. Thanks also to Don Denton, Michael Trotter, Jay Kaser, Fast Signs, and Sherwin-Williams.

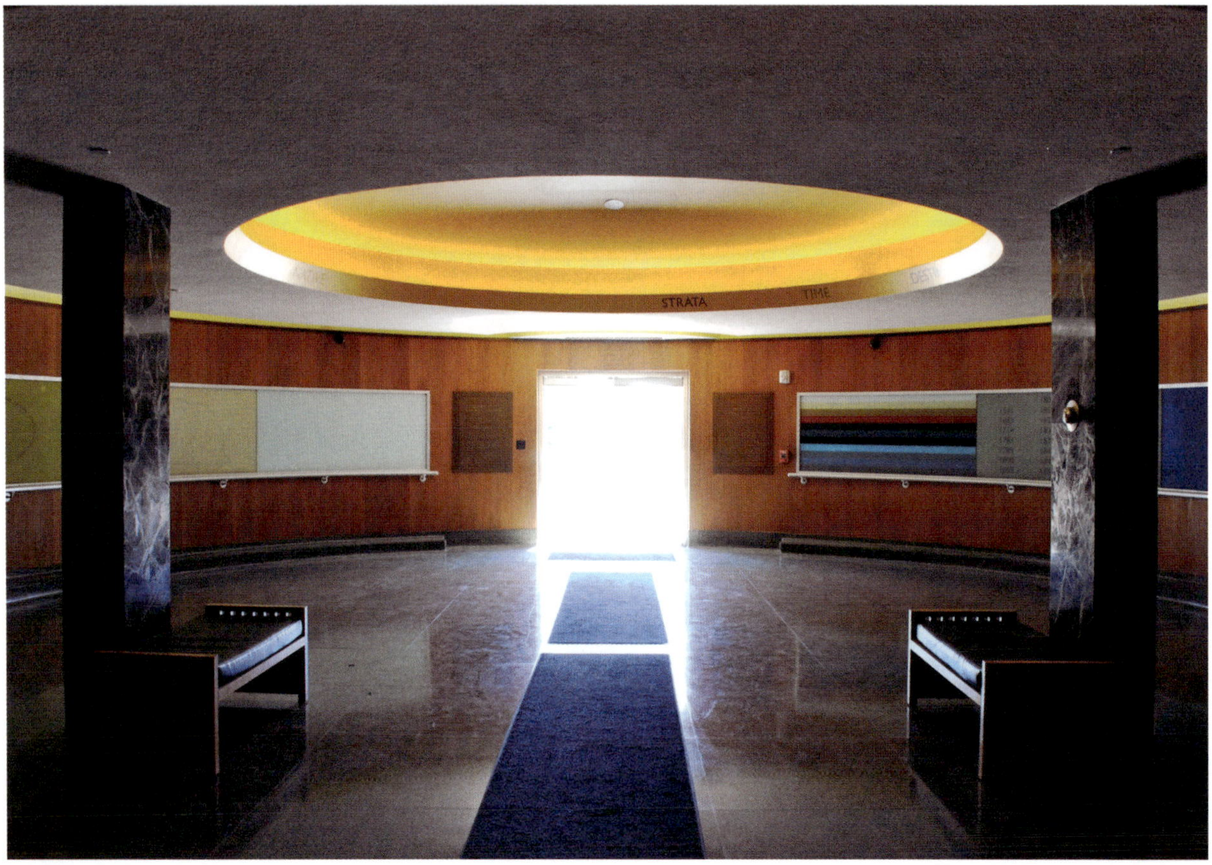

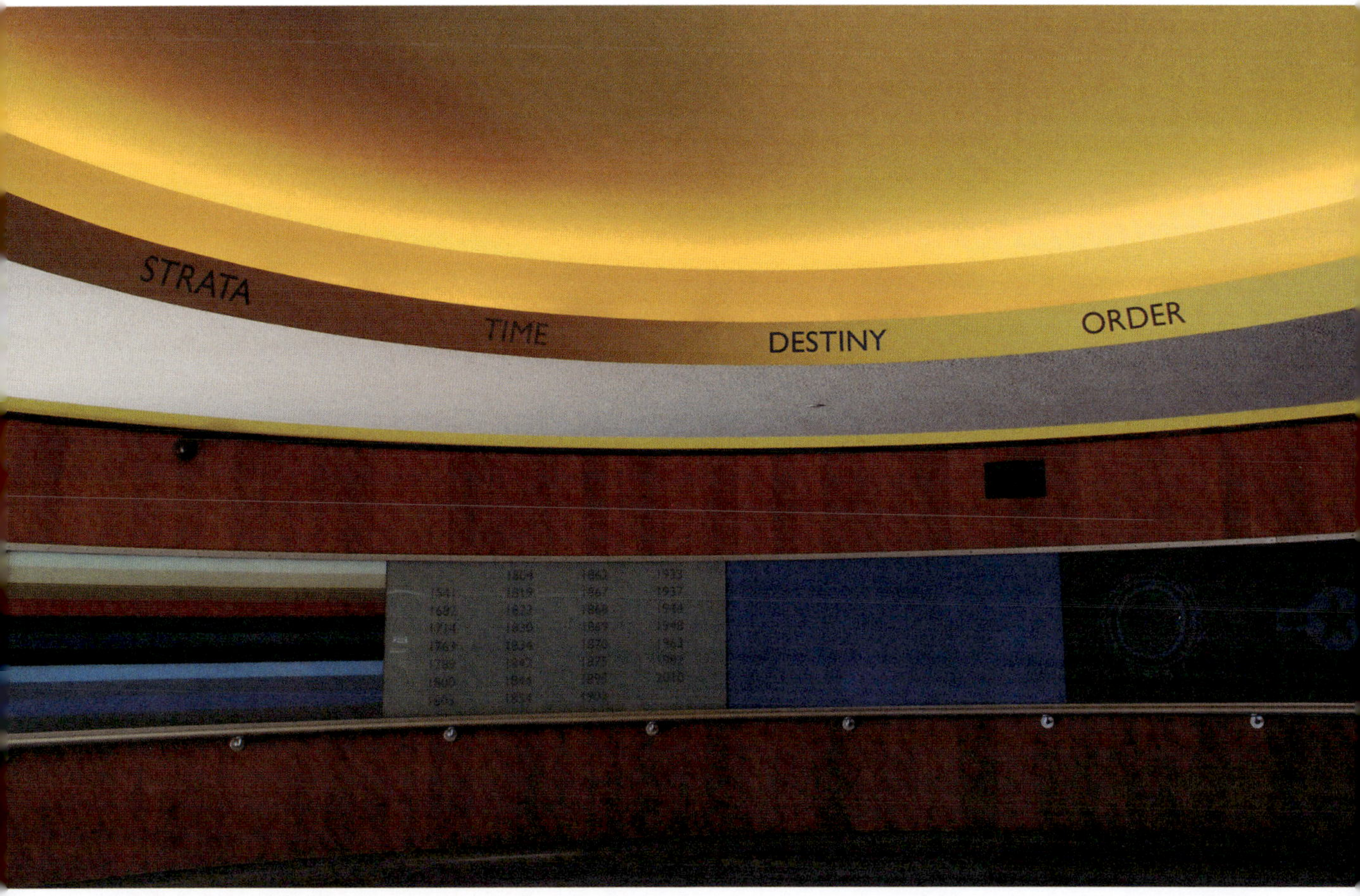
STRATA
TIME
DESTINY
ORDER

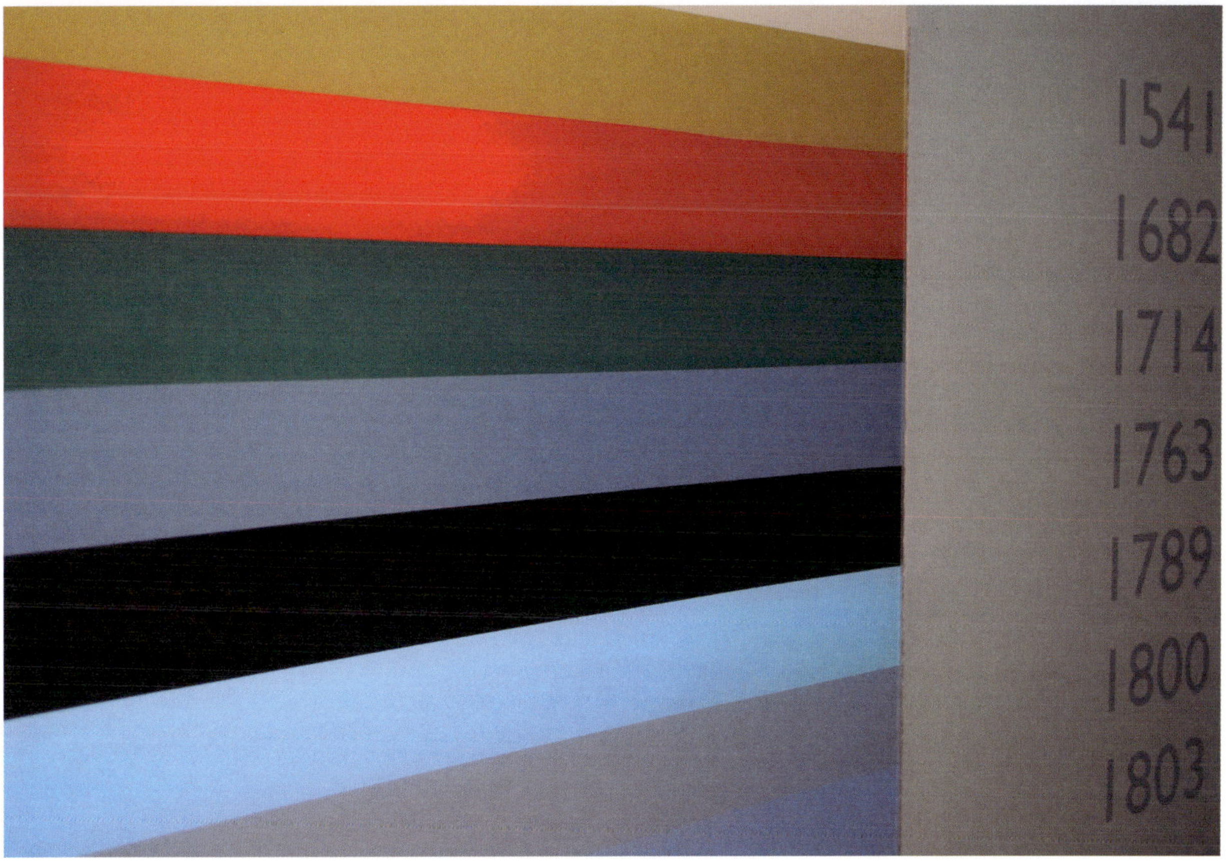
1541
1682
1714
1763
1789
1800
1803

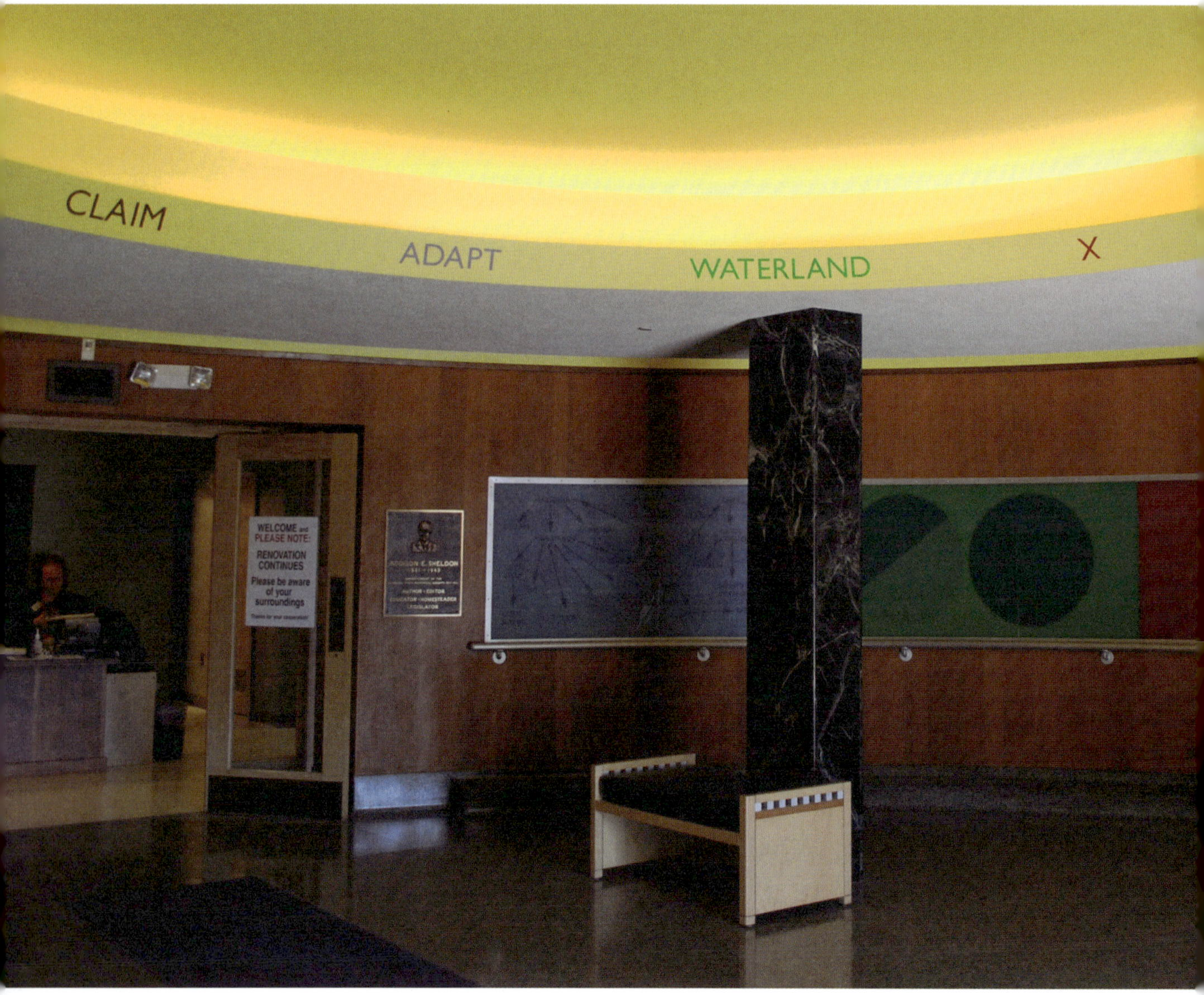
CLAIM
ADAPT
WATERLAND
X
WELCOME
PLEASE NOTE:
RENOVATION CONTINUES
Please be aware of your surroundings

The modernist architecture of the building that houses the Nebraska State Historical Society was the primary and overarching consideration in the formal organization of our installation. The piece is embedded into the existing structure, but we have also worked with the staff of the Historical Society to reinstate the original lighting plan in order to fully realize the intent of the architect, Ellery Davis.

Our view of history is that it is not reducible to a series of "facts." It is not objective. It is never comprehensive; many voices are necessarily left out in the retelling of any historical narrative. Thus, it is a rich maelstrom of competing views in much the same way that art is.

The role of art is not to make a series of statements, but to engage dialogue. Industry of the Ordinary intend this work to engage in a dialogue about history, in general terms, and about Nebraskan history, more specifically. It does not need to reproduce the job already successfully undertaken by the Historical Society and its museum or, indeed, any other institution or collection that celebrates the history of Nebraska.

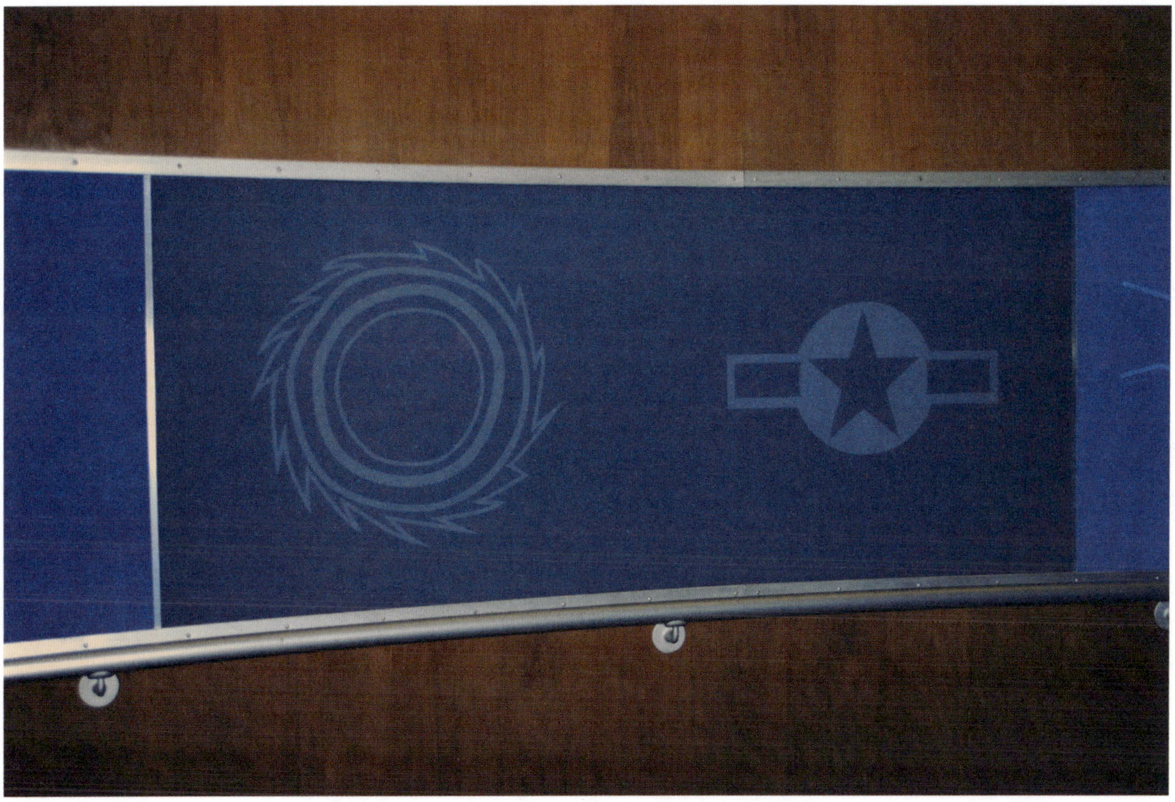

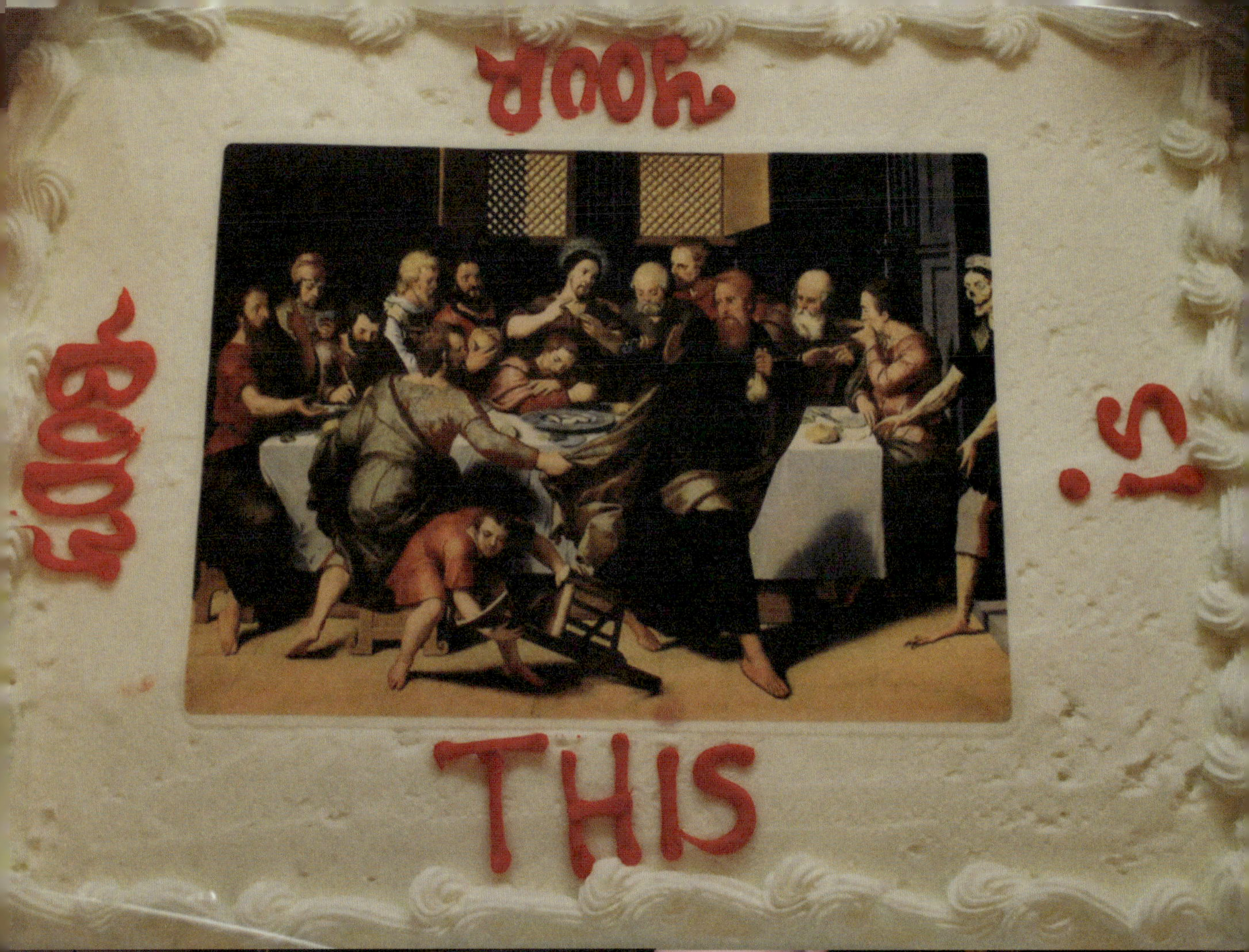
THIS
is
YOUR
BODY

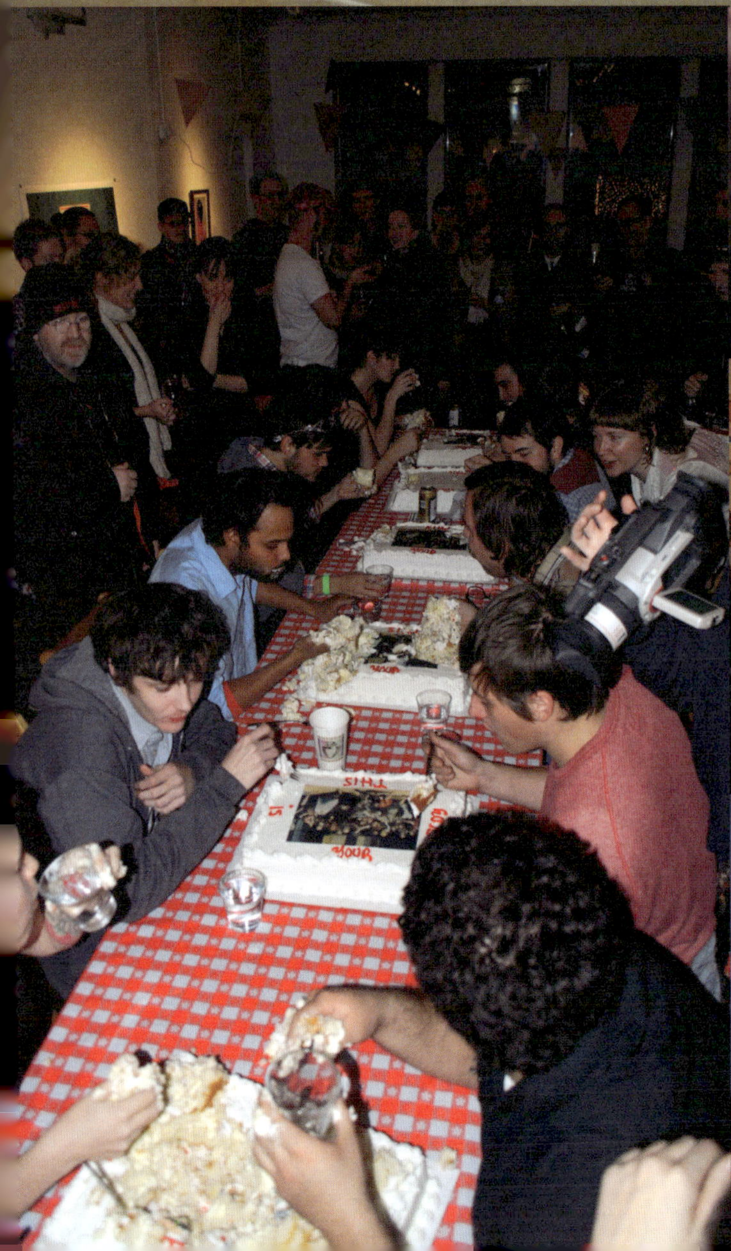

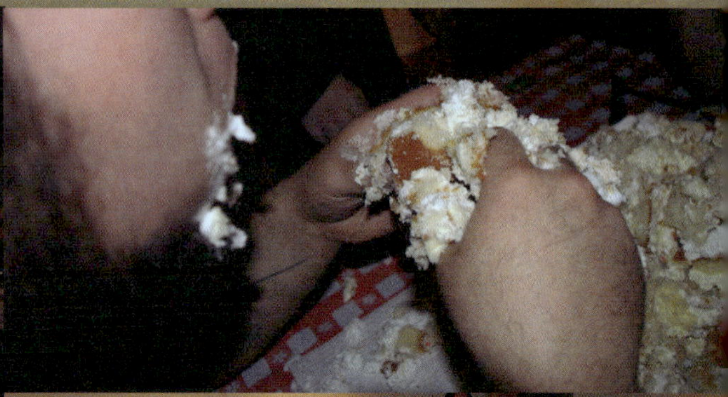

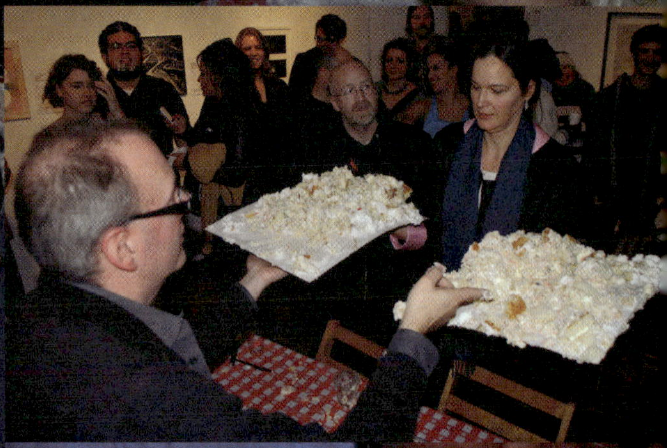

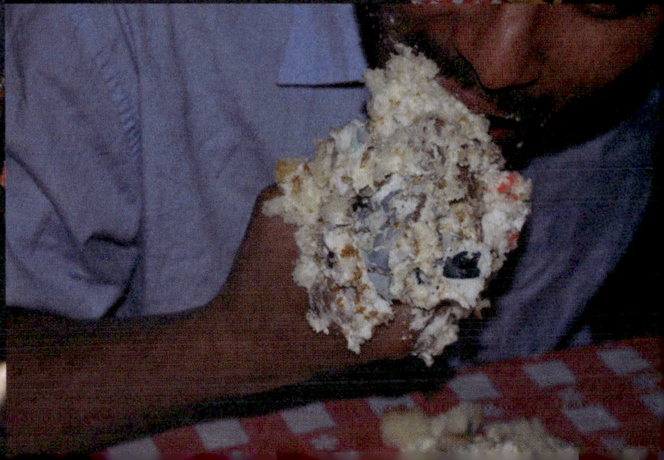

2010

TRANSUBSTANTIATION

Industry of the Ordinary compere competitive corporeal gluttony.

Photography by Greg Stimac. Videography by Alexa Loftus. Thanks to ACRE, Chicago, for hosting.

2010

Impermanent Collection II

Industry of the Ordinary remotely dissect and disseminate the Tate Modern catalog.

Special thanks to JL Murtaugh.

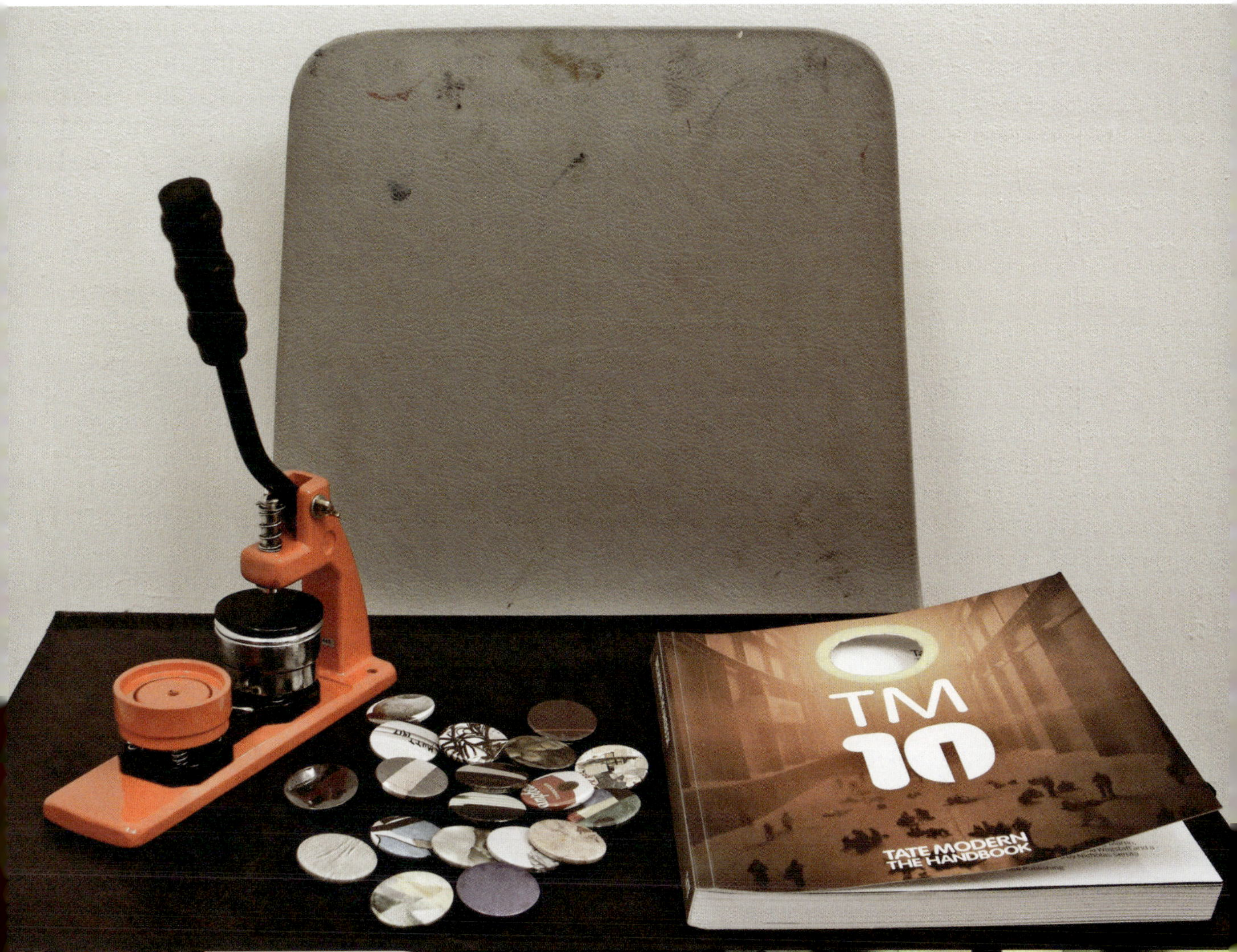
TM
10
TATE MODERN
THE HANDBOOK

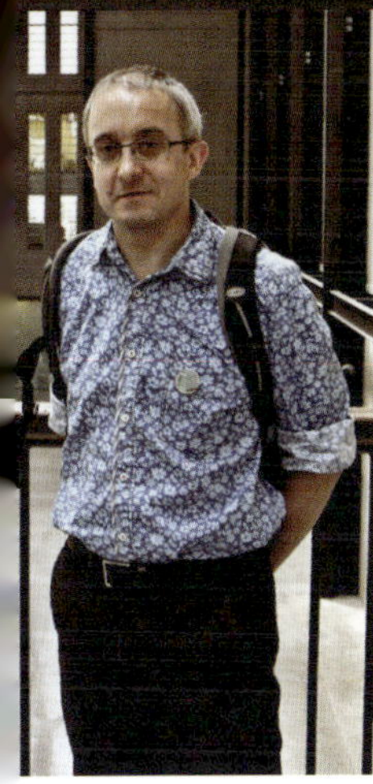

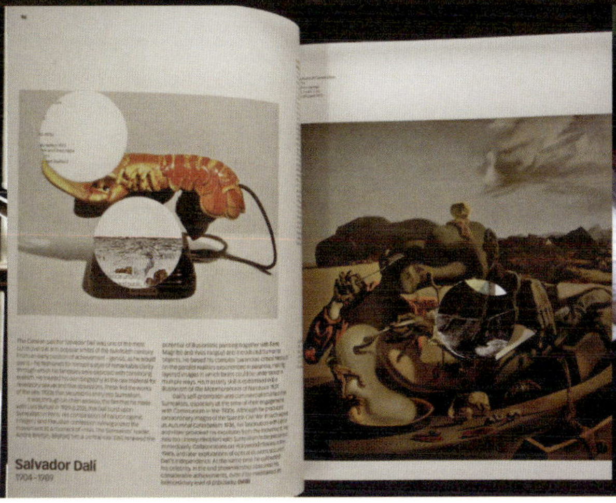
Salvador Dalí
1904–1989

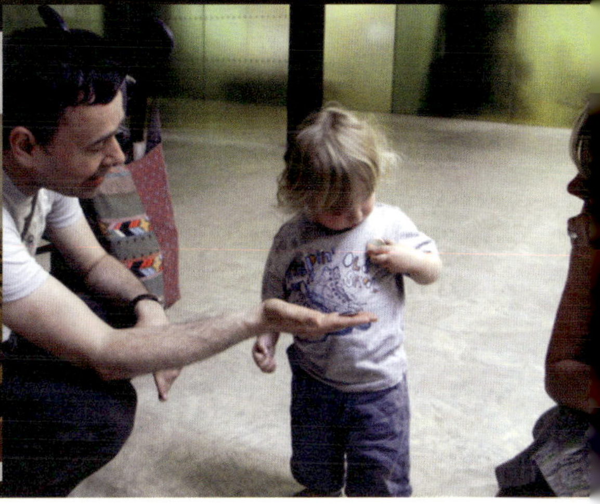

2010

Epilation (Reprise Reprise)

Industry of the Ordinary endeavor to shear down to the skin and face down the Estonians.

Photography by Melody Snyder. Special thanks to Jesse Achramowicz.
Thanks also to Joseph Ravens, Defibrillator, and Tempestt Hazel for her willingness to step up.

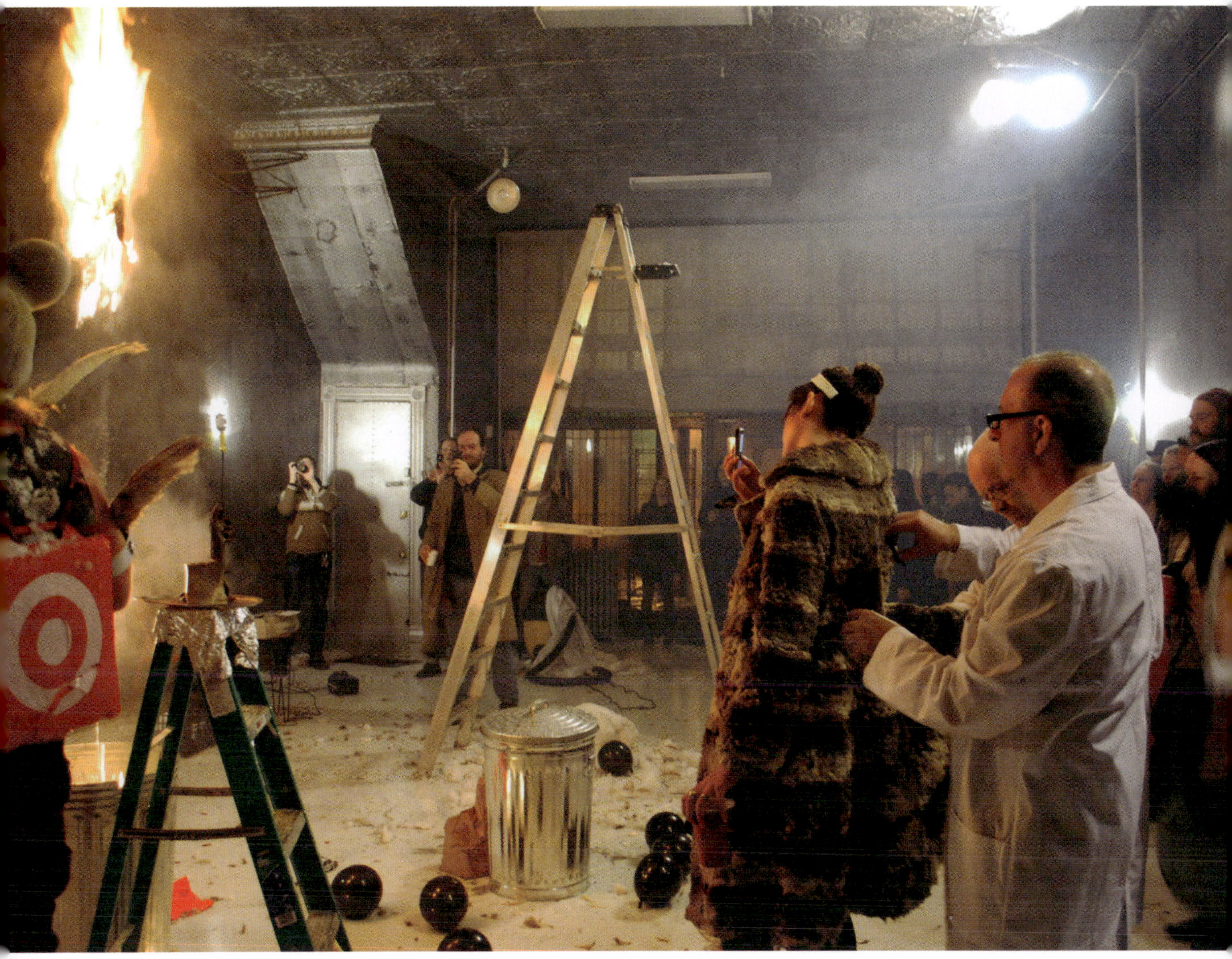

2011

NORMAL

Industry of the Ordinary examine tautology.

Special thanks to Virginia Fabbri Butera and to the people of northern New Jersey.
Thanks also to the Happy Collaborationists.

A question that is not

simple. "What is normal?"

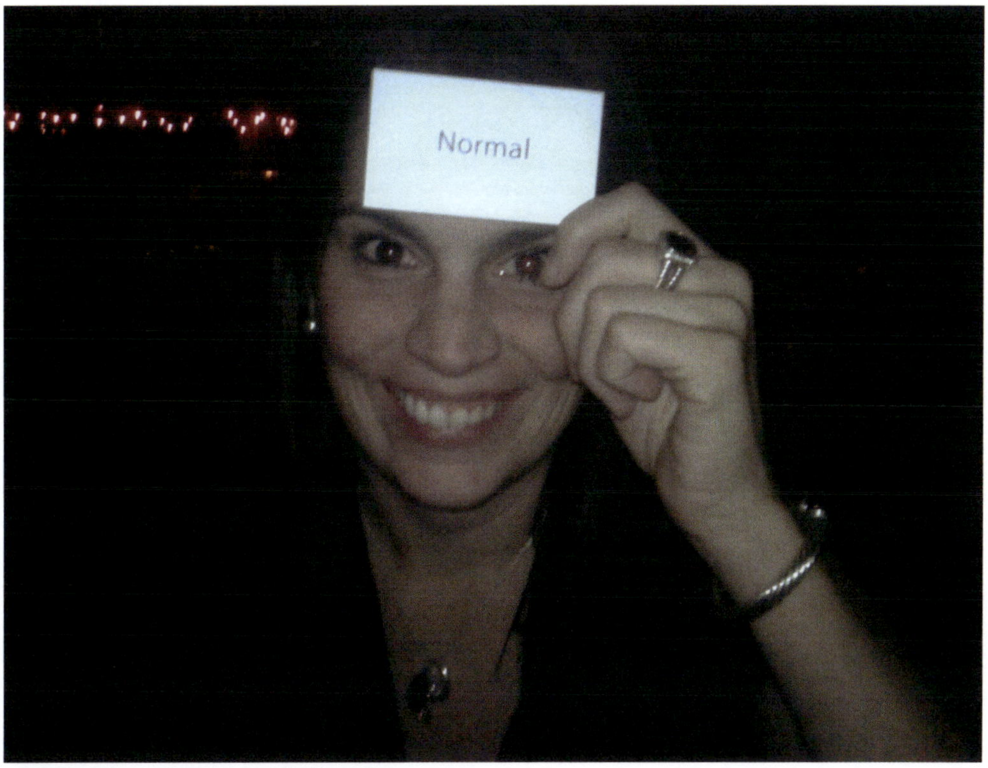
Normal

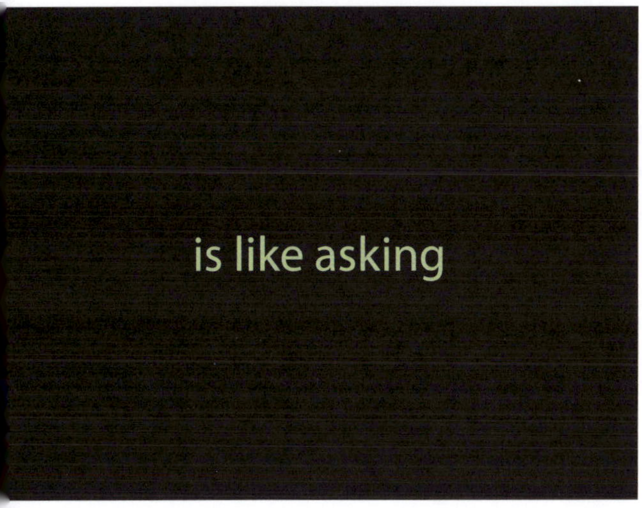
is like asking

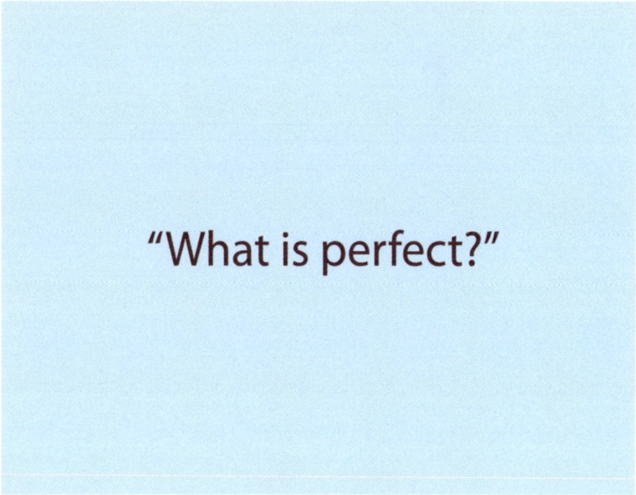
"What is perfect?"

2011

SURROGACY

Industry of the Ordinary seek stand-ins for an absent member.

Photography by Lynda Wellhausen. Special thanks to Anna Trier and Meredith Weber of the Happy Collaborationists, and to Bradley Bergquist for ferrying us around.

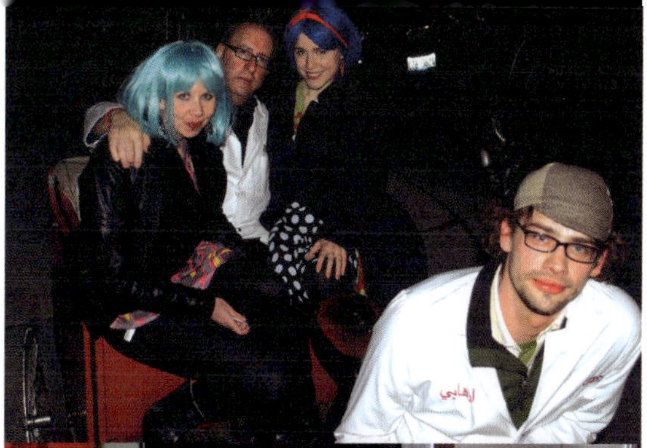

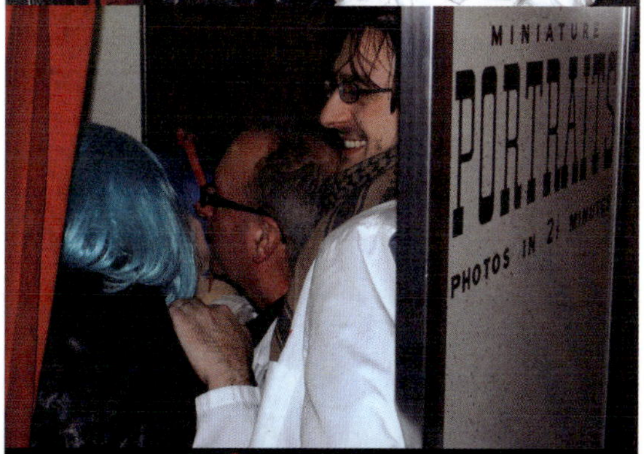
MINIATURE
PORTRAITS

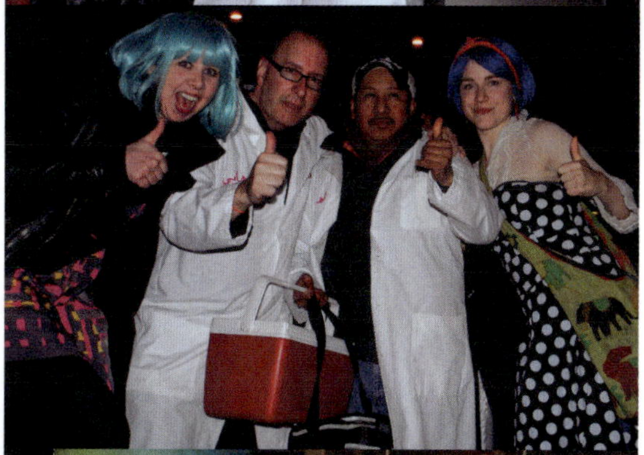

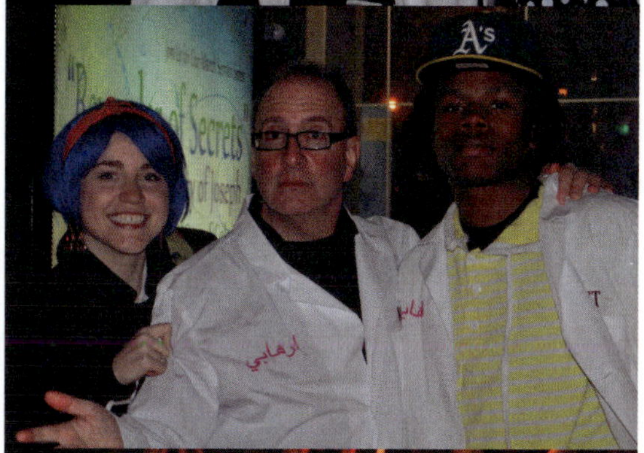
ارهابي

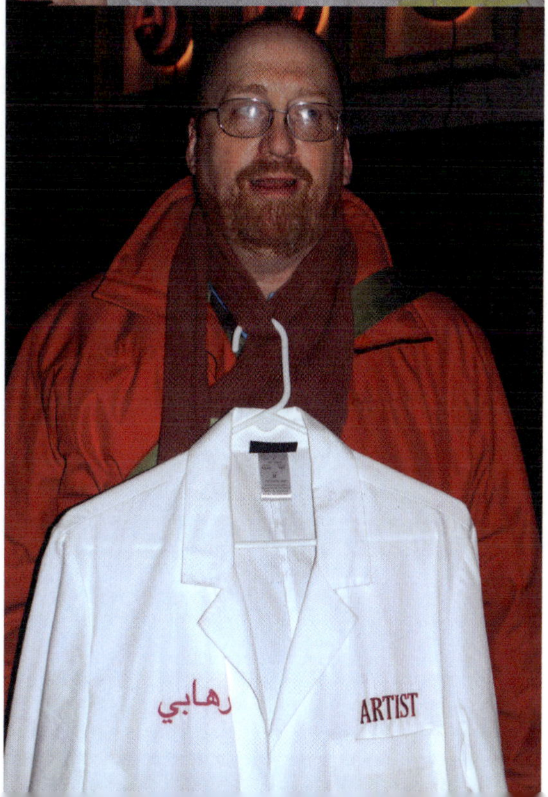
ARTIST

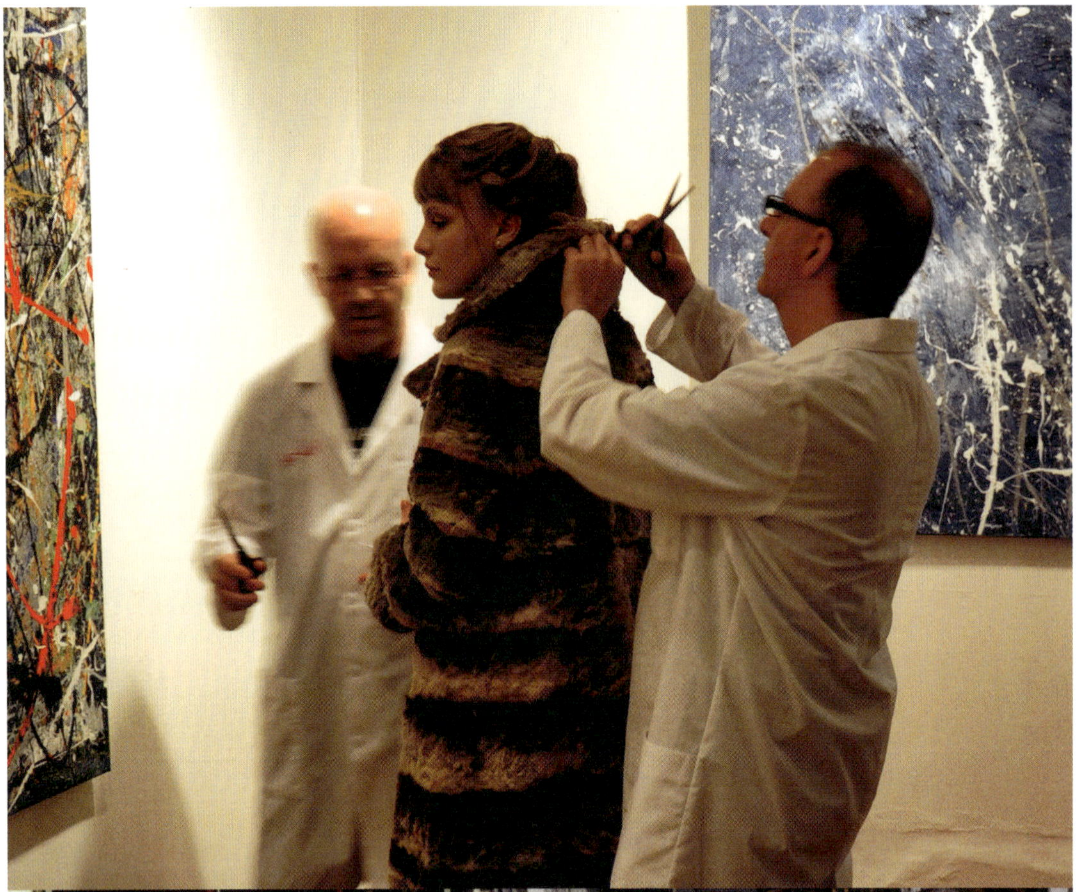

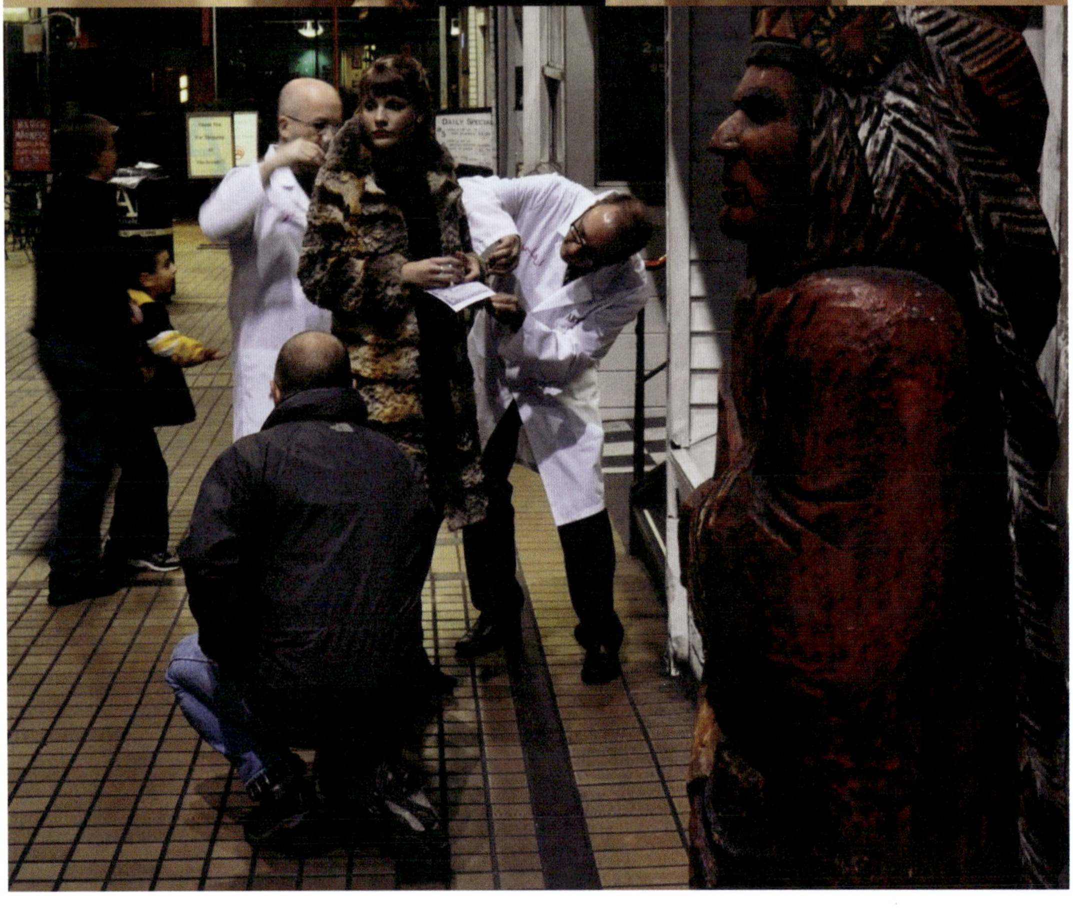

2011

EPILATION (REPRISE REPRISE REPRISE)

Industry of the Ordinary shear in Nashville, Tennessee.

Photography by Jennifer Leach and James Tyler Blankenship. Special thanks to Emily Olds. Thanks also to Brady Haston for all of his facilitation, and to Derek Cote and Ron Lambert.

Two Heads,

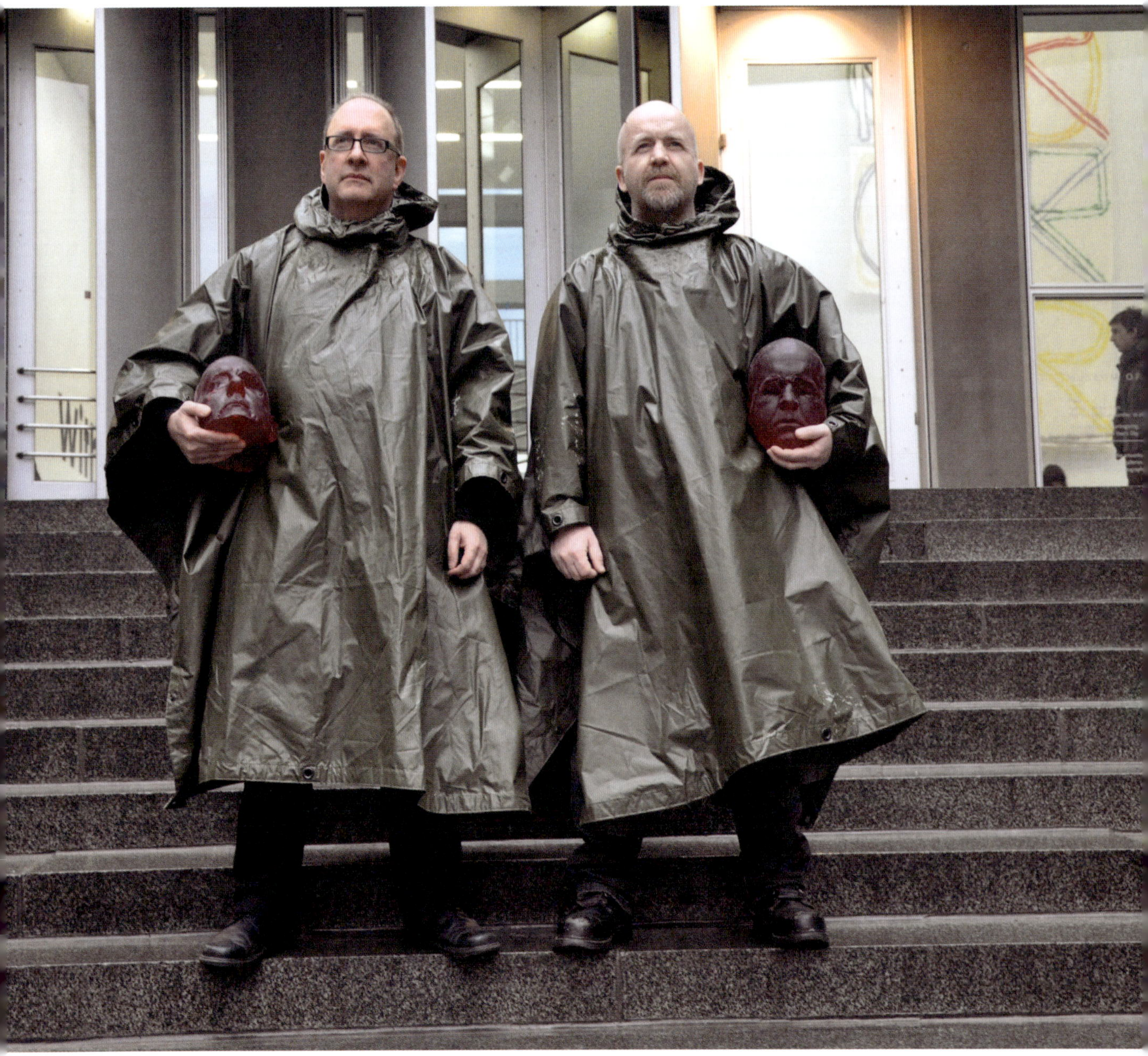

One Goal 2011

Industry of the Ordinary reflect upon the origins of football for the Museum of Contemporary Art, Chicago.

Photography by Melody Snyder, Junn, and Debra Purden. Special thanks to Jim Zimpel for casting expertise, and to Amy Corle at the MCA.

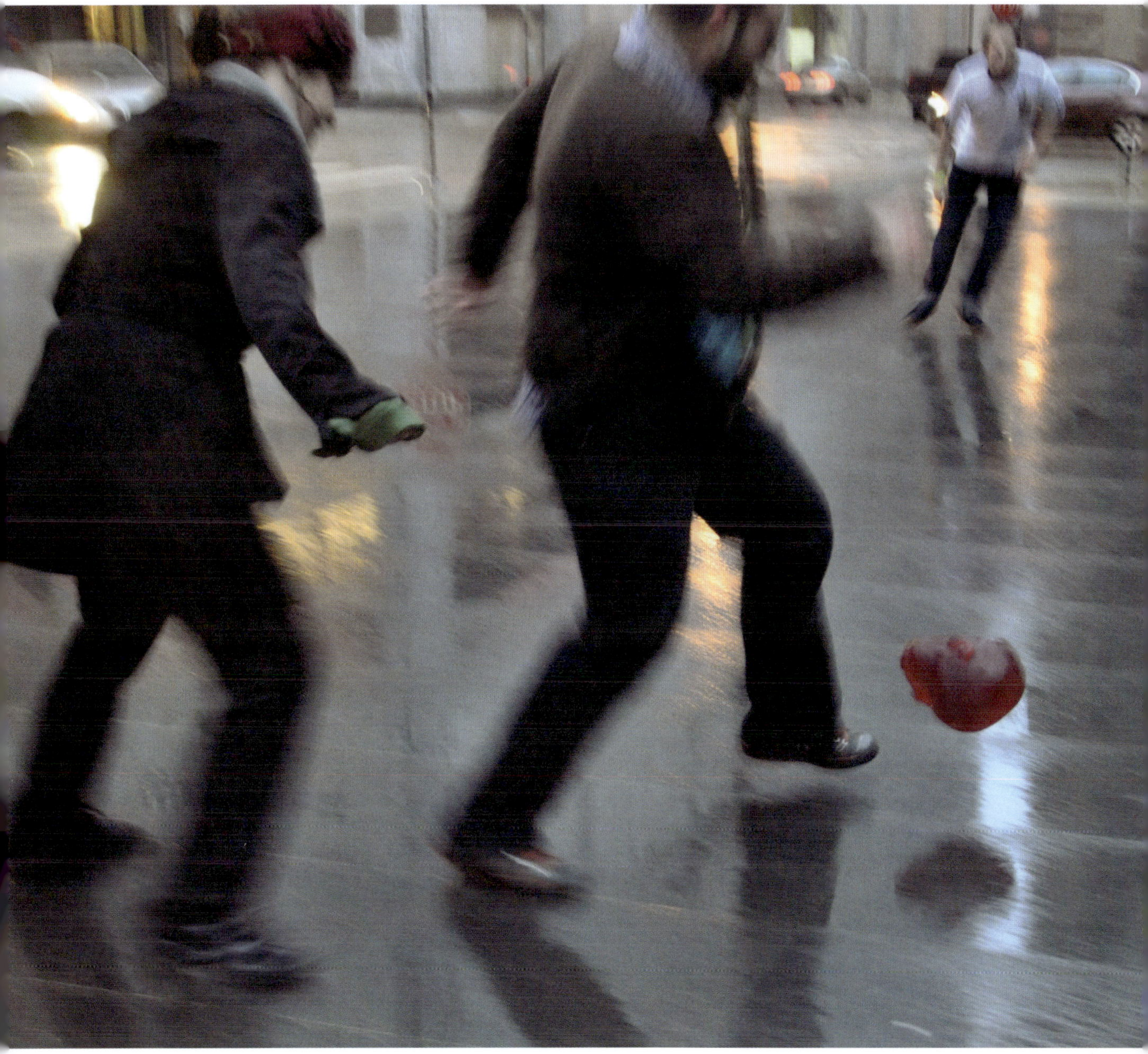

2011

A Paradise of the Ordinary

Industry of the Ordinary mine the Internet for affirmation.

Special thanks to David Jones, Chris Flynn, and James Iannaccone at Anchor Graphics, Chicago, for their support and production assistance for this project.

Heaven would be full of ordinary things: trees, fresh air, lies and infidelities, chattering animals, and sex. What kind of place could it be if there were no ordinary things? Or could we live forever in a limbo of miracles and the constantly renewed fires of the superreal?

We are fascinated by the ordinary and in just about anything in this world and the imagined next. You can't turn around without tripping over the ordinary and its omnipresent power to be more than artifice.

The problem with painting is not just that it celebrates such artifice, but that it has no ambition. A single self-conscious brushstroke, pulled against the grain of the canvas, cannot fail to disappoint. Magnify that number into the millions and you may resuscitate the medium, but who has the time? The painting might be dull, but the pain in the wrist is delightful.

We have to have faith in something. Rauschenberg knew that if he opened his window the world would rush in. Of course this is more beautiful than superstition. Of course it's more tangible than god. We don't mind if god exists because we know the folly of the teleological: we object to heaven.

An algorithm can provide a fascinating and absurd selection. It looks like randomness. It was Cage's genius to recognize this power. To him we owe what we have become. We know this upsets pockets of a previous generation, as well as those younger than cradle dust, but the burden of relevance fails to weigh on the shoulders of fools and the forgotten.

We are passing the age where sex is rewarding and we look past ourselves in mirrors. Man has created god in his own image and there's the morning-after pill for that. Lacking the appropriate contempt for ourselves, we have invented redemption and justice. It's time to throw the baby out too. It's no use just wanting to be ordinary.

FOLLOWING PAGE:
The source material for this series of prints is the result of image searches on Google through which the word "ordinary" is combined with a particular language. Pairings are produced that reflect important historical tensions or other charged relationships between speakers of these languages. IOTO take randomly selected images that result from these searches and zoom in on a specific section. This close-up is then combined with the close-up from the search of another language, creating a diptych that is printed using photolithography plates. The work is framed in shadow boxes with the word ORDINARY in the correlating languages sandblasted on to the glass. A key frame incorporating all images from the searches straddles the diptychs.

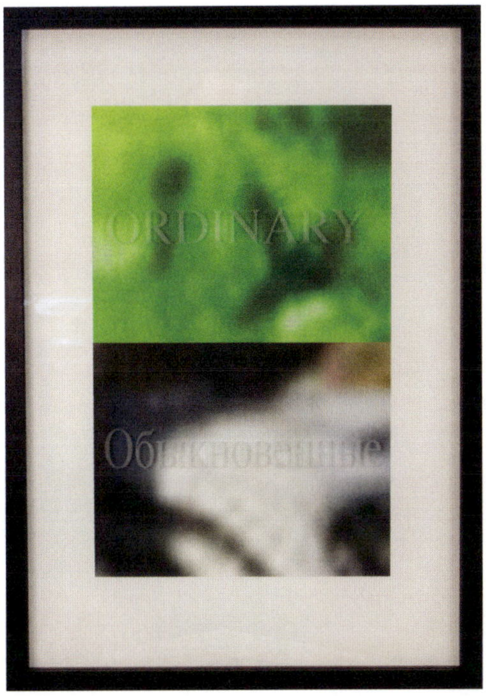
ORDINARY

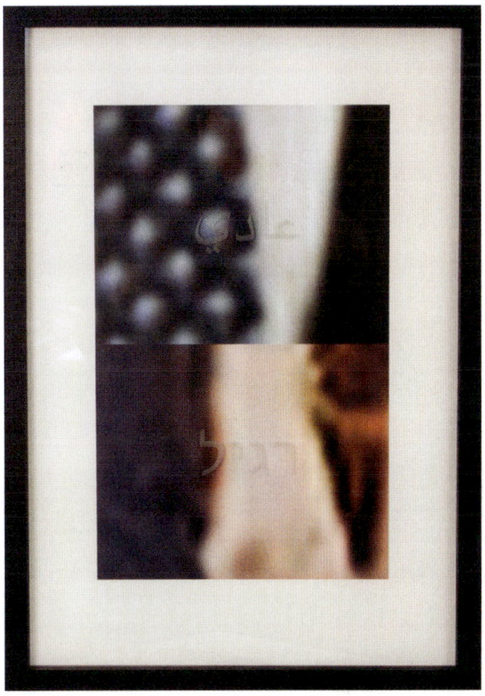

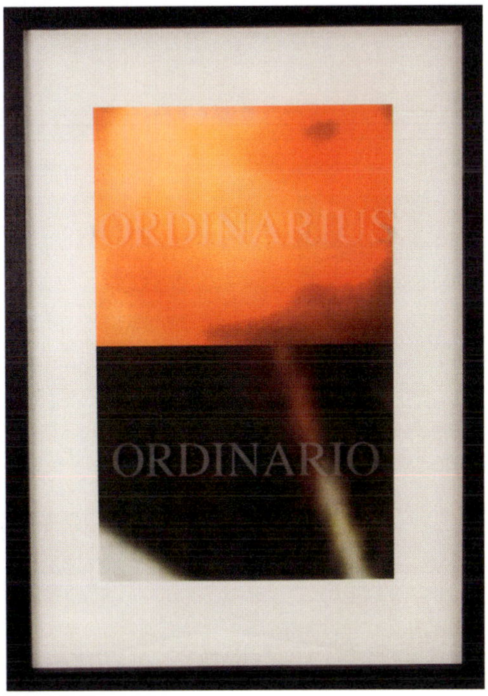
ORDINARIUS
ORDINARIO

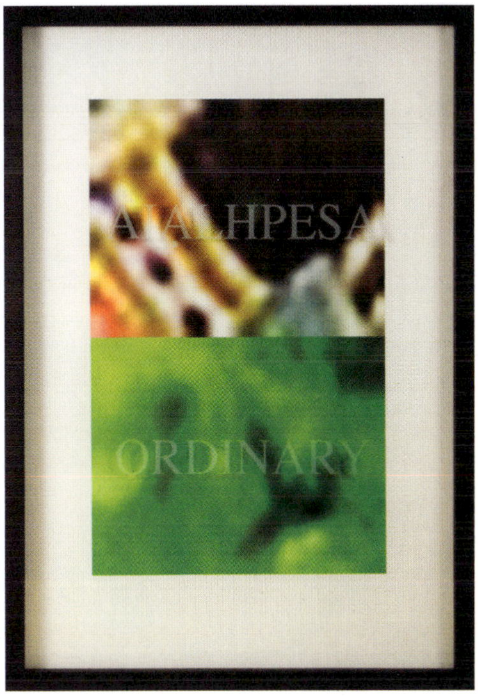
ORDINARY

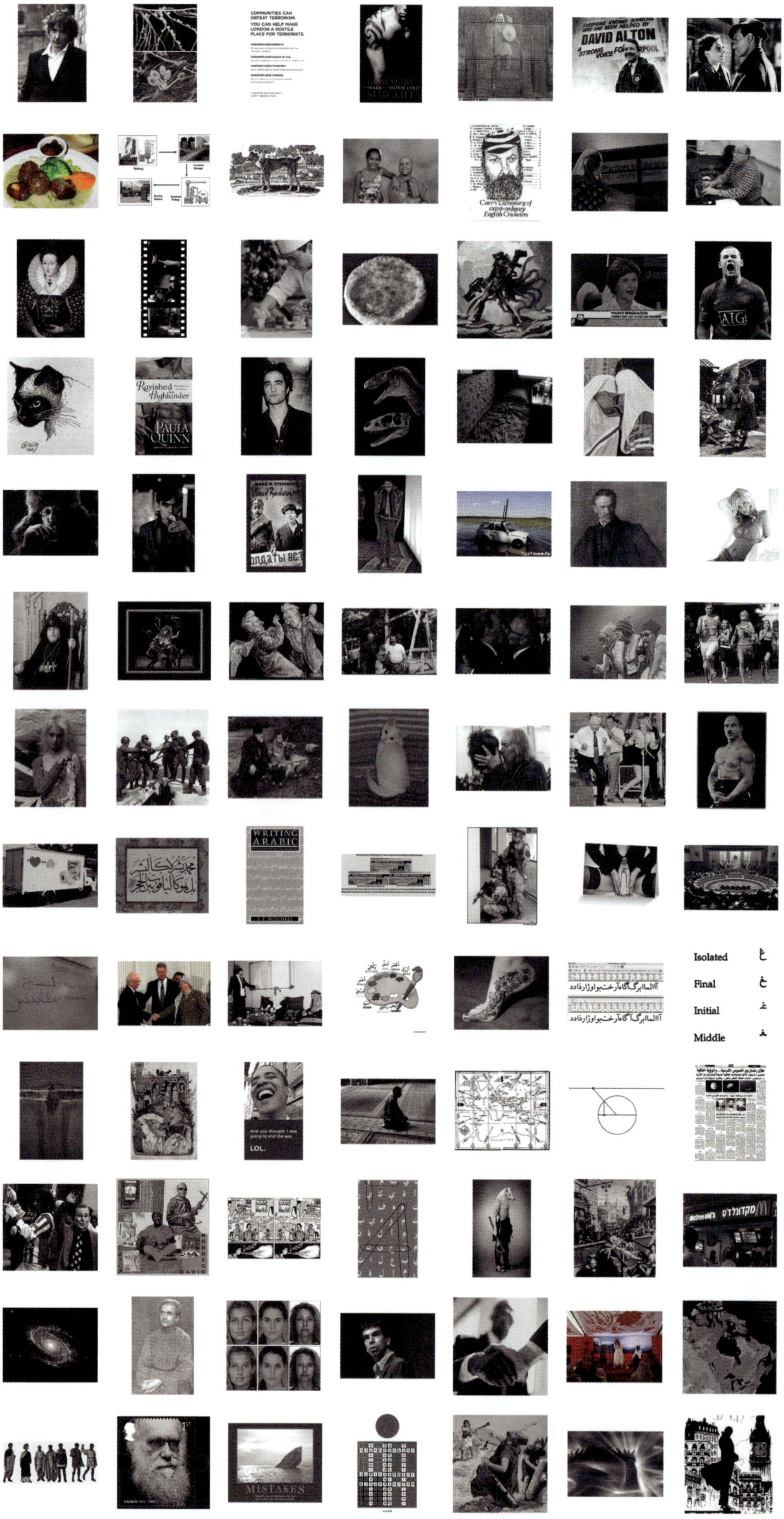
COMMUNITIES CAN DEFEAT TERRORISM.
YOU CAN HELP MAKE LONDON A HOSTILE PLACE FOR TERRORISTS.
DAVID ALTON
Carr's Dictionary of extra-ordinary English Cricketers
AIG
Ravished by the Highlander
PAULA QUINN
WRITING ARABIC
Isolated
Final
Initial
Middle
LOL.
MISTAKES

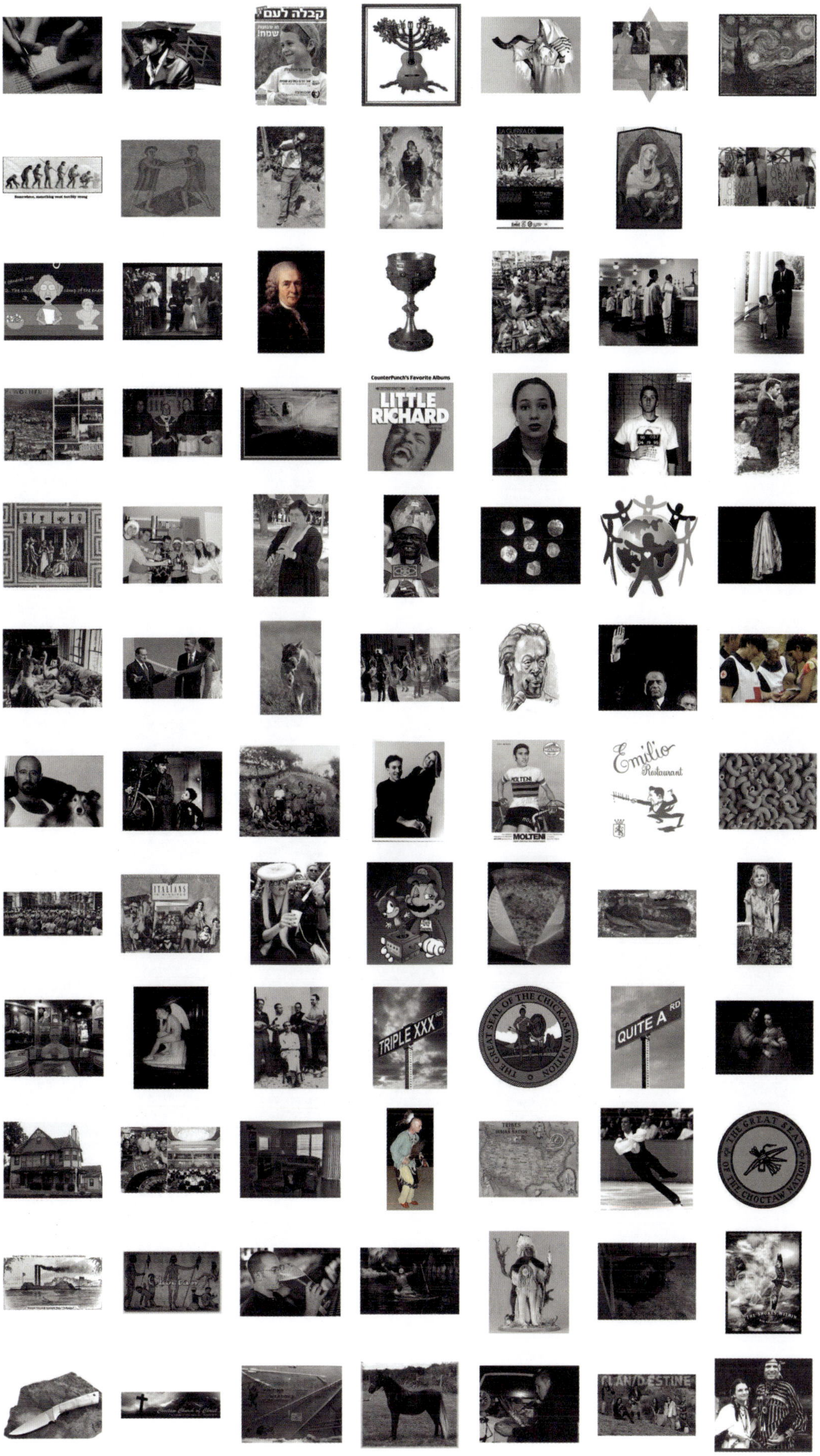

קבלה לעם
CounterPunch's Favorite Albums
LITTLE RICHARD
MOLTENI
Emilio
Restaurant
ITALIANS
TRIPLE XXX RD
THE GREAT SEAL OF THE CHICKASAW NATION
QUITE A RD
THE GREAT SEAL OF THE CHOCTAW NATION
CLAN/DESTINE

2011

Prayer

Industry of the Ordinary spread the good word.

Special thanks to Roger Machin, Doug Snower, Fast Signs, Jessica Wobbekind, and the Bucktown/Wicker Park Chamber of Commerce, Chicago.

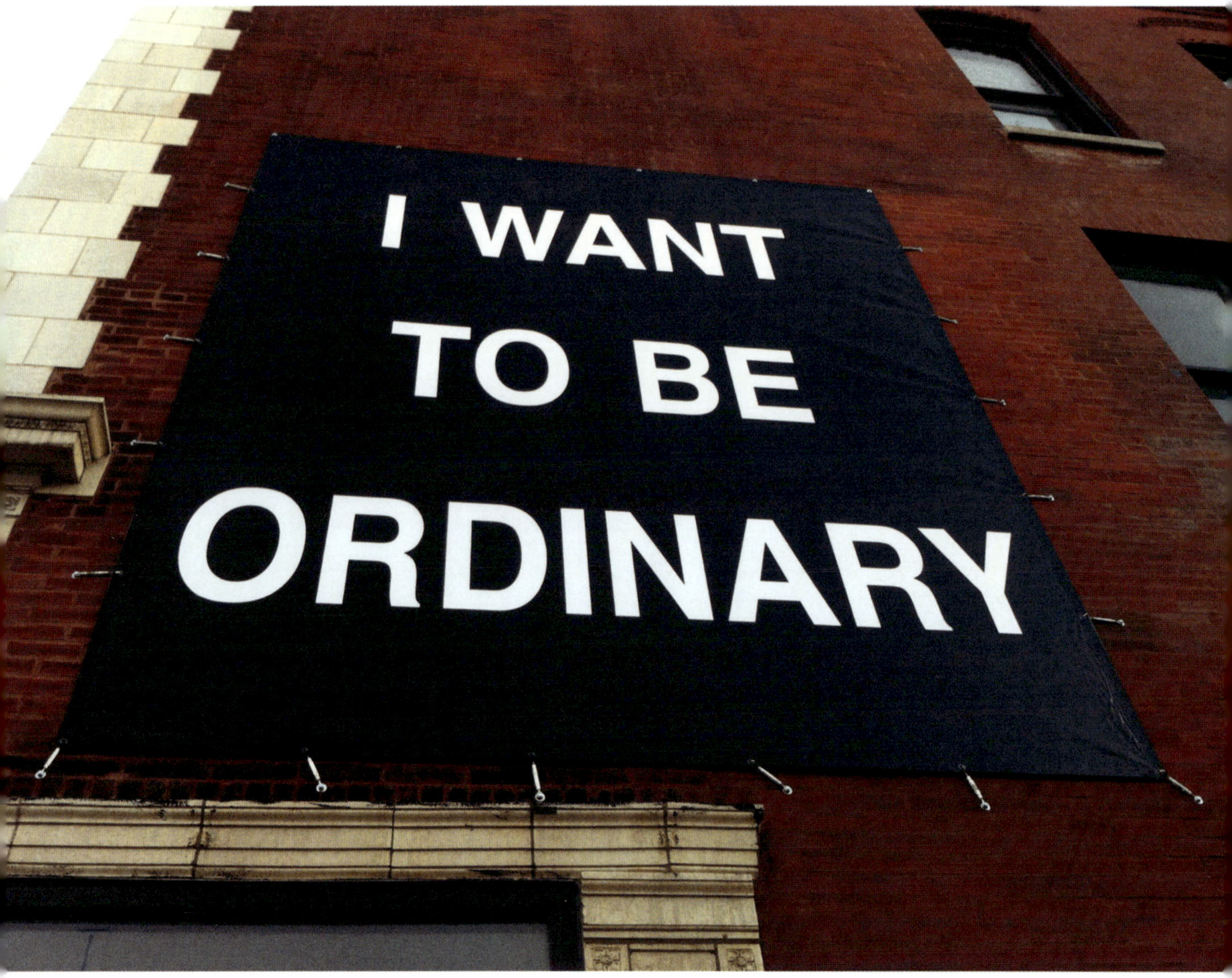

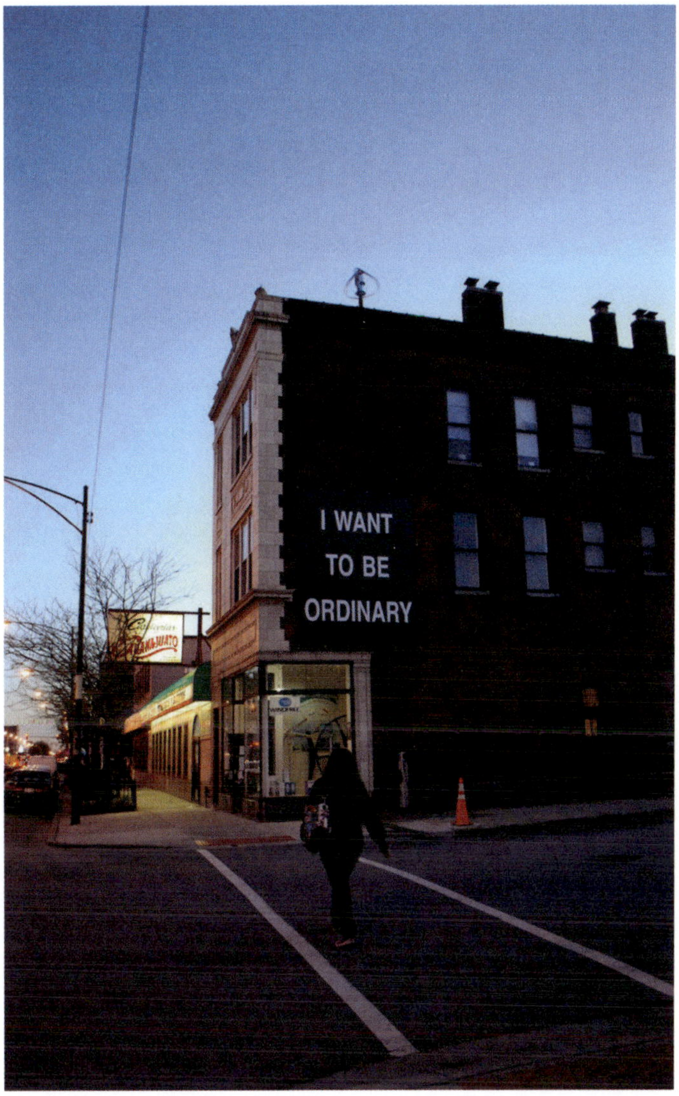
I WANT
TO BE
ORDINARY

WE ARE NOT RESPONSIBLE

For equipment failure, threatened terrorist act(s), terrorist act(s), air raid(s), blackout(s), act(s) of public enemy, earthquake(s), war(s) (declared or undeclared), fire(s), flood(s),epidemic(s), explosion(s), unusually severe weather, hurricane(s), embargo(s), labor dispute(s) or strike(s) (whether legal or illegal), labor or material shortage(s), transportation interruption(s) of any kind, work slow-down(s), civil disturbance(s), insurrection(s), riot(s), or any other similar or dissimilar cause(s) beyond our control.

WE ARE RESPONSIBLE

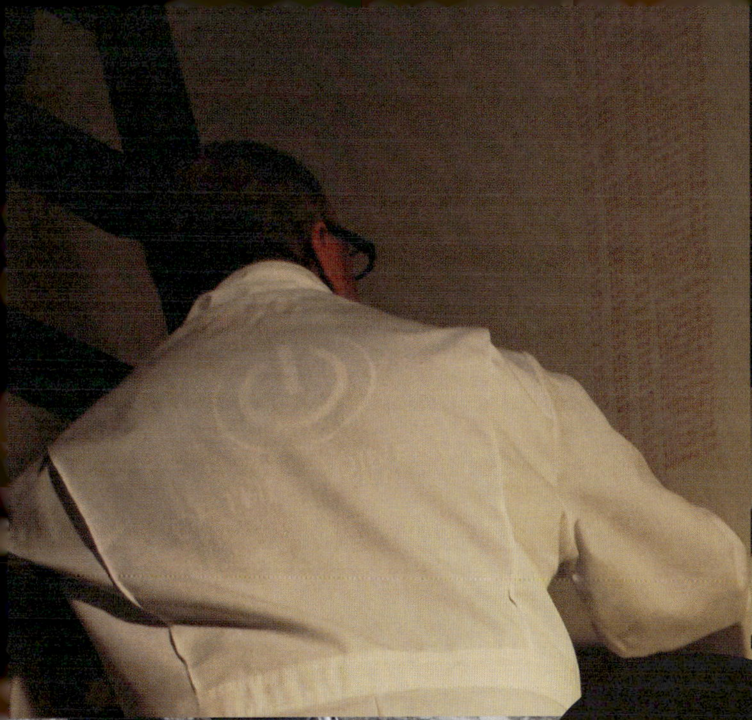

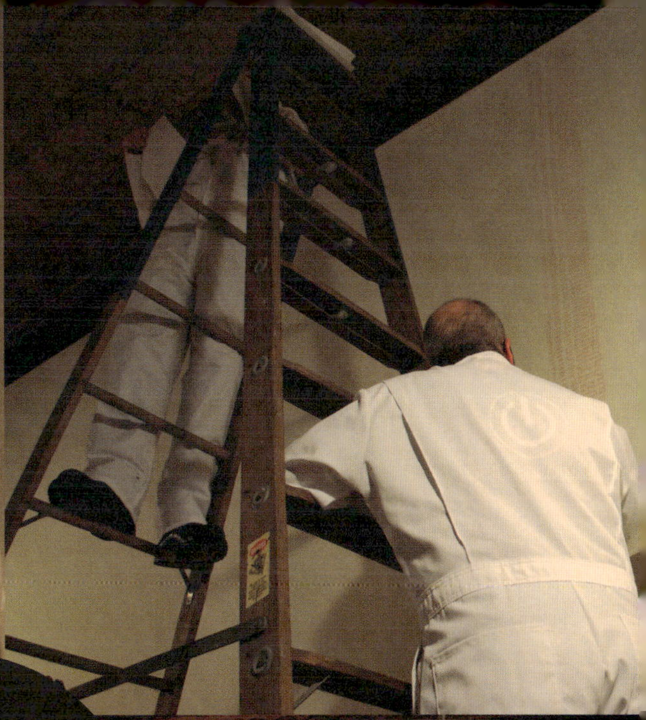

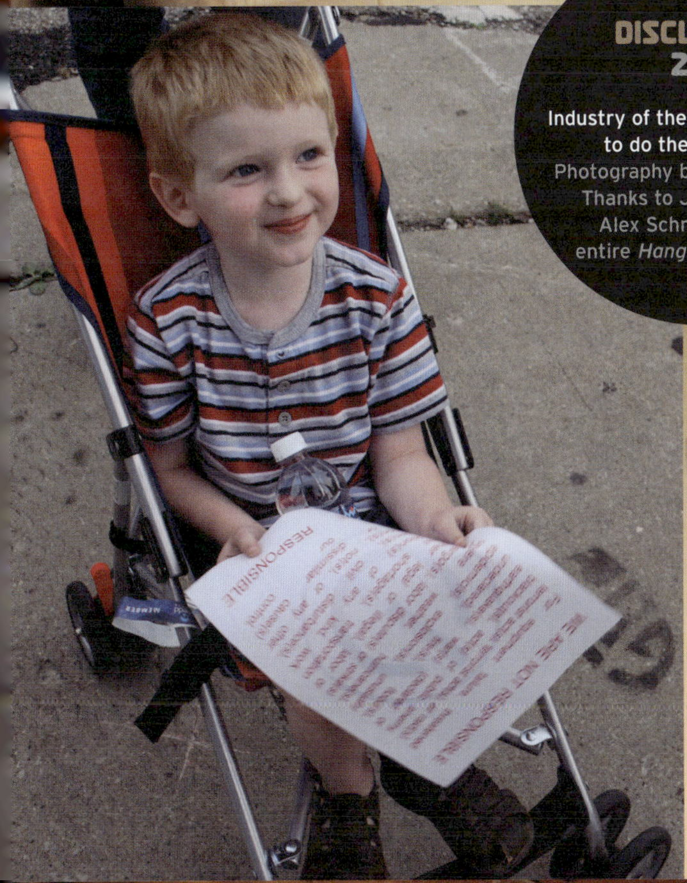

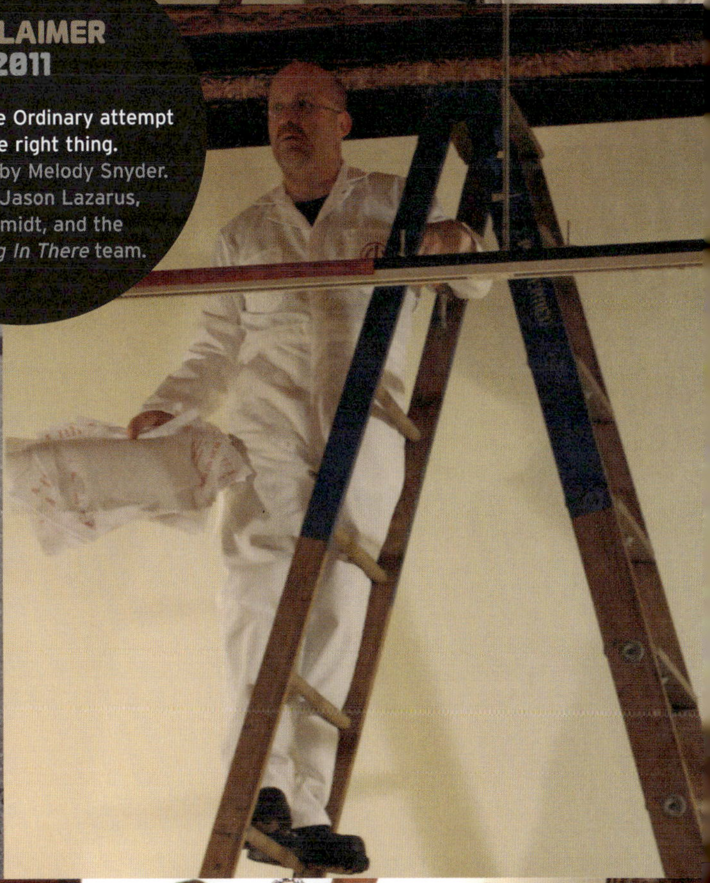

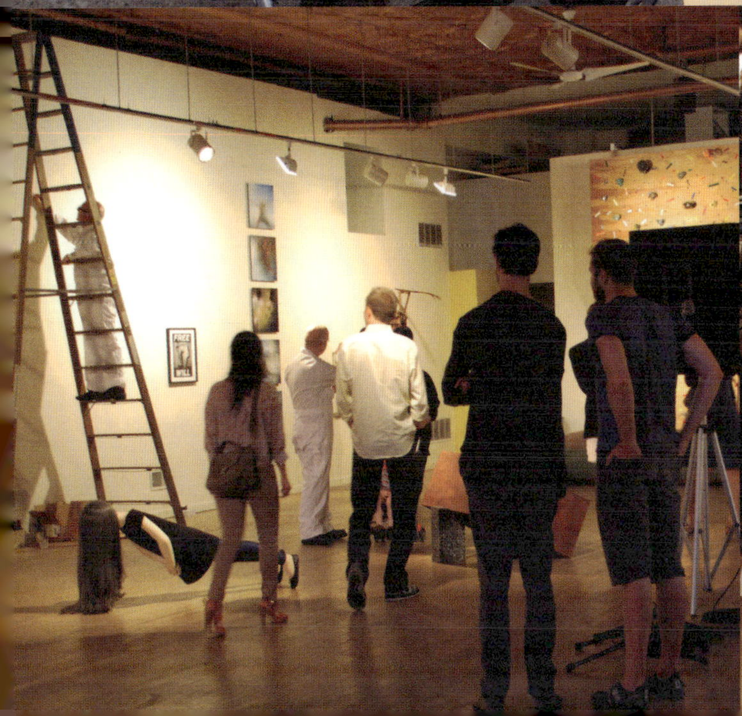

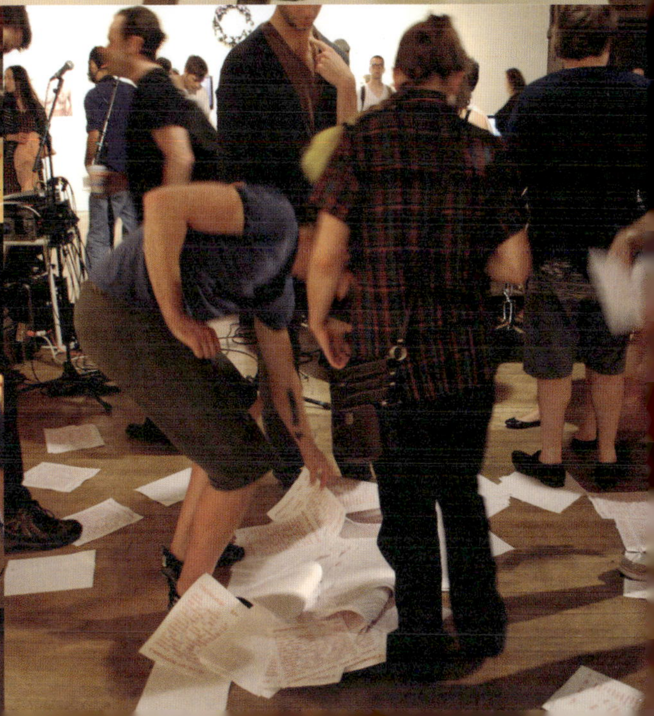

DISCLAIMER
2011

Industry of the Ordinary attempt to do the right thing.
Photography by Melody Snyder. Thanks to Jason Lazarus, Alex Schmidt, and the entire *Hang In There* team.

2011

The Narcissism Chamber

Industry of the Ordinary invite admiration.

Thanks to Jennifer Murray and Meimei Yu.

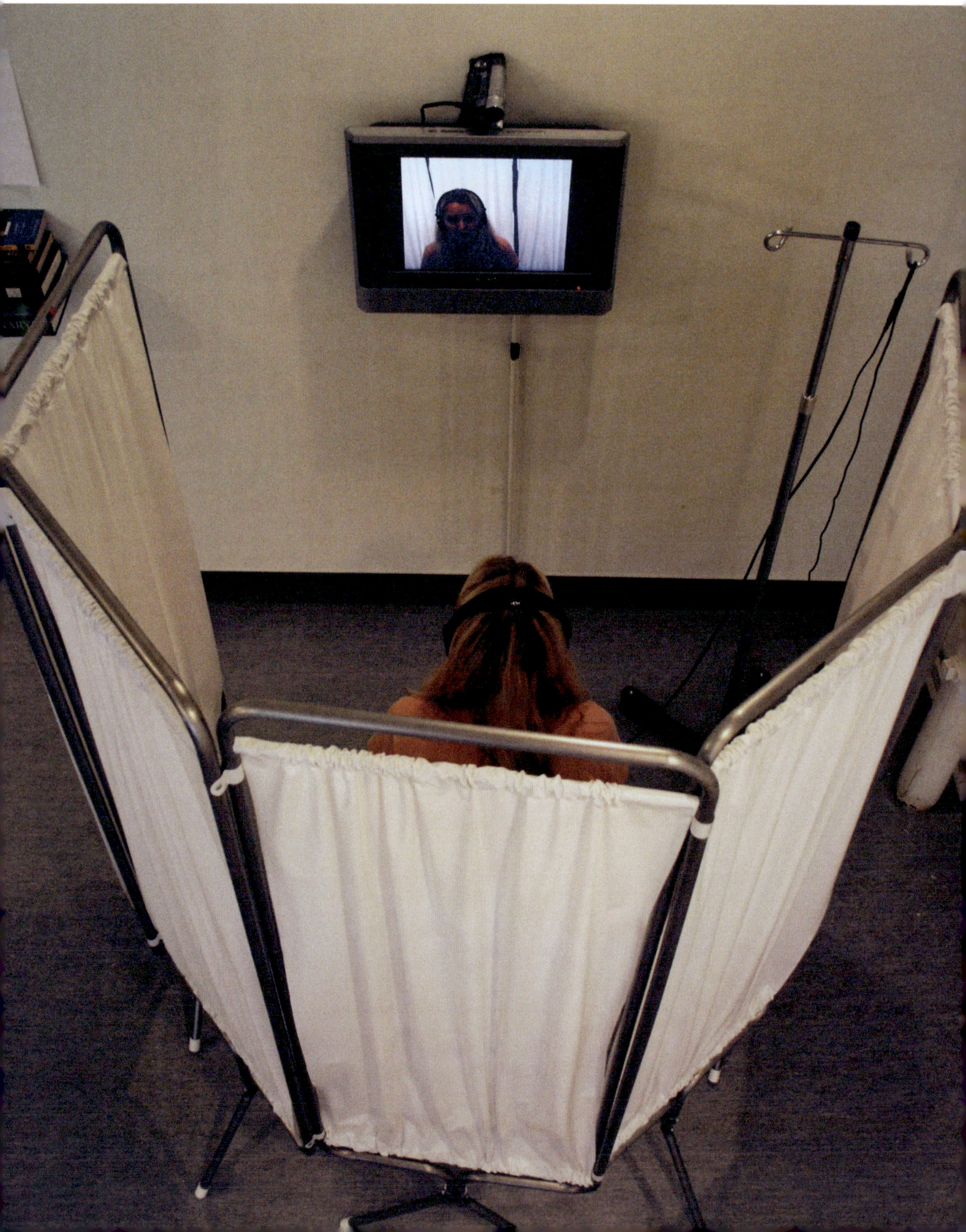

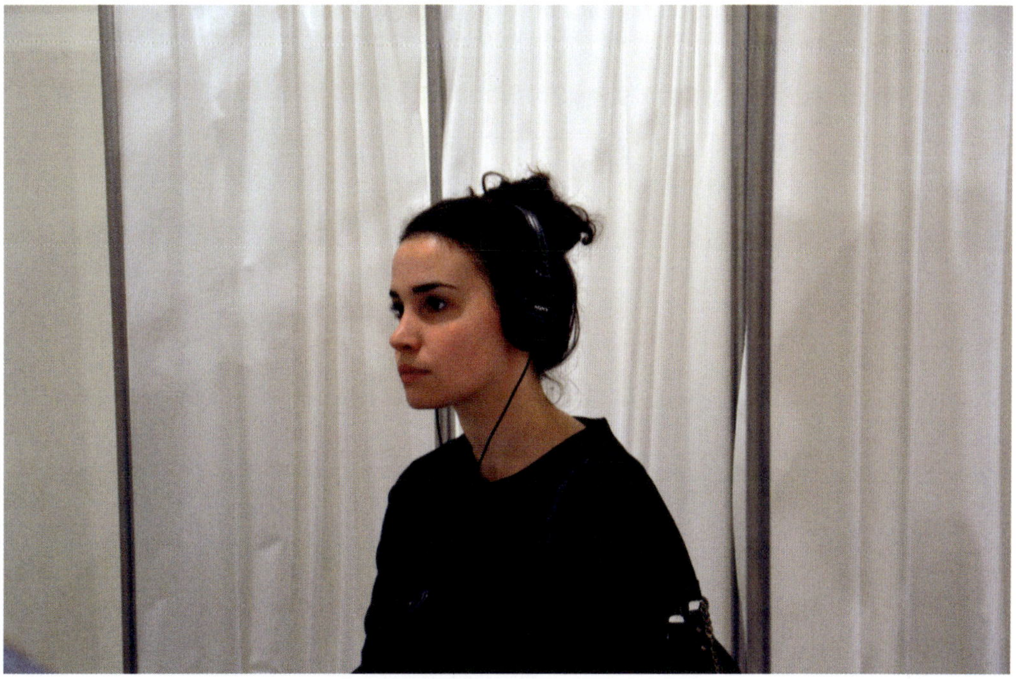

Lyrics for "(I Am) Beautiful"

I am preoccupied with fantasies of unlimited success
Power, beauty, ideal love, or brilliance
I've got a grandiose sense of self-importance
I exaggerate my achievements and my talents

I am beautiful, I'm beautiful
I am beautiful

I am interpersonally exploitive and take advantage of others to achieve my ends
I lack empathy and I'm unwilling to identify with the feelings and needs of others
I am arrogant and haughty in my behaviors
Yes, and I am often envious, and I believe that others are often envious of me (x2)

I am beautiful...

Original text/concept by Industry of the Ordinary.
Lyrics arranged by Elisabeth Blair and Nick Pichet.
Music by Nick Pichet.

Performed by Nick Pichet and Elisabeth Blair.
Produced by Nick Pichet and Elisabeth Blair.
Mastered by Carson Krabbe.

KLEIN BOTTLE (FOR THE SEARCH), 2011

Industry of the Ordinary investigate the state of being internal, protected, and private, while simultaneously external, vulnerable, and public.

Photography by Melody Snyder and Anna Trier.
Special thanks to Jason Lazarus, Shayna Cott, and Josh and Haley.

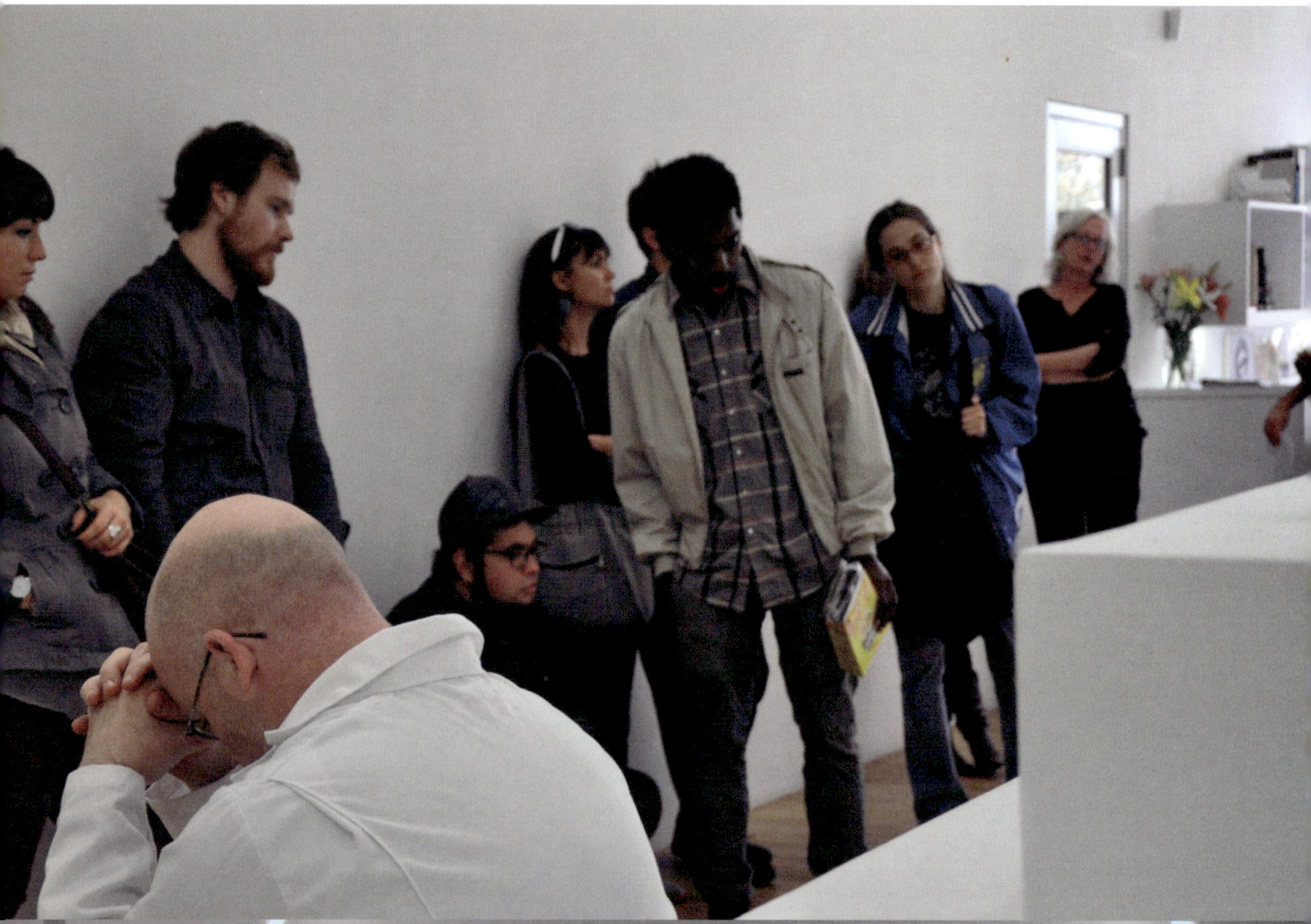

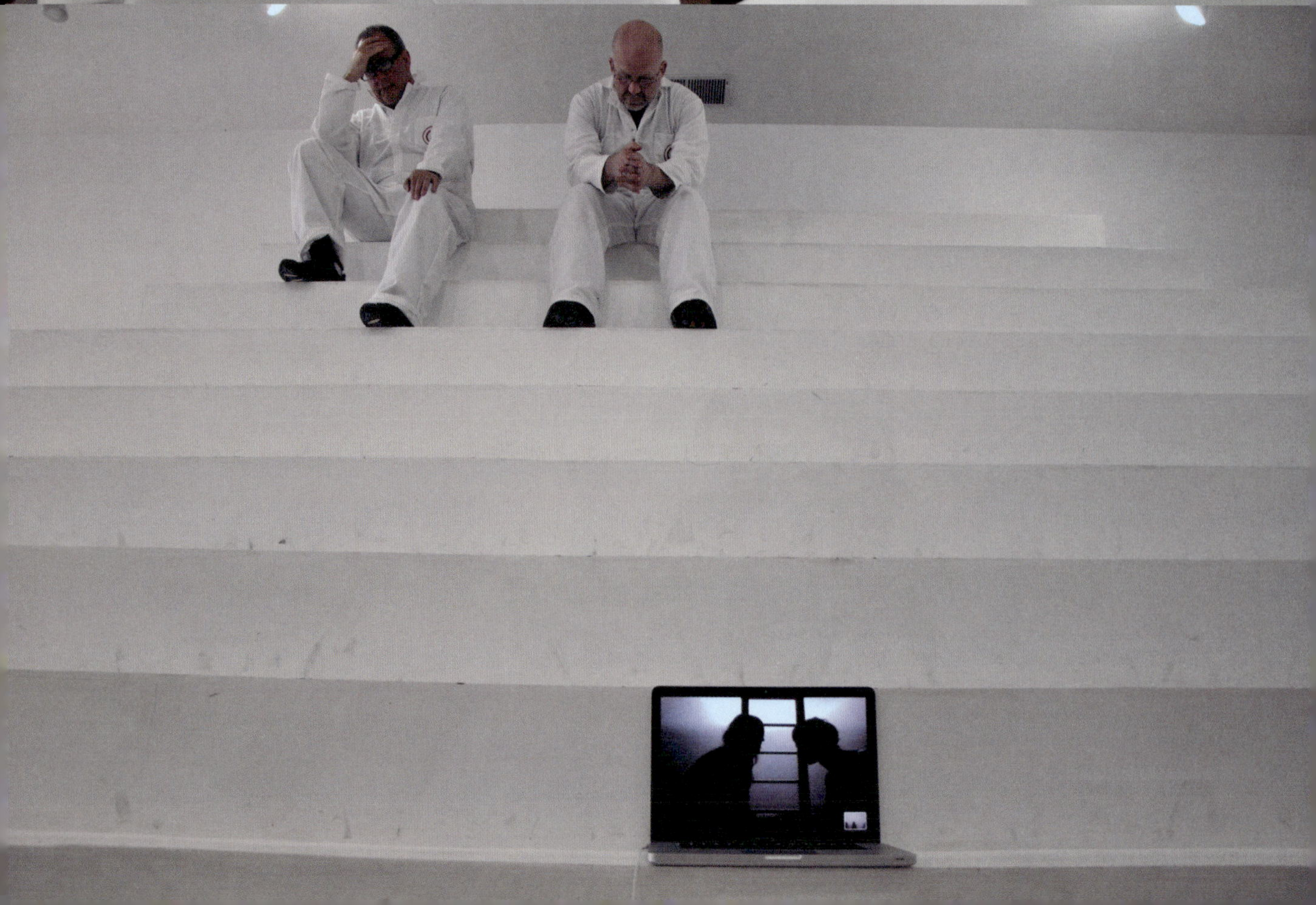

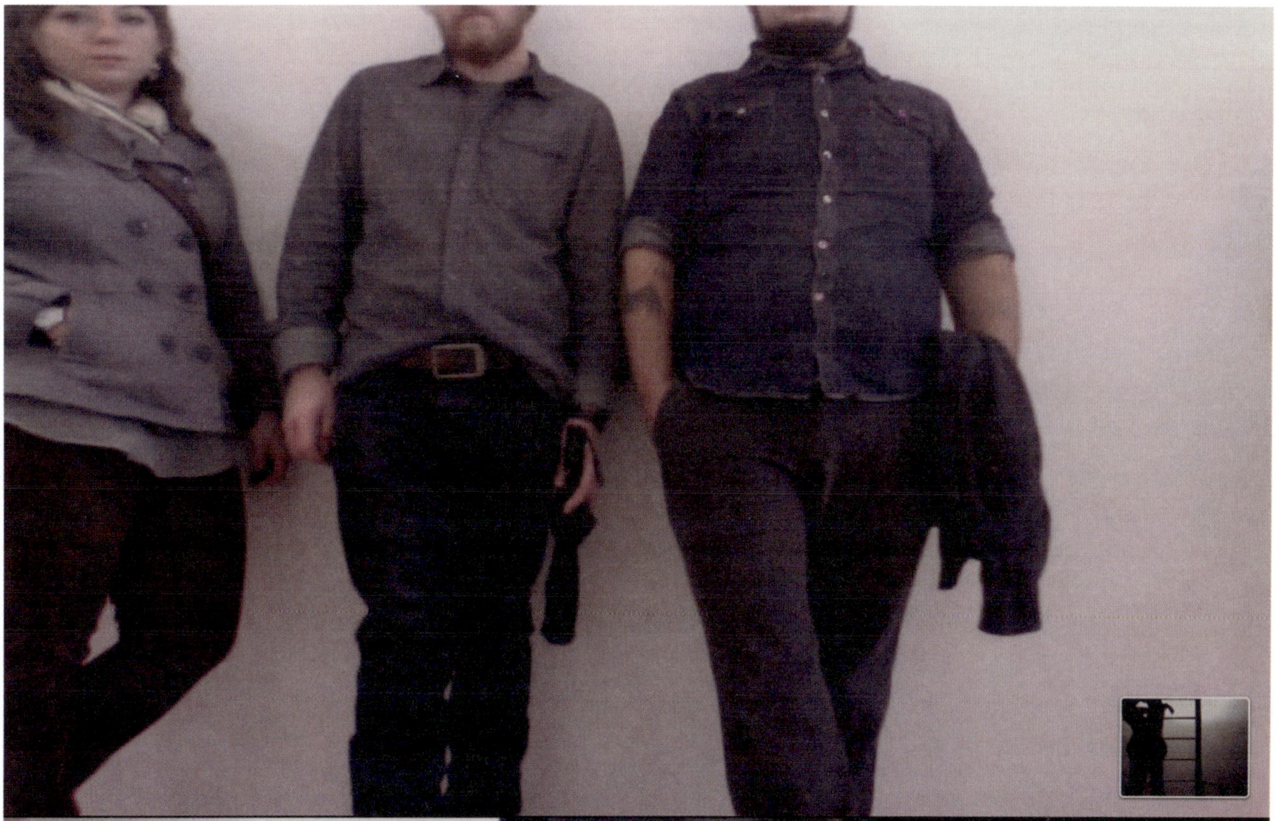

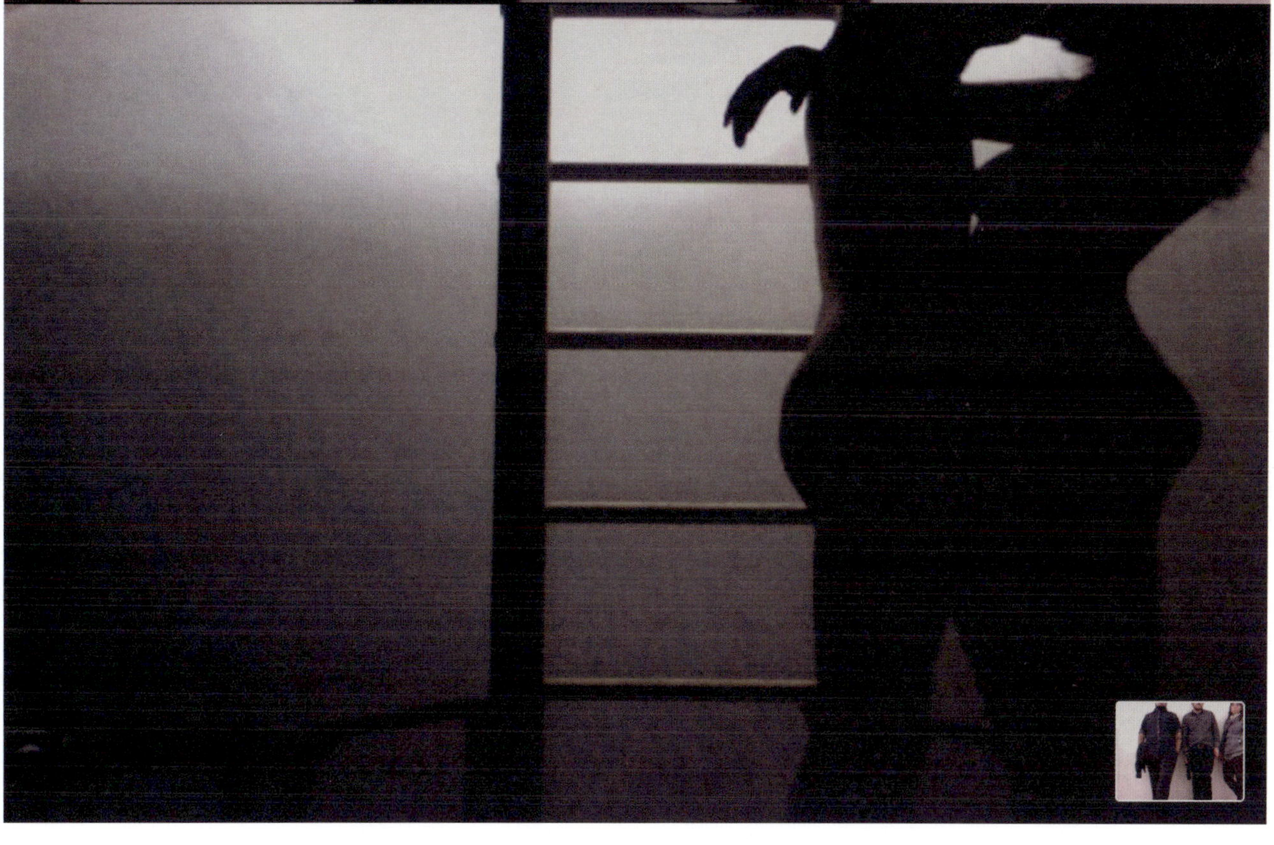

Epilation V 2011

Industry of the Ordinary return to shear in Chicago.

Photography by Melody Snyder. Special thanks to Shayna Cott and Carron Little.

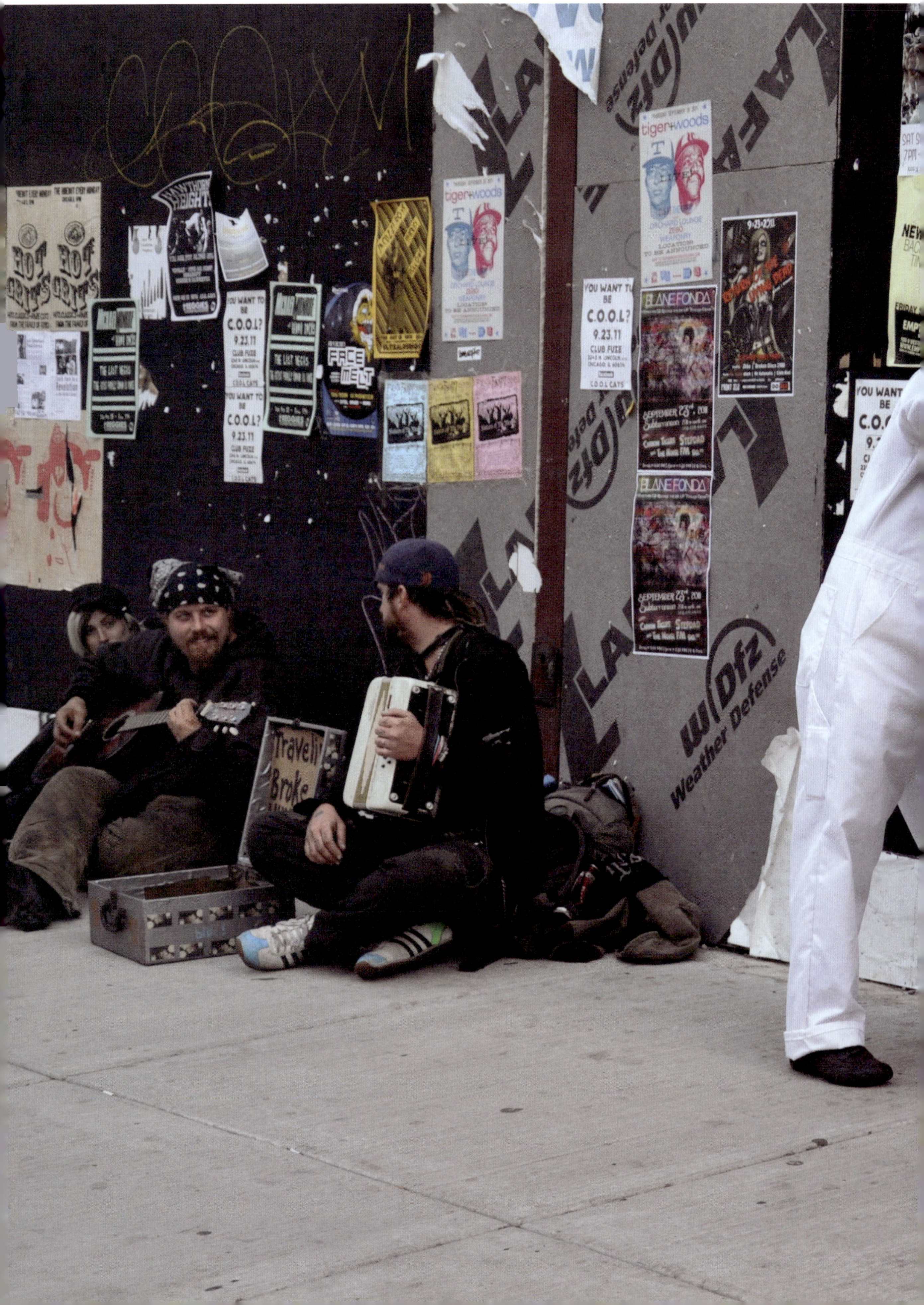

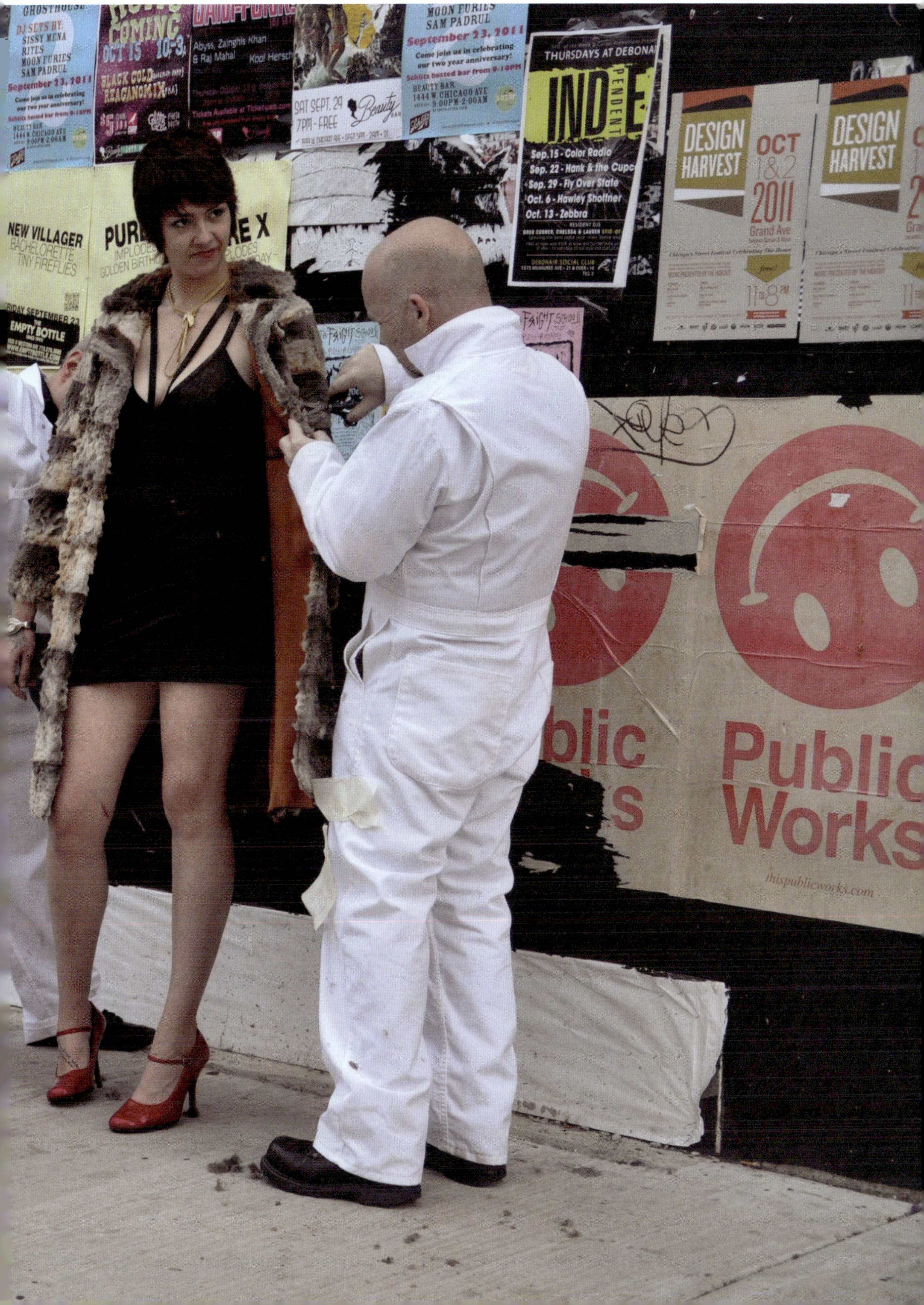
GHOSTHOUSE
DJ SETS BY:
SISSY MENA
RITES
MOON FURIES
SAM PADRUL
September 23, 2011
Come join us in celebrating our two year anniversary!
BEAUTY BAR
1444 W. CHICAGO AVE
9:00PM-2:00AM
OCT 15
BLACK COLD
Abyss, Zainghis Khan & Raj Mahal
Kool Hersch
SAT SEPT. 24
7PM - FREE
Beauty BAR
THURSDAYS AT DEBONA
INDEPENDENT
Sep. 15 - Color Radio
Sep. 22 - Hank & the Cupc
Sep. 29 - Fly Over State
Oct. 6 - Hawley Shoffner
Oct. 13 - Zebbra
RESIDENT DJS
DEBONAIR SOCIAL CLUB
DESIGN HARVEST
OCT 1&2 2011
Grand Ave
free!
11 to 8 PM
DESIGN HARVEST
NEW VILLAGER
BACHELORETTE
TINY FIREFLIES
EMPTY BOTTLE
Public Works
Public Works
thispublicworks.com

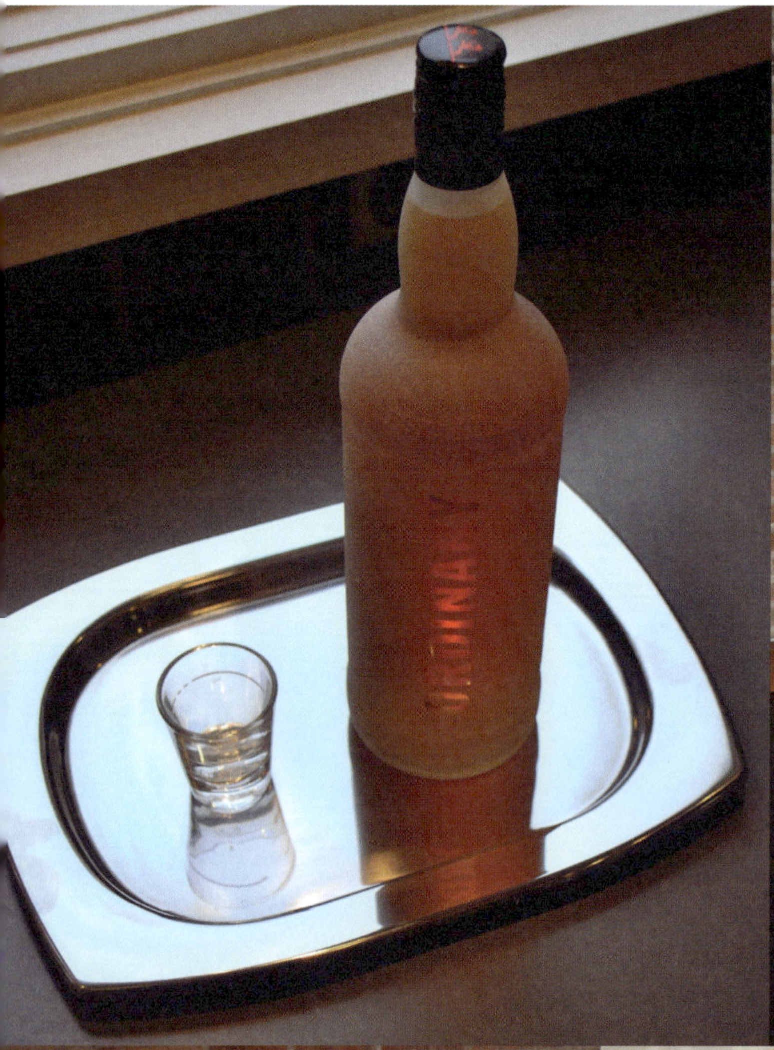

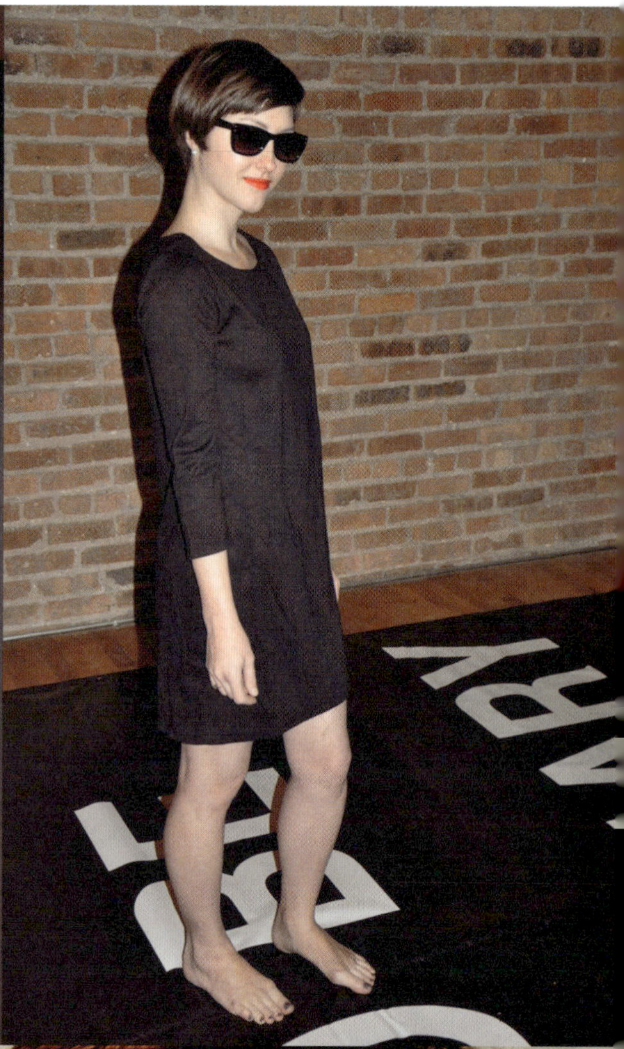

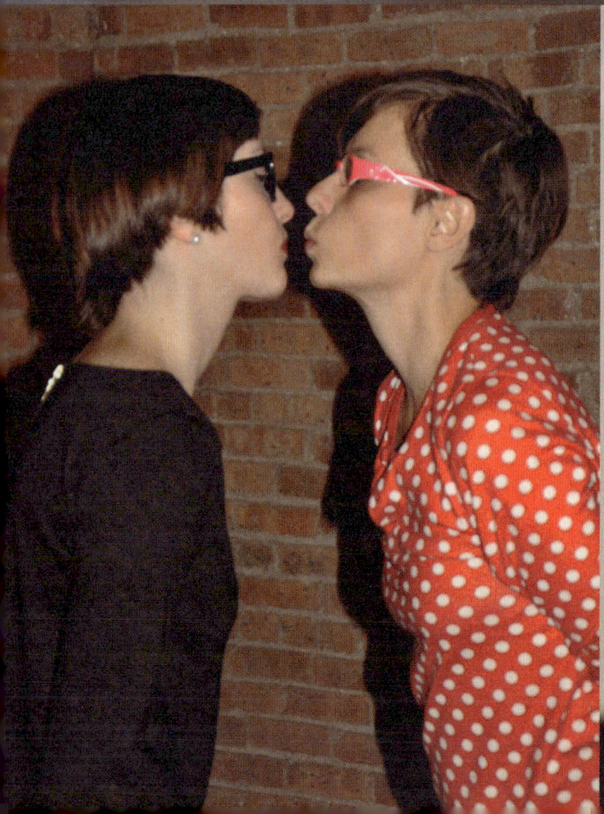

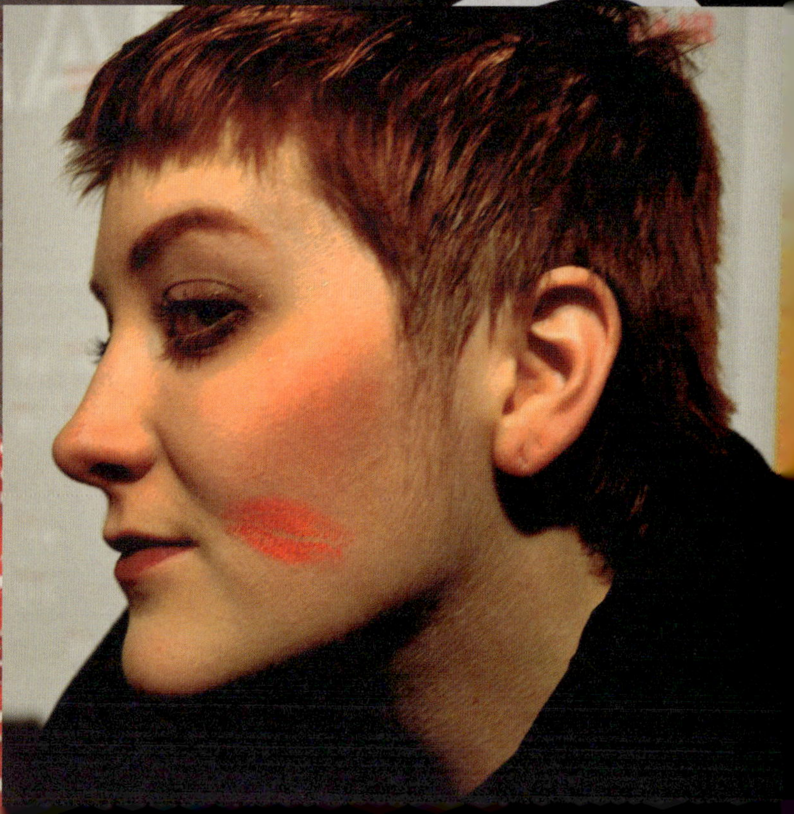

2011

Whiskey and Kisses

Industry of the Ordinary dispense courage and affection.

Photography by Shayna Cott.
Special thanks to Lauren Humphries and the Happy Collaborationists.

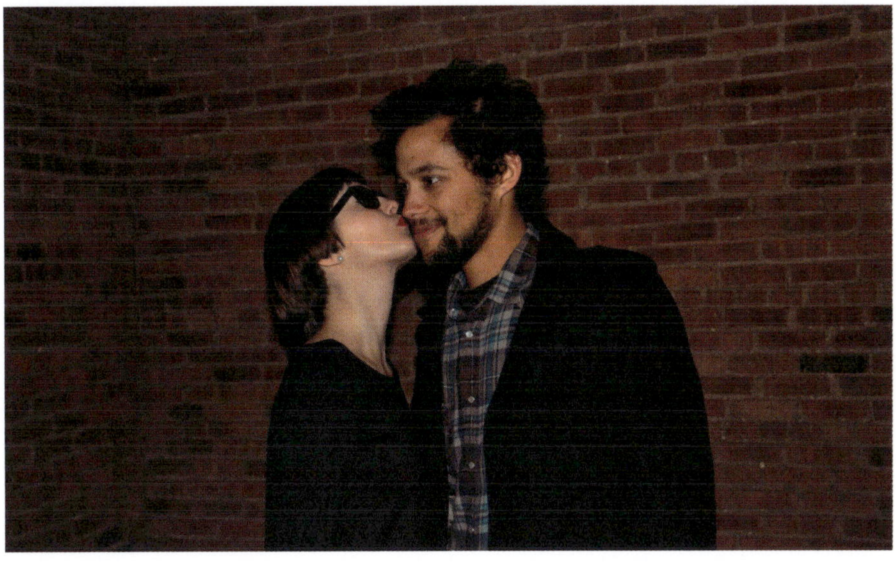

2011

GO-BETWEENS

Industry of the Ordinary explore the boundaries of taste.

Special thanks to Andi Crist and Evan Carrison.
Photography by Melanie Boyna.
Thanks to the Happy Collaborationists.

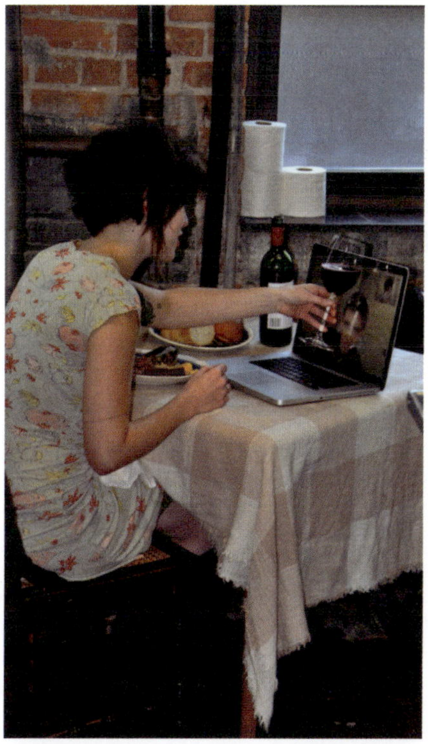

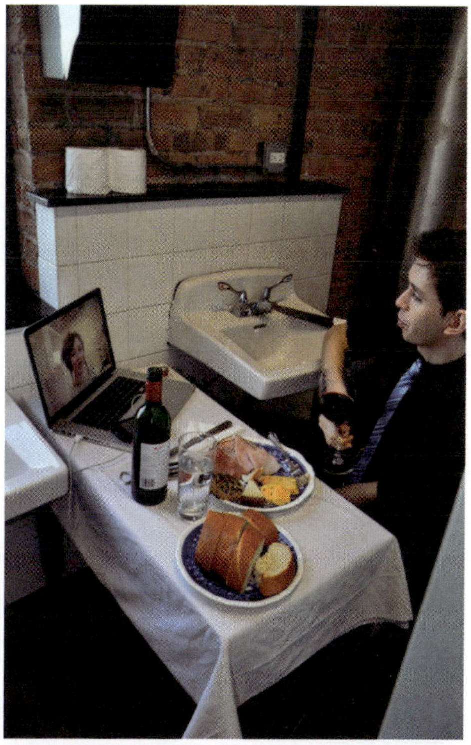

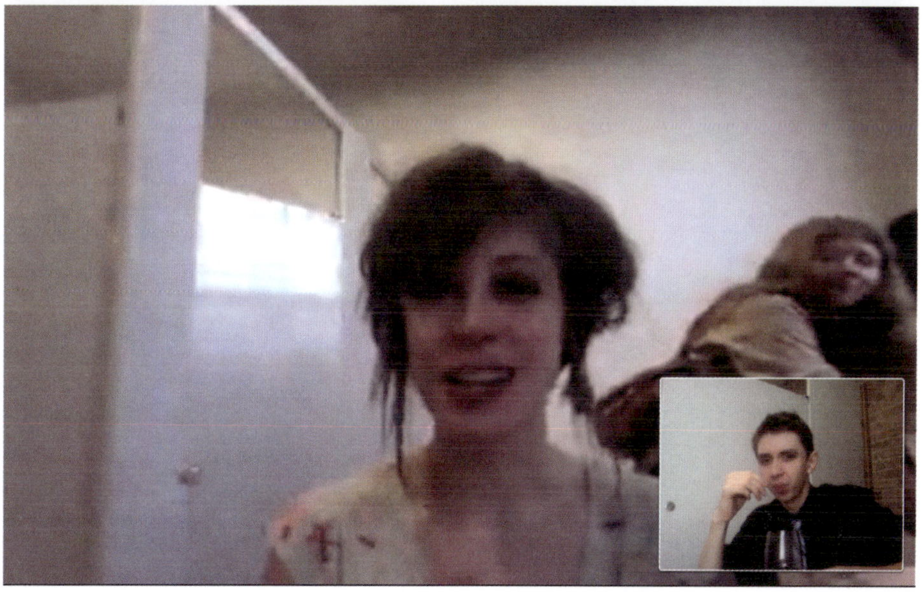

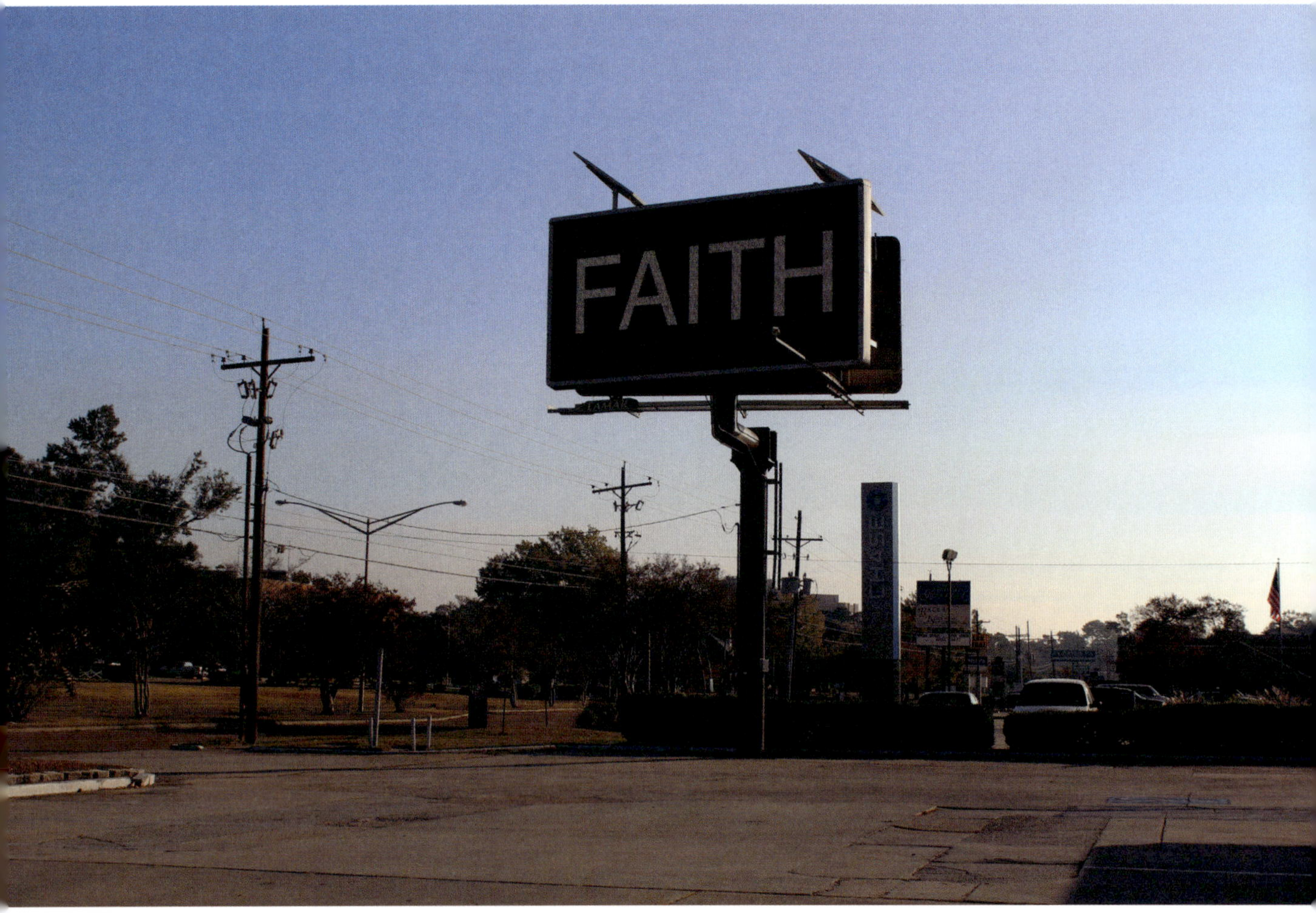

2011

FIDEL (FOR BATON ROUGE, LA)

Industry of the Ordinary suggest a new belief structure.

Special thanks to David Morrison and the Billboard Art Project.

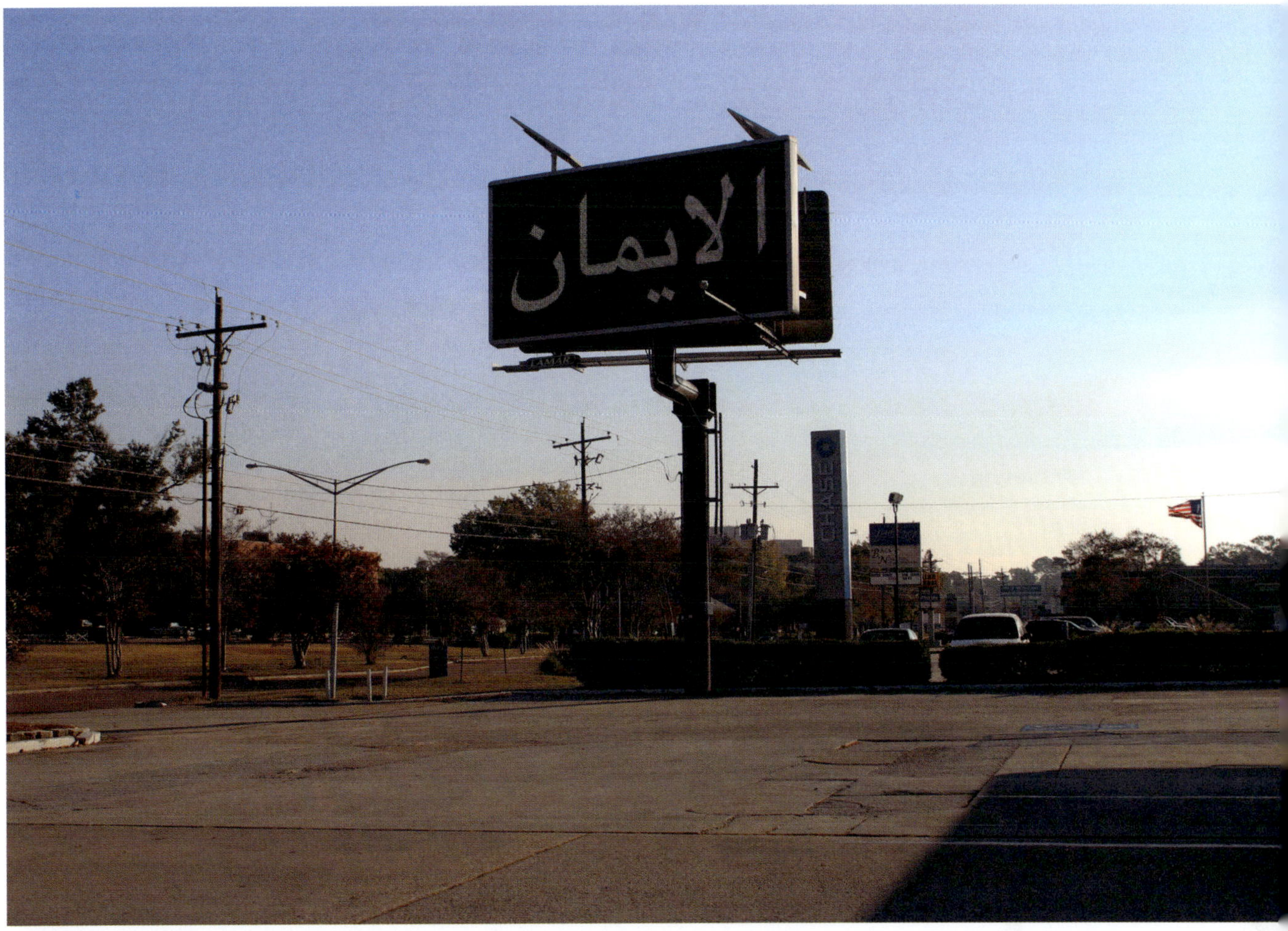
الايمان
CHASE

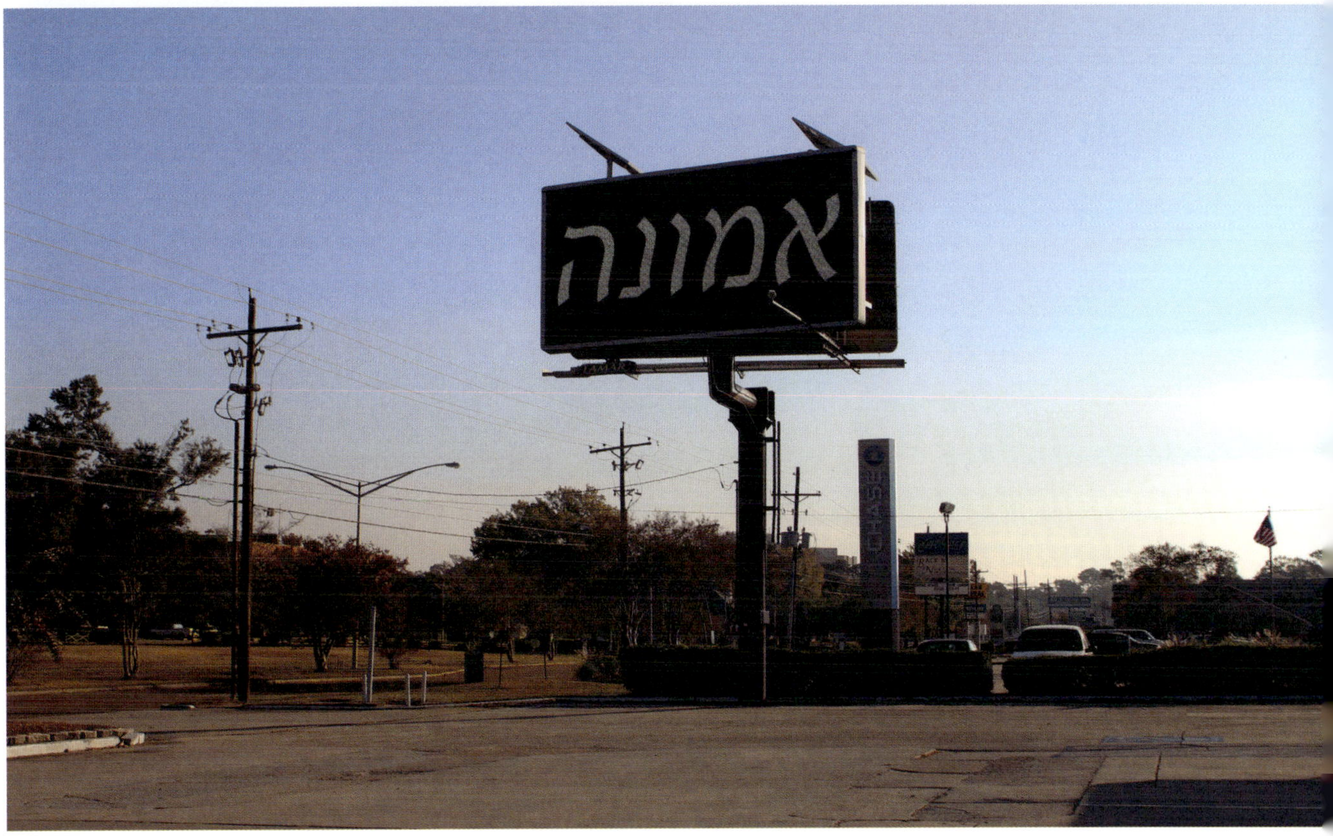
אמונה
CHASE

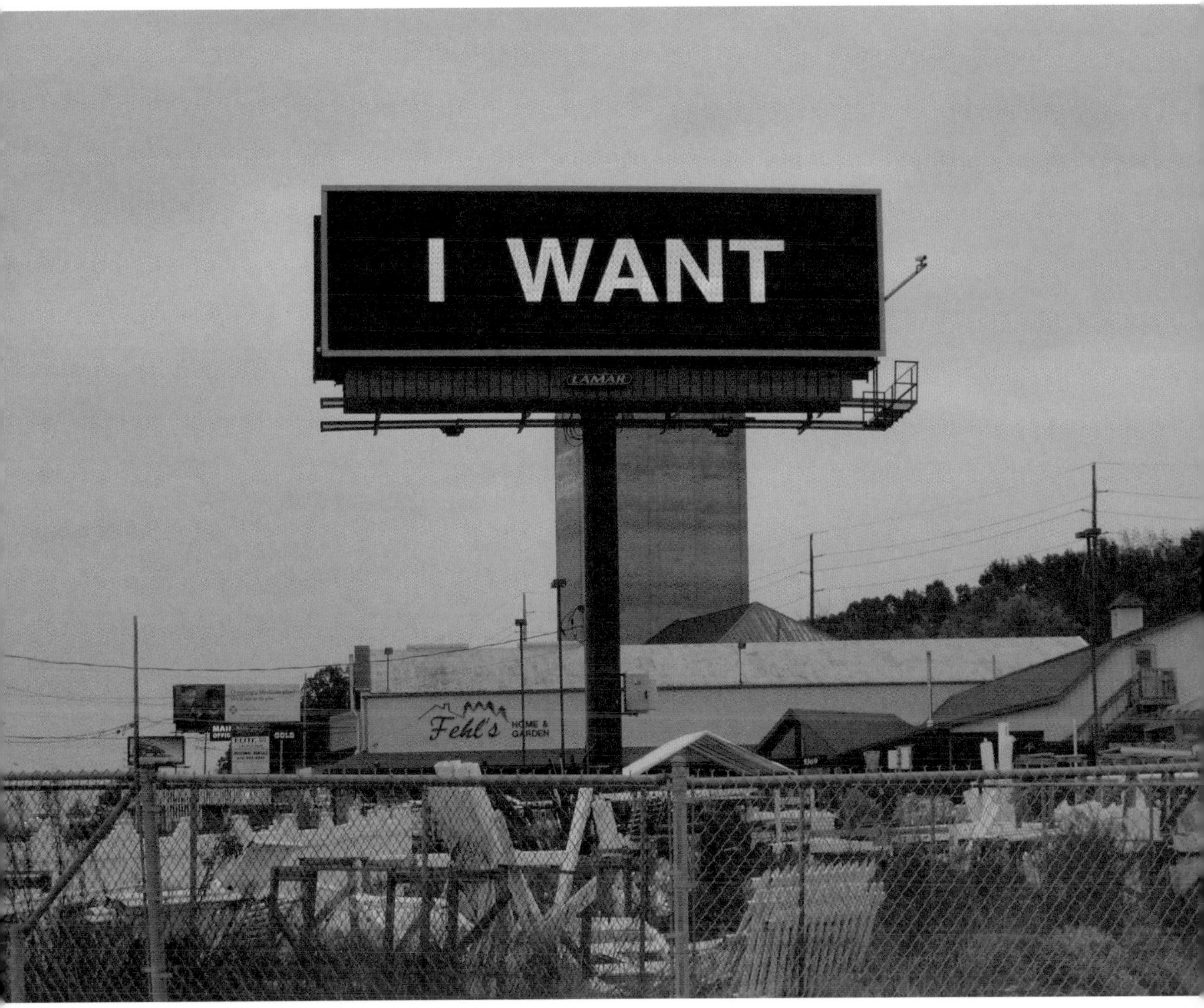
I WANT
LAMAR
Fehl's
HOME &
GARDEN

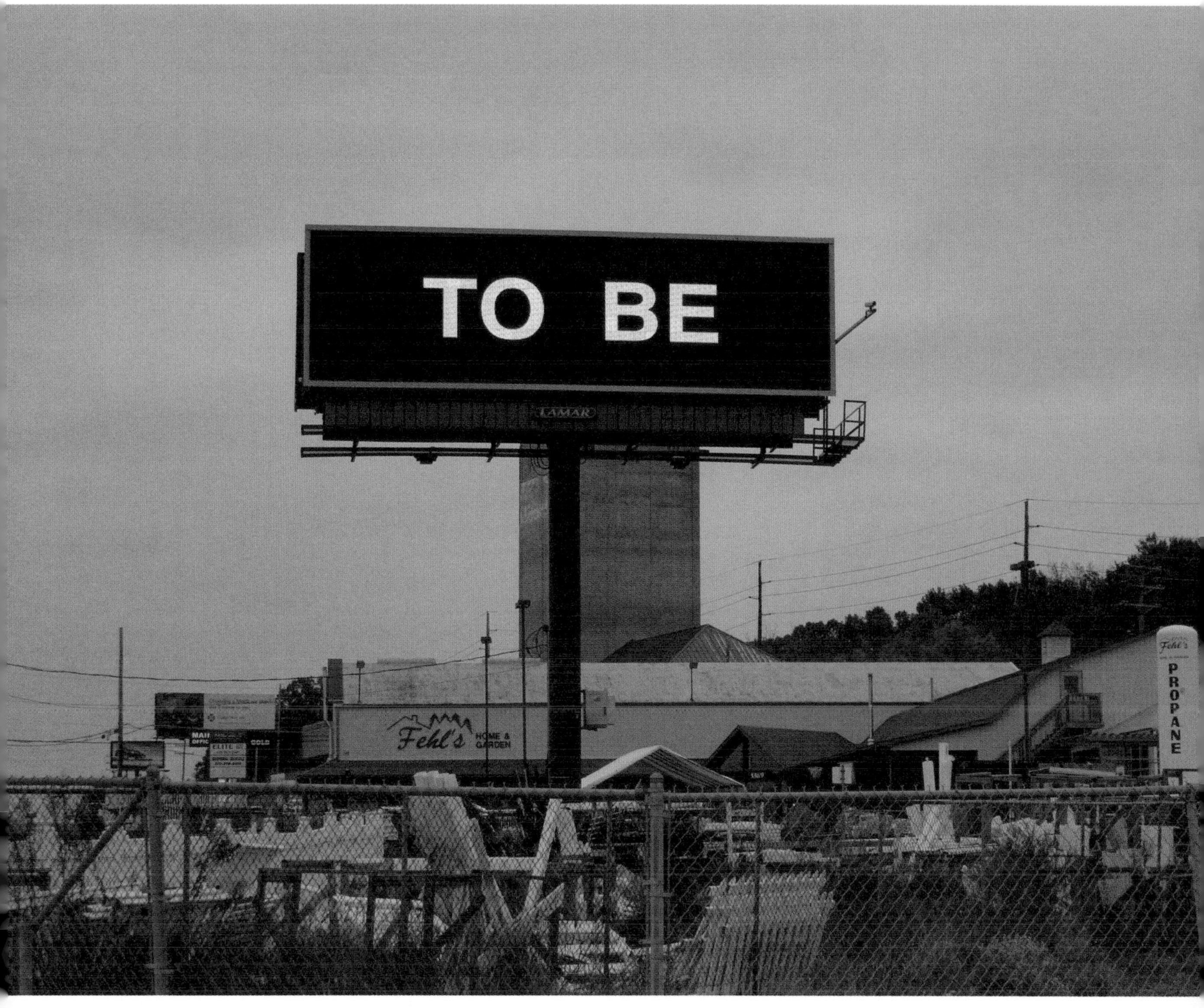
TO BE
LAMAR
Fehl's
HOME & GARDEN
PROPANE

This simple yet provocative phrase intends to challenge the viewer, question their assumptions, and invite them to contemplate the ambiguous nature of the word ORDINARY. Most will first read it in its pejorative sense. In a society that values celebrity above substance and material wealth above simpler pleasures, the desire to be ordinary will commonly be seen as pathetic. However, it can also be read as a resounding affirmation of the power and beauty of the everyday and a rejection of our narcissistic self-obsession: a call to arms.

2011

PRAYER (FOR READING, PA)

Industry of the Ordinary proselytize in the heartland.

Special thanks to David Morrison and the Billboard Art Project.

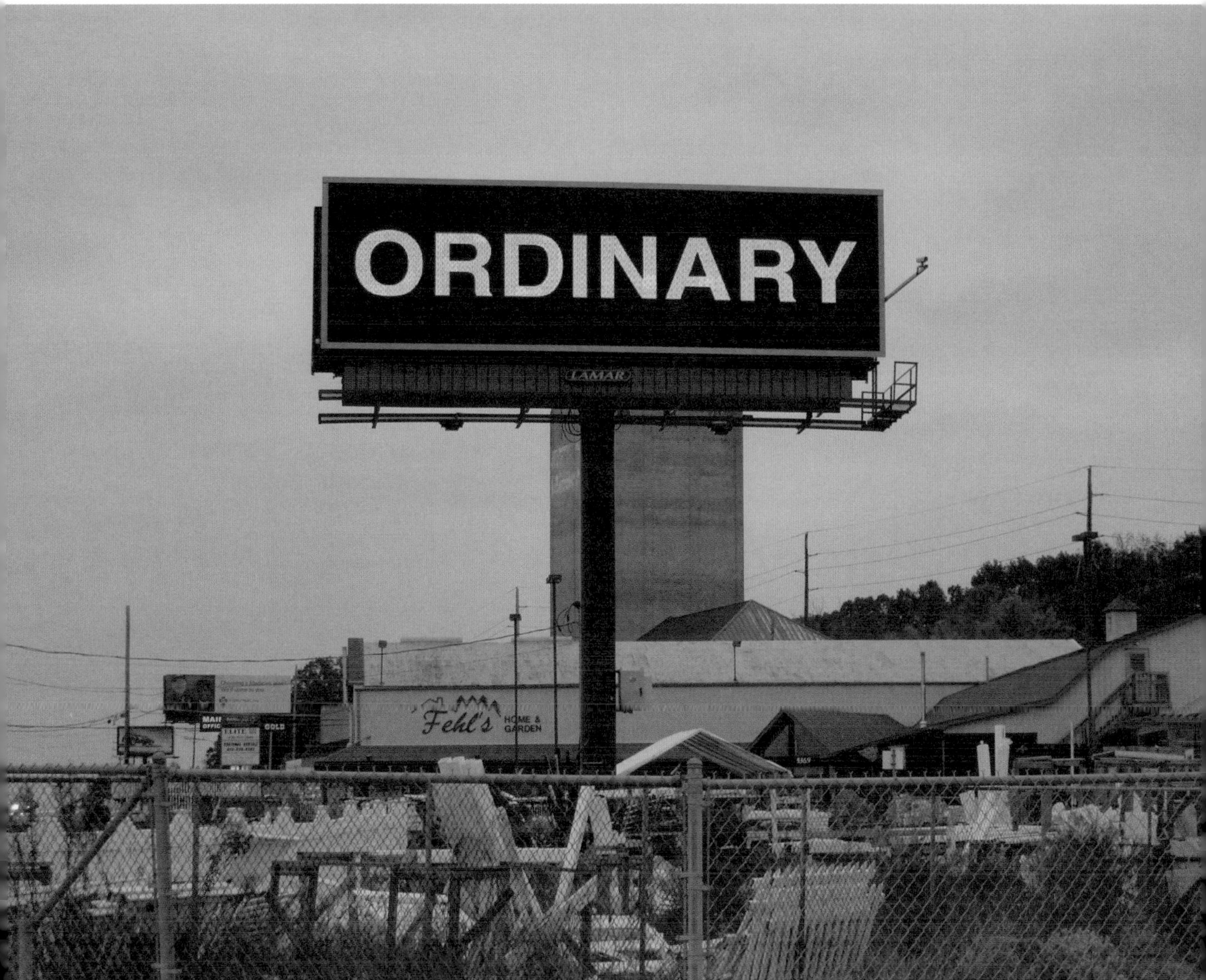
ORDINARY
LAMAR
Fehl's
HOME &
GARDEN

FEELING ORDINARY

Duncan MacKenzie with Industry of the Ordinary

When asked if I would be interested in doing this interview, my sole condition was that we each start with a six pack and, over the course of our time together, drink as many beers as possible. Industry of the Ordinary suggested that this might be a rather irresponsible approach to the task at hand. To which I responded, "Come on, what's more ordinary than three guys getting together to drink beer and talk about what they do?"

Duncan MacKenzie: Let's talk about why you decided to call yourselves Industry of the Ordinary (IOTO). Why not Brooks and Wilson? Please tell me that it was not for fear of sounding like a country and western act.

Mathew Wilson: So, why Industry of the Ordinary? It was one of the longest periods of time that we'd thought about anything. We'd done one action in 2003, which was a starting point, but unsatisfactory for a couple of different reasons. Then we didn't do anything *but* talk about the name. We wanted something that was open-ended because we didn't know what we were going to do. The only thing we knew was that we wanted to work together. We felt sure of that. I think the word "ordinary" was always in the mix, and there were numerous phrases that included the word "ordinary," most of which made us laugh, but were not necessarily useful. A favorite of mine was Industrial Sandwich, although that doesn't, of course, include the word "ordinary." But anyway, most often it was circling around the use of the word "ordinary" because that word encompassed everything around us and did not limit our subject matter. I remember bouncing emails back and forth endlessly for months on this. Industry of the Ordinary was in one of those emails and we were both immediately happy with that.

DM: Has the name shaped what you have done?

MW: Sometimes. I think perhaps more at the beginning. And in all honesty, and perhaps I shouldn't be saying this, I think at the beginning we did think more about it in relation to our actions. Now we're stuck with the name and we just do whatever we want. We make it fit, or we make other people make it fit, or we don't make it fit, but we really don't necessarily care. But perhaps there's a dissenting view from my partner.

Adam Brooks: No, not dissenting. I think that was one of the things we were conscious of when we were choosing the name. That it was catchy and memorable, at least we thought so, but it was also a catch-all. We would be able to do pretty much anything we wanted. So, in that sense, it worked.

DM: I sort of believe you, and don't, because had you been Industrial Sandwich, you would be making pornography, or really ridiculous post-Oldenburg sculptures, or maybe kind of crude "fuck off" drawings, with pyramids and a palette that would best be described as "Neon 80's ski suit." You guys are interested in the "ordinary," in the minutiae that surround our lives. You make art that often speaks to sports, drinking, youth culture, sex, religion, and politics. Those obsessions are in the realm of the quotidian, right? They are the space of our day-to-day lives.

AB: An example: given recent events, the idea of making a piece about Joe Paterno is certainly full of possibility, particularly because an old friend of mine lives a block away from him. She teaches at Penn State and she said it was a fucking nightmare with the media and all of the students chanting. There's something that is really unsettling about this whole affair. That hundreds, if not thousands, of kids at Penn State feel like what they see is this coach being run out of town on a rail. Never mind that the alleged atrocities he enabled through his lack of action were far worse than losing a football coach.

DM: This is a creepy transition but I want to pull it back to you guys rather then a disgraced football coach. I want to talk about history pointing toward a future or affecting the future. So when IOTO crystallized, did it hybridize your personal aesthetics or create its own new visual language? Were there works in your personal histories that, in retrospect, feel like they pointed the way to where IOTO is now?

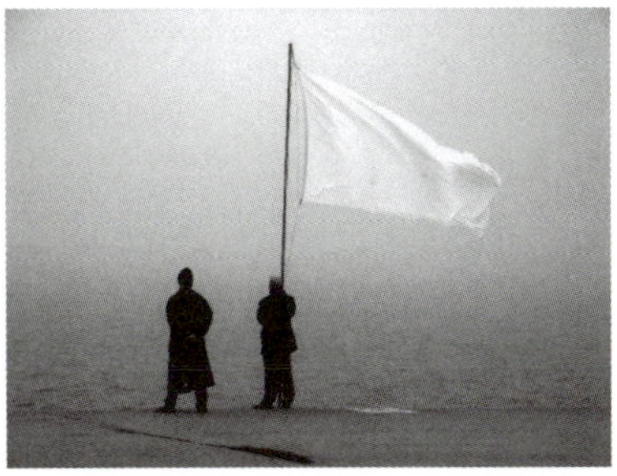

Mathew Wilson, *The Surrender Office*, 2004
Performance

MW: Prior to IOTO most of my work was performance based and most of that was public sited. Actually, my last solo performance ran concurrently with our first twelve pieces in 2004 during the PAC/edge Performance Festival. It was called *Surrender Office*, and I opened up a small office to offer the public this service. I would "surrender" to anything a person wanted me to in exchange for a video testimony about why they were asking me to do this. I remember it as one of the most emotionally exhausting performances I ever undertook—I was at it for several weeks. There are one or two IOTO pieces that cover similar territory, *The Narcissism Chamber*, the *I Want To be Ordinary* series. I like taking something that everyone knows to be true and turning it on its head, I guess. IOTO feels like an extension of the performance work I was doing, but it added object making and a more overt use of popular culture and politics. I like that about IOTO—it's a broader range of activities than I was engaged in before.

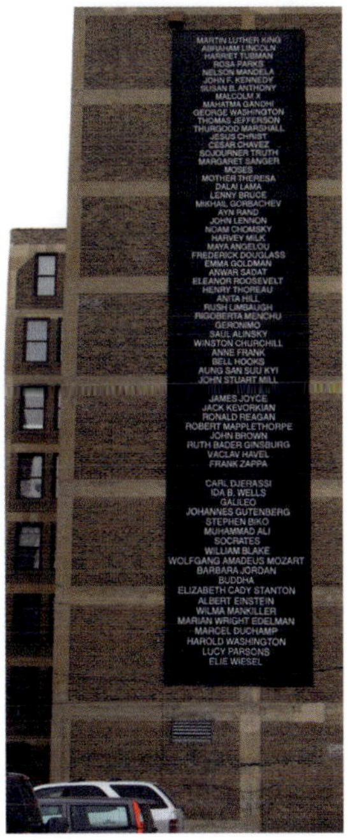

Adam Brooks, *Freedom Wall*, 1994
Enamel on vinyl, 72 feet x 15 feet 6 nches

AB: For me, the public work that I had produced over the prior fifteen years continues to inform certain aspects of IOTO's practice. Particularly the information-gathering process embedded in a work such as *Freedom Wall* (1994), which took eighteen months to evolve and involved hundreds, if not thousands, of respondents. This partially street-based approach to sampling a wide variety of viewpoints resulted in a mural listing the names that the respondents felt embodied the idea of "freedom," whatever that nebulous term meant to them. We have used not dissimilar strategies in projects such as *History as Idea* in Nebraska, and *Journeys* for the Bucktown-Wicker Park Library in Chicago. I agree with Mat that the blending of our prior practices has forced each of us into new and sometimes risky, although ultimately satisfying, behaviors.

DM: On that question of satisfying behavior, I'm curious about how the things you make take on and embody meaning, and present that for an audience's consideration. When is the lab coat just a lab coat and when is it so much more? One of the strengths of the IOTO practice has always seemed to be the way it floats above questions of form and looks more towards an embodied meaning or cultural relation.

AB: We have become interested in the "idea," or we work within the sphere of the "idea." And, actually, the "meaning" can be made by others. We're just doing whatever it is in this multiplicity of ways that you referred to. We're doing what we want to do. And people can take it or leave it. That may be getting ourselves off the hook, and I think, in part, probably the construction of our project from the name onwards gives us that license. People have leveled the criticism at us that we do not stick with anything, although we do circle around processes, materials, and ideas, and come back to them repeatedly. But ultimately, I don't think we're interested in feeling like we have one eye or one-and-a-half eyes on the way that the project is going to be externally perceived. Ultimately, it is something that we're happy if people notice, but we're not standing up there with a loud hailer, what's the—

DM: You mean a bullhorn? I want to take issue with the viewer as author point implied there. That position in which an artist posits that their viewer is going to sketch out the meaning, because meaning is idiosyncratic, and it can only be defined from a personal position and experience, rather than your position as the artists/authors. IOTO actually makes a really aggressive push to situate different kinds of conversations: conversations about death, conversations about war, conversations about soccer. And then you slam them together in a way that sort of normalizes the absurd or makes the normal absurd. Your art plays around that space of the ordinary and the manufacturing of the ordinary. Isn't that your bullhorn?

MW: I think that we're relating it to artist Iñigo Manglano-Ovalle's idea—that the art object accrues meaning. We are very conscious of the territories that we want to be operating in a given piece. We know when we get into an area, medium, or subject that we want to come back to. There are a series of things that constitute a very traditional form of art-making discipline in what we do, but at the same time, there are conscious, controlled ambiguities where we want to respect the intelligence of the audience. We know that they're going to individually add something to the work that requires of them some sort of creative input.

DM: For example, the *Vote for Me* piece?

MW: So, this is going back to 2004. We felt we should run for election. Actually we've run for election twice, so to speak. Once was in Italy. Adam, you can talk about that as you were at campaign headquarters, with dire consequences, as I recall.

AB: It was two years ago at the time of the Biennale and I was teaching a class over in Venice and we wanted to make a piece. Mat wasn't there so it had to be done at arm's length, at least in the bridge between the conception of the work and the execution of it. European elections were taking place simultaneously in Venice and across Italy, and so there were these structures all over the city that had campaign posters on them, and of course, being Italy, most of the candidates were incredibly well groomed and well chiseled, perfectly formed specimens of Italian manhood in the Silvio Berlusconi mold. So we made a campaign poster that said "Vota IOTO," translated as "Vote for Industry of the Ordinary," and then a picture of us that we've used on occasion, which shows us in a pub, each holding a glass of beer, then underneath it, the Arabic "Vote for Me," which added a particular spin, given the xenophobia that is very quick to raise its head in Italy. I put these up around the city and went back and revisited them over the next few weeks. Someone did editorialize on one of them by smearing healthy gobs of dog shit over the surface of one of these posters.

DM: I like imagining you in Italy proposing that people vote for two, you know, laddish English, middle-aged men, and then quietly underneath, in Arabic, suggesting that there might be like some kind of tie-in with the Middle East. How would they make sense of these English pub fans with Arabic scrawled underneath–the potential there must have made people crazy. I'm surprised all that happened was a mess of dog shit.

MW: It was just an odd moment in our political careers. But this all began with an English version and a response to the habit of politicians speaking in the third person. We made a simple neon sign that read "Vote for Me" in English and Adam put it in his bedroom window for several months, causing a bit of a stir in the neighborhood. The next iteration was made during the Iraq war, we decided to translate "Vote for Me" into Arabic. That started a whole series of works, not only the *Vote for Me* pieces, which have become t-shirts and other ephemera, but also a series of works that deal with the beauty of Arabic script, and our (as Americans) inability to read it. So we can look at it and we know that there is something–as you point out, with the Italian campaign, as soon as somebody recognizes that it's Arabic script, it becomes this vague, unnerving, threatening drawing. Few of us in America could possibly know what it means. We don't speak Arabic, we can't read Arabic, and yet it elicits a fear response. So, we've used that many times translating "Vote for Me" first, but also the word "terrorist" itself. So that sort of reinforces those expectations of this being something to be feared, simply through typography. Arabic is often just a scary drawing to us.

DM: I have been thinking about the implications of you two as the institution of IOTO arguing that you should, "Vote for Me." It is complicated both from the personal implications of the "me," in that, outside of grade school, no one says "Vote for Me." They say "Vote Barack Obama" or "Vote Mitt Romney." It is made more elusive when that "me" represents an institutional or corporate entity—a "me" which represents a collective, rather then a more traditional and comfortably understood "heroic individual." In your case, it's further complicated, or maybe just made more overt, through the "Industry" in your name. How does one vote for an industry? How could we elect an institution? Can we individually empathize with a corporation?

MW: And sadly, we're still waiting for our landslide victory.

DM: What percentage of the vote did you see floating your way?

MW: We'd like to consider that we might have had a chance of a handful of voters stepping up.

DM: Did you get any percentage of the vote? Were you a write-in on the ballot?

MW: I don't think that we were there long enough to be able to ascertain that.

DM: It was more like you were tweaking people's experience of the Italian election.

MW: We were doing what we always do, which is...

DM: For the record, Mat said, "playing" quietly, and Adam concurred. But you play with things like casting your own heads in red rubber and using the "heads" as balls in a soccer match. Or you play with our fear of Arabic as a loaded and pop-culturally threatening language. You play with signs like they are language grenades.

MW: But doesn't that keep us interested? And alert? We've said ourselves that we do what we do mostly because we think it's funny and engaging. There's a great deal of humor in the work, and much of it even in more serious subjects. The conversation begins out of humor. We laugh about the world because that's a fairly healthy way to deal with the world.

AB: Because we're deeply skeptical about the world in general, and rather than sitting around and becoming paralyzed by the feeling that something is deeply flawed within everything we see around us, the healthier response is to leaven that skepticism or that pessimism with humor.

MW: It's a consequence of the relationship that we have. Through humor we deal with the world, but that doesn't mean that all the works are supposed to operate at that level. We have been, in the past, referred to as pranksters. In some of the work, it's fine to label us as such. But there is also very serious stuff that we work through that's not intended, ultimately, to be funny.

AB: And this brings up an interesting question, I think, given the fact that, apologies to any future audience who may look at this as stale and old news, the Maurizio Cattelan show that opened at the Guggenheim Museum in New York, and has elicited a major backlash against his work because of his ego, obviously. But the charge that's leveled against him is that he does not have the ability to really take anything seriously. Even though he takes the entire world as his subject, there is something that is interesting in the context of what we do. I'm thinking about the project we did for Nebraska the summer before last.

DM: When you say Nebraska, you mean *the* Nebraska?

AB: By association. It was actually for the state or an arm of the state, the Nebraska State Historical Society. We made what is probably our most considered and complex work as a result of that process, which certainly has some of our dark humor. But because of the venue and context of the work, and the strong suggestion that the work should be digestible. Our competitors, as finalists for this commission were, all three of them, very traditional muralists who presented notions of history and chronology in an incredibly expected way. And luckily we had an advocate on the selection panel that believed that we could do something that was entirely different. That was a fascinating project, and I think we feel that it was a project that really stretched us. We're good at creating gestures and making work that is easily digestible, but for us, this was the result of an almost year-long process of traveling around the state, talking to people, thinking about not only the specificity of the place and the people that we were coming into contact with, but also, in a larger sense, how history is constructed, what it means to even be making a work for a historical society that purports to be the repository of both official and unofficial histories, and how one can possibly ever be equal to the task of doing something like that.

DM: How could any individual be equal to the task of somehow exemplifying and embodying a culture's history? How did you approach the challenge?

AB: We stepped back and realized that what we needed to do was deflect that task and reconfigure our investigation into a series of more oblique subject areas that dealt with larger questions: "How is history constructed?" "Who constructs it?" "Who is the beneficiary?" "Who is excluded?" And through a long series of interviews, follow-up investigations, and research on our part, and a lot of thinking and talking while driving back and forth across the state, we were able to synthesize those, as you say, impossible tasks into twelve distinct areas that started to take apart the mechanics of the construction of meaning, history, importance, and the pedagogical way we're taught that history is something that is immutable. Our essential premise from the beginning was that that was a flawed position to consider starting from. And so, as we continued to have these dialogues with people and between the two of us, and then other individuals and entities that we came to through this elongated process, we realized that obviously it could never be complete. It had to be something that was aestheticized in a certain way so that people would be engaged, but it also had to work through a clear mechanism, and not make a claim to be comprehensive in any regard. All we wanted to do—and I think this is true with all of our work, whether it uses that aforementioned element of humor or not—is that we want people to look at what we're doing and have a think about it.

DM: That actually raises a really interesting point about the nature of IOTO and universality. The ideas you take on as subject matter and content are huge, thorny, and contentious. I'm thinking about you guys dressed up as God and Adam playing foosball out in a storm as the water from the beach threatens to wash both of you away.

AB: A quick clarification, it's Young God and Old God. So it's the two parts of God. The senile...

DM: I thought the foosball was the Holy Spirit?

AB: The father and the son were clearly there. Perhaps, to quote Duncan, the "awesome" nature of nature that day was the other implicit part of the trinity, because we were almost swept into the lake.

DM: Again and again you take on subject matter that is seemingly universal. In Nebraska you're trying to synthesize the universality of the state's culture and history, while recognizing the impossibility of any attempt to situate a universal, or even arguing for a universal in culture. It's funny. That tweek is similar to the *Vote for Me* piece and similar again to kicking around that soccer ball head or when the two of you drag the Ten Commandments as a melting ice sculpture down Michigan Avenue from one museum to another while bottling and distributing the run off. You take something that makes a claim to universality and you problematize it. You resituate it in a way that makes it comical, accessible, participatory, and hard to read as universal.

MW: A lot of the work comes from, I suppose, our studio practice which is conversational. IOTO has to be understood, in part, by the fact that it's a collaboration. It's two people with some things in common. We both have long histories and have spent a long time in England. We've both come to America. We've spent our adult lives and our professional lives here in America. So there's that, and there's the sense of humor that we've already mentioned. But these works, especially the serial works, the things where you notice we've stayed on the same subject for several pieces, are a consequence of hours upon hours of conversation.

The *Ten Commandments* and other works, *Old God and Young God, Match of the Day 2*, that have to do with faith, were a consequence of an experience that I was having that I dealt with through these conversations. We came to a series of gestures that somehow externalized a lot of occasionally very uncomfortable, certainly not funny, experiences with the subject.

But we also like to use wit to hook an audience. We feel that that is a strategy that we know well and it's a way of getting a lot of people who might otherwise be intimidated by contemporary art into the conversation. So neither of us see any problem in using humor, but if it's only humor... Of course, this was our reaction to being called pranksters. Performance art can be accused of this, especially publicly sited performance art, as just a couple of guys goofing around, and dismissed accordingly. Humor is a hook, but there is so much more under that–at least as far as we're concerned. The end product might be quite a simple gesture. It may even be very funny, but that's the end of a very long process, at which point it's for the audience to add the next part of the conversation. So while it might be funny, it's certainly often very serious to us.

DM: So I want to talk a little bit more about this position of prankster because, to me, the position of prankster is really important, right? It's Shakespearean in its role, it's the role of...

MW: Fool.

DM: It's about that position of speaking truth to power. But I feel like in the art world the position of making people laugh is not a good position to hold because it doesn't wash with the serious kids. I have this mental construct of the art world as kind of grade school where there are all these kind of cliques that somehow run parts of it. There's that serious kid group, they would be the aspirants to the *October* school, so rigidly serious about everything that they think laughing might endanger their precious hold on a title or some kind of power over the other kids. It's upsetting to me to think that we have built a community in which funny is a pejorative. Not all comedic acts should be understood as the juvenile whoopie cushioning of a classmate. One can be an intellectual and funny and use those tools to seek a wider engagement.

AB: The art world is a peculiar place and your characterization of it is quite on the money. I don't know that we're—we're certainly not stand-ups—interested in that. Mat probably could do it, and he has done it. He's the stand-up of the two of us. His comic timing is quite well honed, whereas mine, I can't tell a joke and I fall over myself trying to get the information out.

But it's not something that we've premeditated. Certainly we do share—and I know it's not genetic—a culturally produced gene that enables us to look at everything as potentially absurd. You know, we both look to Monty Python as the original model of taking everything much too far and then taking it even a bit further than that. In the same way that we might be called pranksters, and I don't want to necessarily compare ourselves to them, Python took the entirety of human endeavor as their subject matter and put it through an unbelievably harsh ringer of scrutiny and humor. Nothing was outside of their potential fodder mill.

MW: The only thing I've got to add to that is that we believe that irreverence is an important thing that we should all remember to trade in. You know, we shouldn't take up—I'm being careful here because I have a capacity to get fired occasionally—but nothing is holy. So everything is potentially a subject, and finding humor in things is entirely appropriate; we do that through the work and at a personal level, and that's a good thing. Nobody should be considered beyond question, beyond reproach. All of the big subjects where reverence and respect are asked for are the very subjects that we are attracted to first.

DM: War, death, politics, nationalism...

MW: Terrorism. God.

DM: You somehow cover them all. Do you feel that same way about your collaborator? Do you feel like nothing is sacred, including each other?

MW: Oh, absolutely. I mean, the humor itself is self-deprecating. I know his reputation, but...

DM: What is Adam's reputation? Cad? Gadabout?

MW: He's a small-time Mafioso, a small-time operator, a card shark.

DM: Fair enough. Let the record show Adam referred to himself as the Joe Pesci of the Chicago art world.

MW: He wishes.

DM: I myself work with the Ray Liotta of the Chicago art world.

MW: Damn right, for the record.

AB: So where does that leave the two of you?

DM: I'm going to end up in a shallow grave is the end of that story.

MW: We're on our way to Vegas. We find humor in everything. I think that's just our personalities, and there's a very healthy self-deprecating process that occurs. We make fun of ourselves first, each other next, then the rest of the world. And I think that's probably the right way around.

We don't agonize. And the reason that we don't agonize over the work—although Adam sometimes agonizes over the tempest that is my private life—but the work comes smoothly almost invariably for two reasons. One, despite everything that we say about each other publicly and at great volume, we respect the fact that we both know what we're doing. And the other thing is trust. If I send an idea, and it's usually via e-mail, that's the way we do things. If I send an idea and he's like "nah," it won't be a complete breakdown. Actually, maybe is the word that usually says nonstarter to me. If he comes back with "I like that," then we're on. We're doing it. And the same is true in reverse, we both know when that's an IOTO piece. I think that's always been the case.

DM: That actually brings me very comfortably to one of the other things I wanted to talk about: the relationship between your work and various kinds of design practices. A relationship to design seems to be almost a necessity for artists and collaboratives who work in a post-studio way. For IOTO that seems particularly urgent when you are making signage, murals, labcoats, t-shirts, wine glasses. Your production often results in ephemera and designed objects, but in such a way as to direct the read of them toward the space of art. It is a kind of battle zone that you guys seem to be very comfortable in, as though your work could somehow bridge a dialectic?

AB: Well, let me ask you this Duncan, as someone who is certainly more than competent to voice his own opinion about these things, how do you look at the succession of objects and other kinds of stuff that we put out there in the world as designed objects? Does it work? Are they beguiling enough to hold their own in the massive flow of stuff?

DM: Sure. Of course, but what's maybe more interesting to me about that space is not whether once an object enters our collective imagination it's successful as a designed object, although certainly many of the signage pieces, the t-shirts and that sort of stuff are. The question to my mind is, What is the meaningful difference between designed objects and art work? And how do those things situate themselves in a useful or meaningful way? Is there ultimately a meaningful difference between the two. And if so, what is it?

AB: I don't think I see any meaningful difference except in the ascribed value and, hopefully, the chasm between the two will become somewhat diminished. Because as we all know, value in the art world is something that is from the land of unicorns and wizards.

DM: For me, there is a difference. It comes back to that prankster thing. And it's that position which I would find highly complementary because your work, even when it looks like ephemera or graphic design, embodies a position of problematizing, of looking to... I kind of want to use the word subvert, but it's really not exactly what I mean, but what I mean is sort of taunt, or like English archers flashing their two fingers in a V. A kind of way that screams "We can still be human under all of these circumstances and we will continue to represent ourselves in these ways despite all of the machinations of all of your industries and all of your institutions, and power excursions. That's the position of prankster that is amazing, the ability to take the power to speak, to lead, and then to release it just as easily.

AB: We would like nothing more than for the mayor to declare a particular day as Ordinary Day while our show is up at the Chicago Cultural Center, and have 50,000 people walk down Michigan Avenue with "I Want to be Ordinary" t-shirts on, and hearing everyone else shouting, "Why? No! Wrong!"

DM: That, again, is a kind of knock at the heroic, right? A little nudge towards the value that is found in the quotidian, toward the value that is found in a people's history of a state, or our normal day-to-day humdrum existence.

MW: The most heroic people that I've ever known didn't claim anything of themselves. They just went about what they had to do in their lives, things that we all have to deal with, in a just beautiful and dignified way. They were surrounded by the same things as the rest of us. Things have gotten perverted to the point where value accrues around really stupid shit. If we can just remember for a moment to luxuriate in the things that are right there in front of us: they're wonderful and they're beautiful. This is what life is. It doesn't get any better than that. People might suggest to you, or trick you, or you may trick yourself into believing you're going to be happier if the tree is ten percent bigger, but at the end of the day if you can't find happiness without it, you're screwed.

10TO PORTRAIT PROJECT

"Every portrait that is painted with feeling is a portrait of the artist, not the sitter." —Oscar Wilde

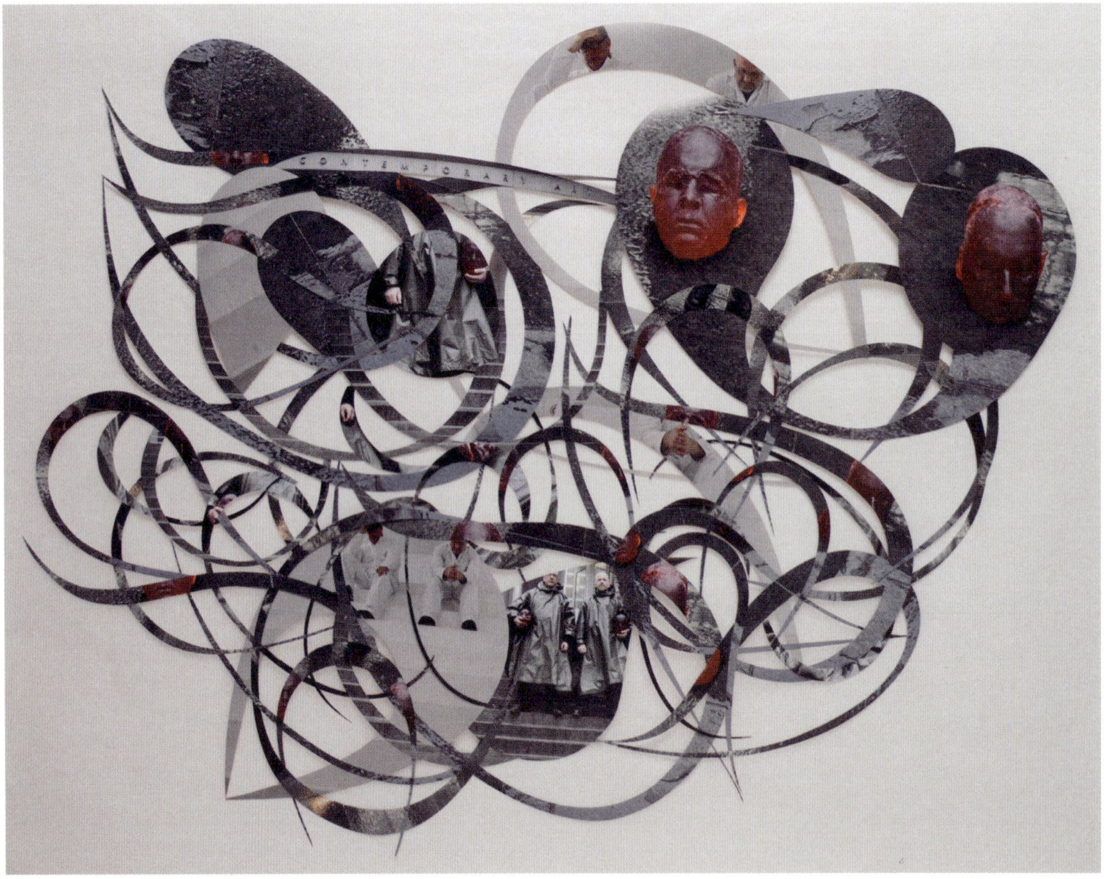

AIMÉE BEAUBIEN
Thoughts of "Two Heads, One Goal," 2012
Collage with pigment prints

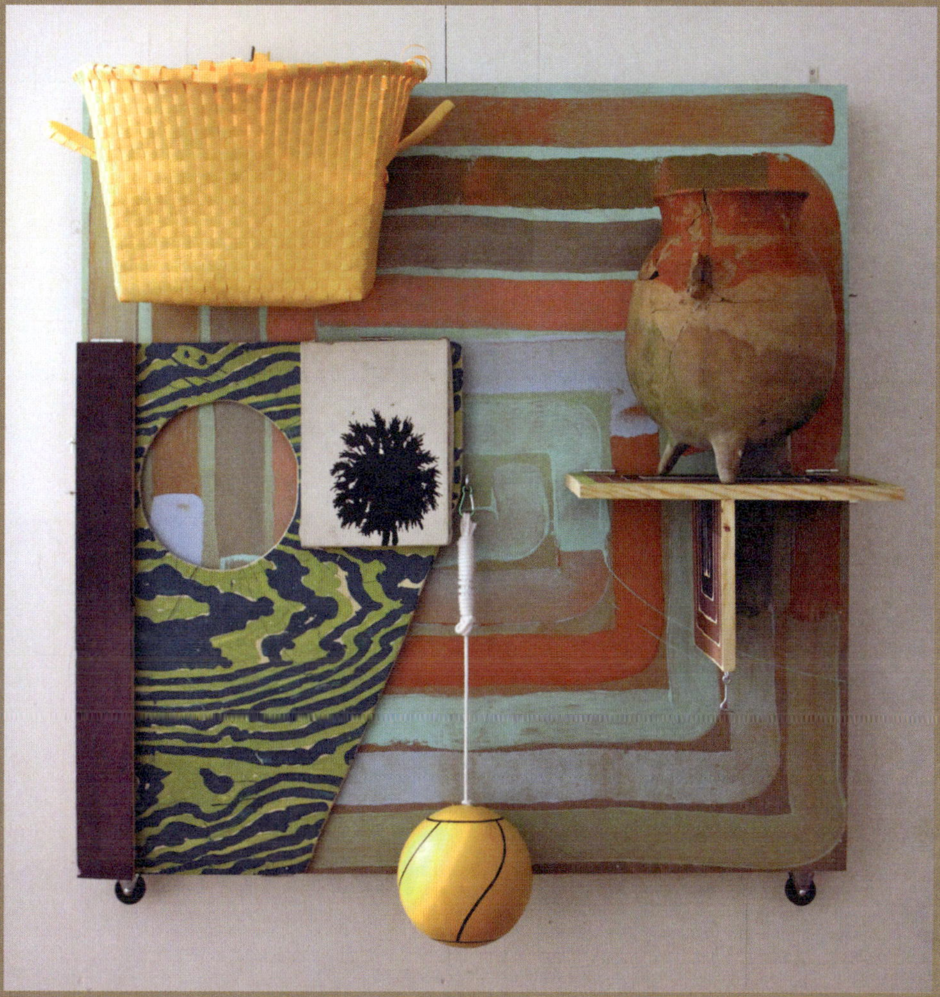

ALBERTO AGUILAR
Boliche Che-Che, 2012
Wood, latex paint, hardware, a laundry basket, and a clay vessel

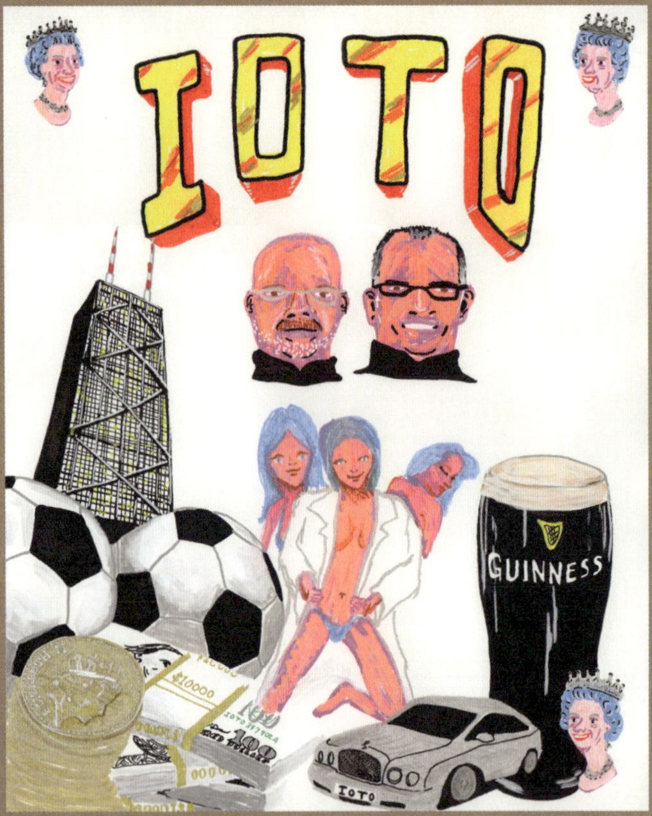

CHRIS KERR
IOTO, 2012
Acrylic poster markers on Bristol board

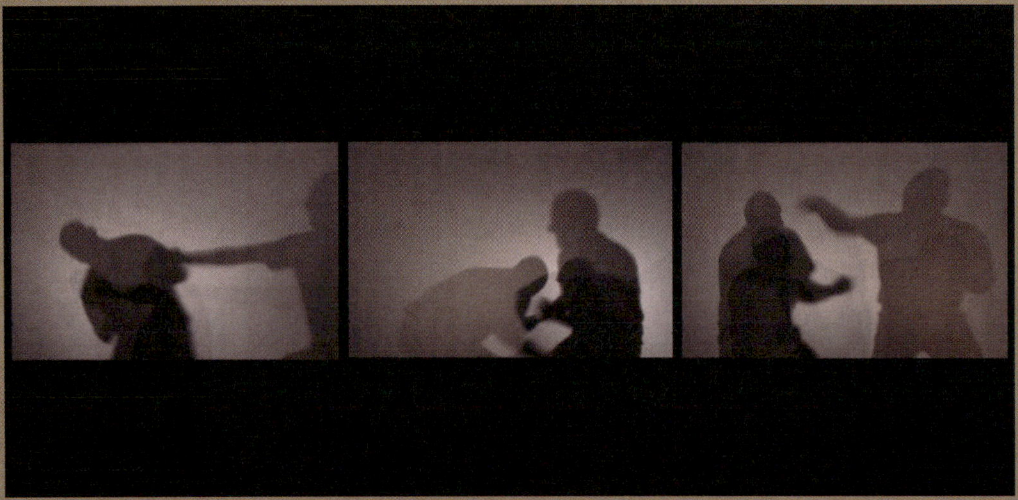

ED, JR.
(a Chicago-based collective, comprised of Edra Soto,
Deborah Boardman, Jeroen Nelemans, and Ryan Richey)
Clinch, 2011, still from video portrait

HEIDI NORTON

I Want to Be Ordinary (Adam's Anthurium Plant), 2012
I Want to Be Ordinary (Mat's Cat-Chewed Plant), 2012
Archival pigment prints

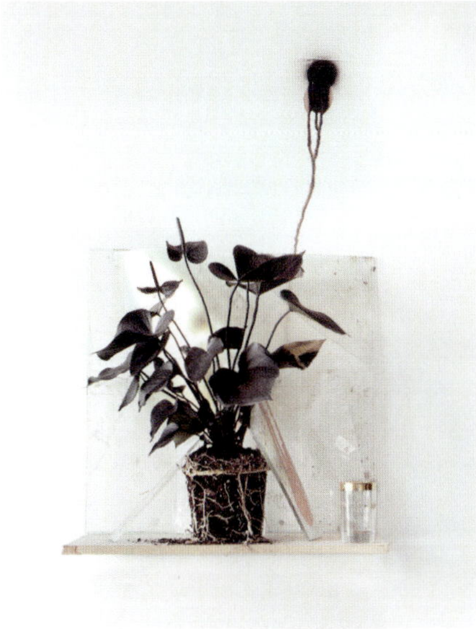

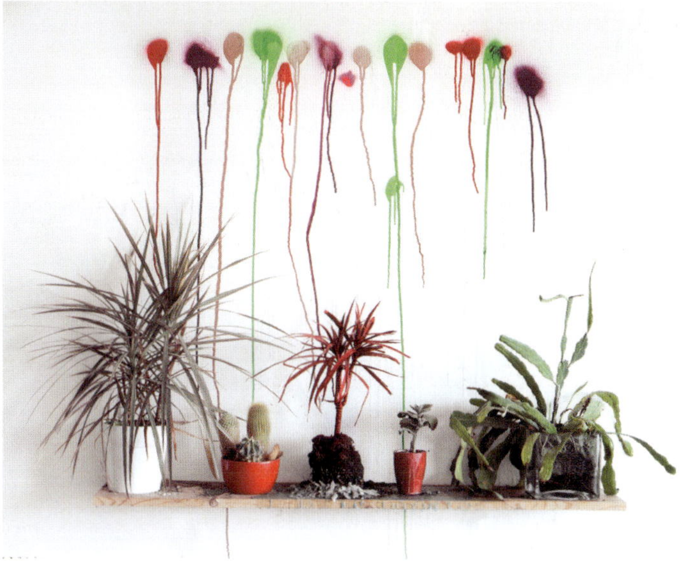

We smoke them occasionally.
We prefer them to people.
Photosynthesis rocks.

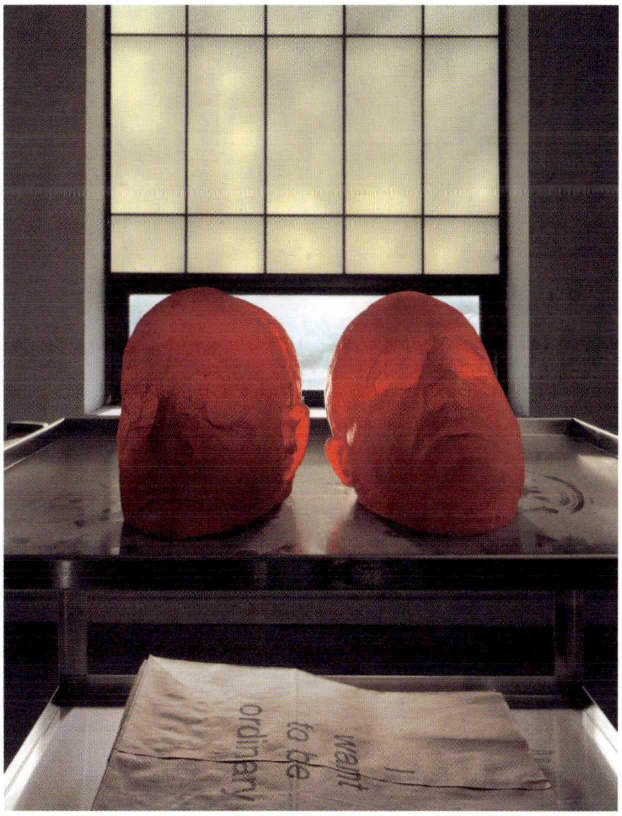

JAY WOLKE

Two Footballs, 2011
Archival digital inkjet print from 4x5 color negative

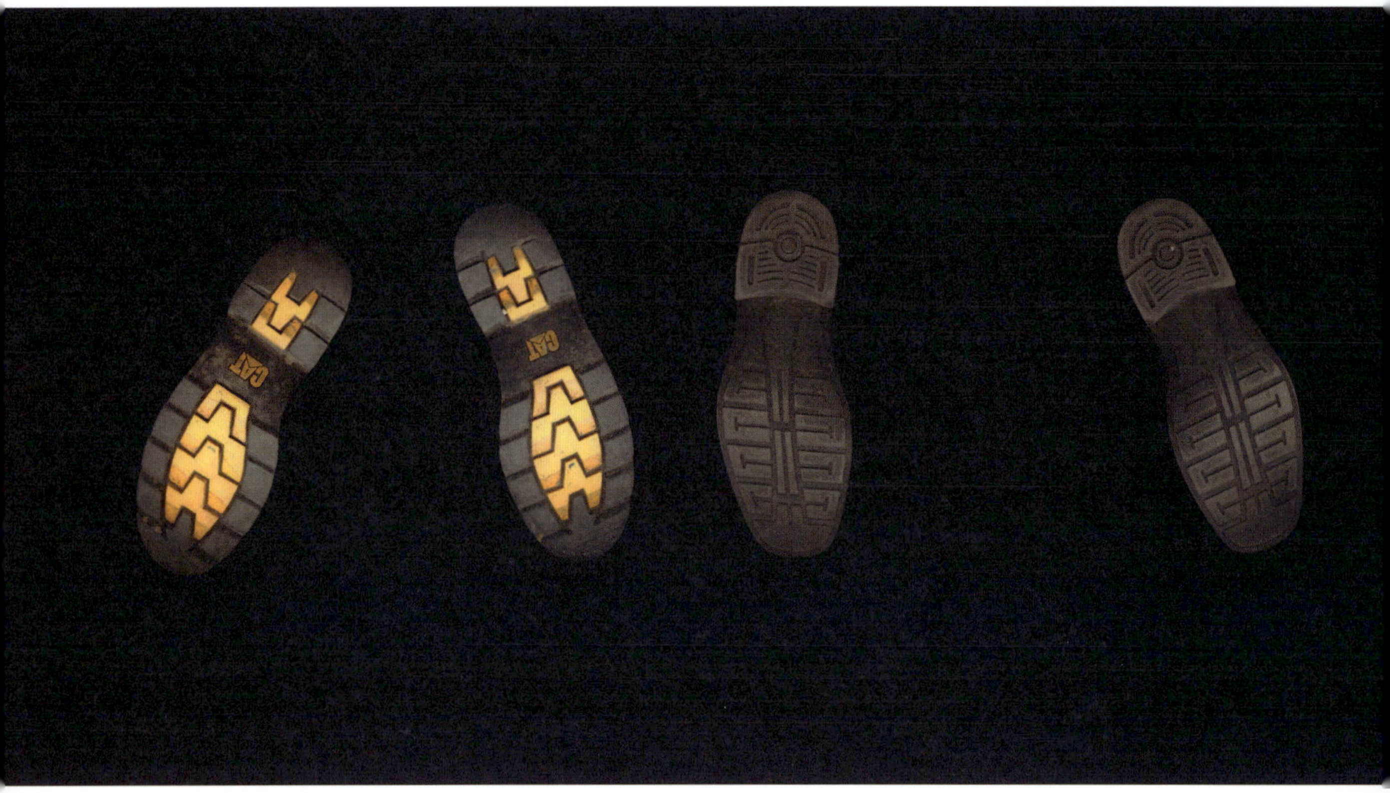

JO HORMUTH
The Soles of the Industry of the Ordinary, 2012
Lambda print

CARRIE SCHNEIDER
Round, 2012
Video loop on monitor

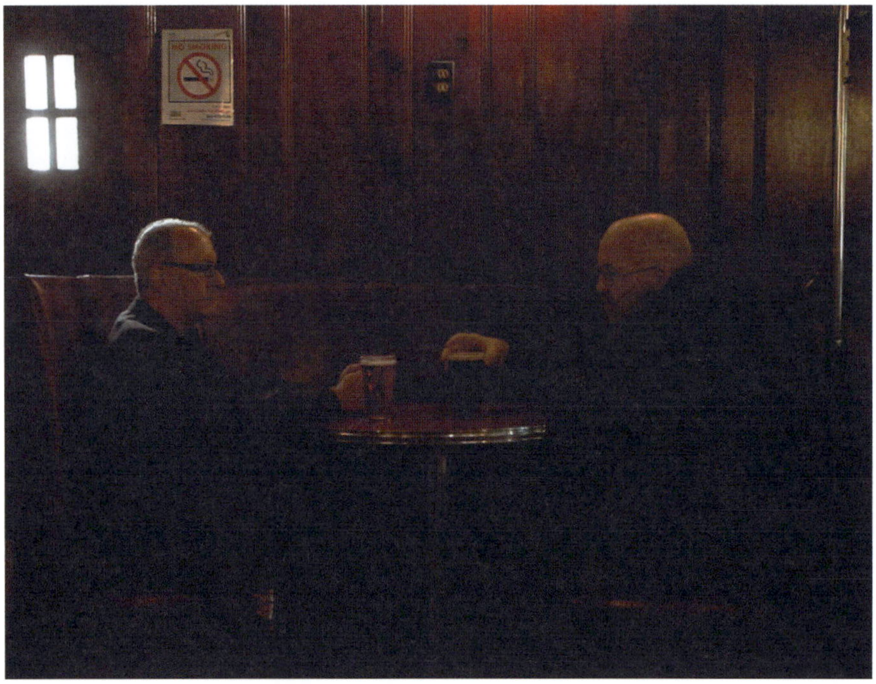

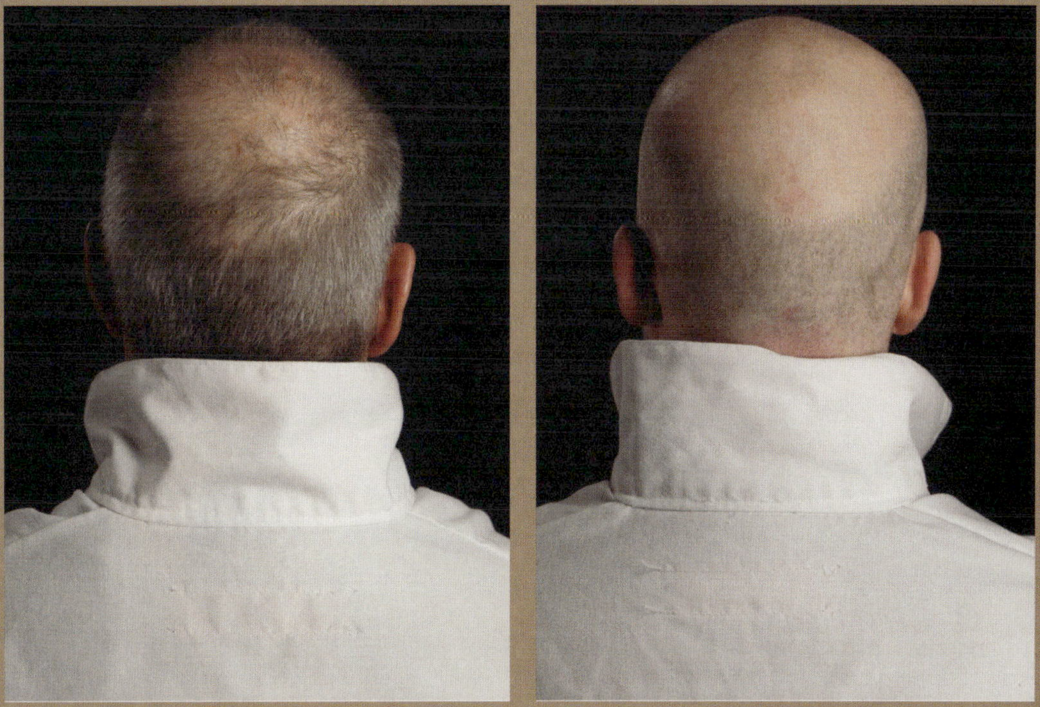

JORDAN SCHULMAN
Oh, I recognized you from the back of your head, 2012
Color photographs

JUDY NATAL
We are but Stardust, 2012
Archival inkjet on rag paper

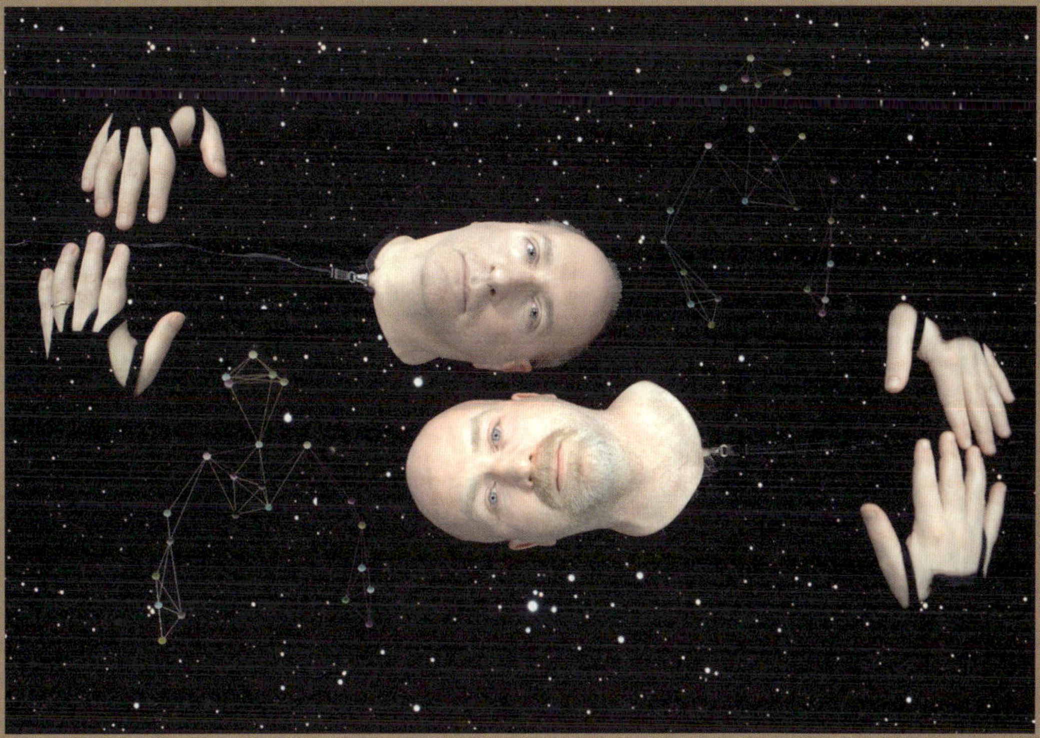

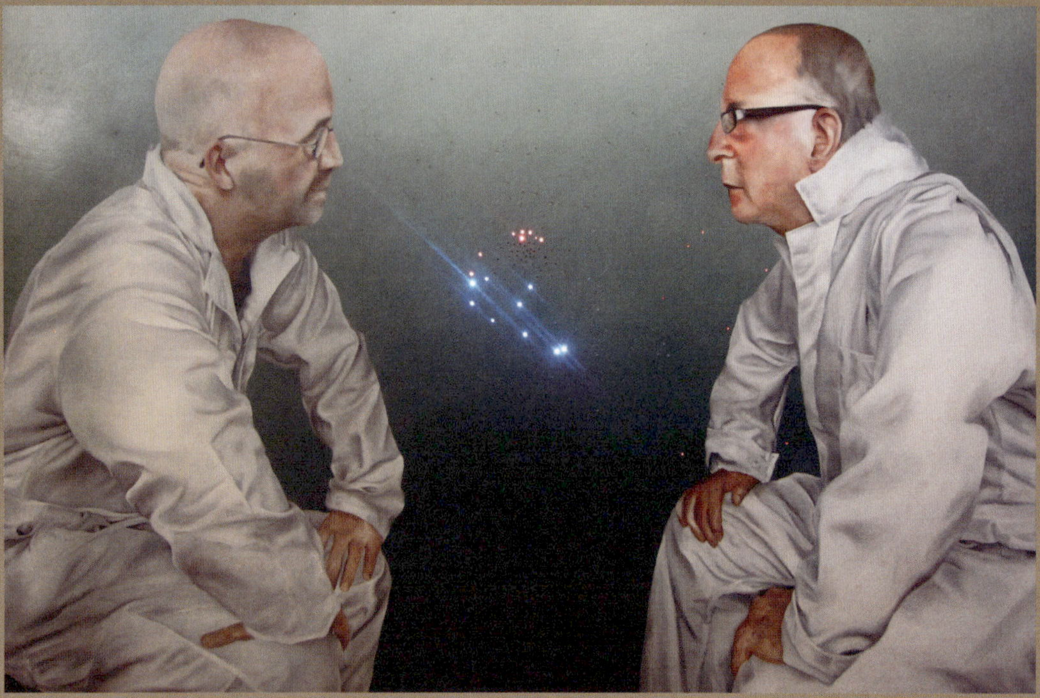

JULIA HAW
Generation of an Idea: IOTO, 2012
Oil, fiber optic cables, wood, LEDs

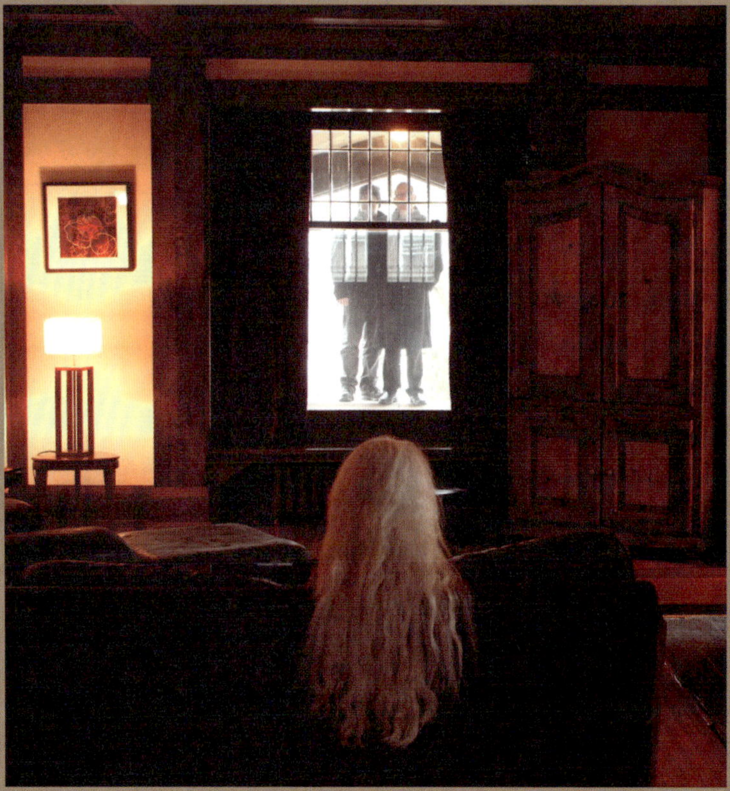

JULIE LAFFIN
Visitation, 2012
Photograph

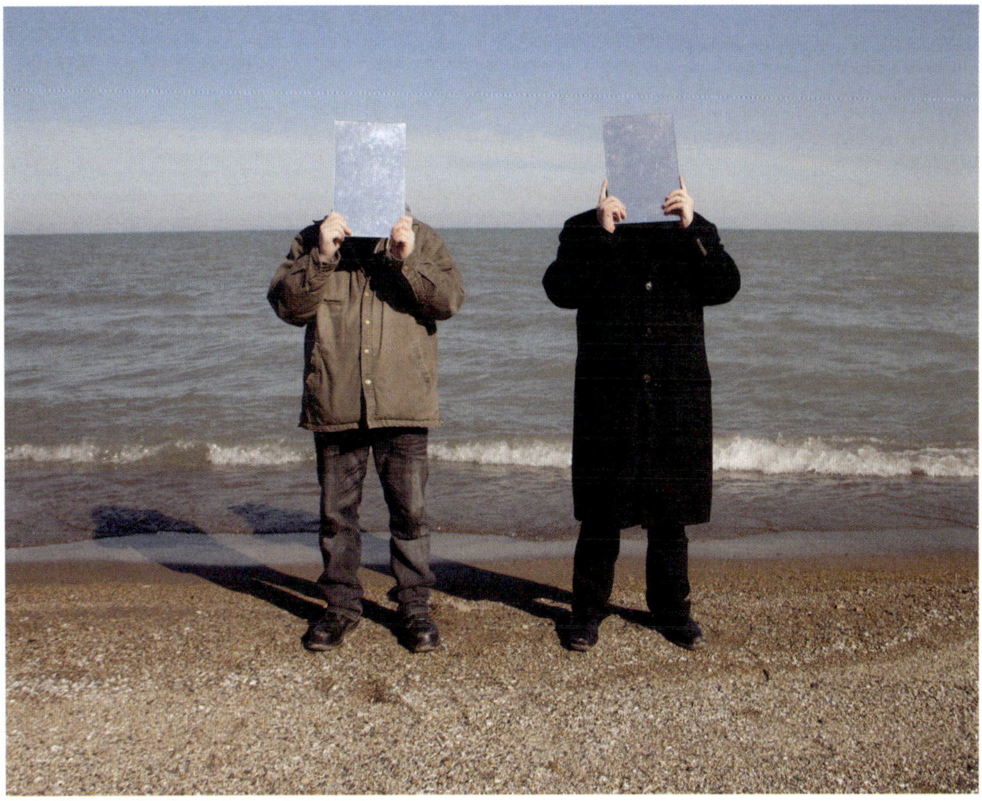

KELLY KACZYNSKI
Twinning a thing it is not, a(n ordinary) hole (Lake Michigan), 2012
Archival inkjet print

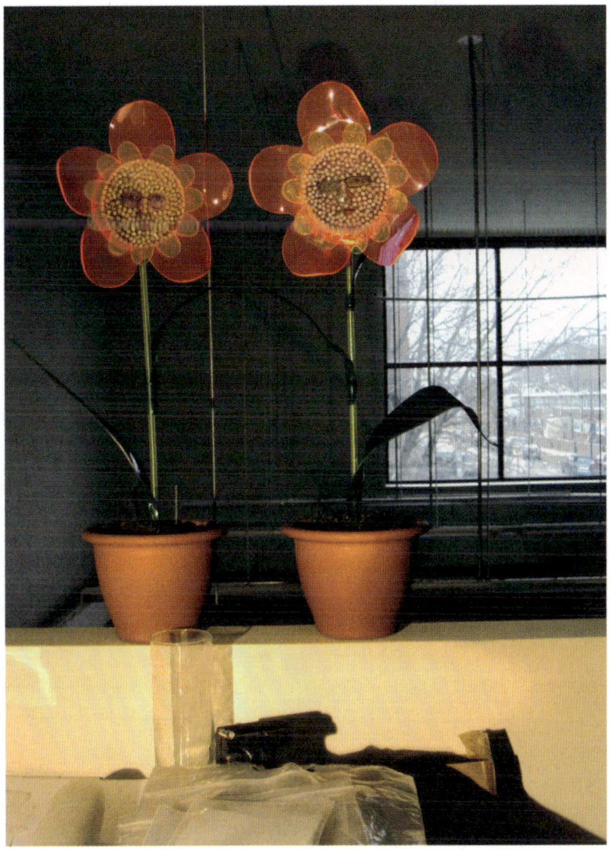

KERRY JAMES MARSHALL
Untitled (two potted plants), 2012
Mixed media (fluorescent acrylic, acrylic, potting moss, plastic flower pot, photographs)

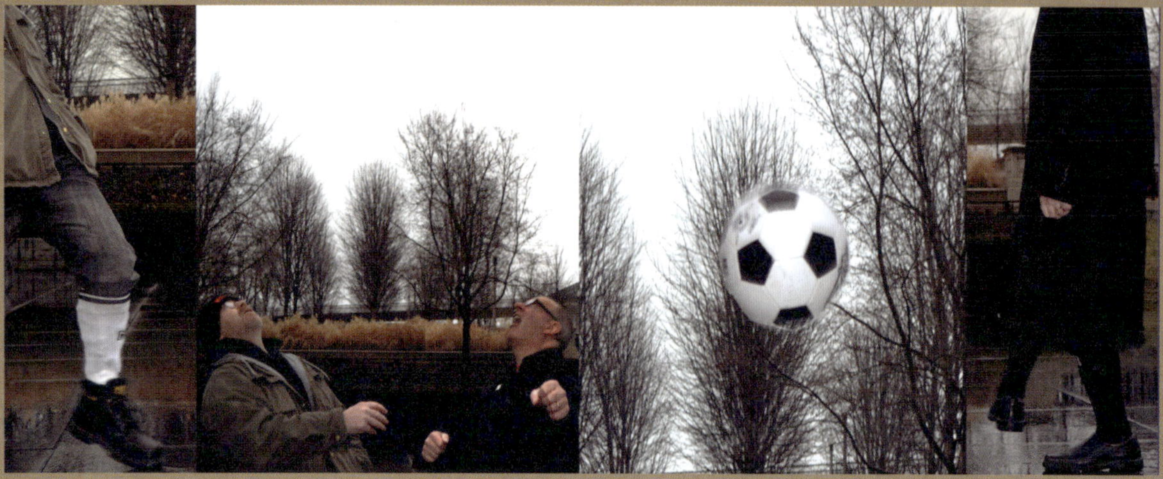

KIRSTEN LEENAARS
Proper Football, 2012
Digital C-print

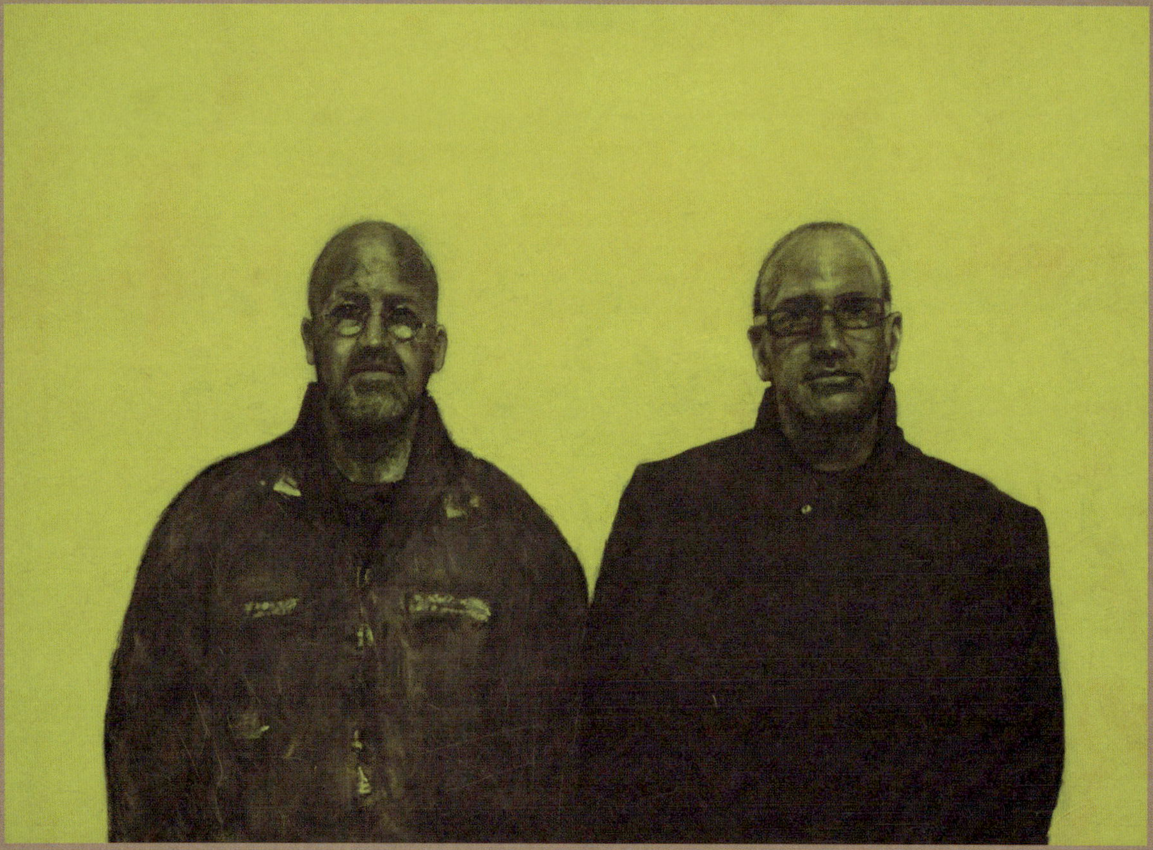

TIM ANDERSON
Industry of the Ordinary, 2012
Oil and graphite on canvas

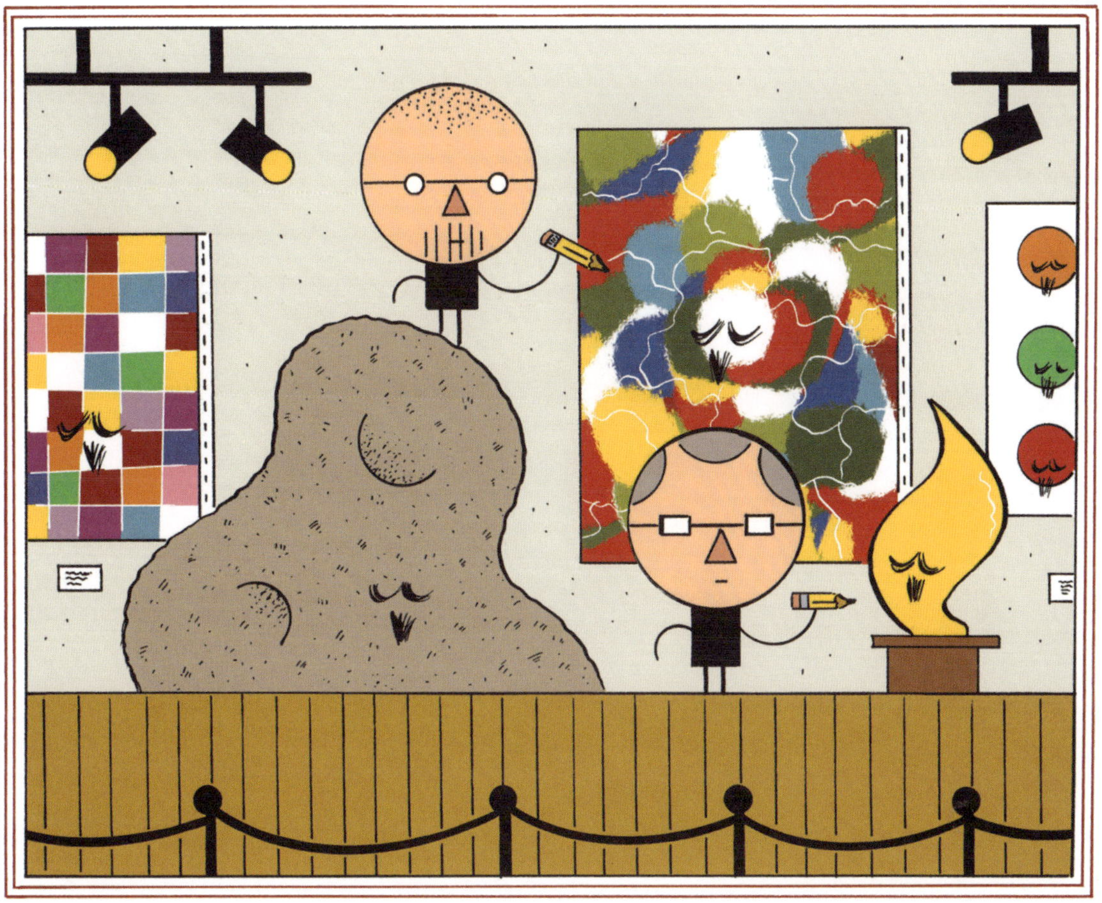

IVAN BRUNETTI
Portrait of Industry of the Ordinary, 2012
Inkjet print on Bristol board

IÑIGO MANGLANO-OVALLE
Bluff (the artist invites Adam Brooks and Mathew Wilson to play strip poker in a dark room), 2012

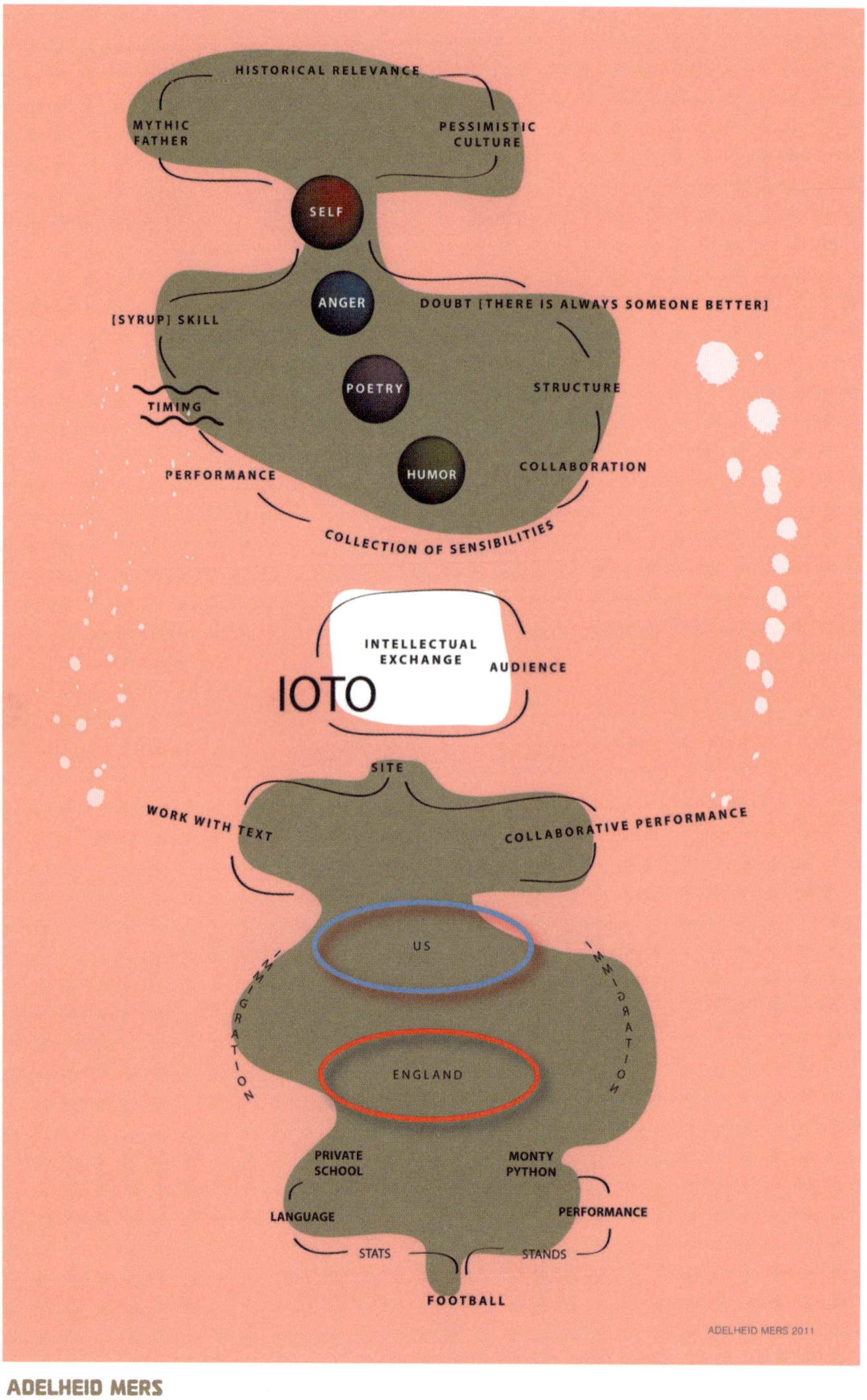

ADELHEID MERS
Conversation about his practice with Adam Brooks, December 4, 2011
Conversation about his practice with Mat Wilson, December 4, 2011
Digital file, dimensions variable

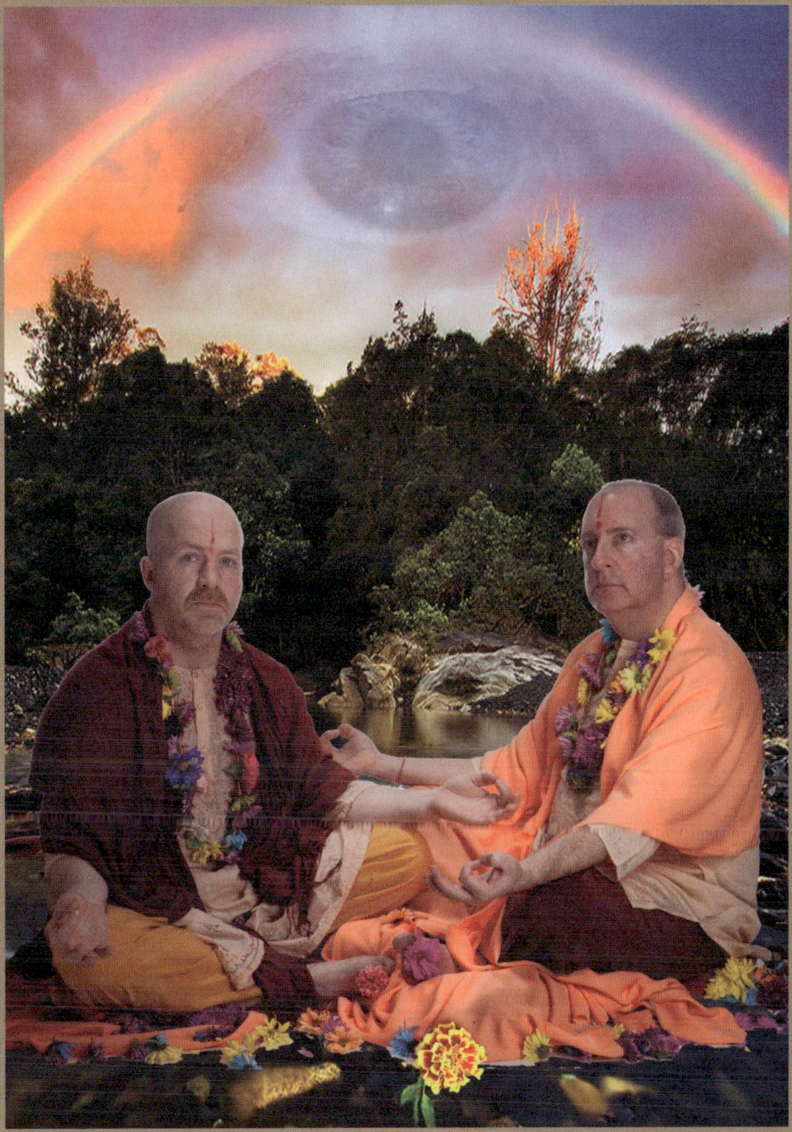

SABINA OTT
Rainbow, 2012
Pigment print on paper
Photo: Megan Taylor Noe
Costume and set: Alaina Moore

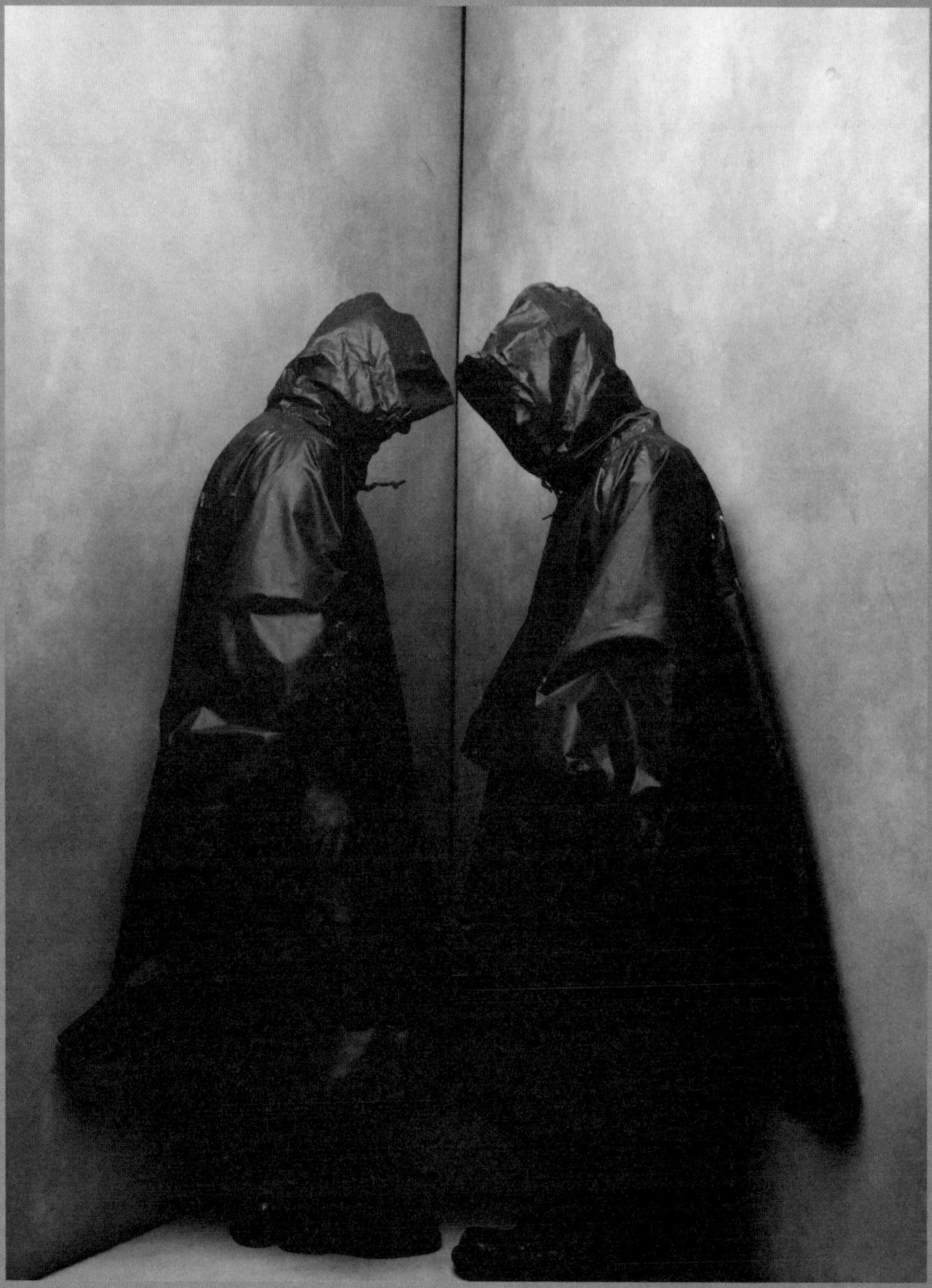

MARC HAUSER
Portrait of Ordinary Guys, 2011
Fine art giclee print

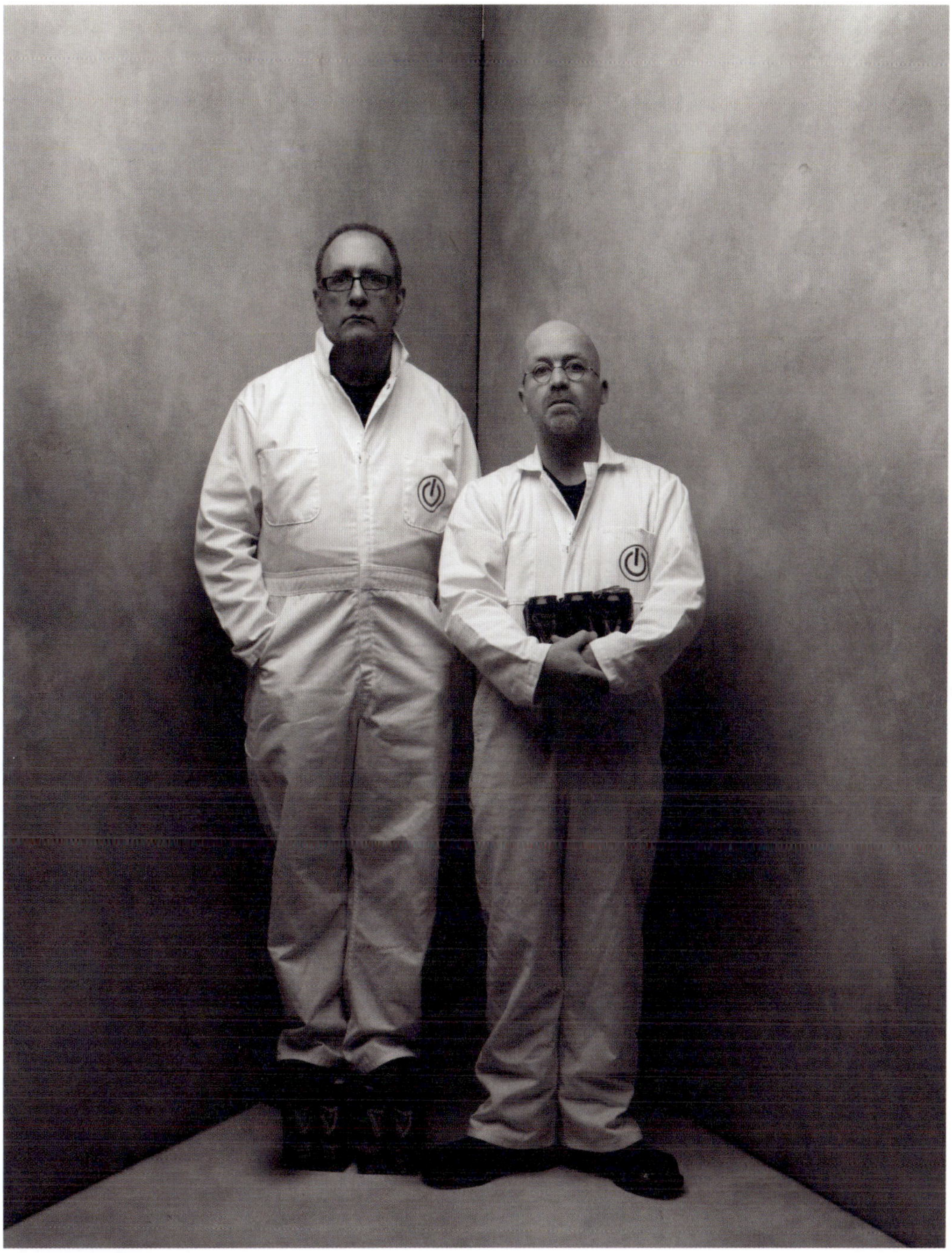

MARC HAUSER
Portrait of Ordinary Guys, 2011
Fine art giclee print

Eleanor Heartney is a Contributing Editor to *Art in America* and *Artpress,* and author of numerous articles and books on contemporary art including *Critical Condition: American Culture at the Crossroads* (1997), *Postmodernism* (2001), *Postmodern Heretics: The Catholic Imagination in Contemporary Art* (2004), and *Art and Today* (2008). She is co-author of *After the Revolution: Women Who Transformed Contemporary Art* (2007). She received the College Art Association's Frank Jewett Mather Award for distinction in art criticism in 1992, and was honored by the French government as a Chevalier dans l'Ordre des Arts et des Lettres in 2008. Heartney is a past President of AICA-USA, the American section of the International Art Critics Association.

Duncan MacKenzie is an artist, pundit, educator, and a founding member/producer of Bad at Sports (badatsports.com), a project he began with Richard Holland in 2005. Bad at Sports is one of the US's largest online arts resources, currently sharing an archive of 350 hours worth of audio documenting the art history of Chicago, New York, and San Francisco, and over 2000 posts by the best art writers in Chicago. His art works have appeared in galleries all over the world, including Canada, Australia, the United States, New Zealand, Estonia, and England, and have been discussed in *Flash Art, Artforum, The New York Times, Time Out,* and many other venues. He is the author of over 250 interviews and has worked with Rodney Graham, Kerry James Marshall, Francesco Bonami, Luc Tuymans, James Elkins, Julie Ault, Carol Becker, James Rondeau, Jeff Wall, and Gavin Turk. He currently enjoys a posting as an Assistant Professor in Art + Design at Columbia College Chicago.

Dominic Molon is Chief Curator at the Contemporary Art Museum, St. Louis, where he has organized exhibitions of the artists David Noonan (2011), Emily Wardill (2011), and Christodoulos Panayiotou (2012). In his previous position as Curator at the Museum of Contemporary Art, Chicago, he organized the thematic exhibitions *Production Site: The Artist's Studio Inside-Out* (2010) and *Sympathy for the Devil: Art and Rock and Roll Since 1967* (2007), as well as solo exhibitions of Susan Philipsz (2011), Liam Gillick (2009), Wolfgang Tillmans (2006), and Sharon Lockhart (2001). Molon has contributed to numerous publications including *Art Review, Whitewall, Art on Paper, Contemporary,* and *Tate: the Art Magazine,* as well as to exhibition catalogs and monographs for the artists Karin Mamma Andersson, Ashley Bickerton, Elmgreen and Dragset, Karen Kilimnik, and Banks Violette. He also sits on the acquisition committee of the FRAC Nord-Pas de Calais, Dunkerque, France.

Ciara Ennis is the Director/Curator of Pitzer Art Galleries at Pitzer College, Claremont, where she has curated the exhibitions: *Antarctica* (2007); *Narrowcast: Reframing Global Video 1986/2008,* co-curated with Ming-Yuen S. Ma (2008); *Veronica* (2009); *Capitalism in Question,* co-curated with Daniel Joseph *Martinez* (2010); *Euan MacDonald: Kimball* (2011), *Synthetic Ritual,* co-curated with Gabi Scardi (2011); and *Liz Glynn: No Second Troy* (2012). Previously, she was Curator of Exhibitions at the University of California Riverside/California Museum of Photography. Ennis was Project Director for Public Offerings, an international survey of contemporary art, at MOCA, Los Angeles in 2001, and then Associate Curator at the Santa Monica Museum of Art, where she initiated the Project Room. Ennis's curatorial practice blurs fact with fiction, and focuses on storytelling as a means to explore the fluidity and fragility of identity, revealing the subtleties of the social, political, and the cultural issues that impact our lives.

Industry of the Ordinary:
Sic Transit Gloria Mundi
2003-2013
17 August 2012 – 17 February 2013

ISBN 978-0-9852964-0-7
Library of Congress Control Number: 2012904017

Layout + Typography by Jason Pickleman for the JNL graphic design, Chicago
Typeset in Interstate, Forma Solid and CR2 Regular.

This book was printed in an edition of 1000 copies on 120gsm paper with a 150 line screen.

Facebook: www.facebook.com/IndustryoftheOrdinary
Twitter: @IOTOrdinary
www.industryoftheordinary.com

Printed in China